Experience and Memory

Contemporary European History

Editors:
Konrad Jarausch, University of North Carolina, Chapel Hill
Henry Rousso, Institut d'histoire du temps présent, CNRS, Paris

Volume 1
Between Utopia and Disillusionment: A Narrative of the Political Transformation in Eastern Europe
  Henri Vogt

Volume 2
The Inverted Mirror: Mythologizing the Enemy in France and Germany, 1898–1914
  Michael E. Nolan

Volume 3
Conflicted Memories: Europeanizing Contemporary Histories
  Edited by Konrad H. Jarausch and Thomas Lindenberger with the Collaboration of Annelie Ramsbrock

Volume 4
Playing Politics with History: The Bundestag Inquiries into East Germany
  Andrew H. Beattie

Volume 5
Alsace to the Alsatians? Visions and Divisions of Alsatian Regionalism, 1870–1939
  Christopher J. Fischer

Volume 6
A European Memory? Contested Histories and Politics of Remembrance
  Edited by Małgorzata Pakier and Bo Stråth

Volume 7
Experience and Memory: The Second World War in Europe
  Edited by Jörg Echternkamp and Stefan Martens

Volume 8
Children, Families, and States: Time Policies of Childcare, Preschool, and Primary Education in Europe
  Edited by Karen Hagemann, Konrad H. Jarausch, and Cristina Allemann-Ghionda

Volume 9
Social Policy in the Smaller European Union States
  Edited by Gary B. Cohen, Ben W. Ansell, Jane Gingrich, and Robert Henry Cox

Volume 10
A State of Peace in Europe: West Germany and the CSCE, 1966–1975
  Petri Hakkarainen

Volume 11
Visions of the End of the Cold War
  Edited by Frederic Bozo, Marie-Pierre Rey, Bernd Rother, and N. Piers Ludlow

Volume 12
Investigating Srebrenica: Institutions, Facts, Responsibilities
  Edited by Isabelle Delpla, Xavier Bougarel, and Jean-Louis Fournel

Volume 13
Samizdat, Tamizdat, and Beyond: Transnational Media During and After Socialism
  Edited by Friederike Kind-Kovács and Jessie Labov

Experience and Memory

The Second World War in Europe

Edited by

Jörg Echternkamp and Stefan Martens

First published in 2010 by
Berghahn Books

www.berghahnbooks.com

©2010, 2013 Jörg Echternkamp and Stefan Martens
First paperback edition published in 2013

Originally published as:
Der Zweite Weltkrieg in Europa: Erfahrung und Erinnerung
©2007 F. Schöningh Verlag

All rights reserved.
Except for the quotation of short passages for the purposes of criticism and review, no part of this book may be reproduced in any form or by any means, electronic or mechanical, including photocopying, recording, or any information storage and retrieval system now known or to be invented, without written permission of the publisher.

Library of Congress Cataloging-in-Publication Data

Zweite Weltkrieg in Europa. English
 Experience and memory : the Second World War in Europe / [edited by] Jörg Echternkamp and Stefan Martens.
   p. cm. -- (Contemporary European history ; v. 7)
 Papers from an international colloquium held in Paris, France, in April 3-4, 2006.
 Includes bibliographical references and indexes.
 ISBN 978-1-84545-763-1 (hbk. : alk. paper) -- ISBN 978-1-78238-093-1 (paperback) -- ISBN 978-1-78238-094-8 (retail ebook)
   1. World War, 1939-1945--Social aspects--Europe--Congresses.
 2. World War, 1939-1945--Europe--Historiography--Congresses. 3. World War, 1939-1945--Influence--Congresses. 4. Experience--Social aspects--Europe--History--20th century--Congresses. 5. Collective memory--Europe--History--20th century--Congresses. 6. War and society--Europe--History--20th century--Congresses.
 7. Violence--Social aspects--Europe--History--20th century--Congresses. 8. Europe--Social conditions--20th century--Congresses. I. Echternkamp, Jörg. II. Martens, Stefan. III. Title.

D744.7.E8Z8 2010
940.53'4--dc22

2010038740

British Library Cataloguing in Publication Data

A catalogue record for this book is available from the British Library.

Printed in the United States on acid-free paper

ISBN 978-1-78238-093-1 paperback   ISBN 978-1-78238-094-8 retail ebook

Contents

List of Illustrations ... ix

List of Abbreviations ... xi

Chapter 1
A New Perspective on the War ... 1
  Henry Rousso

Chapter 2
Conceptualizing the Occupations of Belgium, Luxembourg, ... 10
and the Netherlands (1933–1944)
  Benoît Majerus

Chapter 3
The Role of the War in National Societies: The Examples ... 21
of Belgium, Luxembourg, and the Netherlands
  Chantal Kesteloot

Chapter 4
Myths and Realities of the "People's War" in Britain ... 40
  John Ramsden

Chapter 5
"We Can Take It!" Britain and the Memory of the Home Front ... 53
in the Second World War
  Mark Connelly

Chapter 6
Experience and Memory: The Second World War in Poland 70
  Piotr Madajczyk

Chapter 7
Remembering and Researching the War: The Soviet and 86
Russian Experience
  Sergei Kudryashov

Chapter 8
Bombing and Land War in Italy: Military Strategy, Reactions, 116
and Collective Memory
  Gabriella Gribaudi

Chapter 9
Italy as Occupier in the Balkans: Remembrance and War Crimes 135
after 1945
  Filippo Focardi

Chapter 10
Brest under Bombardment (1940–1944): Being in War 147
  Pierre Le Goïc

Chapter 11
Experiences of War, Memories of War, and Political Behavior: 161
The Example of the French Communist Party
  Philippe Buton

Chapter 12
The Air War, the Public, and Cycles of Memory 180
  Dietmar Süß

Chapter 13
The Long Shadows of the Second World War: The Impact of 197
Experiences and Memories of War on West German Society
  Axel Schildt

Chapter 14
The War in Postwar Society: The Role of the Second World War 214
in Public and Private Spheres in the Soviet Occupation Zone
and Early GDR
  Dorothee Wierling

Chapter 15
Violence and Victimhood: Looking Back at the World Wars   229
in Europe
   Richard Bessel

Chapter 16
The Meanings of the Second World War in Contemporary   245
European History
   Jörg Echternkamp and Stefan Martens

List of Contributors	271
Selected Bibliography	273
Index of Names	293
Index of Places	295

LIST OF ILLUSTRATIONS

Maps

1	Election results for the PCF in 1924	162
2	Election results for the PCF in 1928	162
3	Election results for the PCF in 1932	163
4	Election results for the PCF in 1936	163
5	Distribution of PCF members in 1937 by *département* (per 10,000 inhabitants)	164
6	Election results for the PCF in 1946	165
7	Distribution of PCF members in 1946 by *département* (per 10,000 inhabitants)	165
8	Distribution of PCF members in 1952 by *département* (per 10,000 inhabitants)	167
9	Distribution of PCF members in 1979 by *département* (per 10,000 inhabitants)	167
10	Election results for the PCF in 1951	168
11	Election results for the PCF in 1958	168
12	Election results for the PCF in 1967	169
13	Election results for the PCF in 1973	169
14	Election results for the PCF in 1978	170
15	Election results for the PCF in 1988	170
16	Election results for the PCF in 1997	171
17	Comparison in the growth of the PCF, 1937–1945	172
18	Distribution of volunteer *Résistance* fighters in 1944 by *département*	172

19	Distribution of PCF members in 1945 by *département*	174
20	Summary executions per inhabitant during the liberation	174
21	Death sentences during the liberation	175

Photograph

| 1 | Battle of the Bulge, Houffalize/Belgium 1945; CEGES (Brussels), picture no. 13037 | 247 |

LIST OF ABBREVIATIONS

AFHRA	Air Force Historical Research Agency
AG	Aktiengesellschaft
ANPI	Associazione Nazionale Partigiani d'Italia
AP	Associated Press
ASN	Archivio di Stato di Napoli
ATS	Auxiliary Territorial Service
BBC	British Broadcasting Corporation
BRD	Bundesrepublik Deutschland
CAB	Cabinet
CDU	Christlich-Demokratische Union
CEGES	Centre d'Études et de Documentation Guerre et Sociétés contemporaines Brussels
CLN	Comitato di Liberazione Nazionale
CNRS	Centre national de la recherche scientifique
COGIS	Kenniscentrum Vervolging, Oorlog & Geweld
CVR	Combattants volontaires de la Résistance
DBD	Demokratische Bauernpartei Deutschlands
DC	Départementale communiste
DCA	Défense contre avions
DDR	Deutsche Demokratische Republik
DM	Deutsche Mark
DP	Displaced Persons
ed.	Editor
E.K.	Eisernes Kreuz
EDC	European Defense Community
EVG	Europäische Verteidigungsgemeinschaft
FDGB	Freier Deutscher Gewerkschaftsbund
FFI	Forces françaises de l'intérieur
FFL	Forces françaises libres
FRG	Federal Republic of Germany

GDR	German Democratic Republic
Gestapo	Geheime Staatspolizei
GHI	German Historical Institute
GLAVLIT	Glavnoe upravlenie po delam literatury i izdatv
GULAG	Glavnoje Upravlenije Ispravitelno-trudovych Lagerej
HJ	Hitler-Jugend
HO	Handels-Organisation
HZ	Historische Zeitschrift
ICODO	Informatie- en Coördinatieorgaan Dienstverlening oorlogsgetroffenen
IfZ	Institut für Zeitgeschichte
IHTP	Institut d'histoire du temps présent
IPN	Instytut Pamięci Narodowe
ITV	Independent Television
KGB	Komitet Gosudarstvennoy Bezopasnosti)
KP	Kommunistische Partei
KPD	Kommunistische Partei Deutschlands
KPdSU(B)	Kommunistische Partei der Sowjetunion (Bolschewiki)
KZ	Konzentrationslager
LDPD	Liberaldemokratische Partei Deutschlands
MGFA	Militärgeschichtliches Forschungsamt Potsdam
MGZ	Militärgeschichtliche Zeitschrift
NATO	North Atlantic Treaty Organization
NDPD	Nationaldemokratische Partei Deutschlands
NIOD	Netherlands Institute of War Documentation
NKWD	Narodnyj komissariat wnutrennych del
NS	Nationalsozialismus, nationalsozialistisch
NSDAP	Nationalsozialistische Deutsche Arbeiterpartei
NWDR	Nordwestdeutscher Rundfunk
OBOP	Opinii Publicznej i Studiów Programowych
OKH	Oberkommando des Heeres
OLG	Oberlandesgericht
PCF	Parti communiste français
POW	Prisoner of War
PREM	Premier / Prime Minister
PRO	Public Record Office
PSC-CVP	Parti social chrétien - Christelijke Volkspartij
RAF	Royal Air Force
RAI	Radiotelevisione Italiana
RF	Russische Förderation
RGASPI	Rossiiskii gosudarstvennyi arkhiv sotsial'no-politicheskoi istorii
RJM	Reichsjustizminister
RKKA	Raboche-Krest'yanskaya Krasnaya Armiya

SBZ	Sowjetische Besatzungszone
SD	Sicherheitsdienst
SED	Sozialistische Einheitspartei Deutschlands
SFB	Sonderforschungsbereich
SOMA	Studie- en Documentatiecentrum Oorlog en Hedendaagse Maatschappij Brussels
SOZ	Soviet Occupation Zone
SS	Schutzstaffel
SSSR	Sojus Sowjetskich Sozialistitscheskich Respublik
SU	Sowjetunion
TASS	Telegrafnoe Agentstwo Sowjetskowo Sojusa
TGV	Train à grande vitesse
UdSSR	Union der Sozialistischen Sowjetrepubliken
URSS	Union des républiques socialistes soviétiques
US	United States (of America)
USA	United States of America
USAAF	United States Army Air Forces
USSR	Union of Soviet Socialist Republics
VE Day	Victory in Europe Day
VGK	Oberkommando der russischen Streitkräfte
VNV	Vlaams Nationalistisch Verbond
VRP	Volksrepublik Polen
WRAF	Women's Royal Air Force
WRNS	Women's Royal Naval Service
ZfG	Zeitschrift für Geschichtswissenschaft
ZK	Zentralkomitee
ZZF	Zentrum für Zeithistorische Forschung Potsdam

Chapter 1

A New Perspective on the War

Henry Rousso

Like memory, the writing of history is as much a product of the past as it is a child of its time. Even when dealing with such a momentous event as the Second World War, the different narratives certainly depend on the past as it "truly happened," but they also depend on the contexts in which they were crafted after the actual events. These narratives change depending on the available sources, current research questions, and on each new generation of observers. This remark may sound trivial, but living this experience is surprising time and again.

The present volume, as well as the international colloquium from which it resulted, illustrates this point well. How can we contribute anything new on a topic that has already received so much attention? How can we avoid the risk of a mere listing of new facts and punctual revisions? In comparison to previous conferences and colloquia on similar topics,[1] the changes are clearly noticeable: on the one hand they result from the questions posed above, on the other from current historiographical developments. Taken together, this allows for a new perspective on the Second World War.

I.

This new perspective does not primarily focus on political and ideological interpretations, which historians used to emphasize when referring to the special character of this war. It rather tells the story of the war from a social angle while attempting to capture its dynamics as closely as possible. Indeed, it combines a "top-down" and a "bottom-up" perspective. Strategic decisions, war objectives, as well as the policies that brought about the war (and were implemented in its course) are systematically

---

Notes for this chapter begin on page 8.

placed in the context of the actors on the ground and the experiences of combatants and civilians who, if anything, became "non-combatants" in the course of the conflict. Contemporary wars, and the Second World War in particular, can no longer simply be explained in terms of commanders or nations – even if these are understood as collective or abstract concepts. Wars concern individuals with faces. These individuals belong to social groups that existed prior to, or developed in the course of the conflict (such as prisoners of war, for example). From a geographical viewpoint, they live in places that are either at the center of the fighting or located far away from the battlefields. With regard to the Second World War, the French experience illustrates this point well – some regions were directly affected by the war, while for others it was merely a far-away phenomenon (see Philippe Buton's chapter). Whatever the specific situation may have been, social groups and individuals were shaped by specific experiences during the war, which were frequently characterized by the suddenness of events (such as the defeat of Poland or of France), by fear and uncertainty, sometimes even by fatalism, but at times also by a certain excitement in the face of the extraordinary nature of the events. Hence the importance of the contemporary witness, a figure that dominates the postwar era(s) of the twentieth century – post-1918 as well as post-1945; hence also the necessity to analyze the economy of individual emotions during the war as a preparatory step in order to understand the subsequent memories of the war (Pierre Le Goïc).

The war experience, a logical consequence of the culture of war, is therefore the essential key to understanding what precisely was implied by the totalization of the war, a term preferable to that of "total war," as the latter is too closely tied to the aims of the Third Reich. However, even if all segments of a society share the experience of war and can thus become objects of investigation, not all of them attain the same level of "appropriation," nor do they internalize this experience in the same ways (Jörg Echternkamp). Henceforth, the challenge of writing a social history of the war involves not so much describing its effects on people, but rather studying the state of "being in war" in its social, temporal, and spatial dimensions, including varying degrees of involvement, consciousness, approval, and especially violence, as well as varying degrees of resistance, passivity, and even individual "apathy" (Axel Schildt).

II.

Most of these terms originate from the historiography of the First World War, which has likewise undergone a process of renewal in recent years. Today, the "First World War" – a teleological definition that only came into being after 1945 – is a necessary stage on our way to understanding the Second World War.² One of the most striking results of this volume was that the comparison can be subdivided into three complementary but separate sections: the direct connection, the contemporary referential, and the historiographical model.

The direct connection ties a historical knot between the two conflicts that can thus be analyzed as two parts of the same belligerent sequence that lasted from 1914 to 1945. The history of the occupation of the border regions between France and Germany is a good illustration of this point: "A young Belgian may have experienced the occupation of his region by German soldiers between 1914 and 1918 and then, after the signing of the Treaty of Versailles, may have himself taken part in the occupation of the Ruhr Area and the Rhineland. Twenty years later, he could again have found himself under the domination of a German administration" (Benoît Marjerus). Comparable situations can also be found in Central and Eastern Europe.

The contemporary referential emphasizes that the war experience of 1939 to 1945 was, first and foremost, based on the experience of the previous war, which had been very formative for the majority of its protagonists. Fascism and National Socialism in part evolved as a result of the bitterness brought about by the defeat of 1918. These ideologies were shaped by negative recollections and by the desire to revise history. The memory of the "Great War" was, however, still vivid among the opponents as well – be it in defeated France of 1940 which offered its services to Pétain, the "Victor of Verdun," or in Great Britain which, still under the impression of the ubiquitous victory of 1918, decided to confront Hitler around the same time (Mark Connelly). The war experience was thus primarily based on memories of the preceding war: it resulted from depictions of the past as well as the immediate present – at least initially. This is a trait shared by everyone's war experiences, not only those of its strategians.

The historiographical model originates from yet another field. Whatever similarities, nexuses, and differences may exist between the two wars, historians tend to employ similar concepts in analyzing them – together or separately. Even the term "war experience," provided that it has a universal meaning, has recently been explored particularly by historians of the First World War. Moreover, the relatively new concept "culture of war," which should not be understood as a mere consequence of the societies involved in the war, but rather as their true "matrix," is primarily an interpretation of the First World War.³ In turn, we should note that the fashionable concept of "brutalization" does not play a significant role in this volume, even though it was specially created in order to describe the preconditions for the Second World War.⁴

III.

In order to be able to regard these two global conflicts together, however, the notion of the "violence in the war" occupies a prominent place among the "imported" or only recently created concepts. Only a few years back, this phrase was considered a pleonasm. However, it describes a clearly defined field of research: the differentiated analysis of the concrete practices aimed at weakening or annihilating the enemy – combatants as well as civilians, on the collective as well as the individual level. It takes into consideration the inflicted as well as the suffered violence, the actual as well as imaginary violence, in collective consciousness.[5] This volume contains various examples of this, especially in the contributions on the "forgotten victims": the German prisoners of war after 1945, the victims of allied bombardment in Germany and – a less well known episode – in Italy, where the terror strategy was explicitly aimed at weakening the population's morale (Gabriella Gribaudi). The policies of the Italian occupiers in the Balkans, which were in some cases similar to those of the National Socialists, also play an important role, however (Filippo Focardi). These are various historical examples that until recently were still considered too "delicate" to address openly or even regarded as "taboo," since they had been instrumentalized by the defeated countries after the war or hushed up entirely in the service of the necessary establishment of positive myths: the "good Italian" versus the "bad German," the "decent Wehrmacht soldier" versus the "sadistic Nazi," etc.

In collective memory as well as in the historiography of the past twenty years, the various forms of violence that shaped the Second World War have been subsumed under the extreme and unprecedented violence of the Genocide of European Jewry – a topic that is very well researched. The fact that the Holocaust plays a less central role in this volume than in past publications is certainly not the result of specifications to that effect nor indeed an agreement between the authors. Perhaps historiography, if its perspective is less tainted by this dark shadow, can not only take into consideration other traumatic experiences and other victims of the war, but also finally regard the "Final Solution" in a broader context, relating it not only to National Socialism and anti-Semitism, but also to the history of the war itself. The final step toward genocide – or even the murderous intention – can neither be separated from the reality of strategic war decisions nor from the specific conditions of the violence that surfaced in this context. This violence was particularly aimed at the Jews, but also at other groups or categories of people. This topic undoubtedly also gives rise to controversies: should past research have focused "less" on the extermination of the Jews in order to bring to light other categories of victims as well? Is there not the risk of measuring all the victims of the war with the same yardstick? Can the German victims of 1945 be placed on the same level as the victims of National Socialism? Certainly not in a moral sense, but the question remains how a serious history of the last great global conflict, if it hopes to truly understand the events, can continue to neglect the fates of several millions of people. This silence and these taboos have, after all, weighed heavily on the memory of the protagonists and involved nations. This history should, however, be treated with due accurateness and caution, if only to avoid political revisionism (Dietmar Süß).

IV.

The situation of the Germans "resettled" after 1945 relates to another important topic addressed in this volume: ending wars or "exiting wars," a concept borrowed from the French notion of "sorties de guerre." Here we must also note that the term has only recently come to be widely used and thus requires some elucidation.[6] "Exiting wars" not only refers to a simple state, a given situation at a certain point in time, such as the term "postwar era," but rather a process, a development that encompasses social dimensions of great scope and in a certain sense can be understood as a continuation of the war – on the national as well as the international level. The term thus avoids a clear-cut distinction between "before" and "after," which is characteristic for legal documents that define specific states of war or peace, ceasefire, capitulation, or armistice, and that assume a clearly defined temporal caesura. Certainly these elements must be part of a historical analysis, and certainly they play a decisive role in the outcome of the war, but they do not suffice to explain the concrete social situation or the various historical processes at work here. Not everybody arrives at the war's end at the same time, or under the same circumstances, or even with the same short-, mid-, or long-term consequences. The demobilization of body and mind depends on the social situation, the circumstances of the conflict, the extent of the preceding mobilization, and the degree of the totalization of war.[7]

It is thus not surprising that there is no consensus on the precise point in time the Second World War ended – except on the observation that the year 1945 may not necessarily be the most appropriate date. Should we rather take the year 1947, which can be regarded as the beginning of the Cold War? Or should we, at least for Germany, consider the monetary reform of 1948? Perhaps we should even contemplate the very late year 1989? Of course it depends on the events we wish to accentuate. For the majority of people, the war generally ended with the end of rationing and the return to normal sustenance, i.e., around 1948/49. For the combatants, the war did not end with physical demobilization, but rather with the possibility of returning to a normal social and psychological life – if this was indeed possible at all. For many veterans, this return to "normality" took years. As far as the prisoners of war of the defeated nations are concerned, the chronology is again completely different. We can even assume that many victims never exit from the war. The abuse suffered during the war was followed by a time of traumatization – a key to understanding the anamnesis of memories of the Second World War.

V.

The recent and ongoing interest of historians in the outcome of the war is already a significant development in itself. In the 1920s and 30s as well as in the 1950s and 60s, research primarily focused on the causes of war and the reasons for its outbreak. Half a century later, the beginning of the war appears less interesting than its end. This is undoubtedly the result of the culture of memory and remembrance that has evolved in Europe in the course of the past twenty years or so, and which tends to construct the Second World War as never-ending. This political and cultural trend has contributed to a new perspective on the Second World War that concentrates more on its lethal dimension, is marked by perceptions of the reality under National Socialism and its aftermath, and in consequence focuses more on the fates of individuals.

Regarding this question also, which is at the heart of the volume, there is a shift in perspective. Contrary to established assumptions, the beginnings of memory are not to be found at the war's end. Memory is no longer understood as isolated – as an element detached from the actual history of the events. On the contrary, it has come to be understood as central to the events themselves and in this way makes sense of the direct connection between the actual experience and its memory. These developments moreover prompt historians to regard the war and its aftermath in unison, without any artificial distinction. This type of approach is absolutely essential if we want to distinguish between myth and reality (John Ramsden). It is moreover indispensable if we want to understand the very topical and increasing phenomena of "victimization." During the war and in the immediate postwar years – even into the 1960s – official remembrance in countries such as France, Great Britain, and Belgium tended to accentuate the figure of the hero, the sacrifices made by the combatants, and the martyrdom of the resistance fighters. Forty years later, the nations of heroes have turned into nations of victims (Chantal Kesteloot, Richard Bessel), and the officially recognized victims of today are no longer the same as directly after the war. The Jewish victims of the Holocaust still occupy the most prominent place. However, other victims who were treated with contempt in the euphoria of victory or, conversely, in the shame of defeat (among them prisoners of war, forced laborers, displaced persons, and homosexuals who suffered persecution) have come to resurface in collective memory in the more recent years.

We must continually call to mind, however, that these phenomena do not develop simultaneously, or in the same ways, across Europe. Indeed, a unique memory of the war prevails in the countries of the former Eastern bloc. In Russia, despite the falsifications of history that were asserted during the Stalin era (and which many people continue to believe), the heroization of the "Great Patriotic War" is still the dominant paradigm (Sergei Kudryashov). In Poland, on the other hand, interest in this historical era has markedly decreased since the demise of communism and the weakening of the national paradigm – a development that has also led to some positive changes, however. For one thing, the image of Germany has become more positive among broad segments of society and there is a better understanding of the fates of the victims. Moreover, a discussion has ensued about topics that were previously taboo, such as Polish collaboration with the National Socialist occupiers (Piotr Madajczyk). Last but not least, Germany is a unique case since the same experience has produced two separate depictions and two diverging forms of memory and remembrance in the former GDR and the FRG before the *Wende*, respectively (Dorothee Wierling). In all of the countries of the former Eastern bloc – and this constitutes a significant difference to the Western European countries – the memory of the Second World War cannot be regarded as separate from the traumas inflicted by the Soviet system, which was strengthened by the victory of 1945. While the memory of communism is lacking in the debates about past crimes in the West, it is still very present in the East.

In fine, these conflicts of memory should alert us to the illusion that a homogenous history of the Second World War is possible. Certainly historians should be capable of transcending their own national frames and of developing a non-Manichean and comparative perspective on the conflict – particularly this conflict. A social and cultural history of the war and the postwar era allows for this sort of perspective, although we should avoid a viewpoint too strongly shaped by political and ideological considerations, as in the past these have all too often facilitated "nationally-centered" approaches in historical analyses. Apart from that, today there is a strong political will to construct a united European memory of the Second World War, in the course of which some authors have even proposed to regard the holocaust as a negative myth that forms the basis for the contemporary values of the European Union, which was created from the rubble of Europe dominated by National Socialism.[8]

Among other things, an important conclusion of this volume is that the ruptures that resulted from the varying war experiences persisted into the postwar years and in some ways even cast their "shadows" into the present. If the necessity to remember appears to be prevailing everywhere as a new moral imperative and a new human right, this certainly does not mean that the contents of these various depictions of the past will be the same. Historians must hence guard against a holistic approach that levels all differences in the name of a universal definition of "combatants," "victims," and "violence," as well as against an exclusively national perspective, which in turn erases all differences and cleavages on the local, social, and cultural level that the war had forced on the societies in question. The more the memory of the war tends to produce an increasingly abstract and purely cognitive perspective on the actual war experience, the more we must bear in mind that this war was more than just a "Great War": it was the cause of partitions, divisions, and deep wounds, some of which are only slowly beginning to heal.

Notes

1. This introduction is based on my remarks at the end of the colloquium which took place in Paris, 3–4 April 2006. To previous conferences cf. especially the (unpublished) colloquium conducted by the Netherlands Institute of War Documentation (NIOD): Memory and the Second World War in International Comparative Perspective, Amsterdam, 26–28 April 1995. See also the conference conducted by the Comité international d'histoire de la Deuxième Guerre mondiale: "1945: Consequences and Sequels of the Second World War, Montréal, 2 September 1995, 18e Congrès international des sciences historiques," in *Bulletin du Comité international d'histoire de la Deuxième Guerre mondiale*, 27/28 (1995); "The Second World War in XXth Century History, Oslo, 12 August 2000, 19e Congrès international des sciences historiques," in *Bulletin des Comité international d'histoire de la Deuxième Guerre mondiale*, 30/31 (2000). Cf. also earlier conferences on similar topics conducted by the German Historical Institute Paris: Claude Carlier and Stefan Martens, eds., *La France et l'Allemagne en guerre. Septembre 1939–novembre 1942, actes du colloque de Wiesbaden, 17–19 mars 1988* (Paris, 1990); Stefan Martens and Maurice Vaïsse, eds., *Frankreich und Deutschland im Krieg (November 1942–Herbst 1944), Okkupation, Kollaboration, Résistance* (Bonn, 2000).
2. Cf. Stéphane Audoin-Rouzeau, Annette Becker, Christian Ingrao and Henry Rousso, eds., *La Violence de guerre, 1914–1945. Approches comparées des deux conflits mondiaux* (Brussels/Paris, 2002); Bruno Thoß and Hans-Erich Volkmann, eds., *Erster Weltkrieg. Zweiter Weltkrieg: Ein Vergleich. Krieg, Kriegserlebnis, Kriegserfahrung in Deutschland* (Paderborn, 2002); Nicolas Beaupré, Anne Duménil and Christian Ingrao, eds., *1914–1945. L'ère de la guerre*, 2 vols. (Paris, 2004).
3. Cf. Stéphane Audoin-Rouzeau and Annette Becker, *14–18: Understanding the Great War* (New York, 2003). See also Martin Van Creveld, *The Culture of War* (New York, 2008).
4. Cf. George L. Mosse, *Fallen Soldiers. Reshaping the Memory of the World Wars* (Oxford, 1990).
5. Similar studies in a rapidly growing field of literature include: Joanna Bourke, *An Intimate History of Killing: Face-to-Face Killing in Twentieth-Century Warfare* (London, 1999); John Horne and Alan Kramer, *German Atrocities, 1914: A History of Denial* (New Haven, 2001); Audoin-Rouzeau et al. (see note 2); Omer Bartov, Atina Grossmann and Mary Nolan, eds., *Crimes Of War: Guilt And Denial In The Twentieth Century* (New York,

2003); Alf Lüdtke and Bernd Weisbrod, eds., *No Man's Land of Violence. Extreme Wars in the 20th Century* (Göttingen, 2006).
6. See for example: Stéphane Audoin-Rouzeau and Christophe Prochasson, eds., *Sortir de la Grande Guerre. Le Monde et l'après 1918* (Paris, 2008); Bruno Cabanes and Guillaume Piketty, eds., »Sorties de guerre au XXe siècle«, special issue, histoire@politique, 3, November–December 2007.
7. On this question, see in particular: "Démobilisations culturelles après la Grande Guerre," in *14–18. Aujourd'hui. Today. Heute*, no. 5 (May 2002).
8. On this question, see: Daniel Levy and Nathan Sznaider, *The Holocaust and Memory in the Global Age* (Philadelphia, 2006); Henry Rousso, "History of Memory, Policies of the Past : What For?, in Konrad Jarausch and Thomas Lindenberger, eds., *Conflicted Memories. Europeanizing Contemporary Histories*, (New York, 2007).

Chapter 2

CONCEPTUALIZING THE OCCUPATIONS OF BELGIUM, LUXEMBOURG, AND THE NETHERLANDS (1933–1944)

Benoît Majerus

When Germany invaded Belgium in August 1914, its preparations had largely been limited to the realm of military operations. At some point, there certainly existed long-term plans concerning the fates of the occupied territories, but nobody seemed to have given much thought to how the mid-term administration of these regions was to be organized. During the preparations for the impending war, the partial occupation of France after the war of 1870 was never mentioned. Only in October 1914 did the German general staff for Belgium – and later for Poland – resort to occupation structures directly modeled on the experience of the Franco-German War. Thus, in 1914 it became necessary to "reinvent" this occupation. The chaos that ensued during the first weeks of the occupation shows that decision makers were quite unclear about the future fates of the territories. They had assumed that the war would be over soon and therefore had not devised any detailed administration plans.[1]

When, 26 years later, German forces crossed the Rhine River a second time and occupied Belgium, Luxembourg, and the Netherlands, the situation was completely different. Occupation had become a Europe-wide experience. Especially in the border regions between Germany and France, occupiers and occupied populations had encountered one another on various occasions; the roles were sometimes even reversed in the course of a few years. Many a young Belgian had experienced the occupation of his region by German soldiers between 1914 and 1918 and then, after the signing of the Treaty of Versailles, had himself taken part in the occupation of the Ruhr Area and the Rhineland. Twenty years later, he

---

Notes for this chapter begin on page 18.

again found himself under the domination of a German administration. On the German side, many generations had been shaped by similar experiences, which significantly contributed to the evolution of a national identity in this border region between France and Germany.

This chapter traces the conception of the occupation of the Benelux countries the Germans developed at the time. It is not primarily interested in the views of the National Socialist functional elite, but rather in the networks between administrators, historians, and other intellectuals who had an interest in these regions. Wittingly or unwittingly, these individuals took part in a thought process that facilitated German plans for the reannexation of these territories between 1940 and 1944.

In this context it is important to distinguish between two levels of historical time: space of experience (*Erfahrungsraum*) and horizon of expectation (*Erwartungshorizont*) (Reinhart Koselleck).[2] The concept space of experience is particularly suitable for this analysis in that it combines two significant terms: space in its geographical and experience in its temporal connotation. Combining these two elements for the region in question, which encompasses Germany, Belgium, Luxembourg, and the Netherlands, we can discern three important aspects: the First World War, the occupation of the Rhineland and the Ruhr Area, and *Westforschung*.[3] Space and time are intimately interwoven here. Moreover, these aspects had multifaceted impacts on the planning and implementation of Germany's occupation policies in Western Europe from 1940 onwards.

Three possible spaces of experience

The first space of experience is the First World War. In the West, there existed two occupation regimes between 1914 and 1918. The first was in Luxembourg, whose political elite had remained in the occupied territory: the Grand Duchy retained its neutrality during the occupation. Due to its policy of accommodation, it could more or less remain autonomous politically. Moreover, the Germans did not have to invest a lot of personnel into the surveillance apparatus, which in fact remained quite small over the four years of occupation.[4] German publicists, however, paid this model little attention during the interwar years (and historians neglect it to this day). Belgium, in turn, was ruled directly as a general government (*Generalgouvernement*), replacing the Belgian king and government, which went into exile. This model was characterized by a very languid administration. Not only did it require a great number of personnel – which was henceforth no longer available for service at the front – it was also not very successful. During the interwar years, the high expenditure, especially the deployment of so many administrators, was repeatedly juxtaposed with the little benefit it had yielded.[5] As most of the analyses are from the 1920s, very few authors believed that these experiences might serve some practical purpose in the near future. At this point in time, the horizon of expectation hardly encompassed the possibility of their utility in the mid term. As we shall see, this changed in 1939. In addition, many men who held power positions in Nazi Germany had experienced the First World War as young soldiers – among them Adolf Hitler, who regularly visited Brussels. This was also the case for administrators who served in Belgium, Luxembourg, and the Netherlands between 1940 and 1944. Alexander von Falkenhausen, the military commander in Belgium and northern France, was not only the nephew of the last general governor in Belgium during the First World War, Ludwig von Falkenhausen, he had also fought at the western front. Bodo von Harbou, the future chief of the general staff, had taken part in the capture of Liège in August 1914. Eggert Reeder, the future head of administration of the Military Commander in Belgium and Northern France, had fought at the western as well as eastern front. They all, consciously or not, experienced the administration of the occupied territories, be it on the way to the front or be it on a short leave.[6] On the one hand, they were thus able to develop their own conceptions of life at the base, which is generally identified with the occupation. The numerous accounts of this "being in between," of life between home and front, some of which were written during the war, but most after 1918, have to this day not been sufficiently analyzed. On the other hand, these young soldiers developed conceptions of the "Other" on their travels through Luxembourg, Belgium, and northern France that significantly shaped their views and perceptions in the long run.[7]

The second space of experience is the occupation of the German border regions from 1918 onwards, i.e., the occupation of the Ruhr Area and the Rhineland as well as the mandate over the western Saarland. As Gerd Krumeich has recently pointed out, the occupation of German regions after the signing of the Treaty of Versailles was a continuation of the war in a certain sense.[8] The reversal of roles between occupiers and occupied is obvious, particularly in the realm of everyday life. The regulations imposed on the Germans by the French and the Belgians had been adapted almost literally from the German regulations enforced in these countries between 1914 and 1918. This experience of occupation had to be incorporated into the new order all the more as many of the former German officials came from precisely those regions that were occupied by French and Belgian forces during the 1920s. Without considering their own practices as occupiers during the First World War, the Germans portrayed the French and Belgians as particularly barbaric.

The third space of experience encompasses what is known as *Westforschung*. In the Weimar Republic, an academic school came to evolve that concentrated on Belgium, Luxembourg, and the Netherlands. Universities of cities such as Aachen, Bonn, Cologne, and Münster, all in close proximity to the borders of these three countries, developed a science in itself that was based on a blend between history, geography, and folklore (i.e., "folklife"). Scholars involved in *Westforschung* did not, however, limit their efforts to the academic realm, but rather regarded their work as a contribution to the revision of the Treaty of Versailles. At home in the western part of Germany, already during the Weimar Republic and the early years of National Socialism they led a proxy war with their colleagues in Belgium, the Netherlands, and Luxembourg.

These last two spaces of experience – the occupation during the interwar years and *Westforschung* – are geographically connected, as they concern the same territories. Men such as Franz Thedieck experienced the interwar occupation, pursued *Westforschung*, and took part in devising the future German occupation apparatus. In this sense, they can be regarded as a "point of intersection" between the three spaces of experience. Born in 1900, Thedieck belonged to a generation that was too young to serve in the First World War. Under National Socialism, these men received a "second chance." In 1923, Thedieck became the director of the counter-espionage department of the Prussian ministry of the interior against separatism (*Abwehrstelle des Preußischen Innenministeriums gegen den Separatismus*) in Cologne, where after the occupation of the Ruhr he struggled against the presence of French and Belgian troops on the right bank of the Rhine River. In the 1930s, he was employed in various regional administrative bodies in what is today Rhineland-Palatinate. Among other things, he was active in organizations that pursued a pro-German cultural policy in the regions Eupen-Malmédy. Moreover, his name appears in numerous initiatives affiliated with *Westforschung* before, during, and after the Second World War.[9]

The planning and implementation of the occupation

In contrast to the First World War, the future occupation of the territories to the east and west of Germany during the Second World War was carefully planned and coordinated from the second half of the 1930s onwards. The German Army High Command (*Oberkommando des Heeres* – OKH) created task forces that were assigned the job of planning the future war in the West. After the bitter experience of the Polish campaign, where the Wehrmacht had been unable to prevail, the OKH wanted to be better prepared for the new western front. In the army groups A and B, commissions also considered the possible problems a long-term occupation of Belgium, Luxembourg, and the Netherlands could entail.

The example of the commission of the army group B illustrates the significance of the three spaces of experience mentioned above. Eggert Reeder, the future head of the administration department, was in charge of this commission. In May 1933, a few months after Hitler's seizure of power, he was named district president (*Regierungspräsident*) of the city of Aachen. As the chief administrator of a region bordering Eupen and Malmédy, which were ceded to Belgium in 1919, he fraternized with *Westforschung* circles. In 1936, he was relocated to Cologne, where he held the same post. During the war, he established contact with a group of high-ranking German officials around Werner Best.

At least three adherents of *Westforschung* were also represented in this commission: Franz Petri, one of the most productive scholars in this field, who wrote a handbook for German administrators in Belgium, Luxembourg, and the Netherlands in the framework of the commission;[10] Rolf Wilkening, whose dissertation on the German minority in the Liège region was advised by Martin Spahn, the director of the Institute for Space Policy (*Institut für Raumpolitik*) in Cologne; and Werner Reese, who in 1939 wrote a habilitation on "The Netherlands and the German Empire" in Berlin.[11] Other scholars were indirectly affiliated with the commission. For one, the Special Group Student (*Sondergruppe Student*) supported the commission. Its members' task was to confound the enemy behind the front lines in the Netherlands and in Belgium. They also took part in the commission's preparatory studies. One member of this special group testified after the Second World War that the experiences of the First World War were extensively discussed at these meetings. Among these young men was also Ludwig Pesch, whose dissertation on "People (*Volk*) and Nation in the Intellectual History of Belgium" was advised by the already mentioned Franz Petri in Cologne in 1939.[12]

Two civil servants who had already served in the military administration in Belgium during the First World War also participated in these preparations and made "valuable contributions based on their past experiences to the quartermaster general's first requests."[13] Although the authors' names are not known, it is very probable that one of them was Robert Paul Oszwald, as the commission met on the premises of the Dutch Institute in Cologne, which Oszwald, among others, had founded.

The first few weeks of occupation threw the models worked out by the commission into some disarray. However, the military succeeded in putting its plans for Belgium into action by establishing a military administration. Various members of the preparatory commission, such as Petri, found posts in this new administration. Others came from the border region and had been involved in *Westforschung*: Eggert Reeder, the head of administration, Franz Thedieck, his general secretary, and Harry von Craushaar, the director of administration. Incidentally, these men were all from Cologne.[14] The topicality of the First World War also becomes apparent in numerous details: for example, all situation reports of the president of the civil administration during the First World War, Maximilian von Sandt, can be found in the stock AJ40 of the French

National Archives in Paris, which contains the German files on Belgium and the Netherlands from 1940 to 1944.

In 1941, in his résumé of the first year of occupation, Reeder as the highest administrator in Belgium points out two important levels: "In its work method, the military administration strives to learn from (1) the successes and failures of the German administration in Belgium during the [First, B.M.] World War, (2) the conduct and administration of the Allied occupation powers in the occupied German territories."[15] Precisely what sorts of "learning processes" did this imply? Reeder distinguishes between four different aspects: Flemish policy,[16] economic policy, administration, and the treatment of the population. According to Reeder, the pro-Flemish policy of the First World War, which among other things led to an administrative splitting, had "encouraged the opposition of the civil servants and the economic leadership to a degree that made the additional deployment of a substantial number of German personnel necessary."[17] During the First World War, attempts had failed to "sufficiently put the Belgian economy and Belgian labor into the service of the German war economy. ... Exploiting these negative experiences, labor and economic performance have now largely been activated."[18] Reeder moreover criticized that the administration of the First World War was marked by an "excessive degree of organization as well as a lack of clear-cut competences in the various assignments."[19] In order to underline his various points, he relied on the literature from the interwar years mentioned above. He was particularly inspired by a book Ludwig Köhler, head of the section commerce and industry, had published in 1927. As far as the treatment of the local population is concerned, nowhere did the author mention the atrocities committed by the Germans in August 1914 – they are simply denied. Rather, he writes about the "Victor airs ... of the enemy occupation powers in the Rhineland," which by their conduct "forced the German people into a serious, unvarying resistance."[20]

No doubt, this historical argumentation served Reeder's own interests. For him, the most important lesson of this first occupation was that the Germans' aggressive stance, particularly in the areas of Flemish policy and economic policy, had made an additional administrative effort necessary. For this reason, Reeder desired greater cooperation by the Belgians under German supervision. He instrumentalized the experiences of the First World War in his dispute with the SS, which demanded a more energetic policy. The lessons that Reeder drew from the first occupation were in perfect accordance with the policies he intended to pursue in the future.

The function of the historical commission founded in June 1943 "on the assessment of the General Government Belgium" was quite similar. Its aim was to write a history of the general government that could be instrumentalized to serve present goals.[21] At the outset, various topics were touched upon: Flemish policy, the organization of the administration, the attitude of the Belgian police, and the use of Belgians in the German army. By the end of December 1943, the commission's work began to falter due to the growing problems at the fronts and a rising need for soldiers. However, the commission completed a total of three studies: on Flemish policy, on the stance of Cardinal Mercier, and on the Belgian legal system. Petri's analysis of Flemish policy was even read by Himmler.[22]

In the Netherlands, the continuity between the three spaces of experience is partly disrupted due to the fact that the military leadership suffered a defeat in their opposition toward the political option of installing a civil administration under the leadership of Arthur Seyss-Inquart. In contrast to Belgium, the Netherlands were not so much governed by administrative elites that came from the border region itself. However, as detailed analyses of this question are still pending, it is difficult to gain an impression of the precise composition of the German administration in the Netherlands. Judging by the few available documents, the apparatus behind the Austrian Seyss-Inquart was also dominated by Austrians.[23] Seyss-Inquart himself moreover relied on different personal experiences regarding the organization of a country's occupation. He had been the mastermind of the Austrian "Anschluss," and as the first Reich governor (*Reichsstatthalter*) was among those responsible for the incorporation of Austria into the Reich. At the end of October 1939, he was transferred to Poland as deputy to General Governor Hans Frank. Although in the case of Austria we cannot speak of an occupation proper, the Germans were nonetheless confronted with similar problems in the administration of the Netherlands, especially regarding the attainment of legitimacy and the conferment of sovereign rights. The different geographical orientation most likely explains the lower significance of men from the field of *Westforschung*, although they were represented here as well. The most prominent figure in this respect is undoubtedly Robert Paul Oszwald. As a member of the political section of the administrative apparatus operating in Belgium between 1914 and 1918, he had attained a reputation as an expert on the Flanders region during the interwar years. Among other academic institutions, he worked at the Provincial Institute for Westphalian Regional and Folklife Studies (*Provinzialinstitut für westfälische Landes- und Volkskunde*) in Münster, where shortly before 10 May 1940 he was assigned the task of compiling maps of the Netherlands. He was also actively involved in the negotiations with Dutch elites that agreed to cooperate with the Germans before he returned to Berlin in October 1940.[24]

Another, less well-known case is that of the research assistant Wilhelm Josef Bodens, who pursued archeological and ethnological research at the University Bonn after 1935. From August 1940 onwards, he found himself employed at the Reich commissariat (*Reichskommissariat*) as an academic advisor.[25] And Walter von Stokar, who worked as an archeologist at a local community museum prior to the invasion of the Netherlands, participated in conceptualizing cultural policy in the occupied Netherlands.[26]

In Luxembourg, the situation rather resembled that in Belgium, although the army was unable to prevail in the Grand Duchy. The military administration barely lasted for two months. Indeed, at the end of July 1940, Hitler decided to transform the administration of the Grand Duchy into a civil administration. Parallels to the Belgian case can essentially be found on two levels. For one thing, many administrators also came from the bordering regions. The head of the civil administration, Gustav Simon, was district leader (*Gauleiter*) of the district Koblenz-Trier. Since the second half of the 1930s, he had professed his interest in Luxembourg. Many other administrators came from the other side of the Mosel River, which marks the border between the two countries. Thus, the head of the district propaganda department (*Gaupropagandaleiter*) of Koblenz-Trier was simultaneously the head of the Reich propaganda department (*Reichspropagandaamt*) in Luxembourg. The mayor of the city of Trier, Konrad Gorges, became the mayor of Luxemburg City in 1943.[27] As had been the case in Belgium, individuals from the field of *Westforschung* were involved in devising the occupation apparatus. One of the most important figures in this context is Josef Schmithüsen. As a geographer at the Institute for Historical-Regional Studies of the Rhinelands (*Institit für geschichtliche Landeskunde der Rheinlande*) of the University Bonn, he worked on Luxembourg from 1933 onwards. He argued that the Germanic border did not end at the rivers Mosel and Rhine, but rather extended to the Ardennes and thus included Luxembourg and parts of Belgium. In 1940, he published a new study entitled "The Land of Luxembourg – Nature, Customs and Traditions, and the Rural Economy."[28] In the same year, he was involved in the establishment of a collaboration movement in Luxembourg, the Movement of Ethnic Germans Living Abroad (*Volksdeutsche Bewegung*), that brought together various groups that were willing to collaborate with the Reich. At the end of 1940 he left Luxembourg for Russia, but his academic work continued to serve as a justification for the "Germanization" policies pursued in Luxembourg and its incorporation into the *Moselland*, as the occupiers termed it. His studies became the basis of a book that appeared in 1942, portraying the Grand Duchy as an integral part of the Third Reich.[29] It was published by Paul Hermann Ruth, who was also responsible for the publication of the "Hand Dictionary for the German Populations in the Border Regions and Abroad."

Summary

When the Second World War broke out in 1939, various spaces of experience influenced how people perceived the new situation and, accordingly, how they acted. The few examples introduced in this contribution describe experiences at the meso level. There can be no doubt that at the macro level, the National Socialist paradigm shaped the general patterns of occupation policy. Notwithstanding the argumentation of more recent studies, which advocate a reevaluation of German repression policies, the differences in the treatment of the populations in the eastern and western territories can be explained by the racist character of the National Socialist ideology.[30] At the micro level, a different logic and individual mindsets determined people's behavior. As already mentioned, the experiences described here are situated on the meso level as far as both the individuals in question and their ideologies are concerned. For Belgium, Luxembourg, and the Netherlands, three spaces of experience appear particularly significant in this context: the First World War, the occupation experiences in the Ruhr Area and the Rhineland, and *Westforschung*.

Notes

1. Benoît Majerus, "Von von Falkenhausen (Ludwig) zu von Falkenhausen (Alexander). Die deutsche Verwaltung Belgiens in den zwei Weltkriegen – Brüche, Kontinuitäten und Lernprozesse," in Günther Kronenbitter, Markus Pöhlmann and Dierk Walter, eds., *Besatzung. Funktion und Gestalt militärischer Fremdherrschaft von der Antike bis zum 20. Jahrhundert* (Paderborn et al., 2006), 131–33.
2. Reinhart Koselleck, *Vergangene Zukunft. Zur Semantik geschichtlicher Zeiten* (Frankfurt/M., 1989), 349–75.
3. Translator's note: *Westforschung* was an academic branch that focused on the history, geography, and "folklife" of the countries and regions to the west of Germany.
4. Gilbert Trausch, "La stratégie du faible: le Luxembourg pendant la Première Guerre mondiale (1914–1919)," in Gibert Trausch, ed., *Le rôle de la place des petits pays en Europe au XXe siècle* (Baden-Baden, 2005), 45–176.
5. Franz Anholt, *Die deutsche Verwaltung in Belgien* (Berlin, 1917); Heinrich Waentig, *Belgien* (Halle, 1919); Ludwig von Köhler, *Die Staatsverwaltung der besetzten Gebiete*, Vol 1: *Belgien* (Stuttgart et al., 1927); and Robert Paul Oszwald, "Errichtung des deutschen Generalgouvernements in Belgien 1914," in *Staat und Gesellschaft. Erich Brandenburg zum 60. Geburtstag* (Leipzig, 1928), 234–69.
6. As an example of this: Ernst Jünger, *In Stahlgewittern*, 14th edition (Berlin, 1933), 98–9.
7. Klaus Latzel, *Deutsche Soldaten – nationalsozialistischer Krieg? Kriegserlebnis – Kriegserfahrung 1939–1945* (Paderborn et al., 1998).
8. Gerd Krumeich, "'Der 'Ruhrkampf' als Krieg: Überlegungen zu einem verdrängten deutsch-französischen Konflikt," in Gerd Krumeich and Joachim Schröder, eds., *Der Schatten des Weltkriegs. Die Ruhrbesetzung 1923* (Essen, 2004), 9–24.
9. Among others, see the contributions by Michael Fahlbusch, Stephan Laux, Thomas Müller, Klaus Pabst, and Jan Zimmermann in Burkhard Dietz, Helmut Gabel and Ulrich Tiedau, eds., *Griff nach dem Westen. Die 'Westforschung' der völkisch-nationalen Wissenschaften zum nordwesteuropäischen Raum (1919–1960)* (Münster et al., 2003).
10. Franz Petri, *Die Niederlande (Holland und Belgien) und das Reich. Volkstum – Geschichte – Gegenwart* (Bonn, 1940).

11. Marnix Beyen, *Oorlog & verleden. Nationale geschiedenis in België en Nederland, 1938–1947* (Amsterdam, 2002), 86–94. As head of the "branch West" of the Reich Student Leadership (*Reichsstudentenführung*), from 1935 onwards Wilkening worked on Belgium within the German-Flemish Society (DeVlag).
12. Étienne Verhoeyen, *De 'Sondergruppe Student'* (unpublished), 2–3. With gratitude to the author for allowing access to this unpublished work.
13. "Aufgrund ihrer damaligen Erfahrungen wertvolle Beiträge zu den ersten Anforderungen des Generalquartiermeisters." Konrad Kwiet, *Reichskommissariat Niederlande. Versuch und Scheitern nationalsozialistischer Neuordnung* (Stuttgart, 1968), 34.
14. Horst Romeyk, *Verwaltungs- und Behördengeschichte der Rheinprovinz 1914–1945* (Düsseldorf, 1985) does not address this interesting phenomenon, which most certainly affected the administration of the Third Reich.
15. "In ihrer Arbeitsmethode bemüht sich die Militärverwaltung zu lernen aus 1. den Erfolgen und Misserfolgen der deutschen Verwaltung Belgiens während des [Ersten, B.M.] Weltkriegs, 2. der Haltung und Verwaltung der alliierten Besatzungsmacht in den besetzten deutschen Gebieten".
16. The German policy of favoritism toward the Flemish population in Belgium intended to deepen the rift between the Dutch-speaking and the French-speaking populations in Wallonia.
17. "Die Opposition der Beamtenschaft und Wirtschaftsführung in Belgien so stark aktiviert und einen nicht unerheblichen Einsatz weiterer deutscher Beamter notwendig [ge]macht".
18. "Die Wirtschafts- und Arbeitsleistung Belgiens in nennenswertem Umfange in den Dienst der deutschen Kriegsführung zu stellen ... Unter Ausnutzung der negativen Erfahrungen konnte die Arbeits- und Wirtschaftsleistung jetzt weitgehend aktiviert werden".
19. "Überorganisation sowie mangelnde Abgrenzung der Zuständigkeit in den Aufgabengebieten".
20. "Vainqueur-Allüren ... der feindlichen Besatzungstruppen im Rheinland," die durch ihre Haltung das "deutsche Volk zu einem ernsten, einheitlichen Widerstand zusammenzwangen." CEGES, GRMA T 501, roll 104; yearly report of the military administration in Belgium and northern France for the first year of occupation (Jahresbericht der Militärverwaltung in Belgien und Nordfrankreich für das erste Einsatzjahr), A8.
21. Letter of the group Volk/allg. to Reeder from 28 October 1943, cited in Marnix Beyen, *Een bewoonbare geschiedenis. De omgang met het nationale verleden in België en Nederland, 1938–1947*, Dissertation (Leuven, 1999), 164.
22. Els Herrebout, *De Duitse Archivschutz in België tijdens de Tweede Wereldoorlog* (Brussels, 1997), 273–75 and Archives nationales Paris, AJ40, carton 14.
23. Friedrich Wimmer (Vienna) as general commissary for administration and justice, Hans Fischboeck (Vienna) as general commissary for finance and economy, Hans Albin Rauter (Styria) as general commissary for security. There were certainly also various higher administrators who came from German port cities such as Bremen and could thus rely on experiences important for the administration of the Dutch ports.
24. Stephan Laux, "Flandern im Spiegel der 'wirklichen Volksgeschichte'. Robert Paul Oszwald (1883–1945) als politischer Funktionär, Publizist und Historiker," in Dietz, Gabel and Tiedau, eds. (see note 9), 247–90.
25. NIOD, DOC I, Wilhelm Josef Bodens's personal identification file.
26. Uta Halle, "Archäologie und 'Westforschung'," in Dietz, Gabel and Tiedau, eds. (see note 9), 390–4.
27. Mathias Wallerang, *Luxemburg unter nationalsozialistischer Besatzung. Luxemburger berichten* (Mainz, 1997), 56.

28. Josef Schmithüsen, *Das Luxemburger Land. Landesnatur, Volkstum und bäuerliche Wirtschaft* (Leipzig, 1940) (Forschungen zur Deutschen Landeskunde, 34); Klaus Freckmann, "Luxemburg – ein Teil des deutschen Reiches? Zur Kontinuität der landes- und volkskundlichen Kulturraumforschung und ihr Verhältnis zur kulturellen Identität Luxemburgs im 20. Jahrhundert," in Dietz, Gabel and Tiedau, eds. (see note 9), 480–81.
29. Paul Hermann Ruth, ed., *Luxemburg* (Breslau, 1942).
30. Gaël Eismann, "La politique répressive du Militärbefehlshaber in Frankreich, un cas singulier en Europe occupée (1940–1944)?", in *Revue Européenne d'Histoire Sociale – Histoire & Sociétés* 17 (2006), 44–55.

Chapter 3

THE ROLE OF THE WAR IN NATIONAL SOCIETIES:
The Examples of Belgium, Luxembourg, and the Netherlands

Chantal Kesteloot

As an introduction to his dissertation on the significance of the Second World War in the history of the Western European countries occupied by Nazi Germany, Pieter Lagrou raised the question whether the war constituted a fundamental rupture with these countries' recent history and whether it functioned as a catalyst in the development towards a new society.[1] Considering the question from a broad and long-term perspective, he tended to give a negative answer. Nevertheless, more than sixty years after the actual events, we have not stopped commemorating what appears to have become the most important experience of the twentieth century in the public as well as the political realm.

In the course of the past sixty years, our perspective on the Second World War has fundamentally changed: from an emphasis on national and later democratic values, the scenario has shifted to a universal approach that focuses on human rights, with the extermination camp Auschwitz and the paradigmatic notion of "never again" at its center. What kind of a role do national representations play in this general approach? What are the after-effects of this period and what are the questions that seem to dominate today?

This chapter analyzes three national scenarios. These three political spaces are all marked by their own individual particularities and each of them looks back on an occupation experience that is no less distinctive: a simple, straightforward annexation in the case of Luxembourg, a military occupation regime in Belgium, and a civil administration in the

---

Notes for this chapter begin on page 37.

Netherlands. If one were to search for a common ground for all these spaces in terms of how the war is commemorated, one can distinguish between a strong culture of commemoration (*commémorationisme*)[2] on the one hand and emphasizing one's own role as a victim (*victimization*) on the other. For that matter, one could ask whether these two categories are not the inseparable members of a new "couple," united before the altar of the "obligation to remember," a couple that dominates public space whenever there is a representation of the Second World War involved. These phenomena certainly do not appear everywhere and not always to the same degree, but they nevertheless represent the most striking similarity between the three case studies examined here. However, beyond these terms we must also observe the role of the two world wars as an important factor in the evolution of national identities. In this respect, the boundaries between history, memory and ideas tend to be blurred.

Twenty years ago, the historian Lou De Jong, a distinguished expert on the Second World War in the Netherlands, diagnosed that interest in the epoch would not necessarily drown in an ocean of oblivion in the near future, but that it would certainly decrease – albeit without entirely disappearing. This was supposedly the case because the Second World War was something anomalous (in the life of society) that undermined the norms of humanity and the values of a democratic society. At the time, he simply hoped that the omnipresence of the past would not become an element of escape in the face of the complexity of today's world.[3] An amusing detail is that fifteen years before, the very same De Jong had simply proclaimed that "interest in the War would not persist much longer" and that historians should therefore abstain from any predictions concerning the future.[4]

This understanding of the war as a special period in the history of societies is, consequently, nothing new. The notion of a past that "does not pass" (*onverwerkt verleden*) is a phenomenon that arises in the context of the history of the Second World War, but which is not limited to this history: today, it appears as though a similar process is in the making with regard to the colonial past, although this is still far away from affecting Dutch society as a whole – as was the case with the occupation.

This past that is "difficult to digest" is told in different ways in the Netherlands, in Belgium, and in Luxembourg. But, even more so than in the respective political structures, this becomes apparent in the area of public opinion, in representations, in different notions and depictions and particularly in the realm of remembrance.

Over the years, the practice of remembrance has conquered various domains: literature, culture, media, and, of course, politics. Initially perceived as a sort of representation of the time from 1940 to 1945, memory became a subject of history itself before it conquered the field of politics. At a time when historians began to distance themselves from memory, politicians appropriated this field so thoroughly that commemoration ceremonies marked by litanies on the "duty to remember" came to occupy the place of history.

From heroes to victims: making sense of the Second World War

Immediately after the war, it was considered good form to emphasize one's own role as a resistance fighter. The myth that "everyone was a resistance fighter," which prevails in several European countries, can be encountered in a Luxembourgian and Dutch version as well. In Belgium, however, the resistance movement had a negative connotation from the very beginning: that of resistance fighters who, towards the end of the war, temporarily took the law into their own hands to enforce public order and to assault (actual or supposed) collaborators.

The "Heroes of the Nation" and the "Nations of Heroes" – to use a phrase coined by Pieter Lagrou – prided themselves on having played a positive role in the liberation of their countries, and thus in their history. Today, sixty years later, these very same heroes would prefer to identify with the "Nations of Victims" who are to be revered not on account of their deeds, but rather on account of their suffering. Between the words that were addressed to a survivor of the Genocide in the Netherlands in 1945 ("Well, there are many like you who came back. You are lucky not to have stayed here. We suffered terrible hunger."[5]) and the speech given by the Belgian president of the National Confederation of Political Prisoners and Entitled Persons (*Confédération nationale des Prisonniers politiques et Ayants droit*) in 2003, there seems to be a strange and shocking continuity that fits into what is today most often termed the "competition of victims":

> People talk a lot about genocide, but not enough about the suffering of our citizens who fought in the Resistance and their incarceration in National Socialist prisons and concentration camps. Many of our friends died there from total exhaustion. But we, the survivors, are still suffering from the physical and psychological after-effects, and nobody talks about it anymore. ... There is also a big difference between the Belgian political prisoners, who, as a result of their patriotic activities, died exhausted by hunger and forced labour in the German concentration camps, and the majority of Jews, who were killed in the gas chambers directly after their arrival – all due to racial reasons. Thus, they did not suffer as much as the Belgian political prisoners.[6]

This written (not spoken) "faux pas" – the remarks were certainly exaggerated and the author has apologized – clearly corresponds with a widespread way of thinking among former resistance fighters who feel robbed of everything: the legitimacy of their commitment, the visibility of the resistance, and of their home or the ideology they once fought for. Since the normative hierarchy has been reversed – what some term "remembering the dead," which has replaced concern for the living – and since the victims (particularly of the genocide) are now preferred to the resistance fighters, the latter are left with little more than to present themselves as victims too ... before they dare claim that they are simply the victims of the omnipresence of Auschwitz.[7] This question not only concerns the generation of those who were active in the war; in the case of those persecuted on account of their "race," the trauma can span generations and thus affect the second and even the third generation as well. This is a phenomenon that does not apply to the resistance movement. The child of a hero cannot in principle be a victim, although studies dealing with the children of resistance fighters who died during the war have shown that these children do feel like victims, or at least felt that way at some point in their lives.[8]

Even more so than in Belgium, in the Netherlands the symbolism of Auschwitz, which has almost attained the status of a civil religion, is central to people's conceptions of the past: firstly because, at seventy-five percent, the percentage of Jewish victims is the highest in all of Western Europe, secondly because the stance of the Dutch population, which was initially regarded as a source of pride, has since become an element of shame, and thirdly because the discourse of victimization has clearly become the dominant paradigm in the Netherlands and has acquired some very special undertones. This point will be revisited later in the chapter.

In Luxembourg, Auschwitz never really dominated commemoration – for the simple reason that in Luxembourg there are also other victims worthy of honor: displaced populations and forced draftees (*Zwangsrekrutierte*) of which about one third – 3,150 of the 10,000 approximately who were drafted – died. In short, they were all victims who belonged to the "national community." In light of these circumstances, the "competition of victims" takes on a different form here. The various groups crafted their own forms of remembrance and cultivated their own legitimacy and symbolism (which went as far as founding their own respective research centers)[9]. In this context, the "competition" does not juxtapose resistance fighters and victims of the genocide, but rather resistance fighters and forced draftees.

In Belgium, the term victim often acquires strange connotations. On the Flemish side, and especially on the Catholic-Flemish side,[10] those who were persecuted by law immediately after the end of the war (a process referred to as the "repression") are regarded as victims of the Belgian – i.e., francophone – state aiming to dissolve the Flemish movement via the judicial apparatus. This reveals a strange reversal of conceptions in which the victims are defined contrary to our expectations. This certainly does not mean that the Flemish confess to having collaborated, but rather that the collaboration is regarded as an aberrance of an elite and of a youth whom the Belgian (francophone) state had granted neither upward mobility nor cultural legitimacy. This discourse is still prevalent in some circles. In 1997, the Catholic parliamentarian Herman Suykerbuyck (born in 1934) proposed a draft for an act to the Flemish parliament to compensate the victims of war and repression. This was – to put it mildly – a wayward combination to which he later also added the victims of the Spanish Civil War as a concession to win the support of the left. With this draft, he put the victims of war on the same one level with the victims of repression; in other words – resistance fighters and collaborators. This proposal, which mixed up two very different things, provoked a wave of protest from the French-speaking population. The circumstances under which the ballot was conducted, however, were even more outrageous. In the end, the act was actually passed by an "alternative" majority with the cooperation of the Vlaams Blok – the Flemish extreme right – in open contradiction to the so called *Cordon sanitaire*, the mutual agreement between the democratic parties in the Flanders region not to form alliances with the extreme right. However, the act was never implemented because it was overruled by the Arbitration Court. "War victims" thus remain within federal jurisdiction in Belgium. Regardless of the controversies it sparked, this incident clearly illustrates how the term "victim" has become a filter for all sorts of recognition.

Incidentally, not only individuals can be recognized as victims. On the occasion of the commemoration of the sixtieth anniversary of the end of the war in Belgium, the honorary degree "city or municipality, victim of the war 1940–1945" was created. Following the conception of a linguistically subtle definition, 103 places of memory were selected: 40 in Flanders, 53 in Wallonia (a result of the German Ardennes Offensive), and 10 in Brussels. In all areas the vast majority (85 in total) were cities or municipalities. This provided plenty of opportunities for politicians to practice themselves in the so called "duty to remember."

What sort of developments led to this shift? How can it be reconciled with the various national experiences and how do these respectively grasp this phenomenon?

From exaltation to profanation

After having been written mostly by the actors themselves, the experiences of societies during the war became an object of historical research – a shift that set in only during the 1960s in the Netherlands, in the 1970s in Belgium, and even later in Luxembourg. The first academic studies led to a profanation, but also to a specific sort of recognition of these experiences.

Never before had public interest in, and research on, a conflict allotted contemporary witnesses such a prominent role. The First World War had opened the door for contemporary witness accounts as a source, but not for the contemporary witnesses themselves as human beings made of flesh and blood. The Second World War provided a previously unknown visibility for the "witness" who, transformed into an "icon," now occupies a firm position in public space and will shape the history of other conflicts in times to come. Moreover, relying on oral history was important for our understanding of certain aspects of the history of the Second World War at a certain time – namely when the archives were still closed or in cases where relying on classical sources proved to be problematic (for example when researching underground activity).[11] Thus, historians validated contemporary witnesses as legitimate sources while taking care to develop a critical approach toward oral accounts and, with regard to a "scientific" historiography of the Second World War, to contextualize them as one among various types of sources.

This scientific approach led to the question of these witnesses' commitment in a broader, more global perspective. In the case of Belgium, a frame was gradually constructed for the discourses of the contemporary witnesses, which until then had been missing: from *goed* (good) to *fout* (bad) via the term *moindre mal* (lesser evil). What is more, the opening of the archives by and by allowed for the possibility of a different historiographical approach. Of course, the state of historical research is different in various societies. It is thus not surprising that in comparison to the other two case studies we are concerned with here, the Netherlands were pioneers in this regard, although it cannot be said that Dutch scholars began to write the history of the Second World War very early on. However, this discrepancy undoubtedly says more about the role of contemporary history in that particular society than about the difficulty of writing the history of this war.[12]

The head start in the Netherlands as compared to its two neighboring countries can easily be explained by the favorable institutional circumstances in that country: already in 1945, an institute for the history of the war was founded. In Belgium, such an initiative was not launched until the late 1960s. In Luxembourg – about the competition between victims – we have the Documentation- and Research Center on the Resistance, founded in 2002, and the Documentation- and Research Center on Forced Draftees, founded in 2005.[13]

The special position of contemporary witnesses also has to do with the development of the media, which gave them a third kind of legitimacy (the first coming from written documents and the second from oral history). Via the media, particularly television, the messages of the contemporary witnesses reached ordinary people in their homes: at first in the Netherlands with the pioneer series *De Bezetting* by Lou De Jong, which was conceived as an epos and aired between 1960 and 1965 in twenty-one episodes. In Belgium, series like *De Nieuwe Orde* or *Het Verzet* were made which shocked the viewers. In both cases, these series were broadcast long before the introduction of cable television and at a time when programs were often limited to national productions, which led to extraordinarily high ratings. In the case of the last two episodes of *De Bezetting* (before 1965 there were no means of measurement), the viewer rate was at sixty-five percent (calculated merely according to the viewer audience over twelve years of age at a time when there were 1.3 million television sets in the Netherlands).[14] In the case of the series *De Nieuwe Orde*, broadcast between February and June 1982, there were eight-hundred thousand viewers among 5.5 million overall inhabitants (in Belgium's Flemish provinces). In both cases, it was mostly contemporary witnesses who had their say.[15] However, there is a significant difference between the two series: while collaborators are depicted as anonymous actors in *De Bezetting*, *De Nieuwe Orde* relentlessly exposes collaboration and the collaborators, which more closely resembles later depictions in the Dutch series *Vastberaden maar soepel en met mate*. Through these series, contemporary witnesses came to occupy an important position in accounts of the war. In the series *Jours de Guerre*, broadcast by the francophone Belgian television, the contemporary witness is honored in all of his or her everyday gestures. In other words, they pay homage to the war itself, experienced by ordinary people. Through an increasingly individualized history of the war, it thus provides an even greater potential for identification.

In Luxembourg, this trend starts at a later point in time, but it no less demonstrates the interest in the Second World War as seen through the prism of the contemporary witness account.[16] The documentary film *Heim ins Reich* directed by Claude Lahr and produced by the National Audiovisual Center (*Centre national de l'audiovisuel*), was a blockbuster (two-hundred thousand viewers in six weeks) that even topped the film *Collateral* with Tom Cruise in 2004. Contemporary witness accounts constitute a large part of this film; they define the flow of its narrative. The topic is further elaborated on the homepage of the National Audiovisual Center, which contains short biographies of the contemporary witnesses featured in the film.

However, the academic approach of this history has not stopped the flood of contemporary witness accounts, which, thanks to technological innovations, have now also become important "actors" in various exhibitions dealing with the period. It seems as though the commotion is not allowed to come to an end. "New" (contemporary) witnesses appear – like those men and women who are featured in the Belgian filmmaker André Dartevelle's last film *Leni, la vie après la mort* (Leni, Life After Death), which recounts a woman's experience of the Ardennes Offensive as a child. Other contemporary witnesses write about their experiences or speak about them in an ultimate effort (see the documentary *De laatste getuigen* by Luckas Vandertaelen, 1991) and find allies in the media and in op-ed columns to ensure their visibility and legitimacy. However, their presence is not limited to written and audiovisual media. In Belgium, as well as in the Netherlands and Luxembourg, contemporary witnesses are called upon to speak in front of high school students, ensuring that the individual experience pushes the war into the realm of emotions, dispelling historical analysis and a differentiated understanding of complex factors. Certain politicians even appear to endow these contemporary witnesses with a fateful role as "guarantors of history," the true keepers of memory, and the only ones authorized to pass on what they experienced.[17] This viewpoint is characteristic of the way some of these politicians regard the work of historians.

The role of the war for national identity in times of national values

Questioning national identities

In the three countries analyzed here, the Second World War plays an important role in the (de-)construction of a national identity. In Europe, which is currently undergoing a phase of reconstruction, the question of identities is omnipresent. How can the European dimension be reconciled with national and/or regional realities? How can one retain one's own identity, one's specific values, in a world that is becoming increasingly international? How does the Second World War continue to influence these considerations?

In 1940, the Netherlands as well as Luxembourg appear to have been countries in search of a founding matrix. In 1939, Luxembourg had celebrated its centenary, but obviously it was the war that was to cement its identity in the end: "Luxembourg's historians agree that the deeper significance of the Second World War for the country's history is that it concluded the process of national identity formation."[18] However, as Benoît Majerus has rightly put it, a process of national identity formation never simply comes to a conclusion of its own accord, it is always evolving. The significance of the war for the formation of national identity is nevertheless fundamental – an observation that holds true for all the countries included in this study – but it is expressed according to each country's individual particularities. In the case of Luxembourg, it is important to point out that this was the first time citizens of the country had died "for the homeland." Henceforth, the First World War would appear as a much less significant event for collective memory. This observation also holds true for the Netherlands, as it had remained neutral between 1914 and 1918.

The national history of the Netherlands seemed to lack, in a certain sense, great events that could have served to cement national identity. Since the "Revolt of the Netherlands" (1568–1648), there has hardly been an event that mobilized broad segments of the population; and the defeat in 1830, which led to the independence of the Belgian provinces, was not a triumphant event fit to generate positive national identification. Thus, the Second World War was to replace what is referred to as the Eighty-Year War (*Tachtigjarige Oorlog*) in the Netherlands. We can, incidentally, find elements of continuity in the topics that are generally raised in connection with these two wars: love of freedom, the rejection of absolutism and totalitarianism, and an affirmation of the essential value of justice over injustice.[19] This connection, which began to take hold already during the Second World War, is in accordance with a heroic approach, a strong national identity that came to dominate during the early postwar decades. (This phenomenon is in a way similar to the patriotic commemoration of the year 1914 in Belgium, which was to fuel commitment to the resistance in 1940.) The difficult colonial context of the postwar times (i.e., the decolonization of Indonesia) would further cement the "positive" view of the Second World War. However, developments during the 1960s would gradually shake this image.

Thus, while the war appears to have played a "positive" role in the formation of national identities in the Netherlands and in Luxembourg, the Belgian case demonstrates the opposite. Certainly, behind this somewhat hasty and necessarily simplified assertion, there is a complex and nuanced reality. In fact, depending on the chronology one employs, this reality becomes much more differentiated.

Of all the periods in the history of Belgium, the times of war – the First as well as the Second World War – were clearly the most challenging ones. They entailed political debates, be they on the policies of the institutions (state, church, army) at those times, the actions of collaborators (activists), the role of the resistance, or the general attitude of the population.

Belgium is certainly far from being the only country where such discussions arose in the second half of the twentieth century. Specific for this country is that the national question coincides with the war memory – a phenomenon which goes back to the First World War and was amplified by the Second World War. After a short period of increase in "Belgian nationalism", the war's legacy appears to have become an element of separation, first on an ideological level and secondly – most importantly – between the Flemings and the Wallons. Undoubtedly, it is more the images and not so much the facts that lead to a contradiction in perceptions. They are also much more virulent in societies than in the academic community of historians. However, the latter cannot entirely escape the fragmentation of identities and conceptions; at times they even, wittingly or unwittingly, encourage them.[20]

The most surprising case, however, is the example of the Netherlands. Dutch society looks at the Second World War as a decisive factor in terms of national identity. At the end of the war, the Dutch were proud – proud to have been resistance fighters and proud especially to have contributed to the rescue of Jews. But in the course of the decades, this heroic image became tainted. The Dutch were not the heroic resistance fighters they considered themselves to have been. They saved their Jewish neighbors less often than people in other countries. This process of realization would actually turn into a "trauma," fed by feelings of shame and guilt. The ideas of tolerance and respect toward minorities are, after all, integral parts of Dutch national identity.[21] How then was this memory of persecution to be integrated into national identity? The painful realization of this not so glorious behavior (which is not a moral judgment) produced a traumatic identity. When the past ceases to be a source of pride, it becomes a source of shame and the Dutch began to perceive themselves as the victims of their own lack of heroism. How to integrate this experience into national identity, of which we know from the research of Ernest Renan that it grows out of the ability to forget as well as historical mistakes?[22] In any case, it is to a greater degree reinforced by shared suffering than by shared joy. This shared suffering can be defined, not as that of the Dutch and the Jews, but as the suffering of the former who collectively failed to act according to the ideals of respect and tolerance that define their national identity. This development should be considered as a special context. Nowhere else has the phenomenon of self-victimization found such facilitators, even at the institutional level. Nowhere else was the psychological dimension of suffering underlined so strongly. This phenomenon goes back to the times immediately after the end of the war and then exploded in the 1970s in an interplay between silence and interests, as Jolande Withuis has very fittingly put it.[23] These chronological sequences are not limited to the psychological dimension, however. There are undoubtedly mutual influences: traumatized individuals confess, institutions are created and laws passed (*Wet Uitkeringen Vervolgingsslachtoffers*), followed by the founding of ICODO (*Informatie- en Coördinatieorgaan Dienstverlening oorlogsgetroffenen*), today COGIS (*Kennisinstituut sociale en psychische gevolgen van oorlog, vervolving en geweld*),[24] and historical studies, but mostly radio and television broadcasts, publicize the phenomenon. Regarded from the outside, the significance of the term "trauma" in Dutch culture is puzzling.

As far as the aftermath of the war is concerned, in Belgium this psychological dimension is hardly ever mentioned. However, legislation dates back to the immediate postwar years and at the time mainly physical after-effects were recognized. Up to this day there is a commission at the Administration for War Victims (*Administration des Victimes de Guerre*) in charge of trying to fulfill unsatisfied claims. It is composed of representatives from associations of former resistance fighters and other "war victims" as well as state authorities. For better or for worse, psychological injuries and their repercussions are not among those claims still waiting to be settled. The only category in which this factor was really taken into account is children who were hidden during the war. However, this statute was not included in Belgian legislation until 1999.

In the Netherlands, the psychological dimension touches upon other aspects of the war's aftermath. For example, it is striking to note the attention paid to this dimension in the context of the support for the families of former collaborators after the files pertaining to their family member were transferred from the Central Archive of the Special Administration of Justice (*Centraal archief bijzondere rechtspleging*) to the State Archive of The Hague and made accessible in 2000. A special room and a psychological support team were specially created in order to receive the aggrieved parties.

Neither in Belgium nor in Luxembourg can we observe a similar phenomenon as far as both individual as well as collective behavior is concerned. The culture of trauma as a pillar of national identity is a syndrome in the Netherlands that currently seems to go beyond the Second World War. It is being fuelled by the controversies surrounding the behavior of the Dutch Battalion (*Dutchbat*) in the enclave of Srebrenica in former Yugoslavia in 1995 and the murder of the right-wing populist Pim Fortuyn in 2002. Are these the repercussions of postwar legislation, which was very selective in its politics of recognition? Does the fact that the Dutch have not experienced foreign aggression in more than a century (since the French occupation of 1813) or the premature disappearance of ideological antagonisms play a role in this tendency? It could also be the weight of a Protestant culture that has a different concept of suffering – the strange mix between a very individualized society and collective dimensions of suffering (consider the significance of Auschwitz as a sort of civil religion). Or are we facing the internalization of a notion of mental health directly imported from the United States in the concept of post-traumatic stress syndrome? These questions remain to be answered.

In times of democratic values: the Second World War as a history lesson on racism and right-wing extremism

In periods when democratic values seem challenged – at times even threatened – by the revival of the extreme Right, the experience of the Second World War is used as a "history lesson." This vision again is quite characteristic with regard to the way historical research seems to be perceived by politicians. They continue to be blinded by a very stereotypical view of the Second World War – a perception that almost amounts to an epos of good against evil. The fact that the history of the Second World War by far surpasses this vision as far as good and evil are concerned is not acknowledged in political circles. It is almost as if time has stood still, as if their vision of the past was that of their childhood: the times when children were taken on outings to national memorials once a year and shown the local heroes who had died so that we could all stand here today. In this scheme, the war is regarded as external aggression and the struggle of the "heroes" as a fight for democracy. To be sure, the modalities have changed in today's commemoration culture as compared to past rituals: visiting war memorials has gone out of fashion. Practices have become more subtle and include visiting sites where important events took place during the war, or even a trip to Auschwitz. The perfect mixture for media success seems to be to assemble a few young people, contemporary witnesses, politicians, and of course a few journalists in order to ensure the visibility of the event.

Belgian politicians were eager to convey this message particularly during the 1990s when the extreme Right celebrated its comeback on the political stage. However, this does not seem to have yielded significant results as the extreme Right still attracts every fourth voter in the Flanders region of Belgium and every third voter in Antwerp, the most important Flemish city.[25] This is the case despite the fact that politicians have taken special measures by establishing the Center for Equal Opportunities (*Centre pour l'Égalité des Chances*), the action group Democracy or Barbarianism (*Démocracie ou Barbarie*), the Committee 8 May (*8 mei comité*), and the Historical Pole of Defense (*Pôle historique de la défense*) – a multitude of institutions to ensure the continuation of commemoration.

Public funding and commemoration

The attention political decision makers pay to the analysis of the Second World War – in particular the funds they allot to this purpose – is of course an important indicator in measuring the topic's political significance. In the past few years, all three countries have invested substantial efforts into the creation of special institutions and pursued a specific museum policy.

Immediately after the end of the war, there were several proposals for the foundation of museums. Usually, it was associations of former resistance fighters who put forward these proposals as they were keen to underline their commitment. For a long time, the museums that were founded in this light retained their original forms and purposes. However, due to the lack of sufficient funding and qualified staff, they became outdated at some point. In this area also, the changes of the past thirty years are remarkable. Cultural tourism has developed and the wars – the First as well as the Second World War – have become a "stable" value in this respect.

It is no coincidence that the latest book on twentieth-century places of remembrance in the Netherlands begins with the Anne Frank House.[26] In 2004, almost a million visitors visited this site alone. In 1995, around three-hundred thousand visitors saw the exhibition *J'avais 20 ans en 1945* (I was twenty years old in 1945) in Belgium – an unprecedented success for a historical exhibition. We must add, however, that Belgian politicians and other prominent public figures set an example, among them the king of Belgium. In his address on 21 July 1995, the Belgian national holiday, he called upon his fellow citizens to visit the exhibition as a "patriotic duty."

New sites were created and already existing ones were renewed in order to meet the demands of an increasingly critical public. The Dutch Resistance Museum in Amsterdam was founded in 1985, fairly late, by former resistance fighters worried about the appearance of right-wing extremist groups in the Netherlands.[27] In 1999, the museum's concept was thoroughly revised: it moved to new premises and a new exhibit was developed according to the latest museology. In Belgium, it was the national Mémorial de Breendonk, now the National and International Memory Center (*Centre national et international de la Mémoire*), that was thoroughly redesigned (at a cost of more than two million euros) in order to meet the purportedly high demands of the public. The will to implement a scientific approach is clearly visible. Certainly, the means available today cannot be compared with what used to be the standard. Museology has become a discipline in its own right, employing historians, exhibit decorators, and interior designers. Both public and private funding is, of course, essential. Certainly, the risk of interference and lapses as well as the reformulation of the message according to political requirements cannot always be avoided. The controversies regarding the future of the Jewish Museum of Deportation and the Resistance in Malines (Belgium) illustrate this point. It almost became a Flemish Museum of the Holocaust and will perhaps yet become a "Transit Mechelen."[28] In any case, it is exemplary for the difficulties inherent in a coherent policy and raises the question surrounding the risk of political interference when museums rely too strongly on public funding. In Belgium, the future of the Jewish Museum mentioned above raises the sensitive question regarding the authority responsible for the symbolic site of the barracks in Dossin, which are located in the Flanders region, but were for the most part not used for Flemings, Walloons, or Belgians, but rather as a transit camp for Jews.

In Luxembourg, an exhibition entitled *Et wor alles net esou einfach* (It was not so easy) opened in 2002. This exhibition was part of a chain of events guided by the desire to found a scientific perspective on the war. Based on an interdisciplinary approach, the exhibition focused on ten questions that avoid neither collaboration nor genocide, neither fear nor one's own heritage. The accompanying catalog, based on scientific findings, also openly addresses these questions. This is a commendable effort in a country in which the question of collaboration was swept under the rug or at least evaded for such a long time. In 2005, these topics resurfaced, this time in the framework of the exhibition *The Great Plundering* on the difficult topic of expropriation. This initiative was a follow-up exhibition to the first one and carried the subtitle *New Questions on Luxembourg and the Second World War*. Both projects shared the intention of addressing the questions they outlined in a problem-oriented approach that would induce visitors to further think about them. Behind all these initiatives is the question of Luxembourg's national identity – a historical question that goes far beyond the history of the Second World War. This question is also at the center of the research project *History, Memory, and Identities* on places of remembrance in Luxembourg, which in turn is part of the larger project *Living in Luxembourg Tomorrow*.

Let us commemorate, commemorate, commemorate – in times of universal values

While the commemoration festivities on the thirtieth and fortieth anniversaries of the end of the war were still held in the context of the bipolar world order, the fiftieth and sixtieth (undoubtedly the last anniversaries that contemporary witnesses will experience) were quite different. However, new groups of contemporary witnesses such as war children and the children of resistance fighters have recently started to play an important role. These commemorations have never been spontaneous events; today they have become completely institutionalized. Moreover, new public holidays have been created and it is sometimes difficult to keep them apart. May 8, the symbolic date for the end of the Second World War, is not a public holiday in the Netherlands, Belgium, or Luxembourg. In the Netherlands, it is May 4 (Remembrance Day) and May 5 (Liberation Day); in Belgium and Luxembourg, on May 8, the end of the Second World War is commemorated, but it is not a public holiday. In Belgium, only November 11 is a public holiday. Before January 27 was designated to commemorate the liberation of Auschwitz, Belgium had already decided that May 8 also had to become a holiday "to commemorate the victims of the Genocide committed by the National Socialist ideology."[29] However, Luxembourg tops it off: on the occasion of the war's sixtieth anniversary, it created a National Day of the Resistance (on February 27), a Commemoration Day in Honor of Luxembourg's Veterans and *Maquis* Fighters (May 8), a Commemoration Day for the Shoah and Luxembourg's Jewish Community (July 3), a national Commemoration Day in Luxembourg's Schools (October 10, the day on which the citizens of Luxembourg had declared their opposition to the German occupation in a referendum organized by the National Socialists in 1941), and last but not least a Remembrance Day of the Forces Enlisting and of the Return of the Luxembourgish Prisoners of War (November 12).

And historians?

To what degree do these turbulences surrounding commemoration, this influence of politics, and this omnipresence of the war affect historians? In the long run public funding, foreshadowing the influence of political decision makers, was clearly essential in the foundation of the institutions charged with the history of the Second World War.[30] All in all, these institutions enjoyed – and still do – a great deal of freedom as far as their research is concerned.

However, historians do not live in an ivory tower. "All historical research is embedded in a social context," Michel de Certeau observes. Historical research is always influenced by social implications and political demands. On the one hand, this is a form of recognition, on the other hand, it requires constant vigilance toward those who envisage a history in the service of power (or other aims). Of course the relationship between historians, society, and the political realm cannot be painted black or white. In all three of the national experiences described above, the individual war experiences and particularly the ways in which these diverse societies have cultivated a specific relationship with the past ("the texture of memory," as James Young has termed it) have influenced the research conducted by historians. The fact that Luxembourg's collaboration was such a difficult topic to address must certainly be attributed to the country's (small) size, where "everybody knows everybody," but also to the delicate question of the occupation regime and its forced draftees. Until this day these are generally regarded as victims even though some of them were members of the notorious 101st police regiment whose detrimental role in Germany's eastern occupation territories Christopher Browning has thoroughly analyzed. By contrast Flanders in the questions of collaboration was much easier to address (even though the fundamentally fascist character of the VNV, the Flemish National Union, is often disregarded in this context). This is due to a great degree to the attitude of the Flemish population toward the collaboration, more than to the abundance or lack of interest of historians on this topic.

There is more than just a chronological convergence between the omnipresence of the genocide and the work of historians. The persecution of the Jews has become one of the most important historiographical questions in Belgium and the Netherlands. However, in the Netherlands it is much more pronounced than in Belgium due to the special Dutch situation, i.e., the very high percentage of Jewish victims. In Belgium, "inner-Belgian matters" prevail in the country's remembrance of the war.

In Luxembourg, as we have seen, other groups of victims dominate the realm of commemoration. Despite these differences, ad hoc commissions were created in all three countries in order to investigate the question of Jewish wealth. These commissions made access to previously closed archives possible. The field of new claims also encompasses forced laborers – claims that will again challenge the prevalent concepts concerning war victims in these countries.

Thus, in a way, the demands of society and historical interest have come to intersect. However, this sort of research raises the question of the historian's independence. Political decision makers tend not to think in the long run, but rather act according to the requirements of the present situation. They pose questions that demand clear answers: yes or no, right or wrong. Thus, they work in a way contrary to that of historians. The latter, in turn, are often faced with the request to write history upon demand, on the basis of questions that are not their own. Therefore they are tied to aims that have more to do with remembrance tourism than with history. At best, historical research can inform political representations. But the aims often diverge. In Belgium, for example, the work of the historian Lieven Saerens on the Jewish community of Antwerp has sparked no less than two parliamentary initiatives.[31] However, it was less the quality of historical research than Saerens's disclosures that caused these controversies, as they underscore the idea of a (fascist) "black Flanders." There are also disputed aspects between the two "communities" of decision makers with regard to the genocide, a particularly sensitive question in this respect. The sudden interest of certain Flemish decision makers in providing vast funding for a project initially entitled the "Flemish Holocaust Museum" can be analyzed in the framework of a regional pattern: the aim was to show that Flanders cannot be reduced to the extreme Right and that, on the contrary, it intends to combat and condemn the return of right-wing groups by providing generous funding for this sort of initiative.

As far as the freedom of academic research is concerned, this sort of political interference is not without risk if the directions in which research is supposed to go are predetermined. This can be observed in the establishment of various special commissions and other research assignments. However, besides often providing access to closed archives, this sort of interference is also a source of additional funding, although in a very problematic context.[32]

In the Belgian case, the most recent developments involve plans for the establishment of a "special commission in order to research the relationship between public administrations, historical research, and the demands of society regarding history and memory."[33]

The majority of these sorts of initiatives do not really spark a new élan and are mostly based on a duty to commemorate – a search for emotions. In the long run, there is certainly the risk that they will unbalance historical research by pushing questions into the foreground that historians themselves would not have pursued, questions that are dictated by current political necessities.

These debates remind us just how important it is to continue to critically reevaluate history, all the more so when doubts arise in societies. It is a positive phenomenon that supply and demand diverge in the case of history. This contributes to reassessing old convictions, exposing stereotypes, and creating awareness for the fact that memory and identity are constantly in flux – a process on which historians have only a modest, but nevertheless tangible influence. Resorting to history enables a perspective on the life and survival of groups – on the material, but also on the cultural and psychological level. In order to ensure this life and survival, the concepts of group and community must be recognized. The historian does not always appear as the guarantor of this existence and even less as someone who sets the course for a constructivist approach to the past. Rather – and fortunately – the historian ensures that questions do not go around in circles. While societies and politicians can privilege a certain preferred version of history, historians analyze and interpret the past and its weight. Can historical research enter into a dialogue with politics without compromising these aims? This is just one in a long line of important questions that historians must perpetually ask themselves. However, it is a positive signal as it reflects the unavoidable dialogue in democratic societies which cannot simply disregard their own histories.

Notes

1. Pieter Lagrou, *Beyond Memory and Commemoration. Coming to Terms with War and Occupation in France after 1945* (London, 2003), 9.
2. In French, the term *commémorativite* is also widely used in this context.
3. Lou De Jong, *Het Koninkrijk der Nederlanden in de Tweede Wereldoorlog, Epiloog* (Amsterdam, 1988), 189.
4. "Want de belangstelling voor de oorlog zou toch niet lang meer blijven duren," as quoted in Chris Vos, *Televisie en bezetting. Een onderzoek naar de documentaire verbeelding van de Tweede Wereldoorlog in Nederland* (Hilversum, 1995), 9.
5. Lagrou (see note 1), 230.
6. François De Coster, "Nouvel An 2003," *L'Effort*, no. 1 (2003), 1.
7. See Rudi Van Doorslaer, "Gebruikt verleden. De politieke nalatenschap van de Tweede Wereldoorlog in België, 1945–2000," in Gita Deneckere and Bruno De Wever, eds., *Geschiedenis maken. Liber amicorum Herman Balthazar* (Gent, 2003), 227–66.
8. See Isabelle Ponteville and Chantal Kesteloot, "Dossier: Enfants de résistant ou de collaborateur: grandir sans père ou mère," in *'30 –'50. Bulletin du CEGES*, no. 37 (Brussels, 2002), XL.

9. See Benoît Majerus, *Besetzte Vergangenheiten. Erinnerungskulturen des Zweiten Weltkrieges in Luxemburg – eine historiographische Baustelle*, forthcoming. Gratitude is expressed to Benoît Majerus for allowing the author access to the text prior to publication.
10. In the Flanders region, the Christian Social Party dominated until the end of the 1970s. 1978: 43.5 percent of votes, 1981: 32 percent. On the national level, the PSC-CVP was part of almost all coalition governments between 1945 and 1999, except from 1945 to 1947 and 1954 to 1958.
11. Just regarding the Belgian case, Gie Van Den Berghe alone has secured sixteen hundred written accounts of National Socialist concentration camps from contemporary witnesses (numbers from 1994). For Luxembourg, 265 book publications can be found on the topic between 1945 and 1985, the majority of which were written by contemporary witnesses. See Guy Thewes, "La recherche historique sur la Deuxième Guerre mondiale au Luxembourg. Orientations et perspectives," in *"... et wor alles net esou einfach." Questions sur le Luxembourg et la Deuxième Guerre mondiale: contributions historiques accompagnant l'exposition* [exhibition book] (Luxembourg, 2002), 16–20, here 16.
12. "De huiver ten aanzien van de contemporaine geschiedenis was tot de Tweede Wereldoorlog blijven voortbestaan: een afstand van twee à drie generaties werd algemeen noodzakelijk geacht. Ook in dit opzicht leidden de oorlog en de ontstaansgeschiedenis van het instituut tot een doorbraak. De overheid aanvaardde met haar opdracht de contemporaine geschiedenis als volwaardig object van wetenschappelijk onderzoek. De discussie onder de vakgenoten laaide op. Vele jaren duurde het nog voor de wetenschappelijke bestudering van de jongste tijd als algemeen aanvaard kon worden beschouwd." Abraham Harry Paape, "Veertig jaar Rijksinstituut voor oorlogsdocumentatie," in David Darnouw, Madelon De Keizer, and Gerold Van Der Stroom, eds., *1940–1945: Onverwerkt verleden? Lezingen van het symposium georganiseerd door het Rijksinstituut voor Oorlogsdocumentatie, 7 en 8 mei 1985*, (Utrecht, 1985), 13.
13. See Majerus (see note 9).
14. See Vos (see note 4), 108.
15. "De liefst 197 getuigen die De Jong in zijn serie opvoerde, waren voor het overgrote deel uit de maatschappelijke elite afkomstig, voor zover die een rol in het verzet en de bezetting hadden gespeeld. Door deze getuigen met hun presentatie een zo prominente plaats te gunnen in zijn programma, werd *De Bezetting* niet alleen het verhaal van De Jong, maar ook het verhaal van de Nederlandse elite voor en tijdens de bezetting, waarbij velen van hen de gelegenheid werd geboden om een eigen evaluatie van hun functioneren te geven," ibid., 82.
16. In the 1980s, three Luxembourgian films had already addressed the Second World War. See Majerus (see note 9), 6.
17. "Dans quelques années, il n'y aura plus de témoins directs de l'Holocauste en vie. Il se peut que le révisionnisme et le négationnisme, et plus encore l'ignorance et l'indifférence, affectent la mémoire collective des gens et effacent lentement mais sûrement, le souvenir du passé." Patrick Dewael, *Respect mutuel. Les dangers du Vlaams Blok* (Brussels, 2002), 24; "By 2040 only a handful of centenarians will be left who have any first-hand memory of the war. And they are the end of the line. Once they have gone there will be no one who actually lived through the war, no eye-witnesses to describe what it was like growing up during the occupation, or being confined in a German or Japanese concentration camp, or what it was to live in hiding in an attic, no one who survived a death camp to find himself alone, without friends, without relatives and not even a photograph to remember them by. All that will be left are films, books, letters and other documents to inform us, and emotion." *World War II and the Aftermath in the Netherlands. The Victims, the Benefits, the Remembrance and the Lessons to the Future* (The Hague, 2000), 31.

18. "Les historiens luxembourgeois s'accordent pour dire que la signification profonde de la Seconde Guerre mondiale pour l'histoire du Luxembourg réside dans le fait qu'elle achève un processus de formation de l'identité nationale qui a commencé en 1939," Thewes (see note 11), 16.
19. Statement by the historian Madelon De Keizer in "Vrijheid, blijheid," *De Groene Amsterdammer*, 17 May 1995.
20. See José Gotovitch and Chantal Kesteloot, *Collaboration, répression. Un passé qui résiste* (Brussels, 2002).
21. See Ido De Haan, *Na de ondergang. De herinnering aan de Jodenvervolging in Nederland 1945–1995* (The Hague, 1997), 230.
22. "L'oubli, et je dirais même l'erreur historique, sont un facteur essentiel de la création d'une nation, et c'est ainsi que le progrès des études historiques est souvent pour la nationalité un danger," Ernest Renan, *Qu'est-ce qu'une Nation?* (1882), Chapter 1.
23. See Jolande Withuis, *Erkenning. Van oorlogstrauma naar klaagkultuur* (Amsterdam, 2002).
24. COGIS is a center specializing in the after-effects of persecution. It has eighteen regular and a number of temporary employees. See *Cogiscope*, no. 1 (2005), 41–42.
25. See the barometer of public opinion for the last trimester in *La Libre Belgique*, 27 March 2006 (25.7 percent intended voters for Vlaams Belang in Flanders, 9.4 percent for Front national in Wallonia, 3.4 percent for Front national and 6.6 percent for Vlaams Belang in Brussels).
26. Wim Van Den Doel, *Plaatsen van herinnering. Nederland in de twintigste eeuw* (Amsterdam, 2005).
27. *Het Verzetsmuseum in Amsterdam – The Dutch Resistance Museum* (Amsterdam, 2000), 123.
28. See Gie Van den Berghe, "Geen holocaustmuseum," in *Cahiers d'Histoire du Temps Présent (30/60) – Bijdragen tot de Eigentijdse Geschiedenis (30/60)*, SOMA/CEGES, no. 13/14 (2004), 287–310 and *Transit Mechelen. Museum over vervolging en volkenmoord. Conclusies en aanbevelingen van het Wetenschappelijk Comité*, (15 September 2005).
29. *Annales parlementaires*, Belgian senate, 15 May 1997.
30. "Ces instituts étaient des créations exceptionnelles, avec un cadre institutionnel sans équivalent. Ils étaient prévus comme temporaires, devant être liquidés une fois leur tâche accomplie. Issus directement d'initiatives gouvernementales, ils furent généralement rattachés, à l'époque de leur création, au cabinet du Premier ministre ou du ministre de l'Enseignement et de la recherche. Traditionnellement, pourtant, dans les démocrates parlementaires anciennes comme la France, les Pays-Bas et la Belgique, l'État n'avait pas un rôle prépondérant dans la recherche scientifique en général et encore moins dans la recherche historique." Pieter Lagrou, "Historiographie de guerre et historiographie du temps présent: cadres institutionnels en Europe occidentale (1945–2000). The Second World War in the XXth Century History," in *Bulletin du Comité international de la Deuxième Guerre mondiale*, no. 30/31 (1999/2000), 191–215.
31. Lieven Saerens, *Étrangers dans la Métropole. Histoire des Juifs d'Anvers* (Brussels, 2005).
32. On this topic, see the document signed by 151 Belgian historians entitled "Pléthore de mémoire: Quand l'État se mêle d'histoire," published in *La Libre Belgique* and *Le Soir*, 25 January 2006; and in its Dutch version "Geschiedenis is meer dan herinneren," in *De Standaard* and *De Morgen*, 25 January 2006.
33. Legislation draft introduced to the Belgian senate by Alain Destexhe and Isabelle Durant, Belgian senate – sessions 2005–2006, session on 14 March 2006.

Chapter 4

MYTHS AND REALITIES OF THE "PEOPLE'S WAR" IN BRITAIN

John Ramsden

Though it may seem both triumphalist and chauvinistic, a British historian has to begin any review of this topic by noting that, ever since 1945, both the greatest reality and the greatest myth about the Second World War for the British people has been the fact that "we won." Historians do not of course understand "myth" to mean what that concept conveys to the non-historian (at least in common English usage), where a myth is a popularly-believed untruth about the past – legends of King Arthur or Robin Hood, for instance. Historians rather use "myth" to denote the way in which memories of the past have been selectively organised, an agreed version of the past that explains how a people came to be what they believe themselves to be in the present. In that sense, "the myth of the Second World War" for the British – and one that has been rarely forgotten – is the fact that they were defeated neither in 1940 nor in 1945. Moreover, this is seen as something that somehow sets them apart from the rest of Western Europe – perhaps alongside the United States with whom that myth of the "good war"[1] of 1939–45 can be shared, perhaps merely different in themselves. Winston Churchill had after all assured both MPs and radio listeners in 1940 that were the British Empire to last for another thousand years – a palpable dig at Hitler's prediction of a thousand-year Reich – the Second World War would nevertheless be remembered as its "finest hour." This was reinforced in due course by his own *War Memoirs*, one of the best-selling book-series of all time, but also one that helped to fix a specifically Churchillian interpretation of the recent war in the popular consciousness.[2] The second volume, covering Britain's decision to fight on "alone" in 1940, the Battle of Britain, the Blitz, and the first evidence of a fight-back against the Axis powers in the Mediterranean, was itself titled "Their Finest Hour."

Notes for this chapter begin on page 50.

More than that, it has often seemed to the British that the world owed Britain special favors for her sacrifices in 1940–41, a view rarely expressed openly by British leaders but all too often central to their thought-world. This idea was frequently reinforced by their reception around Europe after 1945, when there was indeed in many countries a widespread gratitude to Britain for its liberating role during the recent war. When in 1946 Churchill asked the Labour Prime Minister Clement Attlee for permission to quote Cabinet documents in his forthcoming *War Memoirs*, he argued that his books "could win sympathy for our country, particularly in the United States, and make them understand the awful character of the trials through which we passed, especially when we were fighting alone, and the moral debt owed to us by other countries."[3] Permission was duly granted, and when the early volumes of Churchill's *War Memoirs* appeared (almost simultaneously published in fifty countries in a dozen different languages), they were often reviewed in just such terms of international gratitude. Or as one American put it, after listening to Churchill's impromptu speech at the Miami Yacht Club in 1946, merely to hear Churchill's voice revived his admiration for "Old England, which has always held aloft the banner of freedom.... . It re-lit memories of those dark days when, huddled with others about a radio in a small United States village, I heard, 'We shall fight them on the beaches'...."[4]

Yet it was not only in the English-Speaking World that such things were said, for wherever Churchill traveled in Europe in the later–1940s he was received with acclamation; statues were raised, streets, bridges and squares were named in his honor, and he received city freedoms and honorary degrees. Speeches delivered at such celebrations invariably referred back to his role as a warrior for freedom in the war years, and to how much Norway and Denmark, France, Belgium and the Netherlands owed to him and to the country that he had led and that he now symbolised internationally. This was both an elite and a popular process. When he visited Copenhagen in 1950 crowds were estimated by the Danish police to be the largest the city had ever seen. The story was reported by the *Daily Telegraph*: "Mr. Churchill welcomed by 100,000 Danes," cheering and shouting "We want Winnie" outside the Town Hall where he addressed them from the balcony. When the speech ended, and after a Danish resistance leader had hailed Churchill as "our great leader in our common fight," the crowd sang "For he's a jolly good fellow." In his celebratory speech, the University's dean hailed "that land which has given us a Shakespeare, a Milton, a Faraday, a Darwin; that England which gave us a Churchill when we needed him, has our love and admiration for ever."[5] The former French Prime Minister Paul Reynaud even argued in 1953 that Churchill was "of all men now living ... incontestably the most generally popular in France",[6] and Edouard Herriot was not far behind in his admiration. Speaking in June 1945, Herriot argued that if in June 1940 Churchill too had, capitulated instead of gritting his teeth and pulling himself together in a gesture of energy, what would we be at this moment? We should not be here today, all united together among friends: there would be the Gestapo instead. We must remain faithful to this old friendship, because the British are a people who love justice and freedom, and perhaps who love liberty more than we do. The British fought for right and liberty.[7]

Churchill's statue was erected in Brussels's Avenue Churchill in 1967, unveiled in the presence of Belgium's Prince Albert and Britain's Princess Margaret by Paul-Henri Spaak with a glowing tribute to Churchill. He was a man who had,

> par son courage, son obstination, sa confiance en lui-meme et dans la peuple qu'il représentait, a été l'élément décisif de la résistance au mal et de la défaite de celui-ci. L'éloge que l'on peut faire de lui se résume en une seule phrase trés courte mais lourde de signification: sans lui l'avenir aurait été différent Churchill fut notre leader à tous. L'immortalité que nous lui conférons en érigeant cette statue qui bravera le temps et empechera l'oubli, c'est aussi celle de la glorieuse aventure que nous avons vécue.[8]

We could pile up hundreds of such quotations, but those few must suffice. It was of course no accident that Churchill's visit to Denmark was so much celebrated in the *Daily Telegraph*, for British papers lapped up such stories, covered them in great detail, and complacently editorialised about them afterwards. As Professor Michael Foot has put it, there was an extraordinary recklessness in wasting such a great national asset of international goodwill by British governments in pursuing foolish foreign policies over the next two decades.[9] That recklessness too is though best explained within the core assumption that the rest of the world, and Europe in particular, had not yet compensated Britain for its moral war debts.

Nevertheless, the British have also regularly fantasised about invasion and defeat in 1940, as did Kevin Brownlow's film *It Happened Here*, the television series *An Englishman's Castle*, and Len Deighton's thriller *SS-GB*. Of the many "allohistories" of World War Two recently analysed by Gavriel Rosenfeld, four-fifths of British alternative histories fantasised about a Nazi victory, compared to under half of American fables and only a third of the German ones. It is as if the British can only bask in the glory of knowing that they "won" by regularly revisiting the dark side of the story, what would have happened had they lost, and how they would themselves have behaved if they had been conquered by the Nazis.[10] Hence the abundance of books and television documentaries about Nazi occupation of the Channel Islands, the only British soil actually conquered in 1940: a *Guardian* columnist in 2004 welcomed the fact that Jersey had "at last" owned up to the islanders' "wartime shame," a long-suppressed story of collaboration in the Holocaust, but she simultaneously bemoaned the reticence of the other islands but had still to come clean.[11] Churchill was as ever rather more magnanimous in victory when it came to issues like collaboration, stating in the Commons in 1947,

> that some consideration ought to be given to ordinary people. Everyone is not a Pastor Niemöller or a martyr, and when ordinary people are hurled this way and that, when the cruel hands of tyrants are laid upon them and vile systems of regimentation are imposed and enforced by espionage and other forms of cruelty, there are great numbers of people who succumb.

Even more generously, Churchill added, "I thank God that in this island home of ours, we have never been put to the test."[12] He was though a lone voice when stressing even within the decade of the "finest hour" the fact that the British did not entirely deserve the moral superiority that they had awarded to themselves ever since 1940, and he was far more often quoted in the opposite sense.

It is of course easy enough to argue that, in the long view of History, Britain did not in reality "win" the Second World War, since the medium-term cost of the conflict was an accelerated ending of the British colonial empire; catastrophic decline of British manufacturing output for export from which the country never entirely recovered; permanent destruction of favorable trade patterns and of overseas investments; subordination to the United States in world affairs; and a period of self-imposed isolation from the main currents of European political development. When the elderly Churchill assured his family and staff, during black moods of depression after 1955, that his entire career had ended in "failure," it was no doubt something much like this that he had in mind,[13] though he did not live long enough to see the story unfold in full. On the other hand, subordination of his father's country to the birthplace of his mother was never likely to seem as negative a factor to Churchill as it did to some others, for he had decided even in 1946 that the United States was now the only place in which a man of talent and ambition would wish to be born.[14]

As the so-called 'British disease' appeared to condemn the country to irreversible decline during the 1960s and 1970s, and as countries which *had* unequivocally endured defeat in 1940 or 1945 came to enjoy higher standards of living than the supposedly victorious British, such questions were widely asked. Had victory in 1945 been achieved at so high a price that it had been worse than a defeat? Had the 'new Jerusalem' of social welfare policies, adopted after 1945 to compensate the British people for their wartime sufferings, increased that price at the very moment when the harsh realities of postwar economic competition ought to have been confronted instead. Fascinatingly though, as that 1970s period of economic decline and that crisis of post-imperial national confidence was painfully reversed during the Thatcher period, the idea that Britain had "won" in 1945 was often and stridently reasserted, not least by Margaret Thatcher herself; all the problems the British had faced in the twentieth century, she often pointed out, had come from Europe, and it had all too often been the British who had had to sort out the mess. When British forces went to war in Argentina in 1982, they were urged by the popular Manchester comedian Bernard Manning to remember "two world wars and one world cup," a slogan that had nothing whatsoever to do with South America and everything to do with Germany in 1918, 1945 and 1966. Once Britain had beaten the Argentinians, national unity helpfully having been strengthened by the fact that the war was once again being fought against fascist military aggression, the British people enjoyed street parties arranged in deliberate imitation of those held by their parents and grandparents in 1945; the official victory concert climaxed with the return from retirement of one of the leading Second World War singers, Dame Vera Lynn, leading a packed London theatre in community songs of the 1940s. "We'll meet again," her greatest hit, had a triple resonance in these circumstances, for the British had indeed met again to re-celebrate 1945 and their finest hour.[15]

Tabloid newspapers have contributed heavily to that national myth of the Second World War, most notably in connection with international football matches against Germany: the *Daily Mirror*'s editor noted in his diary in 1996 that "Germany always brings out the worst xenophobic juices in tabloid editors."[16] British schools' history teaching, situation comedies, popular jokes and cartoons, and the endless diet of televised war films, have all played their part. As a *Daily Telegraph* editorial concluded, sixty years after VE day in May 2005, "we are a nation fixated with the Second World War and are becoming more so ... Thirty years after Basil Fawlty got into a terrible state for mentioning the war once [in *Fawlty Towers*], we have become a country that can hardly stop mentioning it."[17] This makes sense only because the British know that "we won," and it is surely impossible to understand the hang-ups that Britain still has over harmonization within the European community without awareness of the fact, in all its xenophobic grossness. Even in the 1990s, whenever German teams visited British football grounds, they were routinely serenaded by the home fans with the "Dambusters' March," the theme of a 1955 film about the 1943 bombing of Germany. When French, Polish or Czech national teams played in England, they generally received a chorus of "If it wasn't for the English you'd be Krauts," a version of the Second World War that manages to ignore not only European and German resistance to the Nazis, but also the Russians, Americans and British Commonwealth, and even the Scots and the Welsh.[18] If the British people ignored after 1945 the realities of contemporary Europe, realities that were blindingly obvious to everyone else, then, as the historian Peter Clarke has put it, they needed simply to "close their eyes and think of Winston Churchill."[19]

In a rather more populist sense of the word "myth," British historians have for the past twenty years challenged the received narrative of the social experience of wartime.[20] In the heroic version of that narrative, first developed in and soon after 1940, the British awoke from their 1930s torpor after the call to arms issued by Churchill when he became Prime Minister, and thereafter labored selflessly and unitedly for the war effort. In the air-raid shelters of London and in receiving evacuated slum children into the prosperous suburbs and country districts, in the greater fairness imposed by food rationing and in historically high taxation, in volunteering for home defence forces and charitable work, in collectively receiving war news from the BBC and responding to Churchill on the airwaves, the British people achieved an unprecedented level of unity; that sense of wartime sharing together in a common cause in turn radicalised the electorate, so that a Labour government after 1945 delivered advanced social policies, a large public sector in industry and a free National Health Service. So it seemed at the time – or so at least it was proclaimed, and so it was widely accepted by the first postwar generation. As Noel Coward put in the popular song "London Pride" in 1941, the people expressed their unity, "from the Ritz to the Anchor and Crown," from the top people's most expensive hotel to the working class Londoners' pub on the street-corner.[21] The socialist novelist J.B. Priestley, narrating the film *Britain at Bay* in 1940, assured viewers that this was so; although there had been dark spots in the country's pre-war social conditions, they had already been putting them right, and would finish the job when the war ended; in 1965, as narrator of a television documentary on 1940 for the twenty-fifth anniversary of the Battle of Britain, Priestley took almost exactly the same view.[22] Though it now came with some self-deprecating irreverence about the British, inserted to keep the viewers entertained, the essentially heroic tone of the myth remained unaltered. This was very largely the world-view of the BBC's situation comedy series *Dad's Army*, a television comedy series which began only in 1968 but ran for ten years; simple-minded and not very efficient local civilians in a town on the English south coast, drill and practice to meet a Nazi invasion. They are bumbling and incompetent certainly, but determined to die if necessary for their country; the original working title for the series had apparently been *The Fighting Tigers*, and they do indeed achieve at times an impressive unity, despite personal antagonisms, differences in age, class, background and accent. Here was – and in annual repeat television showings still is – the war as self-sacrificial unity.[23] It evoked unusually warm feelings among its audience and in 2004 was voted by viewers the fourth best television comedy series of all time. The feature film spun-off from the series in 1971 captured this mood particularly well in an opening sequence: Anthony Eden, in a broadcast as Secretary of State for War, appeals for the old and the young and civilians in reserved occupations to join a new unit of "Local Defence Volunteers" (later renamed the Home Guard), and in "Walmington-on-Sea" the local police station is absolutely overwhelmed by volunteers who are comically struggling to get in, sign up and do their (entirely voluntary) duty.[24] Yet the reality parodied here was that while the government asked in May 1940 for 150,000 volunteers, three-quarters of a million actually joined, and within a few weeks the Home Guard was a million strong, where it remained for the rest of the war.[25] No wonder there were so many jokes for radio comedians about the government's inability to produce arms and uniforms for a million unexpected volunteers, yet when a Noel Coward satirical song had local defence volunteers asking, "Could you please oblige us with a bren gun? The lack of one is wounding to our pride …,"[26] he was also subtly drawing attention to the fact that the problem only existed because so many men demanded to be in uniform in the first place.

Even in the 1940s, such a heroic narrative was not thought to match very closely to people's personal experience, as wartime radio comedy sketches demonstrated obviously enough. Strikes, crime, profiteering, the black market, evasion of duty and of taxation, the rich fleeing the bombing while the poor stayed on, and similarly "unpatriotic" activity, were all part of the British war experience too.[27] It is on these aspects of the social history of wartime that revisionist historians have more recently concentrated, hoping thereby to prove that the received version of Britain's war on the home front was a fraud, a propaganda untruth imposed upon the people by the authorities. For such revisionist arguments there is plenty of evidence that can be collected and published, for Britain's pulse has rarely been taken so insistently as it was between 1939 and 1945 by social investigators, government surveys, army educationalists, diarists and letter writers. Where the wartime press seems not to support a revisionist interpretation, by for example not emphasising forces that challenged national unity, it can be explained away as the consequence of censorship, the powerful in the media lining up with government to suppress the truth. Such insistent revisiting of wartime experience has undoubtedly modified the received account, but it has also provoked others into the argument on the other side, reasserting a modified version of the traditional view, as Mark Connelly recently did to great effect.[28]

The main problem here is that the revisionists have been guilty of taking the heroic myth too literally and thus making it an all too easy target, but if it is viewed more flexibly it becomes rather easier to defend. What is extremely hard to explain away is the extent to which ordinary people at the time seem themselves to have felt that they were living through a quite special moment of history, a time when the people they knew behaved more selflessly than in the past, when the country meant more to them, and the usually inarticulate British said so rather more often than usual. Any perusal of the masses of wartime diaries and letters is likely to lead to that conclusion, but two or three examples must suffice. Clara Milburn, a Midlands housewife, was writing in her diary in August 1940 about another local housewife, who, having no proper shelter, was putting her family under the stairs for protection against bombing, but had hung two union jacks there too; in September, after reading of Churchill's visits to bombed areas, she noted the cheers he had received from working-class bomb victims, adding that people were saying that Hitler could never have made similar visits in Berlin without "an armed bodyguard."[29] Richard Brown, an engineer in Ipswich, received the news of the defeat of France angrily ("Damn and blast the ruddy French!") but also stoically: "we are in for a tough time, but we shall weather it." A few days later he was cheered by the news that church bells would ring, and beacons be lit, only if Britain were invaded, since that had been the system adopted when England had defeated the Spanish Armada in 1588. At the end of the war, he concluded that everyone he met knew that these had been "mighty events, we are living in history," exactly the message that Churchill had striven to emphasise ever since 1940.[30]

Visiting his old school, for the annual ceremony of Harrow Songs in December 1940, Churchill was greatly moved to find that a new verse had been added to one of his favorite songs, a verse celebrating his own current achievements, but he nevertheless ventured to correct the way in which they had been described. He explained that there was one word in the new verse that he had asked the headmaster to alter, "Not the less we praise in darker days ... " would now refer to "stern days," for "these are not dark days: they are great days – the greatest days our country has ever lived," In the same year, he contributed a foreword to a reprint of William Pitt's war speeches of the 1790s, welcoming the timely reappearance of "the historic speeches with which Pitt instructed and heartened the British people in their battle for freedom a century and a half ago." It would be "fortifying" for Britons to remember that they had already seen off Philip II, Louis XIV, Napoleon Bonaparte and Kaiser Wilhelm II in their quest for the domination of Europe, and they should now recall Pitt's voice, facing the very real threat of invasion with that "just confidence which neither despises nor dreads the enemy," and bidding the Commons to remember that we were "fighting" "for our very existence as a nation, for our very name as Englishmen, for everything dear and valuable to men this side of the grave."[31] The key word here was "we," the continuous nation, called on once more to perform a historic task, but as the conscious heirs of those who had gone before and prospered.

Like many others on the Left, the Liberal-voting novelist and broadcaster George Beardmore surprised himself after a 1943 household debate on the purpose of the war by finding himself so aware of his "Staffordshire forebears, who go back to the Fifteenth Century. It's a true thing, this Englishness."[32] All too many of the British agreed at the time that war had brought out national unity and made them intensely aware of their history: as the popular crime novelist Dorothy L. Sayers put it in a 1940 poem:

> Praise God, now, for an *English* war –
>   The grey tide and the sullen coast,
>   The menace of the urgent hour,
>   The single island, like a tower,
>   Ringed with the angry host.
>
> This is the war that England knows,
>   When all the world holds but one man –
> King Philip of the galleons,
> Louis, whose light outshone the sun's,
>   The conquering Corsican...[33]

Most contemporaries understood well enough that no single pattern of behavior explained everyone that they met, and that criminals, anti-socials and the merely selfish continued to exist too, but they also felt – and often said and wrote – that such features of life were less common than they had been in peacetime. That view was more often expressed during 1940–41 than in the grim, but less immediately exciting, middle years of the war, though it also reasserted itself in the year after D-Day when victory and the war's end was generally foreseen. To that extent then, we now have a more balanced perspective on British wartime experience, but we also have, once exaggerations are stripped away, a better understanding of why the myth has persisted so strongly since 1945. An imposed, propaganda-driven falsehood could never have obliterated ordinary people's daily experience, as the Nazis discovered in 1944–45, but neither could it have survived the transition to peace in 1945, when people were anyway free to write as they wished.

After 1918, revisionist accounts did indeed flood the British literary market, destroying forever belief in such events as the 1914 German atrocities in Belgium and (with enormous consequences for future wars) the idea that the British army had actually defeated the Germans in 1918, but no such repudiation of the basic wartime myth happened after 1945. Not until fewer people actually remembered the war, during the 1980s and 1990s, did historians offer a significantly different narrative to their readers, and so far they have mainly not convinced them. Revisionist historians have then damaged though not destroyed the heroic narrative of 1939–45, but the wider public (which for this purpose largely includes television producers, book reviewers and the majority of book readers too), remains blissfully unaware of the fact. Ever since Churchill died, every British Prime Minister has been tested against him for acceptability as a national leader; several, of whom Harold Wilson and Margaret

Thatcher provide the best examples, have gone out of their way to claim his mantle, quote his speeches and assume his role in national life.[34] All of that inevitably reminds voters of Churchill's "finest hour" and of their own ancestors' place alongside him in the spotlight of history. Tony Blair was in many ways resolutely un-Churchillian as premier, and (no coincidence) he has little apparent interest in history. Yet, although he is also one of the two most pro-European of the country's recent leaders – the other being Edward Heath – when crisis appeared over Iraq in 2002–3, he unhesitatingly lined up with the Americans and Australians against most of Europe, quoting Churchill liberally along the road to Washington.[35] There Churchill's bust is displayed in George Bush's oval office as a gift from the British Foreign Office, still determined even in 2001 to exploit the world's gratitude for 1940. In September 2002, Michael Cockerell reported the scene in Washington:

> It is seven in the morning in the Oval Office; midday in Downing Street. President George W Bush, fresh from his dawn workout, is on the phone to Tony Blair. His feet are on the desk, a mug of coffee is in his hand and a bust of his hero, Winston Churchill, looks down on the scene. The president is on the hotline to No10: "Good morning Tony. I just thought I'd check in with my friend in London."[36]

The depth and breadth of British commitment to the myth of the Second World War remains profound, sometimes with hilarious consequences. When in 1996, the *Daily Mirror* declared its own "war on Germany," a headline declared "ACHTUNG! SURRENDER. For You Fritz, Zee Euro '96 Championship Is Over." In case this seems all good fun, the editor's now-published diary shows that he used the word "Hun" as synonymous with "German" in his private diary, just as he did in headlines (where the shorter word might possibly have had some tabloid justification).[37] Some months later, the newspaper's senior executives fought with German bankers in the bar of a Sussex hotel. The editor's diary continues, "I regret to say that when one of the bankers shouted, 'You started zis!' I shouted back, 'No ve didn't – you invaded Poland!'" Yet this was a man who for most of a decade edited the British paper with the second biggest daily circulation; and the biggest circulation paper, the *Sun*, is even worse in its insistent reminders to readers about the war. The *Sun* is written to be easily comprehensible so uses only a very limited vocabulary, yet it draws repeatedly on detailed memories of the Second World War, its phrases, images, heroes and villains. When in 1987 stories surfaced about disputes between British and German tourists on Spanish beaches, and were taken up by Germany's *Bild* newspaper, the *Sun* promptly declared war and mobilised every cliché of 1939–45. A headline declared "The *Sun* invades Germany," next to a photograph of Churchill with the caption, "He would have been so proud of our brave invasion platoon." In "Operation Klobber the Krauts," a party of *Sun* journalists would visit Germany to "give those Krauts a lesson to remember;" an accompanying map, parodying the opening credit sequences of *Dad's Army*, showed arrows advancing from Wapping in East London (where the *Sun* is produced) into the heart of the Fatherland (one place indicated on the map being "Luneberg," where German armies had surrendered to Montgomery in 1945). Yet the *Sun* appeals to large numbers of readers in the upper and most educated social groups, and has been claimed to be read by more "top people" than either *The Times* or the *Guardian*, which must therefore also compete with it for customers. Again and again such "quality" papers find themselves drawn into the tabloids' 1939–45-obsessed world, and they too commemorate war anniversaries with equivalent (if somewhat more polite) hostility to both the defeated enemies of 1945 and defeated allies of 1940.[38]

Unsurprisingly then, the British populace seems largely to go along with such insular and often chauvinist views. In Summer 1995, an opinion poll about British self-identity conducted for the *Daily Telegraph*, showed that "the nation's history is ... a central theme. People attach special importance to Britain's defiance of Nazi Germany in 1940 ... ." That issue was cited by 5 percent as very important, and by 28 percent as fairly important, in defining their own Britishness; the only factor ranking higher was "British people's right to say what they think," which was also effectively a comment on traditional perceptions of Britain's war effort, while 40 percent mentioned the British people's ability to "take it," 42 percent the Royal Navy, and 31 percent "Land of Hope and Glory." Taking all these factors together, with their obvious relevance to 1939–45, 86 percent felt proud to be British.[39]

This is in fact a very odd feature of contemporary Britain's self-identity: for as fewer and fewer people actually remember 1939–1945 for themselves, and as the nation becomes ethnically diverse in a way that does not in the least reflect memories of 1940, the war has not faded from prominence in the national mind as would have been expected. Rather it has become yet more prominently fixed in its place. How we explain that has much to do with post-imperial Britain – and especially the post-imperial English – losing an Empire and not (yet) finding a post-imperial role, and very little at all to do with the actual Second World War of historical reality.

Notes

1. The Second World War remembered as "the good war" by those who perceived themselves as victors in a strong moral cause was popularised by the American oral historian Studs Terkel, *The Good War, an Oral History of World War Two* (New York, 1984).

2. John Ramsden, '"That will depend on who writes the History"; Winston Churchill as his own historian', Inaugural Lectures, Queen Mary and Westfield College, 1996; see also David Reynolds, *In Command of History, Churchill Fighting and Writing the Second World War* (London, 2004).
3. Churchill to Attlee, 29 May 1946, quoted in John Ramsden, "Mr. Churchill goes to Fulton," in James W. Muller ed., *Churchill's "Iron Curtain" Speech Fifty Years Later* (Columbia, 1999), 30.
4. Philip C. Clarke to Churchill, 4 February 1946, quoted in *ibid*, 29.
5. *Daily Telegraph*, 10–12 October 1950; Tage Kaarsted, "Churchill and the Small States of Europe: the Danish Case," in R.A.C. Parker ed.,*Winston Churchill, Studies in Statesmanship* (London, 1995), 106–8.
6. Paul Reynaud, "Churchill and France," in Charles Eade ed, *Churchill by his Contemporaries* (Hutchinson, London, 1953), 212.
7. *The Times*, 12 June 1945.
8. *The Times*, 5 October 1967.
9. M.R.D. Foot, "Winston Churchill," in Herbert van Thal ed. *The Prime Ministers* (London, 1975), 686.
10. Gavriel Rosenfeld, *The World Hitler Never Made* (Cambridge, 2005), 2, 10–11, 15, 30, 35, 42–44, 46–58, 62–65.
11. *Guardian*, 24 January 2004.
12. John Ramsden, *Don't Mention the War, the British and the Germans since 1890* (London, 2006), 252–53.
13. Anthony Montague Brown, *Long Sunset, Memoirs of Winston Churchill's Last Private Secretary* (London, 1995), 302–3.
14. Martin Gilbert, *Never Despair, 1945–1965, Winston S Churchill, vol. 8* (London, 1988), 196.
15. Ramsden, *Don't Mention the War*, 367.
16. Piers Morgan, *The Insider, the private diaries of a scandalous decade* (London, 2005), 126–31.
17. *Daily Telegraph*, 11 May 2005.
18. Adrian Thrills, *You're Not Singing Anymore* (London, 1998), 15.
19. Peter Clarke, *A Question of Leadership, Gladstone to Thatcher* (London), 229.
20. See for example Steven Fielding, Nick Tiratsoo and Peter Thompson, *England Arise* (Manchester, 1995).
21. Noel Coward, *The Lyrics of Noel Coward* (London, 1978), 268.
22. *Britain at Bay* (Crown Film Unit, 1940); *1940* (BBC Television documentary, 1965).
23. David Croft and Jimmy Perry, *Dad's Army, the Complete Scripts* (London, 2003).
24. *Dad's Army* (directed by Norman Cohen, 1971).
25. S.P. MacKenzie, *The Home Guard* (Oxford, 1995), 33–35.
26. Coward, *Lyrics*, 273.
27. Angus Calder, *The People's War: Britain 1939–1945* (London, 1969).
28. Mark Connelly, *We Can Take It: Britain and the Memory of the Second World War* (London, 2004); see also Malcolm Smith, *Britain and 1940: History, Myth and Popular Memory* (London, 2000).
29. Peter Donnelly ed., *Mrs Milburn's Diaries, an Englishwoman's day-to-day reflections, 1939–1945* (London, 1989), 54–55.
30. Helen D. Millgate ed., *Mr Brown's War, a diary of the Second World War* (Stroud, Glos., 2003), 52–53, 55, 286.
31. John Ramsden, *Man of the Century: Winston Churchill and his legend since 1945* (London, 2003), 65.
32. George Beardmore, *Civilians at War: Journals, 1938–1946* (Oxford, 1986), 148–49.
33. Brian Gardner ed., *The Terrible Rain: the war poets, 1939–1945* (London, 1966), 45–47.
34. Ramsden, *Man of the Century*, 572–79.
35. *Guardian*, 3 October 2002.

36. *The Sunday Times*, 8 September 2002.
37. Morgan, *The Insider*, 126–31.
38. Ramsden, *Don't Mention the War*, 399–401.
39. *Daily Telegraph*, 27 July 2005.

Chapter 5

"WE CAN TAKE IT!"
Britain and the Memory of the Home Front in the Second World War

Mark Connelly

For the British, the memory and history of the home front has largely been constructed around events in the key year of 1940, the year in which the realities of war came home to the British people, and in which the nation defied the Nazi empire alone. Churchill, Dunkirk, the Battle of Britain, the German aerial bombardment of British cities, and full rationing were all legacies of 1940. The perceived reactions of British people during that year have come to symbolise British wartime spirit, and more widely, British national character as a whole: stoical, good humored, resilient, phlegmatic. The memory and history were also largely constructed around images and interpretations forged during the war itself. Nothing startlingly new was either manufactured or discovered after the war. However, the memory and history have not remained static. Emphases have altered since 1945 in line with contemporary social, cultural, political, demographic and economic trends. In addition, the medium of film, and then television, came to play an increasingly significant role in shaping and detailing popular understandings of the home front.

Long before the war broke out, the British had started to shape it in their collective imagination. A key influence on perceptions was the all-pervasive memory of the Great War. The shadow of the Great War then not only played a role in forming reactions to the Second World War, but after 1945 became an alternative pole of experience by which the "people's war" of 1939–1945 could be gauged and measured. In the immediate aftermath of the Great War the British people expressed their sorrow and pride by erecting war memorials on a mass scale. As the former Director of the Imperial War Museum, Alan Borg, has noted, this represented

---

Notes for this chapter begin on page 68.

the "biggest communal arts project ever attempted."[1] These memorials focused attention on the righteous sacrifice Britons made in the quest to defeat the evil of Prussian militarism. Despite a reaction to this largely conservative and affirming interpretation in the early 1930s, the British never quite lost sympathy with the original message. At the same time, the message of the Great War seemed to confirm deeper isolationist and xenophobic traits in the island British, for the conflict was taken as proof that foreigners could not be trusted, and that even allies, the French in particular, were not real equals of the British. The conflict therefore served to reinforce a sense that self-reliance was the only real guarantee of British security, and that few nations could match the British in a test of stoic self-sacrifice.[2]

For the professionals in the military, the shadow of the Great War was equally significant. Few senior British soldiers could escape the memory of the Western Front, but British planning for a future continental commitment revealed that there was little consistency of thought. Most British generals were anxious to avoid another trench stalemate, and vigorously supported the idea of rapid deployment and action. Although such thinking formed the official doctrine, when the British Expeditionary Force crossed to France in September 1939 it slipped into a mindset the troops of 1916 would have recognised. Trenches were dug along the Belgian frontier, and strong points constructed with the idea of ensuring a stalemate in the west until British mobilisation allowed a combined Franco-British decisive offensive some time in 1943.[3] Even with the collapse in France, the memory of the Great War refused to wilt. British conscripts, citizen soldiers, were often reminded of the comparison particularly in the deadlock of the Italian campaign and later in the bloody battle for Normandy. As the poet Vernon Scannell, a veteran of the North African and Normandy campaigns, wrote:

> Whenever war is spoken of
> I find
> The war that was called Great invades the mind …
> And I remember,
> Not the war I fought in
> But the one called Great
> Which ended in a sepia November
> Four years before my birth.[4]

As noted, the key national traits emphasised by the Great War were taken to be self-reliance, stoicism and self-sacrifice, and these rapidly became the crucial determinants of the British Second World War experience particularly after the fall of France and the onset of the Nazi "blitz" against British cities. Along with the other key images of 1940, namely Dunkirk and the Battle of Britain, the myths of the blitz are vital to British national identity. According to this particular memory, it provided, and continues to provide, proof of the distinct qualities of the island race. It is remembered as the moment when the few of Churchill's island stood shoulder to shoulder, regardless of class or creed, and withstood the "full terror, might and fury of the enemy."[5] Instead of buckling, the people laughed and joked their way through it, full of wonderful British *sang froid*. King and Queen came to know their people and their people them, as all did their bit without murmur. The myths of the blitz are defined by a set of visual images that define London and the provincial cities under bombing. These visual images then impart messages of defiance, solidarity and togetherness, and improvisation in the face of a powerful enemy. By surviving this experience Britain bought the freedom of the world. Like most events of 1940, the blitz is something the British people look back on with pride, and both at the time and since many Britons have felt that the endurance and fortitude of the nation in the face of such an onslaught is something the world should thank them for now and forever more. Thus is the blitz remembered and conceived.

A crucial visual image of the blitz, which has been repeated in countless books and television documentaries since the war, is a photograph that appeared on the front cover of the *Daily Mail* on 29 December 1940. The image, captured by the newspaper's staff photographer, H.A. Mason, showed St Paul's cathedral standing proud while wreathed in smoke and flame. The *Mail*'s headline proclaimed the "War's Greatest Picture," and carried Mason's description of how he captured the moment: "Glares of many fires and sweeping clouds of smoke kept hiding the shape. Then a wind sprang up. Suddenly, the shining cross, dome and towers stood out like a symbol in the inferno. The scene was unbelievable. In that moment or two I released my shutter."[6] Such images as Mason's were joined even during the war by documentary film interpretations, the titles of the best are still well known, *London Can Take It!* (1940), *Christmas Under Fire* (1940) and *Fires Were Started* (1942). Wartime feature films also imagined and reconstructed the blitz, as in *Mrs Miniver* (1942), *In Which We Serve* (1942) and *Demi-Paradise* (1943). A way of framing, recalling and memorialising the blitz had been established which set the blueprint for all future interpretations. Since the war, documentaries, television dramas and films have drawn heavily on this original material, often treating reconstructed scenes as real footage. Like Dunkirk, great reliance has been placed upon relatively few images; a uniform interpretation of the blitz has therefore come down to Britons. Virtually every documentary and drama on the blitz made since the war has used images from *London Can Take It!*, *Christmas Under Fire* and *Fires Were Started*. All three of these iconic films were government backed propaganda products, and all three were made by the same man, Humphrey Jennings, one of the finest exponents of the art of documentary. An artistic, message-laden vision of the blitz was the result, but it does not necessarily follow that it is a mistaken one, a cover-up or a fabrication.

What becomes obvious from the visual record and the way it has been used since the war is that London is *the* city of the blitz. St Paul's cathedral shrouded in smoke dominates the memory just as it once dominated the London skyline. It was the crucial image of the Crown Film Unit's *London Can Take It!* Primarily made to influence opinion in the neutral United States, it had a commentary written and spoken by the London-based American journalist, Quentin Reynolds, and was a great success on both sides of the Atlantic. Opening with a low-angle shot of St Paul's, the dome of the cathedral is confirmed as a symbol of both the capital and the nation. Backed by the majestic tones of Vaughan Williams' *London Symphony*, the film balances the stoic attitude of Londoners against the enormous task of fighting a mighty enemy. "I can assure you that there is no panic, no fear, no despair in London town; there is nothing but determination, confidence and high courage among the people of Churchill's Island." Quentin Reynolds' deadpan, matter of fact style combined with his alleged aloofness ("I am a neutral reporter") gave the documentary a sombre authority. It is an authority buttressed by a knowledge of Britain's affinity for and with its past. "It is hard to see five centuries of labour destroyed in five seconds." But "a bomb has its limitations," Reynolds concludes, "it can only destroy buildings and kill people. It cannot kill the unconquerable spirit and courage of the people of London. London can take it!" This final statement is delivered over an image of Marochetti's statue of Richard the Lionheart, the sword held high bent by bombing, and framed by the smashed windows of Westminster Hall in the background. Thus the film ends with a vision of the medieval past and one that symbolises the unity of monarchy and people in the form of Richard and the Houses of Parliament, and the continuity of British history.

Retitled *Britain Can Take It!* for its domestic release, the film was greeted with enthusiasm. When it was shown in a Scottish mining village, the Ministry of Information projectionist recorded, "*Britain Can Take It!* was by far the most successful film. The reasons, I think, were because of the neutral reporter, the emphasis on the common people and the fact that it showed what the war was like." A Mass-Observation report noted that it was "the most frequently commented upon film, and received nothing but praise."[7] If the actual situation was so very different to that portrayed on screen, then the film would surely have been rejected as patronising and insulting.

History brooded over Londoners during the blitz, but at one and the same time the blitz was becoming part of *History*, as opposed to *history*, in other words the epic story of the nation italicised and capitalised. Past and present were fused. The heavy hand of History was most potently felt in the haunting spectacle of burnt out City of London churches, most of them designed by Sir Christopher Wren in the wake of the disastrous "Great Fire" of 1666. In the winter of 1940–41, Wren's churches took on a double meaning: they became symbols of the glory of seventeenth-century London and of the heroic resistance to the modern barbarous enemy. Therefore the churches were, and are, a reminder of what Churchill called "our long history," emphasising the weight of the past on British shoulders, and an epic moment in the nation's recent history. Muirhead Bone's *St Bride's to St Paul's*, a sketch taken from the roof of a building just behind St Bride's, is an excellent example of this phenomenon. The sketch shows the intense damage inflicted on the few blocks between the church and the cathedral. Fire-bombs have gutted St Bride's south aisle and transept and firemen's ladders still lie in the adjacent lane. Combined with the leafless trees and the snowy pavements (despite the recent fire), it creates a sobering picture of death and destruction. However, it is also a vision of majesty and redemption, for the tower of St Bride's remains intact and soaring, as does the noble dome of St Paul's cathedral, which still dominates the skyline. In 1944 London Underground commissioned a series of posters from Walter Spradberry, one of which showed the dome and eastern apse of St Paul's towering over the rubble. Underneath the image ran the legend "' ... the principal Ornament of our royal City, to the Honour of our Government, and of this our realm' from the 'Letters Patent under the Great Seal of England the 12th day November 1675.'" Commenting on his work, Spradberry noted it was to convey "the sense that havoc itself was passing and with new days come new hopes."[8] The poster implies that the great phoenix of the Great Fires (1666 and 1940) has spread its wings. The message was that London had arisen from its ordeal, an ordeal its history had prepared it for.

"Destiny has given England the torch of liberty to hold," said Quentin Reynolds in *Christmas Under Fire*, "she has not let it slip." Presiding over the blitz was also a profound sense of history having thrown up yet another leading role for the nation in the grand drama of world affairs. London felt this onus with particular force. It was a force that inspired and framed the actions of ordinary people. On 21 September 1940, the Lord Mayor of London made a radio address to the United States, it was a message of Churchillian rhetoric: "Today London stands as the very bulwark of civilization and freedom. These streets of my city will be defended to the last. London City has sometimes been attacked, but never sacked. London has steeled herself for resistance and victory."[9]

London set the standard for the rest of the country during the blitz. The way the London blitz was reported and interpreted ensured that other British cities had to react with equal fortitude, resolution and courage. Here myth and reality co-existed, they fused and informed each other to the point where it becomes impossible and fruitless to attempt to distinguish between them as the debunkers seek to do with such vigor. The highly controlled presentation of London meant a behavioral norm had been established by the autumn of 1940 that demanded emulation by others. In turn, this ensured London's status as *the* city of the blitz, *the* model of survival, and encouraged Londoners to remain cheerful so as not to let the mantle slip. If there is such a thing as the myth of the blitz, then it was not a fabrication devised afterwards, even less was it a fabrication devised by those in power and forced on the majority, rather a blurring occurred: the genuine actions of ordinary people were reported and lionized which created a genuinely popular heroic image few wanted to fall short of. The spirit of the blitz has thus become the heritage and folk memory of the British people and remains impervious to assault because the so-called myth is "soaked into the very first-hand evidence itself."[10]

The provincial blitz revealed just as many local government shortcomings as that on London. Small cities were often overwhelmed by the disaster and morale undoubtedly fell; occasionally those in positions of responsibility failed to do their duty effectively and with fortitude. Unlike the blitz on London, the Luftwaffe rarely visited the smaller cities on a continual basis, night after night. This had a far deeper effect on morale than facing the enemy constantly; just as a city thought it had escaped, the bombers might return jarring and denting fragile nerves. A cockney survivor of the blitz said, "you can get used to it. You can get used to anything."[11] But "getting used to" was a symptom of routine, and the provincial cities were often denied this appalling luxury. But despite these problems British cities remained firm, initial shock and horror was overcome and they "took it."[12]

Of course, at the time the failures of local government and collapses in morale were not covered in the press. This does not mean that people were ignorant of such matters merely that in the final analysis they too preferred the heroic picture and did their best to conform to it; the alternatives held little attraction. Seeing the blitz as an heroic moment added additional chapters to already proud local histories, or created a heritage in new communities. As Malcolm Smith has pointed out, after the war local histories of the blitz proliferated, often published by and compiled from the archives of local newspapers.[13] Very few, if any, criticised civic government or the lack of preparation, but all told of the heroism and endurance of the inhabitants. Such records were clearly accepted by many, as the sales reveal: Plymouth's history, *It Came to Our Door*, was published in 1945, went through three reprints in 1946 and was reissued in 1949 and 1975. January 2002 saw the *Kent Messenger* print the fifth edition of its book, *Kent at War*. Written by a local historian, the author acknowledges his debt to Pratt Boorman's original works published during the war, and the archive of the newspaper. The county motto provides the title for the Foreword, *Invicta* (unconquered), and sets the tone for the book. Lavishly illustrated with the newspaper's wonderful collection of photographs, the book is a proud record of Kent's part in the war. Comedy and pathos intersperse the text, which help to underline the proud memory. Of particular significance is the section covering the Baedeker Raid on Canterbury in June 1942. (Hitler had promised to raze Britain's historic monuments to the ground using the famous Baedeker tourist guides to provide the list of targets.) In attacking Canterbury, the Nazis struck at a vital symbol of England, its heritage and self-perception. But by surviving the attack, the inhabitants and the remnants of the city fabric combined to become symbols of the unconquerable nature of the island race and its centuries of history. The history was said to endure in the spirit of the living; it was proclaimed at the time, and again in 2002, in *Kent at War*:

> As the great clean-up continued, scores and scores of Union Jacks were draped from the windows of damaged buildings. Historic Canterbury had died that night, but the message from its inhabitants was crystal clear.[14]

Stating that such responses reveal nothing more than a Pavlovian response to government-inspired propaganda initiatives misses the subtlety of the elision between myth and reality.

The people who bought the initial wave of books were survivors; they knew the facts, yet they bought histories the debunkers would regard as fatally flawed. "They were surely buying a pattern," Smith has noted, "a local historical map against which they could orientate their personal and family experience, and thus make sense of their own experience as part of a larger story."[15] Making sense of the story is the function the received interpretation of the blitz performs for the British people.

As noted above, histories of the war, particularly local histories, surged out almost as soon as hostilities were over. Such histories usually emphasised reactions to the blitz, the numbers of citizens undertaking national service, and how efficiently local government worked with the willing co-operation of the people. This approach broadly chimed-in with the "people's war" message of the war years, and the sentiment that swept the Labour party to power on a broad reforming manifesto promising to bring a "people's peace" as a reward for the sacrifices so freely given. The sociologist Richard Titmuss then made this interpretation triumphant in his *Problems of Social Policy* (1950). His work stressed the way in which the war forced rich and poor to face up to each other, and how the levelling effects of bombing, evacuation and rationing made Britain a unified nation. Ironically, however, his vision of the home front was rarely seen in popular culture between 1945 and 1960. The British cinema's glorious reliving of the Second World War in the 1950s was not particularly interested in the home front, concentrating instead on the fighting services. By emphasising the armed forces this visualized interpretation of the war stressed hierarchies and masculinity. The democratic equality highlighted during the war drifted away from the foreground. In addition, these films largely relegated the role of women to that of loving wives and mothers rather than as essential, independent, active war workers. When the home front was seen it was often in the military context – airfields and barracks, but usually set in the depths of the English countryside thus buttressing the rural myth of Britain. The urban Britain that was hit by the Luftwaffe was rarely seen except in some Ealing comedies, for example *Hue and Cry* (1946) and *The Lavender Hill Mob* (1951), and thrillers, but then it was in the postwar context.[16]

The 1950s was also the period in which the war children grew to teenage years and adulthood. For Britain this was a far from easy period. Deprived of a stable home life and education for many years, many young men in particular drifted into crime and anti-social behavior, reflected in the film *Blue Lamp* (1948). This was a product of the home front the British were anxious to either forget or reform by emphasizing traditional family life. These anxieties helped crystallize the slowly forming right and left-wing versions of the war, which were highly dependent on images of the blitz and 1940. The left-wing myth emphasizes the collapse of the inefficient, "old guard" of British politics (as symbolized by Chamberlain), and its eclipse by the rise of Clement Attlee, who led the Labour party to a dramatic victory in the 1945 General Election, the triumph of the British people in the face of adversity, and a distinct move towards 1945 and the welfare state. In contrast, the right-wing interpretation stresses the deep patriotism of the British people, the greatness of the island race and its standing in world affairs, and Winston Churchill's stature as leader. According to Smith, in the 1960s the left-wing version came under increasing attack from new left criticisms of the compromises made by the Labour party in wartime and the immediate postwar years; while the new right would come to criticise the Conservative party for not recognizing that the country was being hijacked by the left during the long years of war. The triumph of Thatcherism in the 1980s ensured that a right-wing interpretation would become dominant, playing up the elements of patriotism and greatness while playing down the elements of state intervention and the first shoots of the welfare state.[17]

During the war there was an undoubted surge of radicalism in the British people which made itself felt from 1941 onwards in the intense feeling of admiration for the Soviet people. This chapter in Britain's wartime history is missing completely from the contemporary modern memory. British workers gave the "Tanks for Russia" week their full support when it was launched on 22 September 1941; it was also noted that production always rose and labor relations were more harmonious when the plight of the Soviet Union was invoked.[18] The Ministry of Information was initially fearful of this pro-Soviet feeling, but slowly realized that praise for the Soviet war effort was good for home front morale too.[19] On 22 February 1943, in the aftermath of the Nazi defeat at Stalingrad, British cities celebrated a Red Army Day with pageants, music and passionate speeches (a similar day of celebration in November 1942 had been equally popular); a year later the BBC's special feature on the siege of Leningrad and the Soviet counter-offensive gained 9 million listeners.[20] In the same year Anthony Asquith's quaint celebration of Anglo-Soviet friendship, *Demi-Paradise*, came to cinema screens. Laurence Olivier starred as a Russian engineer, Ivan Kutznetsoff, who comes to Britain to discuss plans for a new form of ship propeller. At first he finds it hard to adjust to English customs but eventually comes to respect and like the people, just as they take to him. By turning Anglo-Soviet relations into a gentle comedy of manners, the film avoided making any point about the profound differences in political cultures. With the advent of the Cold War world and Britain's adherence to a supposed special relationship with the USA, the wartime appreciation of the USSR was quickly squeezed out of the national war story and has never been reinstated.

Another element of the home front missing from the contemporary memory, and in many ways connected to the above, is that of industrial unrest. After the terrible depression of the 1930s and its devastating effect on Britain's heavy industries, the war proved a boon. Full employment was guaranteed thanks to total war, indeed such were the demands of modern war that Britain found itself facing an acute labor shortage, particularly in the coalfields. With full employment came renewed trade union confidence. Workers' rights and conditions could be argued with vigor without fear of the sack and a prolonged period on the dole. Though the Minister of Manpower, Ernest Bevin, endeavored to minimize strikes and industrial unrest by imposing arbitration mechanisms on industry, even his impeccable trade union credentials could not stop tension from boiling over in certain sectors. In 1943, 1.8 million working days were lost in 1,785 strikes, and 1944 saw the loss of 3.7 million days.[21] Coal miners took their chance to press for redress of longstanding grievances. Working in appalling conditions for the most vital of war resources, coal miners were outraged that mine owners continued to stack up vast personal profits while their sacrifices were granted scant reward. As demand for coal rose and the labor available fell, the government took the drastic measure of diverting one conscript in every ten to the mines. The "Bevin Boys," as they became known, valiantly though they tried, were hardly the answer to the structural problems of British mining made so graphically obvious by the war.[22] Despite all its problems, British industry rose to the challenge of war and achieved incredible successes. In the vital struggle for finished war materials Britain outstripped its allegedly better organized Nazi foe with some ease. Tanks, aircraft – particularly bombers – guns, radios, and radar sets poured off British production lines; by contrast Germany did not move into total war production until 1942.[23]

The role of women in the People's War has also had a somewhat uneven profile in the public memory, and is one that has come back into the public consciousness after largely disappearing in the 1950s and 1960s. With the growth of women's history and gender studies in the seventies and eighties, the need to recognize and study the role of women in the Second World War was asserted. Wanting to produce a positive image of women in war, the Ministry of Information enthusiastically supported the successful film production duo Frank Launder and Sidney Gilliat in their plans to make a film celebrating women in the factories. *Millions Like Us*, released in 1943, emphasized the importance of female labor to the war effort. Horrified by the thought of factory work, the young, naïve heroine, Celia (Patricia Roc), is told by another woman, "There's nothing to be afraid of in a factory. Mr Bevin needs another million women, and I don't think we should disappoint him at a time like this. The men at the front need tanks, guns and planes. You can help your country just as much in an overall as you can in a uniform these days." Celia gradually gains confidence and begins to like her job making aircraft components. She finds that living in a government hostel is not so bad and makes friends with a variety of women from different backgrounds. But the film skilfully avoids the trap of patronizing its audience by being too upbeat; the downside is also explored. The foreman tells them, "Now you'd better understand there's not much glamor in a machine shop," and Celia's life is touched by tragedy as she marries a young air-gunner who is soon killed in action. Here was the gritty reality of war: a reality that was not denied by the government because it was impossible to avoid the fact of casualties, but the way this experience was interpreted could be shaped in particular ways. Thus Celia's tragedy can only be palliated by the victory of the just.

Since the war the role of women in factories has become less prominent: though most popular novels and dramas with wartime settings hint at it, they often do little more than that. The reason for this omission from the dominant modern memory is probably because women retreated from the workplace with rapidity in 1945, thus leaving very little evidence of their important contribution to victory. Historians have debated the long-term significance of this movement into the male sphere of employment for many years. Arthur Marwick, an exponent of the idea that war is an engine for social change, believes war work brought women out of their homes and into a wider world which may have been temporary for some but established a significant precedent meaning that the postwar world could never return to its 1939 standards.[24] A more subtle argument has been advanced by Penny Summerfield. She has shown that the Second World War forced the complementary forces of patriarchy and capitalism, prevalent in the powers of the state, to face up to the problem of labor supply which demanded female workers. She contends that in trying to achieve a solution suitable to both capitalism and patriarchy the State often severely constrained the role of women and did little to alter the unequal position of women within British society.[25]

As with factory work, postwar interpretations of female service life are hardly numerous. Lucy Noakes has suggested that the need to maintain the image of women as home makers and mothers was – and continues to be – the dominant stumbling block:

> there is little or no room in this popular memory of Britain at war for women in uniform, although many women served as members of the ATS, the WRNS and the WRAF. Instead, women represent the nation's values, the family at home that the men are fighting to defend. Active images of women in wartime are mediated through the need for women to retain a relative degree of passivity in the public narrative of war.[26]

Proof of this rule can be found in its two most significant exceptions. In the 1950s two popular films provided an alternative history by showing a reality hidden in wartime. *Odette* (1950) and *Carve Her Name With Pride* (1958) revealed what the wartime state could not – that women, mothers, wives, and home front workers for victory, were actually being sent on highly dangerous missions behind enemy lines. Both were big hits at the box office, and the film historian Robert Murphy believes the success of these two films reveals a reaction against the conformist society of the 1950s and provided proof that woman did indeed do great things in the cause of allied victory.[27]

The biggest challenge most British women faced during the war was simply trying to carry on as normal for the sake of their families, and this memory has certainly been passed down. The television series *A Family at War* provided an extremely influential interpretation of the home front in that it was accessed and accepted by millions of viewers. A hugely popular television drama series that ran over five series from 1970, it largely conformed to the myth of a united and heroic people attempting to maintain their ordinary lives in the face of overwhelming disruption and pressure. However, it also explored the darker side of the home front by studying issues such as infidelity and corruption. The main female character, Jean Ashton, is worn down by the burden of war, worrying constantly about the safety of her grown-up children and the ongoing struggle to keep her house and family life alive wears her into an early grave. Derided as a piece of nostalgia by some critics, *A Family at War* was sober and realistic as well as celebratory. Those who, like myself, were at secondary school in the 1980s were also shown the realities of wartime home life, albeit in a much less harrowing way, in the schools' educational series, *How We Used to Live*. Most recently, Channel 4 television scored a great popular success with its series *The 1940s House* (2000), which was accompanied by a special exhibition at the Imperial War Museum and a handsome coffee-table book. The series found a family willing to take on the role of time-travellers and placed them in a house returned to its 1940 condition. Nothing of their modern life was allowed to remain as the series sought to show the reality of the 1940s; here was *How We Used to Live* for adults. A particular feature of the program was the way in which the trials and tribulations of wartime life forced the family to become a tighter unit, and this might explain its success. In our increasingly atomised world, where relationships seem far more ephemeral and fragile, this tribute to community and inter-dependence struck a chord. In a similar vein John Boorman's autobiographical film, *Hope and Glory* (1987), followed the pattern established during the war which stressed that heroism was best defined and exhibited by simply carrying-on as normal. But he also examined the issue of infidelity and marital tensions. At the same time, however, he stressed the eccentricity of the British, and thus maintained a streak of British humor seen most potently in the Ealing comedies of the late-1940s.[28]

Often leading drab and harsh wartime lives, British women vigorously sought entertainment and distraction, and from 1942 this was often found in the form of American servicemen. Both the British and American authorities were keen to present American troops as sober and honorable allies which served to disguise the often riotous effect they had on British communities starved of color and glamor. "Oversexed, overpaid, and over here" became the insult of many British males jealous of GIs who were better paid, had access to goods and foodstuffs under strict rationing in Britain, and dressed in far smarter uniforms. But, as the film historian Sue Harper has noted, official propaganda ensured that "Americans in British wartime features are 'over here,' but they are neither overpaid nor oversexed."[29] Since the war the popular memory has tended to focus on the idea of the GI as a glamorous leading man. Two films released in 1979, *Hanover Street* and *Yanks*, were a curious mixture of wartime genre conventions consciously resurrected, but this time the women who fall for Americans have sex with them too, unlike the officially sanctioned discreet friendships accepted during the war years and reflected in the touching 1945 film, *The Way to the Stars*. *Hanover Street* stars Harrison Ford as an American pilot and Lesley-Anne Down as Margaret Sellinger, an English woman with a husband serving in the forces. Unlike *The Way to the Stars*, however, this relationship becomes physical. *Yanks* became the more famous of the two largely due to the performance, and looks, of Richard Gere. Playing an army cook, he falls for Jean (Lisa Eichhorn), an English woman living near the camp. Emotional upheaval comes in the form of Jean's long-standing engagement to a British soldier. But Jean and Matt are portrayed as having deeper physical desires than her British fiancé and so their relationship becomes the natural one. With the former boyfriend out of the way, the lovers do not find immediate contentment as British prejudices towards American servicemen are highlighted. However, the two survive their troubles, held together by the strength of their love.[30]

Partly inspired by the success of *Yanks*, the ITV network launched a television drama series centering on the lives of American airmen based in a small English village. *We'll Meet Again* came to the screens in 1982 – somewhat ironically, full-page advertisements promoting the drama appeared in British newspapers on the day they announced an imminent invasion of the Falkland Islands.[31] Romance was at the heart of the drama, as British women fell for American airmen. Few of the romances ran smoothly as the village men are shown to be a mostly suspicious and unfriendly bunch keen to keep Yank paws off British girls. The women who fall for the Americans are from a wide range of backgrounds, and include the lady of the manor (Susannah York). Though married to an officer serving in North Africa, she cannot resist the gallant C.O., at least ensuring an affair with someone of similar rank. *We'll Meet Again* hit all the buttons of popular memory – fun loving Americans giving away rationed goods with generous abandon, miserable British men sullenly brooding over the presence of the bloody Yanks and, of course, the strains of the famous wartime singer Vera Lynn. This was a far cry from the 1950s representation of British middle-class women standing stoically by their fighter pilot/naval captain husbands, remaining faithful for months and years on end and ensuring that the children grew up decently.

As can be seen, by the late 1950s television and film constituted two of the most potent agencies of memory shaping. During the 1960s television really began to make an impact, and become the key popular communicator by the middle of the decade. Television histories of the Second World War also reflected the cultural shifts of the decade re-emphasising the democratic forces of the war years so celebrated by Titmuss. In 1963, the BBC made a major documentary entitled *1940*, in which J.B. Priestley, a centre-left writer who was turned into a hero by his wartime radio broadcasts celebrating the genius of the ordinary Briton, spoke the commentary. The documentary was a great success, and stressed the familiar story of heroic banding together on the home front in the face of the common enemy. Then, at the end of the decade, Angus Calder's influential book, *The People's War* (1969), was published in which he sustained elements of the Titmuss thesis, but also argued that the ultimate victor of the war was the civil service which found itself newly empowered to regulate and interfere as never before. Calder's book was a huge best-seller, and ran to many editions becoming a standard text on many university courses, and inspired books aimed at younger students. His book was also, in part, the inspiration behind the highly regarded series, *The World at War*, which first ran in 1972–73, and has been repeated many times since. A comprehensive overview of the war, it was notable for its use of dramatic original footage interspersed with talking heads.

Taking its cue from *The People's War*, it did not rely solely on the testimony of those in positions of influence. Ordinary men and women were also interviewed and played a major role in the series. Significantly, Angus Calder scripted the episode on the British home front.

Calder took a far more controversial line in his 1991 book, *The Myth of the Blitz*. Although he did not seek to undermine the heroism shown by the British people during this trial, he sought to show that it was a heroism informed and shaped by the way the British government controlled and manufactured information and images. He then argued that it rapidly became so deeply entrenched in the British psyche that people began to shape their actions according to this blueprint of "correct behavior," and that ever since the war the British have looked to the blitz as a touchstone of their national identity, characteristics and heritage. According to Lucy Noakes, the blitz is becoming *the* central event in the public memory of the war.[32] She suggests this is because the blitz is an easily understood, dramatic story that does not require much expert knowledge of military, diplomatic or political history. The exciting elements often appeal to children, and, as the blitz was something that affected the home front, it is an experience with which women can empathise. The Imperial War Museum's Blitz Experience is identified by Noakes as an important medium through which people gain knowledge of the campaign. Museums, and especially one as prestigious as the Imperial War Museum, are powerful shapers of perceptions; they confer authority on interpretations of the past. People visit museums in order to gain knowledge and in the belief that the collections of artefacts and explanations are legitimate and learned. Therefore when something like the blitz "become[s] the subject of numerous or particularly important museum exhibitions and displays, aspects of the past can change their meaning. They cease to be just a part of *history* and instead have the potential to become part of our shared, national, *heritage*."[33]

Welcomed by the warm tones of a cockney Air Raid Precautions (ARP) warden, the Blitz Experience allows visitors to sit in a replica of an East End air-raid shelter. Once in the shelter, the warden introduces the visitor to the other occupants and their voices are heard. Bombs fall around the shelter, including one near miss which makes the visitors rock on their benches. A museum guide then leads visitors out into a street which has been wrecked by bombing, while the voices of the shelterers and emergency services personnel annotate the scene. Finally, the ARP voice bids the visitors farewell and tells them not to forget. Although the Blitz Experience allows the visitor to hear the screams of an hysterical woman and states that the East End certainly was not ready to face the aerial onslaught, the overall atmosphere is that of the myth: the voices in the shelter sing "Roll Out the Barrel," cockney humor brightens the more sobering moments and the final words of the ARP man exhorting the visitor not to forget those who endured the blitz are poignant reminders of bravery and stoicism. Significantly, a script emphasising the horrors of the blitz was rejected in favor of this more "upbeat" version.[34] The Blitz Experience is dramatic and moving, and whilst it contains no untruths, it is sanitised. It is also tremendously popular; long queues form outside the exhibit and it is a must for all schools visiting the museum. Knowledge of the blitz is therefore perpetuated and interpreted according to the broad parameters of its myth. Yet people do not get a sense of their heritage through museums alone, and so the many other ways in which the blitz has been perpetuated also need to be examined. Such exhibitions and books like Calder's *Myth of the Blitz* set Clive Ponting's notorious *1940: Myth and Reality* into context.[35] Published in 1990 to mark the fifty anniversaries of the events of that crucial year, Ponting argued that Britain's finest hour was nothing more than a government propaganda exercise which disguised the fact that Britain was divided, afraid and bankrupt. Ponting's deliberately provocative view caused some scandal at the time, but was rapidly forgotten. The British people simply did not recognise it as their war.

By the 1990s the British war generation was dying out, and the children of the war years were also getting old. As this demographic shift occurred, the tight grip the war and the home front once held on the British has begun to relax, or rather it has been transferred onto a different aspect of the war. British society, and in particular schoolchildren and students, is now force-fed the history of Nazism and the holocaust from a very young age. With this has come a distinct lessening of knowledge of the British role in the war which has been replaced by a near obsession with Nazism. Where the home front does play a significant role in national curriculum history it is very much centered on the blitz and rationing with an emphasis on trying to understand whether the "blitz spirit" was an invented phenomenon. But there is still the lingering memory that contains many elements translated directly, if rather loosely at times, from the war. The great mythologized elements are still significant: GIs, rationing, "spivs" (black market racketeers) and the concept of a unified people fighting a People's War. But, this does not mean a simple memory; it is one that acknowledges transgression and shadows. By the same token, there are some significant elements missing: the deep respect and fellow feeling for the Russian people and the Red Army, the fierceness with which political issues were fought and the levels of industrial unrest are hardly understood today. Britain's imagined war is a curious phenomenon; it reflects a desire to see the conflict as "our finest hour" without ever becoming a complete whitewash. It is not a monolithic story and explanation of the war because the war itself did not have a simple, single story or explanation at the time. The real war and the mythical war will therefore always been intertwined. But the great demographic shifts, including a fundamental alteration of the racial mix, mean that the clear features in the British landscape of memory of the home front are now in a period of great transition, and the memory of the war is more fluid than at any point since 1939.

Notes

1. Alan Borg, *War Memorials: from antiquity to the present day* (Leo Cooper, 1991) ix.
2. For details see Mark Connelly, *The Great War: Memory and Ritual* (Woodbridge, 2002)
3. For details see Brian Bond, *British Military Policy Between the Wars* (Oxford, 1980), see also G.D. Sheffield, "The Shadow of the Somme: the influence of the First World War on British soldiers' perceptions and behaviour in the Second World War" in Paul Addison and Angus Calder (eds.), *Time to Kill: the soldier's experience of war in the west, 1939–1945* (London, 1997), 29–39.
4. Vernon Scannell, "The Great War," in Jon Stallworthy (ed.), *The Oxford Book of War Poetry* (Oxford, 1984), 223.
5. Charles Eade (ed.), *The War Speeches of Winston Churchill* (London, 1951) Vol. 1, 188–96.
6. *Daily Mail*, 29 December 1940.
7. Quoted in James Chapman, *The British at War, Cinema, State and Propaganda, 1939–1945* (London, 1998), 99.
8. Oliver Green, *Underground Art, London Transport Posters 1908 to the Present* (London, 1990), 98.
9. *War Illustrated*, 4 October 1940.
10. Angus Calder, *The Myth of the Blitz* (London, 1991), 143.
11. *The World at War*, Episode Four: "Standing Alone: Britain, May 1940–May 1941" (Thames Television, 1973).
12. See Tom Harrisson, *Living Through the Blitz* (Harmondsworth, 1990 edition) 132–276, for a discussion of the effect of the blitz on British provincial cities. It is clear that despite the problems with morale, people "bounced back" as they had in London.
13. Malcolm Smith, *Britain and 1940: history, myth and popular memory* (London, 2000) 86.
14. Bob Ogley, *Kent at War* (Westerham, 2002) 124.
15. Smith, *Britain and 1940*, 85–86.
16. For postwar British cinema see Sue Harper and Vincent Porter, *British Cinema of the 1950s: decline of deference* (Oxford, 2003).
17. Smith, *Britain and 1940*, 93.
18. Angus Calder, *The People's War* (London, 1969) 262.
19. Sian Nicholas, *The Echo of War: Home Front propaganda and the Wartime BBC, 1939–1945* (Manchester, 1996) 170.
20. Calder, *People's War*, 347–49, Nicholas, *Echo of War*, 169.
21. Calder, *People's War*, 395.
22. Calder, *People's War*, 431–42.
23. John Keegan, *The Second World War* (London, 1989) 170–78.
24. See, for example, Arthur Marwick, *British Society Since 1945* (London, 1982) 67–71.
25. Penny Summerfield, *Women Workers in the Second World War* (London, 1984). See also Penny Summerfield, *Reconstructing Women's Wartime Lives: discourse and subjectivity in oral histories of the Second World War* (Manchester, 1998).
26. Lucy Noakes, *War and the British* (London, 1998) 120.

27. Robert Murphy, *British Cinema and the Second World War* (London, 2000) 118–19, 205–7.
28. See Mark Connelly, *We Can Take It!: Britain and the memory of the Second World War* (Harlow, 2003) 28–29.
29. Sue Harper, "The Representations of Women in British Feature Films, 1939–45" in Philip M. Taylor (ed.), *Britain and the Cinema in the Second World War* (Manchester, 1988)168–202, 183.
30. See Murphy, *British Cinema*, 257–61.
31. See *Daily Mail*, 2 April 1982.
32. Lucy Noakes, "Making Histories: Experiencing the Blitz in London's Museums in the 1990s" in Martin Evans and Ken Lunn (eds.), *War and Memory in the Twentieth Century* (Oxford, 1997) 89–104.
33. Noakes, "Making Histories," 89.
34. Noakes, "Making Histories," 99.
35. Clive Ponting, *1940: Myth and Reality* (London, 1990).

Chapter 6

EXPERIENCE AND MEMORY:
The Second World War in Poland

Piotr Madajczyk

Research on Nazi Germany's occupation policies was strongly encouraged in Poland for political reasons and because society at large was very interested in this topic. Already the earliest studies were of high academic quality. As a basic principle, the context of this research, i.e., the Polish perspective on the twentieth century, was and still is quite different from perspectives prevalent in Western European countries. In the Western European view, two great catastrophes shaped the "short" twentieth century from 1914 to 1989: the First and the Second World War. In Polish historiography as well as in the country's collective memory, these two major historical events are strictly kept apart. The First World War was marginalized in collective memory and had only a limited impact: it served as a memory for the rebuilding of Poland as an independent state in the war's aftermath. Thus, the First World War was generally regarded positively because it destroyed the unjust system that had upheld Poland's partition. When the partitioning powers Austria-Hungary, Russia, and Wilhelmine Germany crumbled after the end of the war, Poland received the opportunity to pursue its national interests.[1] This is not merely a Polish, but more generally a Central Eastern European and South Eastern European perspective. It pertains to all nations that had previously been dominated by the European great powers and were able to build nation states after the First World War.

In Poland, remembrance and collective memory predominantly focus on the Second World War. The Polish war experience was different in the sense that *two* occupation powers had annexed large parts of the country's territory. The remaining territory was turned into a "General Government." National Socialist Germany led a war of extermination against the Polish

---

Notes for this chapter begin on page 82.

nation while the Soviet Union "only" combated the Polish class enemy. Both totalitarian occupation powers persecuted Polish leaders (the Soviets generally only non-communists) and liquidated all those who were branded as political enemies. Under the German occupation, entire groups that were deemed undesirable were eliminated: Jews, Poles of Jewish origin, "antisocial elements," Sinte and Roma, as well as many chronically ill people. More than half of the war victims belonged to the group classified as "Jews." Under the Soviet occupation, "class enemies" were liquidated and the occupiers attempted to win as many Poles as possible for collaboration with the Soviet Union (except at the very beginning of the war). Both occupation powers resorted to terror and retaliation, forced people to resettle, or confined them in camps. Living conditions were very harsh under both occupation powers. Food shortage and inhumane working conditions prevailed and there was a lack of education opportunities and medical care. Both occupation powers nurtured national conflicts and used them to their advantage. In this context, the policies of the National Socialist regime were more aimed at splitting up the Polish nation. Think only of the German People's List (*Deutsche Volksliste*) or the notion of a *Goralenvolk*. In the second phase of the war, one of the occupiers, the Soviet Union, changed sides and joined the camp of the anti-Hitler coalition. In 1944, however, it effectively became an occupier again and oversaw the establishment of the communist regime in Poland.

The "political reasons" mentioned at the very beginning entailed that the authorities permitted research on the German occupation period – even endorsed it – in order to obliterate the memory of the Soviet occupation and its policies during the Second World War. Thus, we must also note here that the Soviet de facto occupiers and the communists in Poland first attempted to establish a totalitarian system and then, after 1956, developed an authoritarian system. This system sought its legitimacy in history, which had to be falsified in order to achieve this end: the regime pushed the role of the Soviet Union as an occupation power into the background while highlighting Poland's (actually rather subordinate) role in the liberation from German occupation. This led to a "struggle" between private, collective, and official memory in the People's Republic of Poland, which persisted until 1989. The term "struggle" is perhaps not entirely fitting because it suggests the existence of levels of memory independent of one another. In fact, these three levels influenced each other. In phases when it was strong, the state energetically attempted to implement its view of history; in times when it was weaker, it relented its grip in some areas. Some topics nevertheless remained taboo until the fall of the People's Republic of Poland. Private recollections of the war were politically undesired and were not allowed to be published if they addressed delicate topics. Sometimes people did not even pass them on in their families. This way, the regime forced large parts of society into a defensive stance that made coming to terms with the past, which was difficult enough as it is, even more problematic. Certain topics were made taboo in society and stylized as symbols of Polish independence.

In the immediate postwar years, historical research mostly concentrated on the terror of the German occupation authorities, the martyrdom of the Polish nation, and the struggle against the German occupiers. Since the end of the 1960s, the picture of the war became more complex. Research altered its estimation of the official German occupation policies and came to consider more seriously the interplay between German occupation policies and the Polish resistance as well as the fate of the Jews. However, political history remained the main point of focus; interest in the everyday history of the war was only marginal.[2]

Scholarly interest in the Second World War corresponded to the Poles' vivid memories of the war experience under German occupation. The few opinion polls conducted during the postwar period reveal the significance of these memories. The best-known survey was conducted in 1975, thirty years after the end of the war. The responsible institute – at the time the only institute capable of conducting opinion polls – enjoyed a good reputation. Renowned Polish sociologists conceived and analyzed the survey. The results reveal a fascinating picture of people's recollections of the war in the mid 1970s. One third of the polled families remember that relatives were involved in the resistance. All in all, however, other aspects dominated: Martyrdom under the occupation was the most important aspect (36 percent), followed by terrible experiences in everyday life (25 percent). About 25 percent also remembered various forms of struggle and resistance. As grave experiences during the war, people named hunger (55 percent), forced labor (52 percent), loss of property (38 percent), German repressions (31 percent), war captivity (25 percent), loss of one's dwelling (24 percent), and loss of all possessions (24 percent). Also listed were the forced deprivation of one's citizenship (12 percent), and induction into the *Wehrmacht* (7 percent).[3]

In this context, we must note that the air war did not, and to this day does not, play a very significant role in Polish people's memories of the war as the *Bombenkrieg* for instance in Germany does. Rather, people remembered the German *Luftwaffe*'s air strikes on refugees in September 1939 or the terrible fate of the civilian population in the battles, for example the shelling of the capital city during the Warsaw Uprising in 1944. Forced migration and deportation also inhabited a prominent place in people's memories – under National Socialist as well as Soviet domination – as well as the harsh life in the various camps installed by the two occupation powers. This survey shows, however, that besides martyrdom, the experience of the difficulties of everyday life under the occupations was quite vivid in people's private recollections as well as in collective memory.

In official remembrance, however, two very different images dominate. First of all, since approximately 1948, Polish authorities decided not to emphasize the martyrdom of the Polish civilian population so strongly. Instead, for understandable political reasons, they attempted to give priority to aspects of class struggle. Thus, instead of national ideology, class ideology was generally foregrounded for example on memorial plaques. Moreover, all religious aspects and corresponding symbols were avoided in official representations. The aggressors and occupiers were not Germans, but "Hitlerists," "Fascists," or "reactionaries." Zbigniew Mazur has observed that official rhetoric succeeded in creating a community of Polish victims and fighters who – according to this notion – died in the struggle against the "Hitlerists." Martyrdom and the extermination of the Polish civilian population did not fit into this historical concept.[4] The term "Hitlerists" was firmly established in the Polish language, although after 1956 the national component was again emphasized more strongly. However, a different social aspect that was difficult to reconcile with the policies of the postwar regimes played an important role here: the image of history more strongly shaped by national ideology, by the idea of a national struggle, was – as the 1975 survey indicates – the image of the well-educated, higher strata of society. It was mostly this group that advocated this image in public.

Into the 1970s, scholars researched important aspects of German occupation policies in Poland. The, until today, unparalleled synthesis of German occupation policies in Poland by Czesław Madajczyk appeared in 1970, but had already been completed a few years earlier.[5] The comparative study *Faszyzm i okupacje 1938–1945. Wykonywanie okupacji przez państwa Osi w Europie* (Fascism and Occupations. The Implementation of Occupation by the Axis Powers in Europe 1938–1945) by the same author, which appeared in 1983, can be regarded as the dawn of a new phase.[6] This work, which was published during the difficult first half of the 1980s and at first did not receive much attention, was path-breaking also because up to that point, the national history of Poland during the Second World War had dominated, and more general as well as comparative studies only later gained in significance.

In the mid 1980s, historians lamented the lack of regional studies on the Second World War in Poland.[7] However, all in all the war's history was very well researched even on the regional level. Research encompassed the terrorizing and the extermination of the Poles, forced labor,[8] the economy,[9] the concentration camps, but less so prisons. Since the late 1970s, there has also been an increase in research on forced migration.[10] There are some interesting works on the history of the Polish Church under the German occupation as well as numerous publications on the fate of the Jews, although there are still quite a few deficits in this area. Particularly the lack of studies on the smaller ghettos in the Polish province is lamentable in this regard.

However, research did not address certain other topics until the end of the 1970s, in part for political reasons alone, in part because these reasons were in accordance with collective memory. Some topics were researched in smaller circles, but it was impossible to officially publicize them in Poland, and thus they remained without societal resonance. Already in the 1950s, this was the case for Polish-Ukrainian relations, which the popular Polish émigré journal "Kultura" in Paris dealt with extensively. After 1976, the first independent writings appeared whose impact, however, remained rather limited. In the 1980s, a great change took hold as the state's monopoly on information was largely disbanded after the emergence of the Solidarity movement (*Solidarność*). This time of societal changes also led to a renewed interest in history.

Collective memory was now freed from state pressure and this new freedom was not even revoked during the state of martial law from 13 December 1981 to 22 July 1983 – despite the authoritarian character of the system that until 1989 exerted its control by means of censorship, a strict limitation on freedom of opinion, and a quasi-monopoly on mass media. On the one hand, the changes brought about by the open and candid discussions that were sparked between August 1980 and December 1981 were too far-reaching. On the other hand, the regime was too weak and its power was, for various reasons, too limited to suppress all these independent initiatives again. In consequence, the so called *drugi obieg*, the "second circulation" similar to the Soviet *samizdat*, which encompassed various magazines and books that were printed unofficially and thus free of censorship, continued to exist. The extent of this "second circulation" was considerable and was estimated to encompass approximately 200 magazines as well as 300 books and other publications during the second half of the 1970s. Between August 1980 and December 1981, its numbers rose to 3,000 magazines and around 250 books and brochures. Between December 1981 and 1987, it included approximately 1,700 magazines and more than 3,000 books and brochures. Even though these figures are probably imprecise because it is impossible to capture the many local, small, and short-term initiatives, they nonetheless give an impression of the drastic changes collective memory in Poland underwent at the time. Certainly this was not a democratic system in which collective memory is molded mainly through schools, mass media with high circulation, and official, state-organized events. The unofficial publications described above primarily reached those people who were already politically active.

The historical debate of the time can be regarded as an act of "catching up" after years in which history had been misappropriated and falsified. It was not necessarily academic circles that sparked this debate, however, as research possibilities such as access to new papers and documents from archives were limited.[11] Rather, the debate unfolded in an ever growing public sphere in which long-suppressed war memories now resurfaced – all thanks to increased public interest. In the area of journalism, there was a wave of memoirs and public discussions. The debate mainly focused on the previously suppressed topic of Poland's eastern territories and on the policies of the Soviet Union. (I shall elaborate on the focal topic of Katyń.) Concerning the German occupation, people's interest focused on events that had been portrayed inaccurately in the past such as the role and the policies of the Polish communists and communist partisans in Poland. In the following, I will therefore try to outline the most important aspects of the discussions at the time.

Poland and the Soviet Union

For political reasons, the question of Soviet policies and occupation during the war, especially between the years 1939 to 1941 and during the final phase of the war, were practically not addressed in historical research and official discussions. Now, many topics were heatedly debated: the Soviet assault on Poland on 17 September 1939, German-Soviet cooperation, which lasted until 22 June 1941, Soviet policies in the occupied and annexed Polish territories, the Polish resistance and suffering (deportation) in these territories, the situation of the Polish communists until June 1941, Soviet policies after 1943 (Yalta), the Soviet Union's role in the emergence of the communist regimes after the war, and, last but not least, the suppression of the Polish independence movement. These aspects completed the memory of the Second World War.

In light of these changes, the notions that until then had dominated collective memory had to be reconsidered. At the same time, collective memory began to converge with the state of historical research, although the ensuing discussions were often highly emotionally charged and politicized. At the beginning of the 1990s, 79 percent of the sampled population was convinced that the Soviet Union simply wanted to annex Polish territories when it assaulted Poland on 17 September 1939. Only 9 percent confirmed the official version (which was propagated until 1989) that the Soviet Union had wanted to protect the civilian population in Poland's eastern territories. A significantly higher number of Poles (21 percent) believed that all in all the living conditions under Soviet occupation had been worse than under German occupation (6 percent); and 67 percent believed that they had been "equally bad," which implies that the two occupation powers during the Second World War were more or less regarded as ranging on the same level. Respondents gave similar answers to the question of who had persecuted the Poles more severely: 15 percent stated "the Germans," 16 percent "the Soviets," and 61 percent were of the opinion "both equally." In this survey, 28 percent of respondents remembered the many losses they had suffered as a consequence of Soviet policies.[12]

On the basis of these results, we can see that this aspect in people's recollections of the war (the losses suffered as a consequence of Soviet policies) had been suppressed by authorities in a fourth to a third of the population. We can also clearly see here that the history of the Second World War in Polish collective memory is still that of the confrontation with two totalitarian states, although the question certainly arises in this context if indeed the views expressed in the survey reflected people's private memories or if collective memory was not also influenced by the discussions that pervaded since the 1980s. However, it appears as though these findings really do reflect personal memories or memories passed on within families since people often gave accounts of individual or family experiences such as deaths, the loss of home and property, deportation, camp confinement, and forced labor.

The far-reaching societal changes are most vividly illustrated by the example of Katyń. In this town near Smolensk, Soviet authorities had murdered Polish reserve officers in 1940, for which they had later blamed the "Third Reich."[13] For understandable reasons, this was hushed up after 1945 by the communist regime in Poland. However, it could not be entirely eliminated from public space. Officially, the Germans were the perpetrators, but in private and collective memory, the true story was passed on. However, it is difficult to assess its social impact in retrospect. Katyń became synonymous with the Poles' suffering during the war: with Soviet totalitarianism, which was just as dangerous as German totalitarianism, and with the murder of defenseless prisoners of war, who in many cases had belonged to the higher, more educated strata of society and had fought for their fatherland as reservists during the war. Since the 1980s, Katyń was openly addressed in many spoken and written accounts. The state was thus forced to carefully revise its official version – after consultations with Moscow.

Collaboration

The problem of collaboration with the German occupation authorities was only mentioned at the sidelines in the past for various reasons. For one thing, it had played only a relatively marginal role in Poland.[14] It also did not fit into the picture of martyrdom and resistance the regime as well as society embraced. Moreover, the regime instrumentalized the accusation of collaboration in its conflicts with political opponents.

This question was politically so delicate because an open discussion had to also raise the topic of the collaboration of the Polish communists and parts of society with the Soviet Union. There is no doubt that the

Polish communists indeed collaborated with the Soviets, but there is a fair amount of discussion about when precisely this phase came to an end and a totalitarian or authoritarian regime in its own right was created. Collaboration with the Soviet Union was historically more important than collaboration with the Third Reich. It was also politically more significant because it came to bear on the historical legitimization of the People's Republic of Poland. In the 1990s, these discussions continued in Poland's mass media, where arguments ensued about the meaning of terms such as "deceit" and "collaboration" in assessing the history of Poland's communists and the evolution of the People's Republic of Poland.

National ideology and nationalism

These problems were so difficult among other things because the Second World War had strengthened national and nationalist ideology. In the People's Republic of Poland, this topic was suppressed and made taboo in many areas, especially as it was often closely connected with the question of Soviet policies. The fact that nationalism had been used in order to stabilize the communist system further aggravated matters. Moreover, particularly in the 1960s, nationalism had been used as a weapon in internal struggles within the Polish United Workers' Party. In the 1980s, a public discussion ensued about the conflicts with Poland's eastern neighbors, i.e., Polish-Ukrainian, Polish-Belarusian, and Polish-Lithuanian relations. In this context, we should not forget that the negative experience of these national conflicts was deeply rooted in the collective memory of large parts of Polish society. Decisive for this debate was a small popular-scientific book by Bohdan Skaradziński,[15] which influenced public discussion as well as many historians who would address this topic in later years. Skaradziński wrote about Belarusians, Lithuanians, and Ukrainians:

> The weight of historical conflicts and mistrust bears heavily upon us and we – as well as the other side – have done nothing that could at least partially fill up the trenches of suffering and sometimes even hatred. Perhaps only time can soften the vehemence of the conflicts. However, people still live there [in the border regions/in Poland's lost eastern regions, P. M.] who would fight "to the death" with us, the Poles, over the future of these territories; in situations in which neither we nor the other side were "tricked" by someone else, but acted on our own political and moral responsibility. *Nationally*. It was not always a fair battle ... This was the work of Belarusians, Lithuanians, Ukrainians, and Poles. They have all been victims as well as perpetrators.[16]

A special "chapter" within the larger problem of nationality is dedicated to Polish-Jewish relations during the war. A vast amount of literature has been published on this question, which however does not address some important aspects. Various factors are responsible for this: the separation of "Jews" and "Poles" was in part also a consequence of the ghettoization and persecution of the Jews during the war.[17] After the war, Jews as victims were partially included in Poland's remembrance. "Polish" and "Jewish" recollections nevertheless drifted far apart. For Jews or persons intimately connected with the Jewish religion or tradition, the Holocaust was the basis and the point of departure for all further considerations. In the recollections of many Poles, however, Jews were primarily incorporated into the Polish struggle against the two totalitarian states, whereby the communist commitment of certain Jews or people of Jewish origin was generalized in order to include all "Jews." In this view, "Jews" are considered to have been helpers of the Soviet Union in September 1939 and collaborators in the formation of Poland's postwar communist regime.[18] This tendency was amplified by the fact that the regime in the People's Republic of Poland instrumentalized history and – in a defensive reflex – stylized certain historical events as symbols of the national struggle and suffering.

The suppression of memories that were emotionally difficult to face for Polish contemporary witnesses also plays an important role in this regard. And those who took part in atrocities or enriched themselves with Jewish property were certainly also interested in suppressing these matters.[19]

As far as the problem of nationalities is concerned, since the 1980s it has also become clear how national models of interpretation concerning the fate of the German civilian population in the final phase of the war and during the immediate postwar years have changed. An essay by Jan Józef Lipski sparked this discussion. It first reached only the elite, but in later years also had repercussions in important academic publications and public debates.[20] These discussions on the problem of nationalities have contributed to adding nuances to the Polish understanding of victims and to broadening the perspective on the national past. This process, however, which up to this day has not come to an end and which was certainly not linear, does not encompass society as a whole.

In the 1990s, a new political situation evolved in which the tendencies of interpreting history described above nevertheless persisted. Personal recollections hardly played a role anymore during this time. People who were ten-years-old at the war's end are over seventy-years-old today and out of those who actively participated in the war, only few survive.[21] Thus, collective and official memory has come to play an increasingly important role. After a wave of interest in history during the previous decade, the 1990s witnessed a counter-reaction. In a survey from 1995, only 21 percent of respondents stated that they were interested or very interested in history, 43 percent were somewhat interested, 22 percent not very interested, and 14 percent not at all. Academics, higher earners, and executives as well as city dwellers and senior citizens professed a more pronounced historical interest. Among those less interested in history, unemployed people, rural inhabitants, people with only elementary education, and people without an explicit political opinion dominated.[22] This probably indicates a return to normality after the exceptional phase of the 1980s, but at the same time it implies a great change. At the time, the conductors of the survey also noted that particularly younger people had problems with terms such as patriotism and national identity.

During this time, the picture academic research was drawing of the Second World War became more complex and nuanced. In accordance with the tradition of Polish historiography, the trend toward a political history of the war persisted.[23] However, historians also began to address questions from the field of economic history. The process of reconciling collective memory with historiography continued. This was made possible by new research on the Soviet occupation policies and their societal implications. In newer, comprehensive studies on the history of Poland during the Second World War, the German and Soviet aggression on 1 and 17 September 1939, respectively, the territorial shifts and annexations under the two occupation powers, and the German and Soviet occupation and population policies (naturalization, deportation, and camps) are generally presented alongside one another.[24] In this context, research on the Soviet nationality policies and their impact on the national conflicts in the former Polish eastern territories are particularly relevant.[25]

It also became apparent that the until then dominant enemy stereotypes of the Ukrainians and Germans had decreased in significance. They were eliminated from official recollections and replaced by conciliatory rhetoric. Enemy stereotypes certainly continue to exist in certain segments of society, but they have become less virulent and no longer dominate collective memory.[26] Polish-Jewish questions are still difficult to deal with. Despite the political turn in 1989, they remain complicated due to the reasons outlined above. Detailed discussions of these problems, which have unfolded in past years and received great public attention, are therefore all the more important. The best-known example of this is Jedwabne, the town in eastern Poland where Poles murdered their Jewish neighbors in 1941. It is difficult to pinpoint the attitude of Polish society toward this question. On the one hand, it appears to be difficult for many people to acknowledge that Poles were the chief culprits in this atrocity. It was much easier to attribute the leading role to the Germans. On the other hand, 40 percent of the population (sampled in 2002) deemed the apology of the highest representatives of the Polish state appropriate; 36 percent were against it and 24 percent without any opinion on the topic. More than 80 percent thought it was good that the events of Jedwabne had been uncovered and that schoolchildren now learned that Poles had not only saved Jews, but that some had also murdered them during the Second

World War.[27] For many people, however, the way the public discussion was led turned out to be an obstacle to broadening their perspective beyond their own role as a victim and to accepting a more differentiated view of the past.

The new image of history is not homogenous, but it is also not that of a xenophobic society. It is a starting point for a different conception of victims who were sometimes also perpetrators. The question remains disputed whether or not the victim-perspective, which is quite prevalent in Poland, is helpful as far as academic research is concerned. The corrosion of the black-and-white picture coincides with discussions on the questions of collaboration and resistance. Interest in everyday history is on the rise. Newer studies are increasingly addressing the history of Poland's confrontation with the totalitarian systems – the fascist as well as the communist one.[28]

Soviet policies toward Poland, particularly the active phase of Soviet influence after 1943, have also been researched or at least included in analyses. However, important Soviet sources, without which certain questions remain difficult to answer, are still not accessible. The term "Yalta" is certainly still negatively connoted: "The resolutions of the Crimea Conference were the next defeat for Poland. Decisions were forced upon the Polish Republic that did not bring about positive solutions. The Soviet annexation of Poland's eastern territories was finalized here without guaranteeing compensations for Poland in the West and North. The decision in this question was simply postponed. The formula pertaining to the [Polish] government was ambiguous, and, in light of the de facto occupation of Polish territories by the Red Army, Poland was thus presented with a fait accompli – established with violence."[29]

The final phase of the war and the transition phase during the early postwar years – the phase that was marked by the liberation from the danger of annihilation through the "Third Reich" and at the same time heralded a new era of suppression by the Soviet Union – are better researched. This period is also a point of focus of the Institute of National Commemoration, a state institution dedicated among other things to historical education. We can moreover observe a tendency to question the role of the year 1945 as a decisive caesura in certain central political as well as societal processes.[30]

Conclusion

It is not easy to define the relationship between academic conceptions of history and collective memory – particularly in times of dynamic change. The place the Second World War occupies in Poland's historical memory remains disputed, although we can say for certain that it continues to be an integral part of the country's cultural memory. It is nevertheless difficult to estimate the place it occupies in the "hierarchy of memory." How strongly does it influence political thought among Poles today? We have seen that the influence of the Second World War in certain areas has decreased, for example the defusing of anti-German and anti-Ukrainian stereotypes. In other areas, e.g., the polemics surrounding the plans for the Center Against Expulsion (*Zentrum gegen Vertreibungen*) in Berlin, which is organized in cooperation with the controversial German Federation of Expellees (*Bund der Vertriebenen*), the after-effects of the Second World War are still tangible. However, the circle of victims is widening and today also includes Germans. The change of generations and the rise of educational levels have a significant influence on these developments. In this context, it is worthwhile to reconsider the results of the opinion poll conducted in 2002 on the Jedwabne question and to take a closer look at the respondents' age distribution. The question whether or not it was a good thing for children to learn in school that Poles had not only saved, but that some had also murdered Jews was affirmed by 26 percent of respondents over 60 years of age; in the age group 50–59 years: 33 percent; 40–49 years: 30 percent; 30–39 years: 34 percent; 20–29 years: 55 percent; 15–19 years: 47 percent.[31]

We can thus be certain that collective memory is becoming increasingly differentiated. (On central topics, however, there is generally consensus in Poland.) In part already since the 1970s, this process has also profited from the strengthening of regional identities. People are increasingly taking into consideration the complexity of the past, which often cannot be captured in national concepts of history, as well as the heterogeneity of regional histories.[32] The fact that national minorities and their elites – whose interpretations of the past differ from that of the majority of Poles on central points – have developed a greater self-confidence contributes to this process of differentiation.

Collective and official memory in Poland is currently in a phase of transition. When it became possible to openly address the Soviet Union's role, things got out of balance for a certain time: it sometimes appeared as though the Soviet aggression of 17 September 1939 dwarfed the German invasion of 1 September. In principle, this was also true for estimations of Soviet and German occupation policies. But this tendency has since become a thing of the past itself. Another, more fundamental change has taken hold, however: Polish society has witnessed a "comeback" of historical interest since the beginning of the twenty-first century, particularly concerning the history of the Second World War. This became apparent in 2004 on the occasion of the sixtieth anniversary and, shortly afterwards, in the high visitor numbers of the newly established Museum of the Warsaw Uprising.[33]

Notes

1. Wojciech Roszkowski, *Historia Polski 1914–2001* [History of Poland 1914–2001] (Warsaw, 2002), 8, 17–18 mentions the First World War only as a turning point in the international marginalization of the Polish question, as a conflict of interests between the partitioning powers and as Poland's chance for independence. A similar line of argumentation is pursued in Alicja Dybkowska, Jan Żaryn, and Małgorzata Żaryn, *Polskie dzieje od czasów najdawniejszych do współczesności* [Polish History From the Earliest Years Until the Present] (Warsaw, 1996) and addressed in detail by Tomasz Nałęcz in: Henryk Samsonowicz, Janusz Tazbir, Tadeusz Łepkowski, and Tomasz Nałęcz, *Polska. Losy państwa i narodu do 1939 roku* [Poland. The Fate of State and Nation Until 1939] (Warsaw, 2003), 447–465. General remarks on the important role of the First World War for developments in Europe can be found in Antoni Czubiński, *Historia Drugiej Wojny światowej 1939–1945* [The History of the Second World War 1939–1945] (Poznan, 2004), 7, and Antoni Czubiński, *Druga wojna światowa 1939–1945* [The Second World War 1939–1945] (Poznan, 1999).
2. Tomasz Szarota, *Okupowanej Warszawy dzień powszedni. Studium Historyczne* [Everyday Life in Occupied Warsaw. A Historical Study] (Warsaw, 1973).
3. It first appeared in 1975 as a survey: Anna Pawełczyńska, *Polacy a Niemcy – antagonizm i postulaty* [Poles and Germans – Antagonism and Suggestions], Ośrodek Badania Opinii Publicznej i Studiów Programowych (OBOP), and two years later as a brochure: Anna Pawełczyńska, *Żywa historia – Pamięć i ocena lat okupacji* [Living History – Memory and Assessment of the Occupation Years] (Warsaw, 1977).
4. Zbigniew Mazur, "Niemcy czy faszyści? Dwa konkursy w latach 1948–1949 na upamiętnienie niemieckich egzekucji na polskiej ludności cywilnej" [Germans or Fascists? Two Contests from the Years 1948–1949 for the Commemoration of the German Executions of Polish Civilians], *Przegląd Zachodni* (2005), no. 2: 41–70.
5. Czesław Madajczyk, *Polityka III Rzeszy w okupowanej Polsce*, (Warsaw, 1970). The abriged German version is entitled *Die Okkupationspolitik Nazideutschlands in Polen, 1939–1945* (East Berlin, 1987).
6. Czesław Madajczyk, *Faszyzm i okupacje 1938–1945. Wykonywanie okupacji przez państwa Osi w Europie* [Fascism and Occupations. The Implementation of Occupation by the Axis Powers in Europe 1938–1945], (Poznan, 1983). Cf. also Czubiński (see note 1). There is still a preference for comprehensive overview studies of the history of the Second World War. Cf. among others Piotr Matusek, Edward Pawłowski, and Tadeusz Rawski, *II wojna światowa* [The Second World War] (Warsaw, 2005).
7. Główna Komisja Badania Zbrodni Hitlerowskich w Polsce, *Stan i perspektywy badań historycznych lat wojny i okupacji* (Warsaw, 1988).
8. Many works could be cited in this context that were published since the 1960s; cf. as a bibliography: Główna Komisja (see note 7), 90–91.
9. First works addressing economic problems were already written very early on, cf. Krzysztof Skubiszewski, *Pieniądz na terytorium okupowanym* [Money in the Occupied Territory] (Poznan, 1960); Kazimierz Ostrowski, *Hitlerowska polityka podatkowa w Generalnym Gubernatorstwie* [Hitler Germany's Tax Policies in the General Government] (Krakow, 1977).
10. Czesław Madajczyk, *Zamojszczyzna-Sonderlaboratorium SS. Zbiór dokumentów polskich i niemieckich z okresu okupacji hitlerowskiej* [The SS *Sonderlaboratorium* in the Zamosc Area. Collection of Polish and German Documents from the Era of Occupation by Hitler Germany], 2 vols (Warsaw, 1979). Cf. also the studies by Włodzimierz Jastrzębski, Czesław Łuczak, Janusz Sobczak, and Jerzy Marczewski.
11. A few scholarly books that until today play an important role in Polish historiography also appeared; cf. Krystyna Kersten, *Narodziny systemu władzy. Polska 1943–1948*

(Warsaw, 1984 and Paris, 1986), English title: *The Establishment of Communist Rule in Poland, 1943–1948* (Berkeley, 1991).
12. Survey OBOP, September 1992, Opinions on the Soviet Union's Assault on Poland: http://www.tns-global.pl/archive-report/id/971. According to the survey, 57 percent of respondents thought that this historical event should be commemorated in festivities, 30 percent thought that it should not.
13. Various studies address this problem; cf. the literature overview in Zdzisław Jagodzinski, *The Katyn Bibliography* (London, 1982). Moreover, there are a great number of internet websites on the topic. Cf. the compilation of these sites: http://www.geocities.com/katyn.geo/contacts.html.
14. On the problem of collaboration, which cannot be further explored here, cf. *Okkupation und Kollaboration (1938–1945). Beiträge zu Konzeption und Praxis der Kollaboration in der deutschen Okkupationspolitik*, compiled and introduced by Werner Röhr (Berlin and Heidelberg, 1994) (= Europa unterm Hakenkreuz, Ergänzungsbd 1), as well as Czesław Madajczyk, "Między neutralną współpracą ludności terytoriów okupowanych a kolaboracją z Niemcami" [Between the Neutral Cooperation of the Populations in the Occupied Territories and Collaboration with the Germans], in *Studia nad Faszyzmem i Zbrodniami Hitlerowskimi*, vol. 21, ed. K. Jonca (Wroclaw, 1998), 181–96.
15. Kazimierz Podlaski's book (pseudonym for Bohdan Skaradziński), *Białorusini, Litwini, Ukraińcy* [Belarusians, Lithuanians, Ukrainians] first appeared in 1983, 7th edition (Bialystok 1990).
16. Ibid., 6, author's translation.
17. Cf. Ludwik Landau, *Kronika lat wojny i okupacji* [Chronicle of the Years of War and Occupation], (Warsaw, 1962), vol. 2, 375, 380; Claude Lanzmann, *Shoah. An Oral History of the Holocaust* (New York and Toronto, 1985), 26.
18. Despite his excellent knowledge of Polish history, Klaus-Peter Friedrich overlooked this in his article "Frühe Bestrebungen zu einer 'Katholisierung' des ehemaligen NS-Lagers Auschwitz," *Zeitschrift für Ostmitteleuropa-Forschung*, no. 54 (2005): 216 41. In his interpretation of the "'Polonisierung' der Kollektivvorstellungen über Auschwitz und Majdanek" ["'Polonization' of Collective Conceptions of Auschwitz and Majdanek], he writes about Polish attitudes toward Germans: "Because of Majdanek, because of Auschwitz, because of all their crimes, they must fear retaliation" (238). He ignores, however, that this does not indicate a Polonization, but rather an entirely different collective memory in which "Auschwitz" also has a different meaning. Auschwitz-Birkenau is not a significant element in this memory. On the political connotation of the memory of Auschwitz, cf. also Zofia Wóycicka, "Zur Internationalität der Gedenkkultur. Die Gedenkstätte Auschwitz-Birkenau im Spannungsfeld zwischen Ost und West 1954–1978," *Archiv für Sozialgeschichte*, no. 45 (2005): 269–92.
19. The question of why remembrance of the fate of the Jews had an entirely different meaning in the first years after the Second World War than it does today is not elaborated here because it has already been addressed in detail in many publications and public debates.
20. Jan Józef Lipski, "Zwei Vaterländer – zwei Patriotismen. Bemerkungen zum nationalen Größenwahn und zur Xenophobie der Polen," in *Wir müssen uns alles sagen ... Essays zur deutsch-polnischen Nachbarschaft von Jan Józef Lipski*, ed. Georg Ziegler and Wokół Nas (Gliwice, 1996), 185–228. On the discussions in the press, cf. Klaus Bachmann and Jerzy Kranz, *Verlorene Heimat. Die Vertreibungsdebatte in Polen* (Bonn, 1998).
21. The deaths of two influential personalities are symbolic for this: Jan Karski (cf. E. Thomas Wood and Stanislaw M. Jankowski (eds.), *Jan Karski – Einer gegen den Holocaust. Als Kurier in geheimer Mission* (Gerlingen, 1997)) and Jan Nowak Jeziorański (cf. *Courier from Warsaw* (Detroit, 1982)).

22. Survey OBOP on The Historical Memory of the Poles from April 1996: http://www.tns-global.pl/archive-report/id/592. This survey also posed the question which historical events the Poles could be proud of. In first place ranged the year 1989, Solidarity (*Solidarność*), and the abolition of communism (29 percent). Almost equally often (28 percent), the Second World War and participation in various battles during the war was mentioned.
23. Cf. Czubiński (see note 1).
24. Cf. Roszkowski (see note 1), 88–150.
25. Ryszard Torzecki, *Kwestia ukraińska w polityce III Rzeszy* [The Ukrainian Question in the Policies of the Third Reich] (Warsaw, 1972) paved the way for these questions. Several other authors should also be mentioned, however: Krzysztof Jasiewicz, Dariusz Libionka, Eugeniusz Mironowicz, Grzegorz Motyka, Tomasz Strzembosz, Marek Wierzbicki and Rafał Wnuk. A newer study is: Grzegorz Motyka, *Ukraińska partyzantka 1942–1960* [Ukrainian Partisans 1942–1960] (Warsaw, 2006).
26. This assertion is underpinned by a survey conducted in 2003 on the events in the Volhynia region in 1943. In this Polish-Ukrainian border region, nationalist Ukrainian organizations had carried out ethnic "cleansings" against the local Polish population with the support of certain parts of the local Ukrainian population. It remains disputed whether these events constituted a genocide in the legal sense. The survey revealed that only one third of the Polish population knew in some detail what had happened at the time. Out of this third, 37 percent associated the atrocities with Ukrainian nationalists and not with the Ukrainians per se. 21 percent and 21 percent, respectively, understood the events as a fratricidal war and as a genocide. The majority of respondents were aware of the fact that there had also been Ukrainian victims (http://www.tns-global.pl/archive-report/id/1439).
27. Paweł Machcewicz and Krzysztof Persak, *Wokół Jedwabnego* [Surrounding the Jedwabne-question], vols 1 and 2 (Warsaw, 2002). Survey OBOP, December 2002, Poles on Crimes Committed in Jedwabne, http://www.tns-global.pl/archive-report/id/1345.
28. Piotr Niwinski (ed.), *Opór wobec systemów totalitarnych na Wileńszczyźnie w okresie II wojny światowej* [Resistance Against the Totalitarian Systems in the Vilnius Area during the Second World War] (Danzig, 2003); Stanislaw Poleszak and Adam Pulawski (eds.), *Podziemie zbrojne na Lubelszczyźnie wobec dwóch totalitaryzmów* [Armed Underground Organizations in the Lublin Area in the Struggle Against Two Totalitarian States] (Warsaw, 2005). Instytut Pamięci Narodowe (Institute for National Remembrance – IPN) also suggested focusing on totalitarianism with regard to research on the question of forced migrations between 1945 and 1948.
29. "Uchwała konferencji krymskiej była kolejną klęską sprawy polskiej. Rzeczypospolitej narzucono decyzje, które niczego nie rozwiązały pozytywnie. Zatwierdzono ostatecznie zabór przez ZSRR polskich ziem wschodnich nie przyznając RP na razie konkretnej rekompensaty na zachodzie i północy i dokładając rozstrzygnięcie tej kwestii na przyszłość. Formuła w sprawie rządu była wieloznaczna, co przy faktycznej okupacji ziem polskich przez Armię Czerwoną prowadzić mogło jedynie do dalszych faktów dokonanych siłą," Roszkowski (see note 1), 146. Similarly, as a victory of the Soviet conception: Czesław Brzoza, *Polska w czasach niepodległości i drugiej wojny światowej (1918–1945)* [Poland during the Times of Independence and the Second World War (1918–1945)] (Krakow, 2001).
30. Jan Jerzy Milewski and Anna Pyżewska (eds.), *Stosunki polsko-białoruskie w województwie białostockim w latach 1939–1956* [Polish-Belarusian Relations in the Voivodeship Bialystok in the Years 1939–1956] (Warsaw, 2005); Adam Dziurok (ed.), *Armia Krajowa i konspiracja poakowska na ziemi rybnickiej 1942–1947* [Home Army and Subsequent Conspiration in the Rybnik Area 1942–1947] (Katowice, 2004); Aleksandra Namysło and Tomasz Kurpierz (eds.), *Podziemie niepodległościowe na Podbeskidziu w latach 1939–1947*

[Underground Independence Organizations in the Podbeskidzie Region 1939–1947] (Bielsko-Biala, 2002).
31. Survey OBOP from December 2002. Responses to the question whether the Polish apology for the atrocities of Jedwabne was justified were similar: among older respondents, 30 percent replied "yes"; 40–50 years: 40 percent; 20–29 years: more than 50 percent, 15–19 years: 63 percent.
32. In this regional history, remembrance of the local history of the Second World War plays an important role. Cf. for example Jan Orzechowski, *Aby pamięć nie zginęła. Służba Zwycięstwu Polski, Związek Walki Zbrojnej, Armia Krajowa na terenie powiatu grajewskiego w latach okupacji 1939–1944* [The Memory Should Remain Intact. Service to the Victory of Poland, Association for Armed Combat, Home Army in the Vicinity of Grajewo during the Occupation Years 1939–1944] (Rajgrod, 1997).
33. This does not go hand in hand with an increase in nationalist sentiments. In the same year (2004), 61 percent of respondents affirmed that Polish suffering during the Second World War should be spoken about, but 51 percent held that the suffering Poland inflicted on others should also be spoken about. Survey OBOP, Speaking About Forgotten Things, January 2004, http://www.tns-global.pl/archive-report/id/1345.

Chapter 7

REMEMBERING AND RESEARCHING THE WAR:
The Soviet and Russian Experience

Sergei Kudryashov

The twentieth century proved to be one of the most turbulent epochs in the history of the Russian state. Not only did Russia actively take part in various wars and armed conflicts in which, according to vague estimates, its losses amounted to approximately 45 million lives – only taking into account those murdered. It moreover suffered civil war and revolution. As a result of these upheavals, the political system in Russia was repeatedly overthrown, which always also entailed grand social and economic transformation projects. The new holders of power invariably attempted to instrumentalize interpretations of history for their own political ends. What sorts of experiences shaped the country and its rulers as a result of these events? How did different generations interpret the past? Which things did they remember, which things did they forget, and which things did they wish to forget? How did memory change over the course of time and how did the policies of the authorities influence these developments? Last but not least, how did all of this influence historical research and historiography as a whole? These questions will be addressed in this chapter using the examples of both the First and the Second World War.

Allow me to begin with a few methodological comments. In recent years, the popularity of research on memory and remembrance has steadily increased. Under the influence of post–modernism, scholars are calling for a more interdisciplinary approach. They are appropriating concepts from psychology, sociology, and anthropology in order to analyze human history. Following the classics of the genre,[1] these authors are building on older concepts and developing new ones. In the literature, we often encounter the following combinations of terms: collective memory, individual memory, national memory, social memory, cultural memory, historical memory,

---

Notes for this chapter begin on page 109.

communicative memory, public memory, space of remembrance, and place of remembrance. Each of these terms in its own way reflects certain facets of the complex phenomena memory and remembrance. The proponents of these typologies convincingly demonstrate the changeability and fragility of memory and remembrance, as well as their dependence on various factors, primarily social circumstances.[2] In the case of the Soviet Union and contemporary Russia, especially processes of "remembering" and "forgetting," the evolution of myths and the positions they inhabit in public consciousness, the symbolization of remembrance (e.g., through museums and public holidays), as well as the role of state propaganda in "channeling" memory and remembrance deserve our attention in this context.[3]

However, despite many valuable observations, the conclusions thus far established by research are not altogether convincing. This does not primarily pertain to differences in opinion and the impreciseness of the terminology, but rather to the absolutization of a certain understanding of "memory" and claims to a new, universal knowledge about past and present. In this situation, the professional historian and his or her "outdated" instruments turns into an insignificant and unnecessary figure. It is no coincidence that many works criticize a lack of substantiation in historiography and the subjectivity of the historian's viewpoint.[4] Caught in the torrent of "memory," the individual is not an active participant, but rather a victim or prisoner of the cultural-historical process. However, if, as a matter of principle, we cannot adequately understand history, which either stands in opposition to "collective memory" or is absorbed by "cultural memory," the sense of differentiating moral lessons, however one may define these, is lost.[5] Incidentally, morality itself becomes a relative category in this sense because a change in the social framework of memory also entails changes in moral orientations.

If we apply this approach to certain events in the twentieth century, we will quickly discover that it is far from objective. For example, Stalin and Hitler may thus easily be understood as the victims or prisoners of a tragically entangled epoch. Confined by the boundaries of their "social memory," they had simply misunderstood something or not "remembered" it correctly. As a result, millions of people suffered. Some authors assume that people live in the channeled riverbed of "collective memory," which only captures a segment of the past and does not allow for a deeper understanding of the reality of another era. The absurdity of this logic becomes apparent in the assertion that a person is capable of remembering events that he or she did not personally witness. In other words, the reader absorbs "historical memory" via the available literature and thus becomes its representative.[6] In my opinion, this sort of approach disproportionately broadens the concept of memory. It essentially comes to replace human consciousness and thus to encompass the entire surrounding world. Memory in some ways develops an existence of its own – it acquires knowledge, develops, changes, allows itself to be forgotten, and then returns.

Particularly controversial are the currently fashionable attempts to discern "the collective memory" by means of various surveys, especially among young people. One researcher in the Ukraine, for example, asked young people to write an essay about the Holocaust. After having analyzed these essays, she constructed the Ukraine's "collective memory" of the Holocaust.[7] She ignored the quite obvious contradictions in this endeavor. The term "Holocaust" only arose in historiography in the 1980s. To this day, historians contest the meaning of the term, which precise period it covers, and whether or not it is appropriate to employ it for events other than the extermination of European Jewry. Thus, strictly speaking, in the Ukraine there is a vague memory of the extermination of the Jews during the years of German occupation, but this was rarely openly addressed as a historical problem. Accordingly, young people can only speak about their *perception* of the topic, which they have encountered in the classroom and in seminars, in their families, in books, or through the media. The polled high school and university students did not personally experience the time and are thus in no position to "remember" anything at all. Their essays are indicative of what they know or do not know about the topic. It would be appropriate to reflect the roles of family, school, the state, and mass media in the circulation of knowledge about this topic or in the propagation of certain historical stereotypes. It is not possible, however, to label this "the reconstruction of collective memory."

The pleasing diagnosis of "a return of memory" is abstract and does not explain anything. If we accept it as true, then we must also accept that in the Ukraine, the memory of the Holocaust has "smoldered" under the surface for many years and was suppressed by Soviet domination. After the dissolution of the USSR, this "memory" returned, so to speak. In fact, the underlying reason for this new viewpoint is much more prosaic. Almost immediately following their independence, some of the new post–Soviet successor states (specifically the Ukraine, Latvia, Lithuania, and Estonia) turned toward the history of the Second World War in their searches for a heroic past and a new national idea. In these countries, former members of the SS and the German police, former Wehrmacht soldiers, and seasoned nationalists who had fought against the Red Army entered the stage as "new heroes" and "fervent fighters against totalitarianism." The result was a surprising metamorphosis: not the millions of innocently murdered civilians, not the tortured prisoners of war and resistance fighters were presented as tragic victims and moral role models for the nation, but rather those who had served under National Socialism and in return received land, money, and decorations. In the Baltic states as well as in the Ukraine, this sort of service is often termed "fight against Bolshevism," which is hauntingly reminiscent of the familiar Nazi war propaganda. Leading politicians from these countries have repeatedly voiced their regret and even apologized for these tendencies, but this has not significantly changed the situation. It is not surprising that the heroization of nationalists, some of whom, as it turns out, were actively involved in National Socialist crimes, provokes strong responses. The question surrounding the local populations' participation in anti-Jewish crimes finally came to a head since it touched upon the interests of various political forces. In many post–Soviet successor states, the topicality of the Holocaust has thus significantly increased.

This analysis will thus refrain from using the abstract concepts that capture the various forms of memory described above, but will rather focus on the memories and experiences of the generations that actually experienced the war and can thus tell us something about it firsthand. To be sure, their experiences were often "fixed," i.e., committed to memory, at later points in time. In some areas, their recollections can be biased and in others imprecise. It is paramount to comprehend the spirit and motivation of a memoir author, to point out the interplay between memory and historiography, and to explain the role of state policies and propaganda. The same holds true for our analysis of war experiences. Therefore, this chapter will study these complex phenomena in the context of the epoch.

I.

Visitors to the former Soviet Union immediately sensed this society's particular perception of the Second World War. This still holds true in many ways in present-day Russia. There are numerous quite diverse monuments across the country, ranging from smaller monuments in practically every town to the monumental memorial complexes in Volgograd, Moscow, and St. Petersburg. The tradition to put flowers on the graves of fallen soldiers on holidays or on one's wedding day is still alive among young people. Out of the victorious powers in the Second World War, Russia is probably the only country in which Victory Day still has great political, educational, and cultural significance. Political regimes have changed and the Soviet Union has disappeared from the map. However, many Russians continue to perceive 9 May as a special event – as an occasion for both celebration and mourning.[8] Politicians of all shades even agree that the celebration festivities should serve as a symbol of integration for the entire nation. It is no coincidence that the political leadership under President Vladimir Putin went to great lengths to organize a grand celebration of the sixtieth anniversary of the war's end in Europe. Leading politicians from many states came to Moscow and witnessed the traditional military parade on Red Square. In the victorious history of the Soviet-German war, present-day Russia is searching for a strong foothold for its future. The First World

War, in which the Russian Empire played a key role, has since disappeared from national memory. Its course and its outcome are no longer tangible for people living today. There is not a single monument in the country dedicated to the heroes of the "preceding" war, even though it was also called "Great" and "Patriotic" by contemporary witnesses.[9]

What led to this development? The First World War was never regarded as a distinct historical period in Russia. It was always perceived in combination with other important events: the February Revolution of 1917, the October Revolution, and, first and foremost, the Civil War and subsequent foreign intervention. For this reason, the signing of the Peace Treaty of Versailles, to which Bolshevik representatives had not been invited, never became a significant event for the domestic situation in Russia and the Soviet Union. Even before they came to power, the attitude of the Bolsheviks toward the war had been negative. Lenin and his comrades-in-arms not only called for the subversion of the Tsarist government, they also hoped to be able to use the war as a catalyst for revolution. They perpetuated this strategy after their assumption of power. Russia's withdrawal from the war was widely perceived as a blessing, while its participation in it was considered disgraceful. It is thus quite telling that the "Decree on Peace" was the new Soviet regime's first declaration. As a result, a glorification of the Russian army's military achievements between the years 1914 and 1917 was out of the question. Moreover, we have to understand that in the minds of the majority of Russians, the First World War did not touch upon vital national interests.[10] This became apparent from day one of the war. General Aleksey Brusilov wrote in a bitter tone that the soldiers did not understand the aims of the war. They knew neither about their Slavic brothers nor about Serbia, which had been the reason for Germany to go to war.[11] It is thus not surprising that the war appeared incomprehensible and alien to the majority of soldiers. The longer it lasted, the more indifferent they became and the more the idea of ending it appealed to them. In contrast, all involved parties perceived the Civil War as a fierce struggle over concrete national interests.

In October 1917, the country's history was "divided" into a Tsarist past and a new Soviet epoch. It goes without saying that this watershed did not immediately take hold in popular consciousness. Millions of people could not simply erase the First World War, which had significantly affected their lives, from memory.[12] Despite the revolutionary dictatorship of the early Soviet era and its terror against the proprietary classes, for a certain time a plurality of opinions and thus the possibility to publish personal memoirs continued to exist. Various newspapers and journals appeared in Russian cities. The new rulers had not yet enforced a strict centralization of publishers and the newly installed political censors were still inexperienced.[13] The "old cadres" continued their activities at schools and universities. Turbulent changes took place in the areas of art, theater, and cinema. Public appearances of politicians and poets, including open disputes on various topics, were very popular, particularly among the younger generation. The fact that there were heated discussions within the Bolshevik party itself played an important role in this respect. Several years were to pass until a homogenous view of the past was enforced by the regime. Despite these factors, with every new year the memory of the war became increasingly dependent on the new reality. New public holidays, symbols, and monuments, as well as the renaming of streets and cities, "reminded" people every day of the significance of the October Revolution and the Civil War, including the new order these events had brought about. Very quickly, within the time span of five to ten years, the First World War came to be perceived as part of a distant past, as an odd prelude to the revolutionary changes introduced by the Soviet regime.

Stalin's personal dictatorship established a powerful system of ideological control and steering throughout the humanities and social sciences. First, Stalin "cleansed" the Academy of Sciences and "parted company" with politically undesired economists and philosophers.[14] Then he turned to historiography. Under the modest title "On a Few Questions Concerning the History of Bolshevism," the ascending dictator published a letter in the journal *Proletarskaya revolyutsiya* (Proletarian revolution)[15] in October 1931 that had a tremendous influence on the further development of historical research in the Soviet Union.[16] Disputed questions concerning the relationship between the Bolsheviks and the German social democratic movement as well as the Second International on the eve of the First World War triggered Stalin's pronouncement. He harshly criticized certain historians' request to discuss "axioms of Bolshevism." According to him, these questions had already been settled once and for all. Without providing any clear line of argumentation for his position, the general secretary equated the scholars' doubts with "rotten liberalism" and accused them of "knavery" and "infiltration of Trotskyist propaganda." The rationale behind Stalin's attack soon became apparent. A few days later, there was a wave of organized meetings across the country dedicated to discussing the "letter." Almost all participants praised Stalin's "wisdom" and passionately thanked him for his "letter that came at the right time." Skeptics, waverers, and opponents were relentlessly removed from their positions and later subjected to repressions. Those who "deeply felt their guilt" had to publicly repent. As a result, Stalin practically forced all historians to pledge allegiance to him and to accept his monopoly on the interpretation of history.[17]

For outsiders, this sort of unobjective and petty attention the tyrant paid to historical details may seem absurd. In fact, however, it was the result of a well thought-out strategy. In their struggles with Stalin, almost all of his opponents – among them Leon Trotsky, Nikolay Bukharin and

Grigory Zinovyev – recalled the recent past and their own contributions to Revolution and Civil War. Stalin had not held a key position within the party before or during the war, he had made mistakes, his views had been inconsistent, and he had not always followed the directives of Lenin and the Central Committee. These facts contradicted the image of the wise leader who would lead the peoples of the USSR toward a bright future. Every critically thinking individual who contemplated the Soviet past could not ignore the obvious question: "What did comrade Stalin do at the time?" Differences in opinion and ambiguities undermined the general secretary's aspirations toward intellectual predominance, without which he could hardly have established his dictatorship the way he did. Stalin understood this very early on. For this reason, he not only had his actual, supposed, and potential opponents murdered – he moreover undermined all efforts to research Soviet history which he had not personally authorized. Henceforth, he alone would determine how the country's history was to be depicted.

Stalin's letter to *Proletarskaya revolyutsiyu* was followed by a set of measures that changed the research on, teaching, and propagandistic depiction of history in the USSR. The works of persecuted and politically insubordinate authors were removed from libraries. Some larger libraries established departments with special holdings of forbidden and foreign literature, including memoirs. Only a small circle of specialists received permission to work in these departments and only after their employers had lodged special requests.[18] The country's archives were surrendered to the NKVD. All items dealing with the Soviet era received the stamp "secret" – not to speak of party documents. This way, historians were cut off from archival sources. They were forced to rely on the work of comrade Stalin, on party resolutions, and on Soviet periodicals. A strict censorship of all printed materials was introduced. Following a resolution by the politburo from May 1934, a commission headed by Andrey Zhdanov was instituted. Its main task was to develop textbooks for secondary schools.[19] The first Soviet history textbook for elementary schools was written in 1936. It was sent to all regional party secretaries for examination.[20] A textbook for the tenth grade, the last grade of secondary school, only appeared in 1940.[21] Toward the end of 1938, Stalin's dictate over Soviet history was finalized with the publication of the *History of the Communist Party of the Soviet Union (Bolsheviks). Short Course*.[22] Stalin had personally edited the manuscript and regarded the book as the party's last word that was to dissipate all doubts and bring all quarrels to an end. In order to promote the book among the country's leaders and the intelligentsia, the Central Committee called a large assembly of all Moscow and Leningrad propagandists in September/October 1938 in Moscow. All members of the politburo under Stalin's leadership attended this assembly. When some of the speakers presumed to criticize the *Short Course* – no doubt in complete ignorance of the leadership's true intentions – Stalin interrupted their discourse and explained that the assembly's goal was not to criticize the *Short Course*, but rather to endorse it. All following speakers complied with this demand and agreed to the desired postulate, which was confirmed in a resolution by the Central Committee. Thus, the party and people had been taught a lesson on how to navigate history that "no longer allowed for unauthorized interpretations."[23] This motto captures without exaggeration the relationship between the Soviet Union's highest cadres and scholars up to the perestroika years under Mikhail Gorbachev. It moreover holds true for memoirs published during Soviet times.

The regime thus introduced a precise pattern for the explanation of Soviet history toward the end of the 1930s. It proved to be surprisingly flexible and was applied with little variation to all important events of the twentieth century (hence also the wars). The following "axioms" were integral parts of the pattern: the organizational role of the party under the guidance of its leader, the irreproachability of its policies, and the superiority of the Soviet system toward all other political systems. There was some variation in the ways in which difficulties in the country's development were explained. Under Stalin, internal and external enemies were constantly sabotaging normal development. In this context, the "internal enemies" were invariably charged with spying for foreign secret services. Besides imperialism, the state declared Trotskyism a perpetual enemy. Fear of Trotsky and his ideals haunted the CPSU until its demise.[24] In his first days in power, general secretary Nikita Khrushchev also accused his adversaries of working for foreign secret services. After his criticism of Stalin's "cult of personality" at the Twentieth Congress of the Communist Party in 1956, however, certain problems began to be attributed to Stalin's policies. The Encyclopedia of Soviet Historiography spoke of "mistakes" and "errors of judgment." In order to avoid any mention of the party leadership's responsibility and its crimes, the phrase "objective and subjective reasons" was constantly reiterated – an empty formula that made it possible to explain virtually everything. Under general secretary Leonid Brezhnev, "collective leadership" and the "coalition between people and party" was generally emphasized. Scholars as well as authors of memoirs were forced to employ these templates if they wanted to see their work published.

This standard approach to researching the past that did not allow for other interpretations was only possible in light of the limitation and nondisclosure of information, censorship, and the central control of all research activities. Despite the enormous impact of the dictate of party and state, such a simplified treatment of Soviet history would most likely not have prevailed had it not been supported by at least part of the population. Stalin's regime had its adherents and devotees. The question surrounding the extent of social support for Stalinism has so far not been sufficiently researched. Historians tend to emphasize the roles of the party and Soviet bureaucracy, of the police and army structures, and of a certain segment of the workers, peasants, intelligentsia, and youth.[25] A closer look at the various social strata of the 1920s and 30s reveals that Stalin's supporters came from all sorts of backgrounds, however. Even some prisoners in the Gulag earnestly believed that they had been sentenced by mistake and that this was not comrade Stalin's fault. Stalin's language was simple and clear. His historical explanations did not require serious thought. They were easily understandable for the majority of people who had until recently still lived in an entirely different, more liberal social atmosphere.[26] It is thus worth analyzing how "normal people" gradually adapted their memories to the state's ideology and even participated in the creation of new historical myths. This complex problem, which would necessitate the comparative analysis of an extensive number of sources, has so far not been sufficiently addressed by research. The few available studies reveal the process to have been quite ambiguous. People celebrated the newly created holidays, took part in political life, and went to demonstrations and cultural events. As time went by, they blocked out their positive experiences from pre–revolutionary times. The participants in the Civil War on the Soviet side only remembered heroic events. In the course of the consolidation of Soviet power, the numbers of those who wanted to speak about their personal contributions to the building of the "new life" increased. Thus, an affirmative psychological atmosphere gradually grew "from below." Long before the triumph of 1945, hymns of praise to Stalin, the "great generalissimo," no longer provoked social discord.[27]

It may seem surprising, but to this day we know very little about how the experiences and recollections of the First World War influenced the Bolsheviks' domestic and foreign policy.[28] For example, the Bolsheviks did everything in their power to subvert the Tsarist army and to end the war. Only a few months after the war's end, however, they were forced to mobilize the population against the new "White" foe and against foreign enemies. Not only were they able to gather millions behind their banners, they also triumphed in the Civil War and annihilated an army that was certainly their equal in terms of numbers. How did they accomplish this? The answer provided by Soviet historiography was simple: the organizational role of the party and the people's trust in the Bolsheviks' policies won the war. Newer research, however, reveals that the anti-Bolshevik movement had no fewer adherents, among them many workers and peasants.[29] This situation repeated itself in an almost mirror-inverted way in 1941/42. At the time, the world again believed that the Soviet regime was on the verge of collapse. But it triumphed once more, providing historians and politicians with the opportunity to praise the party's achievements anew. In 1991, on the other hand, there was neither a world war nor a civil war, and the CPSU had a much wider range of options for action at its disposal. It commanded vast armed forces as well as powerful secret services and police forces. However, nobody defended the party or the Soviet Union at the time. How did this metamorphosis come about?

It is possible, even imperative, to turn our attention to coercion and force, which the state exerted in critical moments. The Bolsheviks did not repeat the mistakes of the Tsarist army command and resolutely punished all acts of insubordination. Numerous party documents were emblazoned with the words "arrest and execution." The order that Stalin and Zinovyev signed during the defense of Petrograd in May and June 1919, namely "to arrest the families of all those who defected to the Whites and to shoot on the spot all those who attempt to defect or cause panic of any kind," is symbolic for the Bolsheviks' policies. Similar orders were issued on more than one occasion during the Soviet-German war.[30] To be sure, war and repression have accompanied all of human history, and the Russian experience is certainly no exception. However, Stalin consciously profited from this experience and used cruelty and the fear of criminal conviction as a method of power and as a strategy in his conduct of war – for the most part against his own population.[31] It is startling that during the Second World War, a higher ranking military commander could shoot an officer without a court martial and without a subsequent inquiry. The lives of simple troops counted for even less. Many Soviet soldiers were hanged and Stalin legalized these acts of violence through orders that were read out loud to the troops.[32] These orders were classified and some of them were only made public in the 1980s and 90s. In the course of the interviews conducted by the author, he was struck by the fact that many veterans do not remember the public reading of these orders as something out of the ordinary. They seem to have simply confirmed other everyday practices. The historian, however, recognizes their significance in the compilation of document collections. In this context, the role of Stalinist and Soviet postwar propaganda, which emphasized the "compelling" character of these disciplinary measures and argued that it "would not have been possible any other way," should also not be neglected. To this day, this viewpoint has many adherents in Russian literature on the topic.[33]

The Stalinist leadership drew the wrong conclusions from the experiences of the First World War and the Civil War. For example, Stalin could not believe that Hitler would lead a war on two fronts. He assumed that the coming war would also be a trench- and maneuver war and rejected early mobilization, as this might provoke the enemy. Moreover, he underestimated the roles of the European social democratic movements and the non-Marxist parties. Some generals in the Red Army still favored cavalry. Many apparently believed that the proletarians of the Western European countries would rush to their aid in the event of war. Because they were so strongly influenced by images of revolution and believed

Soviet propaganda, simple citizens thought that proletarian solidarity would not allow the workers of other countries – especially Germany – to fight against the first "proletarian state" in the world. In order to fuel hatred of the enemy in 1941, the Stalinist military leadership was forced to adopt special measures. Memories of the relatively lenient German occupation of the Russian Empire's western territories in 1918 induced unwillingness in many people to evacuate to the interior of the country. This was to prove catastrophic for the Jewish population as well as for the Sinte and Roma. No one but the leadership of the USSR and Stalin personally are to be held responsible for the detrimental early phase of the war with Germany. There was nothing exceptional about the situation in 1941. Had the country's leadership studied the military classics and relied on experts, it could have prevented the catastrophic defeats and the loss of millions of human lives. Convinced of their own extraordinary capabilities, they chose instead to trample common sense under foot and to ignore military expertise. The most talented experts had already been exterminated in the late 1930s.[34] Already in the mid 1920s, Major General Aleksandr Svechin, one of the most renowned specialists of his time, drew attention to the Red Army's neglect of defensive measures, to the detrimental role of dogmas, and to the necessity to move vital industries to the Ural Mountains in the country's interior. He wrote about the strategic vulnerability of Leningrad and pointed out that the massive employment of tanks and air strikes by the enemy would pose a serious threat to the country's political centers, particularly Moscow. Four years after the publication of these considerations, Svechin was confined in one of Stalin's prison camps.[35]

The simplifying views of the former Soviet military scout and later GRU (Soviet military intelligence) defector Viktor Suvorov, alias Vladimir Rezun, which some conservative historians support, are not convincingly confirmed by the available data. The core idea is adapted from National Socialist propaganda. According to this view, Stalin dreamed of world revolution, of conquering Western Europe, and accordingly prepared for the war. Shortly before the Red Army was ready, though, Hitler assaulted the Soviet Union and thus forestalled Stalin's attack. The only thing left to do in this case would be to find Stalin's order with the planned date of the attack. No document of that kind has surfaced thus far, however, which is why the proponents of this and similar views mainly rely on memoirs and flattering remarks adopted from Soviet propaganda. Suvorov alias Rezun searches for contradictions, for deviations from the facts, and for the concealment of certain events in the memoirs of Red Army commanders, and constructs a conspiracy theory of sorts from these conclusions. In fact, the only thing proven here is that human memory is fallible and that memoirs can only be consulted as one type of source among various others. In this sense, Rezun and his adherents are victims of Soviet propaganda. They consider Stalin to have been a purposeful, calculating, omniscient, and all-comprehending politician without discerning any shades and contradictions. Most likely, in 1941 Stalin himself was unsure about what to decide. Although he understood that there was no way to avoid war, at this precise point in time he did not desire it – he feared it. Possibly he envisioned new treaties with Hitler, but did not know how to achieve them. This contributes to explaining the puzzling statement of the press agency TASS, which firmly denied all accounts of a German troop concentration at the Soviet border on 13 June 1941.[36]

II.

Participation and victory in the Second World War became the central event in the history of the Soviet Union. Under the influence of the First World War, the October Revolution had established a new political system in Russia. As a result of the Second World War, the Soviet Union not only abandoned its isolation once and for all, but also became an object of admiration and reverence for many people. At the same time, the war brought about terrible suffering for the people of the Soviet Union. The precise losses (again from the perspective of Stalin and all subsequent Soviet leaders) are so far unknown. According to various estimates, the numbers range between 25 and 32 million. If we also take into account the number of wounded or maimed people as well as orphaned children, which also ranges in tens of millions, we can assume that every family in the Soviet Union was either directly or indirectly affected by the war.[37] The devastation of the country was immense. The material losses of the war years were twenty times higher than the country's national income in 1940, which means that the USSR lost about 30 percent of its national wealth. Of course, events of this magnitude became deeply rooted in the country's memory. The social climate during the postwar years was dominated by the memory of the war. It was omnipresent – in cinema and theater, in literature and art, and at demonstrations and meetings.[38] People remembered the war and its victims on public holidays as well as on normal weekdays. On the radio, there were daily broadcasts on the war and with the rise of television, daily shows on the topic also became standard. Even today, sixty years after the war's end, every day there is still some show dealing with the Second World War to be found on television. In other words: the history of the war and its memory became a stable element in everyday life – public as well as private. In light of the event's enormous significance, it is not surprising that the Soviet regime, starting with Stalin himself, went to great lengths to ensure that the memory of the war and research on the war took on forms beneficial to the regime. This was tremendously difficult because the individual experiences of millions of people would inevitably raise uncomfortable questions.

The country's highest officials were certainly aware of this. Therefore, the entire history of the war was measured by the already established Stalinist yardstick. Like before, Stalin himself determined the principal models of interpretation. Nobody dared draw conclusions without his authorization or prior to his official statements. Stalin's most important speeches, including his radio address to the people on 3 July 1941 as well as some of his orders, were published in 1946 in a brochure entitled "J.V. Stalin on the Great Patriotic War."[39] In 1948, a short biography of the dictator appeared. Stalin had not only personally edited the manuscript, but also supplemented it with "important" sections on his "military genius."[40] In the same year, the brochure "Falsifiers of History – A Historical Rectification" was published.[41] Millions of copies were printed and it was translated into all major languages. The brochure contained some obvious hints concerning the struggle with the Western enemies. These sorts of Stalinist booklets in effect determined the development of Soviet historiography on the war, and the conceptions they advanced continue to influence even contemporary Russian literature on the topic. Stalin explained the defeats and failures at the beginning of the war with Hitler's betrayal of the German-Soviet Nonaggression Pact, the Germans' readiness for war, and the Red Army's lack of time to prepare a defense strategy. He moreover explained the war's long duration by pointing out the necessity of mobilizing resources, the need to adapt the economy to the war's requirements, and the lack of a second front in Europe. The victory is thus attributed to "Stalin's wise leadership," the Communist Party, and the unity of the peoples of the Soviet Union. In principle, the various elements in this model of interpretation added up and fulfilled their purpose. It was reproduced in Soviet literature countless times and with only minor variations. The central point is missing, however: criticism of the country's leadership. As in the case of the treatment of the Civil War in the party's *Short Course*, Stalin himself set the tone and did not tolerate deviating views.

In the first ten years after the end of the war, no serious historical research was conducted in the USSR. The most important works of the time are mostly textbooks, essays, brochures, and a few articles. Although it was not explicitly forbidden to publish memoirs, all those in charge knew that Stalin would disapprove. That is why until the mid 1950s, only veterans published their memoirs. Memoirs of top military commanders only began to appear from the 1960s onwards.[42] The first publications were the memoirs of Marshal Andrey Yeremenko and General Vasily Chuykov.[43] We must remember that during the war it was forbidden for members of the armed forces as well as state officials to keep a diary or to make notes of any kind that reflected their duties. An unofficial exception was made for journalists and writers. To the great disappointment of historians, only few officers and officials dared to break this rule. If someone did make notes pertaining to contemporary or recent events, he would keep them locked up in his safe or briefcase and not speak about them to anyone. An example of this is the people's commissar Vyacheslav Malyshev who served under Stalin. His short but very dense diary was discovered in his study after his death and published posthumously only in 1997.[44]

In the Soviet Union, the printed word attained paramount significance in light of censorship, ideological control, and a limited range of newspapers and journals. Writers, poets, and journalists possessed great authority. Many people took their writing about the war at face value and accepted it as a description of the realities of life at the time. The regime of course attempted to use this circumstance for its own manipulations. As a result, published texts were often styled as thrillers and supplemented with myths and legends, around which entire archives were created. It is difficult to analyze and accurately assess these texts to this day.

An example that shaped commemoration in the Soviet Union over the course of many decades may serve to illustrate this point. During the Wehrmacht's attack on Moscow in November 1941, the Red Army's 316th Rifle Division under the command of General Ivan Panfilov suffered great losses. On 28 November, the literature secretary of the journal *Krasnaya Svezda* (Red Star), Aleksandr Krivitsky, printed the lead article "The Legacy of the Twenty-Eight Fallen Heroes." He wrote that in their defense of the road to Moscow, twenty-eight soldiers from the division had died in the struggle to prevent the enemy from reaching the capital. Leading his soldiers into the final battle with the German tanks, the troop's political officer (*politruk*) supposedly cried out: "Russia is Great – there is no way back – behind us lies Moscow!" Thus, a legend was born that was subsequently reproduced in thousands of Soviet books, articles, and novels, in poems and songs, in the naming of streets and schools, and in memorial complexes. The slogan "Russia is Great – there is no way back!" became a sort of motto for the war, a synonym for Stalin's credo "Not one step back!"

In 1947, it was discovered that not all of the heroes had perished in battle. Some had survived in war captivity and even served in the German police. The Soviet public prosecutor's office (*prokuratura*) conducted a thorough investigation and questioned journalists, writers, as well as soldiers and commanders from the division. Krivitsky, who felt intimidated by his summons to the public prosecutor's office, and his superior David Ortenberg, the chief editor of *Krasnaya Svezda*, admitted that they had made up the entire story. The commander of the 1075th rifle regiment, Ilya Kaprov, confirmed that "there was no battle between twenty-eight Panfilov soldiers and German tanks at Dubosekovo on 16 November 1941. It is pure fabrication." This statement became the foundation for the examining magistrates' report to the public prosecutor's office. The Attorney General of the USSR informed the country's leadership of the investigation's outcome.[45] However, nothing happened. The reputation of the twenty-eight heroic Panfilov soldiers had already spread throughout the entire country by then.

Other authors have already exhaustively dealt with the literary framework of the events and the peripeteia in the lives of the soldiers in question.[46] Let us therefore turn to other aspects connected with the investigation itself. The "story" of this heroic deed evolved without the involvement of higher state authorities at the time. Journalists generally knew what was expected of them and how events had to be described. The death of an ordinary soldier was not interesting. That is why they invented a glamorous example of highest self-sacrifice based on a short four-line front report. The writers knew that they were not telling the truth, but this did not irritate them at all because they were composing their tale in the service of a "higher goal": the mobilization of other soldiers in the merciless battle with the enemy. As a result, a myth was born that was in accordance with Stalin's war propaganda, which implied that it is possible to stop an enemy superior to the Red Army in numbers simply by following orders and by not retreating from taken positions. The soldiers sacrifice their lives in the name of the fatherland. The role of the party is fulfilled by the political officer who cries out a powerful slogan that serves to strengthen cohesion among the soldiers. The common mission of Red Army soldiers of various nationalities demonstrates the unity of the peoples of the USSR. When the story about the Panfilov soldiers attained a greater degree of fame, top officials within the propaganda apparatus stepped in and in the course of a few months, the names of the twenty-eight Panfilov soldiers were being praised all over the country. They were posthumously awarded the title Heroes of the Soviet Union.

When the state leadership found out the uncomfortable truth after the war, it did nothing to rectify the mistake. They realized that the destruction of this myth would have fatal consequences for Soviet propaganda. Thus, in the end, the public prosecutor's investigations came to nothing. Heartened by this change of events, the journalist Krivitsky began to "remember" new details, saw to it that his articles were reprinted on a regular basis, and in the end apparently became convinced of the story himself. In response to questions surrounding the investigation of 1948, he and his superior portrayed themselves as victims of an intrigue in which the Stalinist examining magistrates had "threatened" them and tried to "force" them to deviate from the "truth" about the twenty-eight Panfilov soldiers.[47] At a meeting in 1966, Brezhnev criticized those members of the politburo who doubted the heroic deeds of the Panfilov soldiers. He equated their misgivings with a defamation of the "holy of holies" in the "hearts of our people."[48] In 1967, a museum was built on the spot where the soldiers had supposedly fallen. In 1975, the memorial complex The Heroic Deeds of the Twenty-Eight was erected there. Seven monumental stone figures symbolize the political officer and Red Army soldiers of six different nationalities who fought in the ranks of the Panfilov soldiers. A similar complex was erected in a park in Kazakhstan.[49]

In principle, the Soviet regime had the possibility to get out of the deadlock surrounding the story of the twenty-eight Panfilov soldiers. Severe battles had indeed taken place on this spot. The majority of soldiers and officers fighting in the division in question, including its commander, had indeed perished. Thus, the memorials erected in the 1970s could have been dedicated to the division's heroism as a whole as well as the heroism of all the defenders of Moscow. But the powerful myth surrounding the twenty-eight Panfilov companions was too important for Soviet propaganda. It perfectly illustrated the ideal of patriotism, the willingness to make sacrifices, and the notion of the monolithic character of multinational Soviet society. Perhaps the regime also assumed that the truth about the events would forever be kept safe in the secret archives. During the perestroika years, however, details about the circumstances and inconsistencies in the events came to light. Ivan Dobrobabin, the Panfilov soldier who had been in war captivity and later served in the German police, demanded full rehabilitation, including the title *Hero of the Soviet Union*, which had, after all, been awarded to him as well. After 1991, Dobrobabin succeeded in portraying himself as a victim of the "communist regime," which facilitated his rehabilitation.[50]

An important detail became apparent in the discussions of the 1980s and 90s. The more remote the events of the Second World War became, the more clearly those who had defended the story of the twenty-eight Panfilov companions "remembered" the events "from the viewpoint" of Krivitsky. People who have absolutely no means of assessing the true number of the capital's defenders today vehemently assert that it was precisely twenty-eight. One should assume that after the fall of the Soviet regime, the ideological significance of the old symbols would become obsolete and that people should be able to be more critical toward the past in light of the new facts. In Russia, this process took on some contradictory forms, however. President Boris Yeltsin's administration pursued an openly anticommunist policy and tried to destroy the historical legacy of socialism for a number of years. Cities and streets were again renamed on a large scale across the country and the monuments of Bolshevik leaders were torn from their pedestals. The moral images of leading Marxists (from Marx to Lenin and his successors) were thoroughly revised through the mass media. In the Soviet Union, every student had learned that Lenin was a "great revolutionary." Now he had turned into a "cynical revolutionary who betrayed the country and accomplished the Revolution with German money." At the same time, the new regime rehabilitated the tsars and strengthened the role of the Church.

However, this wave hardly touched the heroization of the Great Patriotic War. One possible explanation for this – the weight of veterans as voters – is only part of the truth. The main reason is obviously a different one. The victorious outcome of the war justified everything the CPSU did. For a certain time, the war had a cult-like status. People could draw new strength from their pride in the county's victory.[51] The official thesis that "the victory proved for all times the superiority of socialism and the party line" was firmly established in the minds of every Soviet citizen from an early age. Thus, after having removed the CPSU from power, the Yeltsin administration was in an awkward position as it did not have a clear position on the history and experience of the Great Patriotic War. Early on, it had abolished the military parades. Then it had limited the number and duration of public holidays and festivities. The war played a less and less prominent role in television and radio broadcasts. Hasty and often ill-considered capitalist reforms plunged the majority of veterans into poverty. Among other things, they no longer received adequate medical care. The mortality rate among this group increased dramatically. Some veterans committed suicide, others began to actively support left-wing or nationalist parties. The situation became scandalous, as the new government's relationship toward history and the veterans evoked strong oppositional sentiments. From 1995 onwards, the Yeltsin administration was thus forced to return gradually to the ceremonial recognition of the history of the war – albeit with some fundamental changes. First of all, the role of the Communist Party was stricken from the heroic past. Its contribution to the war was simply swept under the rug. The thesis surrounding the people's unity remained in place, but now the Orthodox Church was propagated as the unswerving element. This tendency even increased under the Putin administration.[52] Making a show of one's religiousness has become as important in contemporary Russia as loyalty to the party once was in the Soviet Union. Since the loss of the outdated ideals led to discontent among the veterans, a positive role model that would appeal to the Kremlin as well as to the majority of veterans had to be found. Marshal Georgy Zhukov, military commander and one of Stalin's closest associates during the war, seemed to be predestined for this role. In almost no time, the marshal was turned into an idol blessed with every conceivable virtue through an intensive propaganda campaign. An ornate monument was erected right next to Red Square. An official award was created in honor of Zhukov, foundations were established, schools, hospitals, and squares were named after him – all in order to reconcile the older generation with the new historical reality and to at least partially alleviate the psychological pressure caused by impoverishment and decline. It is thus no wonder that for many Russian veterans, the extolment of Marshal Zhukov is tantamount to the recognition of their rightful accomplishments. Accordingly, this "impeccable" image of the marshal has turned into a peculiar ideological bastion: "They've dragged everything else through the mud, but they can't touch Zhukov!"[53]

The susceptibility of many Russians to the idolization of historical figures is indicative of the immaturity of civic institutions and of certain tenacious deficiencies in Russian society. It is symbolic that Zhukov's advocates even portray his worst traits – callousness and cruelty – as merits. This corresponds to the present mood in Russian society: when a commander or superior behaves offensively toward his subordinates, to this day many Russians regard this as a sign of skill and competence. The justification of cruelty implies the covert notion that it is necessary simply to accept the harsh circumstances under which many people are forced to live in today's Russia. For this reason, the Zhukov cult, which has in some ways replaced the Stalin cult and the party cult, is widespread not only among veterans, but among the younger generation as well.

In the new system of historical priorities, the images of heroes from the Soviet period have found a new place and are again being used by state propaganda. Even before the sixty-year anniversary in 2005, the authorities no longer deemed it necessary to limit themselves to the twenty-eight Panfilov heroes. It seemed as though it would be possible to erect a large monument in honor of the achievements of the entire division. However, this did not happen. Existing monuments and museums were simply restored for the anniversary festivities. A part of the funds for this project was supplied by the government of Kazakhstan. On 9 May 2005, the president of Kazakhstan, Nursultan Nazarbayev, visited the city Volokolamsk and declared that people of Kazakhstan "remembered the feats of the twenty-eight Panfilov heroes and held them in high esteem." Even today, their "holy deeds" were a symbol of Russian-Kazakh friendship.

Because human memory is fragile and because people's memories are subject to the tides of time, we must also raise the question of how to interpret memoirs and academic literature from the Soviet era. Can we trust what they convey? The Soviet state went to great lengths to control people's personal pasts and to bring their memories under its sway. An interesting fact is that underneath the officially propagated atheism, many war events attained an almost sacred character. The word "holy" (*svyashchenny*) was incessantly used in the Soviet Union, for example in the phrases "holy victims" or "holy deeds." Thus, only few people dared cast doubt on all these "holy" things or even went as far as to criticize them. The strict selection of possible research topics and political censorship contributed to suppressing pluralism – the contents and methods of most works are strikingly similar. Most authors predominantly focus on the heroic aspect of the war, list dry facts, and do not draw the necessary conclusions. Despite these shortcomings, it would be a mistake simply to dismiss this literature. After Khrushchev's criticism of Stalin at the Twentieth Congress of the Communist Party, the Soviet Union witnesses an outright "book boom." As far as the history of the Second World War is concerned, the years between 1957 and 1967 were probably the most productive period. After society had freed itself of the strict Stalinist prohibitions, it began to actively remember and research the war. During this time of "thaw," thousands of valuable books and articles on various aspects of the war were published. Certainly censorship was not entirely relinquished, but, following the party's lead, it was more lax during this period than in the 1970s and 80s. Thus, it is much more interesting to read memoirs published in the 1960s than those that appeared in the following decades. A surprising paradox of the epoch also played an important role in this context: via the party, the state, academic institutions, and other authorities, the Soviet leadership incessantly demanded that scholars and writers emphasize the role of the party. However, almost all of the country's archives remained closed, which led to the striking situation that despite the rich holdings of the archives, historians in the USSR did not have access to the most fundamental sources at the time. As a result, Soviet historiography on the Second World War largely depended on oral accounts (the recollections of veterans). The regime moreover had a periodic desire to possess their "own" history of the war. Author collectives were put together for large multi-volume projects and tentatively allowed access to a limited number of documents. The results were contradictory. The six-volume work produced under Khrushchev and the twelve-volume work produced under Brezhnev both offer a synoptic depiction of the war.[54] The obvious political aims, the ideological ban on portraying delicate subjects, and the authors' boundless faith in the Soviet government's infallibility certainly diminish the value of these publications. The leaders in the Kremlin themselves provide the most convincing piece of evidence toward this: they were never really satisfied with these treatments of the Second World War. On every anniversary of the Soviet Union, they commissioned a new project. In the end, the last decision of the politburo under Gorbachev to prepare a ten-volume edition was never put into practice.

Thus, in practice, only memoirs fill the documentation void. Even the process of writing them was a special procedure at the time. First, only a very limited number of people had the right to print their memoirs at all. It was essential to be included in a publisher's planning and to have the support of a certain authority. High-ranking officers and generals of the Soviet army who had the support of the Ministry of Defense were in the most favorable positions. Many of them wrote their memoirs in the 1960s. Second, it was important to solve the problems surrounding the confidentiality of documents and the literary production process. The following mechanism was established early on: every marshal or general had an officer – sometimes even a group of officers – from the general staff at his service who was responsible for entire chapters of the planned book. These officers gathered the necessary materials, sometimes showed them to their superiors, but often simply wrote long text segments themselves and then had them authorized. These collective efforts gradually yielded the manuscript, which was then revised by a literary editor and passed on to the censors. The responsible censorship authorities varied according to the status of the author. For example, the military, the Communist Party, the KGB, the Ministry of Defense, etc. each had their own censorship departments. After the undesired themes and facts had been removed, the manuscript was again edited and then passed on to the publisher. Of course this sort of procedure led to a decrease in quality as compared to the original text. The most important thing, however, was that all participants in this process carried their bit of responsibility. Thus, it would be ungrounded to sweepingly accuse all authors of memoirs of deliberate lies or distortions. When these books appeared, many contemporary witnesses were still alive and outright lies would quickly have come to light. One fundamental shortcoming in the recollections of the Soviet commanders in the Second World War is that they concealed many important events, especially if these concerned mistakes of the Army High Command, its relationship to Stalin, or internal frictions and conflicts. The tendency to "touch up" the history of the war and to downplay criticism of Stalin – to even praise him with euphemistic and lofty phrases – dominated in the literature that appeared in the late 1960s and early 1970s. Up to the beginning of perestroika, the memoir genre gradually lost its subtext. In many memoirs, the chronology of victories, the movement of armies and divisions, or the shipment of supplies increasingly came to supersede the war itself. However, as John Erickson has shown, careful and meticulous analysis reveals important information in this literature as well.[55]

What about the "truth of the trenches" – history as seen through the eyes of the simple soldier? Unfortunately, Soviet reality allowed ordinary people only limited possibilities to set out their recollections in writing. Independent publication was extremely difficult. For a simple soldier to be noticed at all, he would have to have played some sort of extraordinary role in a great battle or been involved in the deeds of some renowned hero or commander. There was a tradition in the Soviet press to find and interview some such simple solder in the run-up to anniversaries. Another possibility, the documentary film, somehow sank into oblivion. In the 1960s, the writer Konstantin Simonov produced a television series that depicted the war from the perspective of a simple infantryman, artilleryman, or private. This approach yielded some very sad stories. Narrators as well as viewers often could not hold back their tears. Many veterans moreover regularly visited schools and told students about their experience of the war. This tradition continues to exist in today's Russia. But did simple Red Army soldiers actually feel the desire to express themselves and to convey their memories? Undoubtedly yes. One of the particularities of Soviet society was that people often wrote letters, not only to private persons but also to public institutions. The country's leadership supported this practice, which provided them with a good means of control as well as valuable insights into public opinion. Publications in newspapers and journals, new films and theater plays, or stories and novels on the topic of the Second World War generally evoked avalanches of letters – not least of all from former front soldiers. Some of these letters were kept in the archives of radio and television stations and journals, as well as in the private archives of writers, actors, and directors. These important sources have so far barely been exploited. And yet the veterans who had served as the simple soldiers in the Second World War were lucky in a certain sense. Many talented writers, poets, and cinema directors who expressed the everyday lives of ordinary people during the war through artistic means came from their midst. This literature had a tremendous influence on the perception of the war in the Soviet Union.

The radical changes of the 1990s – the abolition of censorship, the removal of the Communist Party from power, and the appearance of numerous new – also electronic – publications lifted many constraints and opened up the opportunity to remember and to recount what had previously been forbidden. Indeed, many new memoirs appeared around the turn of the millennium, but their quality is generally not very high. In my opinion, only few serious books have appeared. Most of the veterans of the Second World War still alive today were very young men at the time. Their experiences, although extremely important, are nevertheless limited and contribute only one aspect to the complex and multifaceted picture of the war. It is striking that the memoirs that appeared between 1991 and 2009 are certainly not free of stereotypes – they are also subject to tides and trends.[56] While during Soviet times the tenor hardly varied, today it is easy to find various interpretations ranging from simplifying Stalinist clichés to furious anticommunist outbursts. This phenomenon too is yet to be thoroughly analyzed, but it is conjectured that a considerable number of veterans did not react positively to the social and political changes of the 1990s. We can sense pain and insult in their letters and public appearances. They do not like to hear criticism of the country's war past. Many have developed a strong resentment toward the state that has largely come to ignore older people's problems and to abandon them to their fate. This explains the veterans' nostalgia: the "positive" memories of their youth, of the time when they were needed and challenged. In the face of the capitalist chaos and rampant crime of the early 1990s, in retrospect the USSR under Stalin's rule appeared like a haven of order and justice to many people. In recent years, not only the elderly, but also young people – for example members of nationalist or patriotic organizations – have increasingly come to share this feeling. Although the veterans' situation improved somewhat after Boris Yeltsin's replacement by Vladimir Putin as president, perceptions of the war have hardly changed. Approximately seven-hundred thousand Russian veterans who fought in the Second World War are still alive today. Considering the average pension of two-hundred and fifty euros per month, we can hardly speak of a happy life. The current Russian administration has repeatedly stressed that it is aware of the scope of the problem, but that the specifics of Russian capitalism did not allow the state to assist the elderly in the way that developed countries do. That is why both the Putin and Medvedev administrations place great emphasis on the moral and psychological significance of military celebrations. Like in previous eras, the heroic history of the war is supposed to bind together state and nation.

In the early Soviet Union as well as in present-day Russia, there is a noteworthy particularity in the public perception of the war. The same phrase recurred (and recurs) time and again in various publications, at conferences, as well as in radio and television broadcasts: "We have to know the whole truth about the war." There is a deeper meaning to this demand. It shows that despite the numerous academic publications, memoirs, art works, and films, many people to this day do not feel that they know enough about the war. It also means that people are unable to attain the necessary information and to find answers to certain questions. The situation has even deteriorated in comparison to the early post-Soviet era. After 1991, people had access to diverging, even opposing viewpoints. Today, the displays of bookshops are filled with blatant and flashy titles on the topic of the war. Across the bench, they promise the disclosure of "secrets." In their hunt for profit, many publishers are willing to declare any random book as the "first ever study." In order to evade the expectations traditionally associated with academic literature and to protect themselves against accusations of falsifying history, these publishers and authors have invented a specific genre: the so called artistic-documentary exploration or documentary narrative. This way, they can emphasize the purported reliability and veracity of the accounts while allowing for artistic freedom. This genre is attractive especially for members of the Russian military and the secret services. It entails assumptions and value judgments that are impossible to ascertain. For ordinary readers, it is extremely difficult to navigate this sea of pseudo-scientific literature. People do not know what and whom to believe. In the end, all eyes rest upon professional historians. These in turn face the difficult dilemma of having to decide in which directions to pursue their research. In my opinion, two fundamental problems obstruct the development of Russian historiography: the lack of an underlying methodology and the confidential status of most primary sources. The fact that methods are outdated or not well developed is intimately connected with the circumstances of past and present times – among other things political trends. Until this day, there are numerous authors in Russia who are willing to fulfill any given assignment. The exertions of the general staff and the Ministry of Defense to downplay the Red Army's losses during the Second World War and to prove that the losses were approximately equal on the German and Soviet sides are a good example of this. They claim that the ratio was 1 dead Wehrmacht soldier to 1.3 (at the most 1.9) Red Army soldiers.[57] The somewhat higher numbers on the Soviet side are explained by reference to the heavy losses during the early years of the war. In order to attain a favorable statistic, the Russian military explicitly excludes the losses among reservists and partisans. Moreover, it excludes the losses of very bloody battles such as Operation Mars (the Rzhev offensive operation in autumn 1942 conducted by Marshal Zhukov, in which Russian losses exceeded half a million dead), as well as those soldiers who died in German war captivity or army service. All of this is done in order to prove the superiority of the Russian military strategy and art of war. Many authors do not fulfill even the most basic requirements: they do not analyze historiographical problems, do not cite previous works, and are uncritical toward their sources. They compensate their lack of competence through self-confidence, heroic pathos, and the accusation that critics of their work "falsify the great victory."[58] However, we can also observe the opposite tendency: in the spirit of a primitive anticommunism, some authors denounce the entire history of the Soviet Union as criminal. The adherents of this viewpoint generally propagate the doctrine of totalitarianism, equate Stalin with Hitler, exaggerate the Soviet Union's losses in the Second World War beyond measure (their numbers range from 50 to 70 million), underestimate the threat of National Socialism, and do not perceive nuances or contradictions.[59] Neither of these ideologically biased approaches do serious research any service.

The nondisclosure of the necessary documents by Russian archives is currently a much-discussed topic. Actually, the situation today is no longer quite so desolate. Historians and authors of memoirs would not have dreamed about the documents that became accessible after 1991. In particular, this pertains to the archives of the Communist Party, the Komsomol, and certain state organs. In Moscow, one of the most confidential depots of the NKVD, the "special archive," has opened its doors. It contains documents that were confiscated by the Red Army during the Second World War.[60] These records allow for an exploration of various aspects of the war. Thus, historical research is certainly not hindered in its progress. Thanks to the efforts of scholars from many different countries, we are already well informed about the history of the war. It would probably be difficult to find a topic that nobody has addressed so far. Contemporary historiography has made such tremendous progress that its further developments must inevitably collide with the unjustified nondisclosure of many other Russian archives. Concrete questions demand concrete answers. Let us return to the question of war losses as an example: the military leadership refuses scholars access to the pertaining documents. How can we confirm or disprove their conclusions if they do not explain their methods of calculation and do not reveal or analyze their sources? Or let us consider the example of the war at the eastern front: it is known how it began, developed, and ended. In a comprehensive study, historians from the German Military History Research Institute in Potsdam have shown in detail how decisions were made, how they were implemented, and which plans and antagonisms existed within the German military leadership. Comparable Russian studies do not measure up to this analysis.[61] It is, after all, impossible to write a plausible history of even a single battle the Red Army fought during the Second World War when almost the entire exchange of telegrams in code between Stalin and his commanders at the front is subject to secrecy. Like thirty or forty years ago, authors have to rely on the memoirs of top military commanders. Numerous similar questions have accumulated in regard to all periods of the German-Soviet war. The opening of the remaining archives is thus the most pressing problem.

The Russian leadership, however, does not share this assessment. It does not demand to know "the whole truth about the war" because it is entirely satisfied with existing explanations. The disclosure of all records could seriously damage the power of still prevalent stereotypes. High state officials are obviously also not interested in addressing these questions. Thus, the disclosure of documents is not only an internal problem for Russian historians, which they would not be able to solve on their own as it is, but rather a pan-European task. The experiences of the past two decades have shown that the Russian government has allowed access to a wide range of "delicate" topics thanks to the influence of Western partners. For example, this was the case with regard to the Soviet-German agreements, the prisoners of war, repatriation, Katyń, the Holocaust, and the Soviet-Korean war. The current Russian administration wants to be taken seriously as a European partner. It strives to portray itself as civil and democratic and is very sensitive regarding its image abroad. This circumstance can and should be used in order to achieve a transparent archive policy and an approximation to Western standards. Free access to Russian archives would, even if slowly, make it possible to truly research the war on an international scale – without the prejudices and suspicions that grow out of the "buried" secrets of the past.

Notes

1. The best known works include Maurice Halbwachs, *Das kollektive Gedächtnis* (Frankfurt a.M., 1985); Jan Assman, *Das kulturelle Gedächtnis. Schrift, Erinnerung und politische Identität in frühen Hochkulturen* (Munich, 1999); Pierre Nora, ed., *Les lieux de mémoire*, 7 vols. (Paris, 1984–1992).

2. See Henry Rousso, *The Haunting Past: History, Memory and Justice in Contemporary France* (Philadelphia, 2002); Susannah Radstone, ed., *Memory and Methodology* (Oxford, 2002); Harald Welzer, *Das kommunikative Gedächtnis. Eine Theorie der Erinnerung* (Munich, 2002).
3. Kathleen Smith, *Mythmaking in the New Russia: Politics and Memory During the Yeltsin Era* (Ithaca/London, 2002); Edmund Bolles, *Remembering and Forgetting. An Inquiry Into the Nature of Memory* (New York, 1988); Andreas Langenohl, *Erinnerung und Modernisierung. Die öffentliche Rekonstruktion politischer Kollektivität am Beispiel des Neuen Russland* (Göttingen, 2000); Jay Winter and Emmanuel Sivan, eds., *War and Remembrance in the Twentieth Century* (Cambridge, 2000); Igor V. Narskiy, *Zhizn v katastrofe. Budni naseleniya Urala v 1917–1922 gg.* [Life in the Katastrophe. The Everyday Lives of People in the Ural Mountains 1917–1922] (Moscow, 2001); Igor V. Narskiy, ed., *Vek pamyati, pamyat' veka. Opyt obracheniya s proshlym v XX stoletiy. Sbornik statey* [Century of Memory, Memory of the Century. The Experience of Dealing with the Past in the Twentieth Century. Collection of Articles] (Chelyabinsk, 2004); *Pamyat' o voyne 60 let spustya – Rossiya, Germaniya, Evropa* [Remembering the War Sixty Years Later – Russia, Germany, Europe], special issue of the journal *Neprikosnovennyy Zapas* [Iron Ration] in cooperation with the German journal *Osteuropa*, 2–3 (2005).
4. See Peter Novick, *That Noble Dream: The "Objectivity Question" and the American Historical Profession* (Cambridge, 1988); Joyce Oldham Appleby, Lynn Hunt, and Margaret Jacob, *Telling the Truth About History* (New York, 1994).
5. Pierre Nora juxtaposes memory and history. According to him, the true designation of history is the destruction and suppression of memory. Cf. Pierre Nora, "Between Memory and History," in *Realms of Memory: Rethinking the French Past*, ed. Lawrence D. Kritzman, 3 vols. (New York, 1996), vol. 1.
6. Susan Crane, "Writing the Individual Back into Collective Memory," *American Historical Review*, 102 (1997): 1372–86. Translations into other languages often complicate matters: in Russian, the term *pamyat'* describes memories, but also the brain's physical capability to remember. However, *pamyat'* is not synonymous with all connotations of "memory." Both the German and the English languages are more nuanced in this respect. For example, in German we have *Gedächtnis*, *Erinnerung*, and *Erinnerungsfähigkeit*; in English memory, reminiscence, recollection, and remembrance. See Irina Sierbakova, "Landkarte der Erinnerung," *Osteuropa*, 55 (2005): 419–32, 422.
7. Yelena Ivanova, "Konstruirovanie kollektivnoy pamyati o Kholokoste v Ukraine" [The Construction of the Collective Memory of the Holocaust in the Ukraine], *Ab Imperio*, 2 (2004): 369–92.
8. The ceremony of the signing of Germany's unconditional capitulation took place on 9 May 1945 at 12:43 AM, which is why this day was Victory Day in the Soviet Union (and continues to be in present-day Russia).
9. On Stalin's request, the war with Nazi Germany was initially called the "Patriotic War" and later on the "Great War."
10. Olga Yu. Nikonova, "Voyennoe proshloe Rossiy i sovetsky patriotizm: k postanovke problemy" [The War's Legacy in Russia and Soviet Patriotism], in Narskiy, ed., *Vek pamyati, pamyat' veka* (see note 3), 497–99.
11. Aleksey A. Brusilov, *Moy vospominaniya* [My Recollections] (Moscow, 1963), 81–83.
12. From the beginning of the First World War until 1 March 1917, the number of mobilized soldiers in the Russian army reached 15.1 million. The total number of losses was 7.4 million people (among them 1.7 million fallen soldiers) until 31 December 1917. These figures do not include the 3.4 million prisoners of war. The losses were greatly augmented by hunger and the Civil War. Precise figures unfortunately do not exist, but according to estimates, the total losses between 1918 and 1920 amounted to between 14 and 18 million people. Out of these, 5 to 6 million died of hunger, 3 million of illness, and the losses of

the Red and White sides in the Civil War approximately totaled 3 million. About 2 million people fled the country. See Andrey M. Zaionchkovsky, ed., *Rossiya v mirovoy voyne 1914–1918 goda* [Russia During the World War 1914–1918] (Moscow, 1925), 17, 30–31; Vladimir P. Buldakov, *Krasnaya smuta* [Red Turmoil] (Moscow, 1997), 244; Vladimir A. Zolotarev, ed., *Mirovye voyny XX veka* [The World Wars of the Twentieth Century], 4 vols., vol. 1: *Pervaya mirovaya voyna* [The First World War] (Moscow, 2002), 624–42.
13. The main department for literature and art (GLAVLIT) was founded in 1922.
14. Nikolay N. Maslov, "Ob utverzhdeniy ideologiy stalinizma" [On the Establishment of the Stalinist Ideology], in *Istoriya i stalinizm* [History and Stalinism], ed. Andrey N. Mertsalov (Moscow, 1991), 60–66; Loren R. Graham, *The Soviet Academy of Sciences and the Communist Party, 1927–1932* (Princeton, 1967).
15. The journal existed from 1921 to 1941 and was the organ of the Lenin Institute in 1931.
16. Iosif V. Stalin, *Sochineniya* [Collected Works], 13 vols. (Moscow, 1951), vol. 13, 84–102.
17. John Barber, *Soviet Historians in Crisis* (London, 1981), 125–32.
18. The system of departments with special holdings existed until the end of the Soviet Union.
19. Until 1937, there was no history textbook for schools in the Soviet Union at all.
20. Andrey V. Shestakov, ed., *Istoriya SSSR. Kratkiy kurs. Uchebnik dlya 4-go klassa* [Short Course on the History of the USSR. Textbook for the Fourth Grade] (Moscow, 1937). Some party bureaucrats scrutinized the textbook with a magnifying glass, which led to tragicomical incidents. For example, P. Postyshev, first secretary of the regional committee of the city of Kuybyshev, found "strange" blotches on the portraits of Pushkin and Stalin that, according to him, resembled Nazi swastikas. Postyshev believed that he was uncovering secret enemy infiltration, upon which the secretary of the party's Central Committee in Moscow, Lev Mekhlis, examined the portraits. However, he did not detect any blotches. "I do not see any swastikas. Postyshev is looking for enemies in the wrong places," Mekhlis wrote menacingly. Two years later, Postyshev was executed as an "enemy of the people." See *Rossiysky Gosudarstvennyy arkhiv sotsialno-politicheskoy istoriy – RGASPI* [Russian State Archive for Socio-Political History], fonds 17, inventory list 120, file 373, pages 1, 3.
21. Konstantin V. Bazilevich, Sergey V. Bakhrushin, Anna M. Pankratova, and Aleksandr V. Fokht, eds., *Istoriya SSSR. Uchebnik dlya X klassa sredney shkoly* [History of the USSR. Textbook for the Tenth Grade of Middle School] (Moscow, 1940).
22. Komissiya Tsentralnogo Komiteta VKP (B) [Commission of the Central Committee of the CPSU], ed., *Istoriya Vsesoyuznoy Kommunisticheskoy partiy (bolshevikov). Kratkiy kurs* [History of the Communist Party of the Soviet Union (Bolsheviks). Short Course] (Moscow, 1938). From 1938 to 1953, the *Short Course* was published in 301 editions and in 67 languages, with the total number of copies published reaching 42 million. Until 1959, it was the main textbook on Soviet history and the history of the Communist Party. (Translator's note: The correct translation of the title would actually be History of the All-Union Communist Party (Bolsheviks). Short Course, as this was the official party name from 1925 to 1952. The party was only renamed Communist Party of the Soviet Union in 1952. However, the title was imprecisely translated as indicated above in the past.)
23. Stenograph of Stalin's speech at the Assembly of Propagandists from Moscow and Leningrad, 1938. See Iosif V. Stalin, "Stenogramma vystupleniya I. V. Stalina," *Istoricheskiy arkhiv* [Historical Archive], 5 (1994): 4–31.
24. In the textbook for the lower grades, Trotsky was called a "Fascist agent" and in the textbooks for the higher grades, he had even turned into a "British spy" who had "sold the fatherland to the imperialists." During the Soviet-German war, "collaborators" could, among other things, be charged with Trotskyism. Shestakov (see note 20), 207 and Bazilevich et al. (see note 21), 209–10.

25. For different perspectives on the problem, see: Andrey N. Mertsalov and Ludmila A. Mertsalova, *Stalinizm i voyna* [Stalinism and War] (Moscow, 1998); Robert Thurston, *Life and Terror in Stalin's Russia, 1934–1941* (New Haven, 1996); Moshe Lewin, "Bureaucracy and the Stalinist State," in *Stalinism and Nazism. Dictatorships in Comparison*, eds. Ian Kershaw and Moshe Lewin (Cambridge, 1997), 107–34; Stefan Plaggenborg, ed., *Stalinismus: Neue Forschungen und Konzepte* (Berlin, 1998); Sheila Fitzpatrick, ed., *Stalinism: New Directions* (New York et al., 2000).
26. The people's commissar Vyacheslav Malyshev wrote after one of Stalin's speeches: "Even the most complicated, the most incomprehensible things become simple, clear, and tangible." Vyacheslav A. Malyshev, "Dnevnik narkoma" [Diary of a people's commissar], *Istochnik*, 5 (1997): 103–47, 108.
27. Viktoriya S. Tyazhelnikova, "Povsednevnost' i revolyutsionnye preobrazovaniya sovetskoy vlasti" [Everyday Life and the Revolutionary Changes Implemented by the Soviet Leadership], in *Rossiya v XX veke. Reformy i revolyuciy* [Russia in the Twentieth Century. Reforms and Revolutions], ed. Andrey N. Sakharov, 2 vols. (Moscow, 2005), vol. 2, 84–101; Sergey V. Zhuravlev, ed., *Golos naroda. Pis'ma i otkliki ryadovych sovetskich grazhdan na sobytiya 1918–1932 gg.* [The People's Voice. Letters and Remarks of Ordinary Soviet Citizens on the Events of 1918–1932] (Moscow, 1998).
28. Dietrich Beyrau, "Der Erste Weltkrieg als Bewährungsprobe. Bolschewistische Lernprozesse aus dem 'imperialistischen' Krieg," *Journal for Modern European History*, 3 (2003): 96–123; Sergei Kudryashov, "The Impact of War on Russian Society," in *The Great World War 1914–1945*, eds. Peter Liddle, John Bourne, and Ian Whitehead, 2 vols. (London, 2001), vol. 2, 94–105.
29. Nikolaus Katzer, *Die weiße Bewegung in Russland. Herrschaftsbildung, praktische Politik und politische Programmatik im Bürgerkrieg* (Cologne et al., 1999), 91–376, 533–52.
30. Andrey N. Mertsalov, ed. (see note 14), 119–20.
31. Andrey N. Mertsalov and Ludmila A. Mertsalova were the first to thoroughly analyze the problem of cruelty as a method of Stalin's dictatorship: Mertsalov and Mertsalova (see note 25), 336–70; Sergei V. Kudryashov and Andrey N. Mertsalov, "Krasnaya Armiya v gody voyny: Bolevye tochki istoriy" [The Red Army During the War Years: History's Sore Spots], *Rodina* [Home], 6 (2004): 8–15.
32. There were many orders of this sort during the war years. The most notorious among them were order no. 270 of 16 August 1941 and order no. 227 of 28 July 1942. Cf. Anatoliy M. Sokolov, ed., *Stavka VGK: Dokumenty i materialy. 1941–1945 gg.* [Headquarters of the Army High Command: Documents and Materials. 1941–1945] (Moscow, 1996–1999).
33. For a critical discussion of similar views, cf. Sergei V. Kudryashov, "Prikaz Nr. 227" (Order No. 227), *Rodina* [Home], 7 (2005): 11–14, 13–14.
34. Nikolai G. Pavlenko, *Byla voyna* [It Was War] (Moscow, 1994); Andrey N. Mertsalov and Ludmila A. Mertsalova, *A.-A. Zhomini* (Moscow, 1999); Andrey N. Mertsalov, "Podchody k izucheniyu proshlogo" [Approaches to Researching the Past], *Voenno-istoricheskiy arkhiv* [War-Historical Archive], 12 (2005): 146–65.
35. Svechin was arrested in 1930, released in 1933, but again arrested in February 1938 and shot a few months later. See Aleksandr A. Svechin, *Strategiya* [Strategy] (Moscow, 1927); Pavlenko (see note 34), 47–60.
36. Cf. Viktor B. Suvorov, *Ledokol* [Icebreaker] (Moscow, 1993); Gabriel Gorodetsky, *Grand Delusion: Stalin and the German Invasion of Russia* (New Haven, 1999); Bianka Pietrow-Ennker, ed., *Präventivkrieg? Der deutsche Angriff auf die Sowjetunion* (Frankfurt a.M., 2000); Evan Mawdsley, *Thunder in the East. The Nazi-Soviet War 1941–1945* (London et al., 2005), 32–41.
37. Vladimir A. Zolotarev and Grigoriy N. Sevastyanov, eds., *Velikaya Otechestvennaya voyna* [The Great Patriotic War], 4 vols. (Moscow, 1999), vol. 4, 282–84, 294; Yuriy A. Polyakov, Valentina B. Zhiromskaya, and Nikolay A. Aralovets, "'Demograficheskoe echo'

voyny" [The War's 'Demographic Echo'], in *Voyna i obshchestvo* [War and Society], ed. Grigoriy N. Sevastyanov, 2 vols. (Moscow, 2004), vol. 2, 375–85; John Erickson, "Soviet War Losses. Calculations and Controversies," in *Barbarossa. The Axis and The Allies*, eds. David Dilks and John Erickson (Edinburgh, 1994), 255–77; Bernd Bonwetsch, "Die Sowjetunion 1945–1949. Arme Sieger," in *Trümmer, Träume, Truman. Die Welt 1945–49*, eds. Gabriele Dietz, Jürgen Holtfreter, and Irene Lusk (Berlin, 1985), 145–52.

38. Nikolay D. Kozlov, *Obshchestvennoe soznanie v gody Velikoy Otechestvennoy voyny* [Societal Consciousness During the Great Patriotic War] (St. Petersburg, 1995); Elena Yu. Zubkova, *Poslevoennoe sovetskoe obshchestvo: Politika i povsednevnost'. 1945–1953* [Postwar Soviet Society: Politics and Everyday Life 1945–1953] (Moscow, 1999).
39. Iosif V. Stalin, *O Velikoy Otechestvennoy voyne* [On the Great Patriotic War] (Moscow, 1946).
40. (no official author), *Iosif Vissarionovich Stalin. Kratkaya biografiya* [Joseph Vissarionovich Stalin. Short Biography] (Moscow, 1948).
41. (no official author), "Falsifikatory istori: Istoricheskaya spravka" [Falsifiers of History – A Historical Rectification] (Moscow, 1948). This brochure was Stalin's response to the publication of a collected volume of documents in the USA: Raymond James Sontag and James Stuart Beddie, eds., *Nazi–Soviet Relations, 1939–1941* (Washington, 1948).
42. Matthew P. Gallagher, *The Soviet History of World War II. Myths, Memories, and Realities* (New York et al., 1963).
43. Andrey I. Yeremenko, *Stalingradskaya bitva (Iz vospominaniy)* [The Battle of Stalingrad (From Memory)] (Stalingrad, 1958); Vasiliy I. Chuykov, *Legendarnaya 62-ya* [The Legendary 62nd] (Stalingrad, 1958); Vasiliy I. Chuykov, *Nachalo puti* [Der Path's Outset] (Moscow, 1959). The fact that these two memoirs were the first to be published was no coincidence. Both generals fought with Khrushchev, who became general secretary of the Central Committee of the CPSU in 1958. Both books emphasize Khrushchev's contribution in the battle of Stalingrad.
44. Vyacheslav A. Malyshev (see note 26).
45. Communication of the secretary of the Central Committee of the CPSU Andrey. A. Zhdanov to Iosif V. Stalin, Vyacheslav M. Molotov, and other members of the politburo on 13 June 1948. *RGASPI*, fonds 82, inventory list 2, file 890, pages 85–88.
46. Georgiy A. Kumanev, *Podvig i podlog* [Heroic Deed and Falsification] (Moscow, 2000), 125–63; Boris W. Sokolow, "Von Mythen des Kriegs zu Mythen der Literatur. Russische und sowjetische Heldentaten im Ersten und Zweiten Weltkrieg," in *Verführungen der Gewalt. Russen und Deutsche im Ersten und Zweiten Weltkrieg*, eds. Karl Eimermacher and Astrid Volpert (Munich, 2005), 715–31.
47. Georgiy A. Kumanev (see note 46), 152. Kumanev regards the "memories" of journalists who spoke about the events in 1975 as proof of the "truth about the twenty-eight Panfilov soldiers." He disregards the statements of officers who actually served in the regiment, as these do not substantiate his version of the events.
48. From the working protocol of the politburo meeting, item 28 of the agenda: "on questions of ideological work." *Arkhiv Presidenta Rossiyskoy Federatsiy* [Archive of the President of the Russian Federation], fonds 3, index 1, papers 273–74.
49. The 316th division was put together in Kazakhstan and many Kazakhs fought in its ranks.
50. Because Dobrobabin lived in the Ukraine, the Supreme Court of the Ukraine rehabilitated him in 1993. This served as the basis for his subsequent appeal in Russia. In 1997, Dobrobabin was again awarded the title *Hero of the Soviet Union*. However, he had died in 1996. As in the cases of the other Panfilov companions, the title was thus awarded posthumously.
51. Cf. Sergei V. Kudryashov, "Voyna vokrug voyny. Politicheskaya konyunktura, ideologicheskie stereotipy i istoriya Velikoy Otechestvennoy voyny" [The War

Surrounding the War. Political Trends, Ideological Stereotypes, and the History of the Great Patriotic War], *Voenno-istoricheskiy arkhiv*, 12 (2004): 25–40.
52. Natalya A. Narochnitskaya, *Za chto i s kem my voevali* [What For and With Whom We Fought] (Moscow, 2005); *Itogi vtoroy mirovoy voyny. Pokushenie na Velikuyu Pobedu* [The Aftermath of the Second World War. The Great Victory Under Attack] (Moscow, 2005).
53. Cf. Andrey N. Mertsalov and Ludmila A. Mertsalova, *Inoy Zhukov* [The Other Zhukov] (Moscow, 1996); Mahmud A. Gareev, *Marshal Zhukov* [Marshal Zhukov] (Moscow, 1997).
54. Petr N. Pospelov et al., ed., *Istoriya Velikoy Otechestvennoy voyny Sovetskogo Soyuza 1941–1945* [History of the Soviet Union's Great Patriotic War 1941–1945], 6 vols. (Moscow, 1960–1965); Andrey A. Grechko et al., ed., *Istoriya vtoroy mirovoy voyny 1939–1945* [History of the Second World War 1939–1945], 12 vols. (Moscow, 1973–1982).
55. John Erickson, *The Road to Stalingrad* (Boulder, 1975); John Erickson, *The Road to Berlin* (Boulder, 1983); John Garrard and Carol Garrard, "Bitter Victory," in *World War 2 and the Soviet People*, eds. John Garrard and Carol Garrard (London, 1993), 1–13, 7.
56. One can get an impression of this when comparing the memoir publications of two opposing Moscow journals: the *Voenno-istoricheskiy arkhiv* [War-Historical Archive] on the one side, which appears in small circulation and is financed by enthusiasts of war history, and the *Voenno-istoricheskiy zhurnal* [War-Historical Journal] on the other, which is financed by the Ministry of Defense of the Russian Federation.
57. At the beginning of the 1990s, the Russian military insisted on the ratio 1 to 1.3, but then the number gradually rose to 1.9 on the Soviet side. See Grigoriy F. Krivosheev, ed., *Grif sekretnosti snyat': Potery Vooruzhennych Sil SSSR v voynach, boevych deystviyach i voennych konfliktakh* [No Longer Secret: Losses in the Armed Forces of the USSR in Wars, Hostile Actions, and Military Conflicts] (Moscow, 1993); Vladimir A. Zolotarev, ed., *Rossiya i SSSR v voynach XX veka* [Russia and the USSR in the Wars of the Twentieth Century] (Moscow, 2001); Andrey N. Mertsalov and Ludmila A. Mertsalova, "Lyudskie potery RKKA (1941–1945) i istoricheskaya nauka SSSR–RF" [Loss of Human Lives in the Red Workers' and Peasants' Army (1941–1945) and Historical Research in the USSR and Russian Federation], *Voenno-istoricheskiy arkhiv*, no. 10, 58 (2004): 27–44; no. 11, 59: 14–37; S.A. Kropachev, "Evolyutsiya ofitsialnoy otechestvennoy istoriografiy o poteryach SSSR i Germaniy v Velikoy Otechestvennoy voyne" [The Evolution of the Official Patriotic Historiography on Soviet and German losses in the Great Patriotic War], *Voenno-istoricheskiy arkhiv*, no. 7, 79 (2006): 23–50.
58. Anatoliy S. Yakushevskiy, ed., *Velikaya Otechestvennaya voyna (Istoriografiya). Sbornik obzorov* [The Great Patriotic War (Historiography). Collection of Essays] (Moscow, 1995); Makhmud A. Gareev, "Marshal Zhukov: Velichie i unikal'nost' polkovodcheskogo iskusstva" [Marshal Zhukov: The Greatness and Uniqueness of the Art of Military Leadership], *Muzhestvo* [Manfulness] (1997): 163–77; Stepan A. Tyushkevich, *V proshlom ishchut ne pepel – ogon'* [In the Past We Search for Fire – Not Ashes] (Moscow, 2005); Sergey N. Mikhalev, Voennaya strategiya [War Strategy] (Moscow, 2005); V.A. Zolotarev and B.I. Nevzorov, *Istoriya Velikoy Pobedy* [History of the Great Victory] (Moscow, 2005), 617–46.
59. See Yuriy L. Dyakov and Tatyana S. Bushuyeva, *Fashistsky mech kovalsya v SSSR: Krasnaya Armiya i reychsver* [The Fascist Sword Was Forged in the USSR. The Red Army and the *Reichswehr*] (Moscow, 1992); Sergey V. Kuleshov, ed., *Zvezda i svastika. Bolshevizm i russkiy fashizm* [Star and Swastika. Bolshevism and Russian Fascism] (Moscow, 1994), 273–315; Yuriy N. Afanasev, ed., *Drugaya voyna: 1939–1945* [The Other War: 1939–1945] (Moscow, 1996); Boris V. Sokolov, *Neizvestniy Zhukov* [The Unknown Zhukov] (Moscow, 2000); Yuriy L. Dyakov, "Gorkoe chuvstvo istori: za oshibki vlasti rasplachivaetsya narod" [The Bitter Aftertaste of History: The People Pay for the Leadership's Mistakes], in *Rossiya v XX veke. Voyna 1941–1945 godov. Sovremennye podchody* [Russia in the

Twentieth Century. The War 1941–1945. Contemporary Approaches], ed. Grigoriy N. Sevastyanov, (Moscow et al., 2005), 76–100.

60. German military documents kept in the Archive of the Russian Ministry of Defense (fonds 500) are still confidential, or rather semi-confidential. It is hard to imagine that these documents could contain "negative" facts about the Red Army still unknown from the files in Washington, Freiburg, or Moscow. See Georgij Ramazašvili, "Geschichtsreiniger als Beruf. Das Zentralarchiv des Verteidigungsministeriums," Osteuropa, 55 (2005): 407–18.

61. Cf. Vladimir A. Zolotarev and Grigoriy N. Sevastyanov, ed., *Velikaya Otechestvennaya voyna 1941–1945. Voenno-istoricheskie ocherki* [The Great Patriotic War 1941–1945. Studies in Military History], 4 vols. (Moscow, 1998–99); Militärgeschichtliches Forschungsamt Potsdam, ed., *Das Deutsche Reich und der Zweite Weltkrieg*, 10 vols., vols. 4–9 (Stuttgart, 1984–2007).

Chapter 8

BOMBING AND LAND WAR IN ITALY:
Military Strategy, Reactions, and Collective Memory

Gabriella Gribaudi

In order to express their experiences in the Second World War and reappraise their grief, the Italians fashioned a view of the *Resistenza* (Resistance) that rested on myths, rites, and symbols of the First World War. The contemporary national view of the history of the Second World War was shaped by a victimization myth stemming from the *Risorgimento* era and by the topos of blood spilled for freedom and the fatherland. The fighters were at the center of this view of history: the men at arms who defended the fatherland, defeated Fascism, and founded the Republic on their blood. The lists of the dead from the Second World War were added to the columns and blocks that had already been erected in public squares in numerous cities to memorialize those killed in action between 1915 and 1918. The national anthem, too, which replaced the "Royal March" (*Marcia Reale*) in 1946, again thematized the *Risorgimento* values of sacrifice and death for the fatherland: "Let us unite, we are ready to die, Italy has called!" say the lyrics written by Goffredo Mameli in 1847.

But the public view of history had little in common with the wartime experiences of the men and women in many parts of the country. There is nothing about the air raids, the acts of violence perpetrated against the civilian population during the German occupation of the country, and not a word about the arbitrary measures taken by the Allies or the mass rapes that occurred in the towns and villages on the Gustav Line in central Italy, the point to which the Wehrmacht had retreated after the Allies landed at Salerno in November 1943. Recollections and interpretations of the war continued to affect people in the background, in their private lives, and only entered into the foreground of public debate again when the end of the Cold War and its accompanying loss of ideological meaning

---

Notes for this chapter begin on page 132.

challenged the values on which the ideological construction of Western Europe had been founded.

This chapter deals with two contrasting experiences and recollections: one is the massive Allied bombing of cities and strategic objects, the other is the sexual violence perpetrated by the French expedition corps against local women after the great battle at the Gustav Line.[1]

Moral bombing

After its beginnings between 1914 and 1918, bombing from the air become common military practice during the Second World War. Millions of people endured the horrifying experience of bombing raids, which soon became an integral part of people's general view of the war. The air raids were portrayed as the decisive weapon of modern military conflict even if the territory was actually conquered in a protracted land battle which in many ways resembled the trench warfare of 1914 to 1918 – for example in the Allied armies' difficult advance on the Italian peninsula.

While the entire nation had already been tied into the war efforts of the First World War, for which reason it was characterized as the first "total" war, it was only in the course of the Second World War that the civilian population became the declared target of highly destructive weapons. The original idea of bombing raids from the air was to attack the enemy and the infrastructure necessary to the war that was behind the front lines. A further motive for the attacks on Germany and Italy was to inflict such suffering on the civilian population that they would grow weary of the war, hate their governments, and foment peace. Thus, this was also an attempt to undermine the moral resistance of the enemy.

This "moral bombing" was one of the most important strategies the Allies employed against Italy until the armistice of 8 September 1943. From this point of view, the country that from the beginning had been regarded as the weakest member of the Axis was an ideal target. The collapse of the regime and the surrender in summer 1943 seemed to bear out the strategy.

The British and the French met together from spring 1940 onwards to plan their military intervention in view of the declaration of war on Italy and to fix the procedures for a coming air war. Italy was viewed as a vulnerable enemy – because of its sparse air defenses, its poorly trained army, and above all the "Italian mentality," which was not considered to be suited to war. They believed that systematic bombing raids would quickly wear down the Italians. The recommendation was therefore to weaken the morale of the Italians by means of heavy nighttime raids and, if weather conditions allowed, daytime raids on the four most important industrial cities. The targets were to be selected with the aim of undermining morale in the widest possible area.[2]

As a result of the French defeat and in view of the obvious difficulties of the British, who were bearing the war efforts wholly by themselves, the Royal Air Force restricted itself to carrying out raids on limited targets that would weaken industry and infrastructure. Once the United States entered the war, the air war reached its peak with the strategic goal of undermining people's morale. The decision to attack the cities directly and on a large scale came at the beginning of 1942. Destruction through bombing attacks became the most important aim of the Allies' strategy. The leaflets that were dropped in Italy and Germany along with the bombs encouraged the population to call for peace. In Italy, which was in a clear military crisis after its defeat in Africa, the population appeared to be more susceptible to influence. After the first intensive bombardment of cities in northern Italy, the British War Cabinet made the following considerations:

> All our intelligence shows that previous to the recent heavy raids on Genoa and Milan, our bombings of the Italian cities on the whole had a salutary effect so far as the Italian population was concerned ... The demoralization and panic produced by intensive heavy air bombardments no doubt outweigh any increase in anti-British feeling. On balance, therefore, there is everything to be said for keeping up and increasing our heavy indiscriminate raids on Italian cities ... The Italian peoples should be told constantly and with every weapon of open propaganda that Mussolini and the Fascist Party have chosen to link Italy's future with Nazism, that they have thus committed themselves to the same fate as Hitler and that we are determined and assuredly shall defeat and punish the Nazis and every one associated with them. We appreciate that the Italian people were forced into this struggle by the Fascist régime. But if now the Italian people decide to continue along the Fascist road, they will undoubtedly suffer all the woes and penalties which fall to the vanquished.[3]

The Allies were banking that the population would reject the regime more and more strongly and that this would result in a crisis of political leadership. Not surgical strikes on military targets such as bases, but blind bombings that would lead to civilian injury and death were considered the most effective means. The raids should be concentrated on a selection of the most important cities and naval bases. Milan, Rome, Naples, Turin, Genoa, Taranto, La Spezia, and Brindisi were on the provisional list. The monthly total of bombs for the raids on Italy should come to approximately four thousand tons per month. This is comparable to the average weight of the raids on Germany in the last three months of 1942.[4]

From October to December 1942, the large cities in Italy experienced devastating bombing raids. Genoa, Turin, and Milan were attacked in October and November; in December it was Naples. The population became the target in this war: They were to be shown over and over again that if they wished to be rescued, they must put everything they had into separating themselves from Mussolini and Germany; they were to become rebels, saboteurs. Thousands of leaflets were dropped on the Italians in addition to the bombs. Some examples show the tone of the propaganda: The Italian people, "a peace-loving people repulsed by war, who had been implicated in the war by the Fascist regime," should rebel against the dictator. He and his Nazi allies bore sole responsibility for those killed in the air war. If the people were not in the position to rid themselves of both dictators, they would be signing their own death sentence.

In May 1943, for example, one of the leaflets dropped by the RAF declared to the Italians that the war had been lost and listed the English and Allied victories. "People of Italy! You are alone! Whose fault is that?" A list followed of the Italian losses in ships, planes and soldiers who had been wounded, killed, or taken prisoner, and entire divisions that had been wiped out or collectively imprisoned. Written in capital letters were the words: "More than 1,000 bombers over Italy in only one night." Other leaflets put it this way: "Following the end of the war in Africa, we are free to attack Italy with all our strength. We dropped 10,000 tons of bombs on Germany in April alone. Now it is Italy's turn. Why die for Hitler? ... Germany will fight to the end. People of Italy, no one asked you whether you wanted war. But they have sent you to your death. They said to you: Believe – Obey – Fight. Why, for whom, at what cost?" Or: "People of Italy ... From now on we will no longer limit our attacks to your ports and your fleet. Our bombers control your whole country: Day and night, they will attack your factories and your trains that are working for the Axis today. They will be systematically destroyed, as your ports and your ships already have been. Demand peace. Demonstrate for peace." Another reads: "Remember that the only reason for the bombing attacks on Italian cities is your alliance with Germany." And yet another pronounces:

> Hitler and Mussolini have made Italy into a no man's land. No man's land: this is the name strategists use to describe a deserted area found between two opposing fronts in wartime. After the conclusion of the African campaign, the Axis strategy is to use Italy as a shield or buffer zone in which the German general staff can stop the Allied advance while fortifications in the Alps, Germany, and the Balkans are completed ... You will realize what it means to become a no man's land, the center of a modern battlefield that is contested with modern weapons. Italy was thrown quickly and brutally into war when a short-sighted Mussolini thought the war would be easy to win; at the end of its forces, after twenty years of political insanity and administrative disrepute, the country was even unprepared in military terms ... And what has happened so far is nothing compared to what Hitler and Mussolini will trigger in your country. When we say to you that Italy will become a no man's land, we say it in earnest. Your country will be exposed to bombardment, constant attack, and the worst disintegration. The number of houses in flames will be enormous; the

dead will pile up in the cities and the country. Winter cold, summer infections, panic, and hunger will multiply.[5]

The leaflet could hardly have been clearer or more drastic. Containing a threatening message, it was meant to produce fear and herald a tragic end. Such clear wording is surprising: while the later public discourse was restrained, here mere hints or diplomatic formulations were dropped in favor of a brutal style. There was no talk of "surgical" strikes and "collateral damage." Instead, "moral bombing" seems to be the openly employed strategy with the unmistakable announcement of human losses. A further example is the unequivocal title of a document from 1 August 1943 regarding psychological bombing operations with the goal of inducing Italian surrender.

This was on the eve of the large raids on Italian cities in August 1943: Naples on 4 August, Turin, Milan, and Genoa on 8 and 13 August. Although Fascism was abolished when Mussolini stepped down on 25 July, the new government led by General Pietro Badoglio made it clear that Italy would continue to fight in the war on the side of its German allies. So the bombings also ought to be intensified, as a colonel from the Northwest African Strategic Air Force suggested with exceeding severity: The deciding moment had arrived after the fall of the Fascist regime to "shatter the Italians' nerves and destroy their morale." Selected big Italian cities, those that were considered most highly symbolic, should now be attacked with the utmost destructiveness in the most "terrible" way possible.[6]

His suggestions could not have been more explicit. The character of a terror-driven war comes into the open here in the raw diction of the strategists.

It was a dubious assumption that this strategy of destroying territories and demoralizing the population, which was supposed to be "liberated," would lead to a later military victory. The German example seemed to prove the opposite: despite the horrific destruction of numerous cities and especially the firestorm that had burned Hamburg to the ground in late July 1943 and caused the death of hundreds of thousands of residents, Germany remained undaunted. Its system of production continued to function, and though the populace was depressed and listless, suffering under the extreme conditions, they had neither the strength nor the opportunity to rebel. The policy of destruction did not diminish the terror of the nihilist Nazi leadership either, which was determined to plunge the entire population into ruin. In contrast, the "moral bombing" in Italy appeared to be working: dictator Benito Mussolini did not control the country alone and the deeply divided political leadership was looking for a salvaging way out. What's more, from the beginning of the war onwards, the population seemed to be less and less convinced by the warmongering propaganda. Their agreement with the regime had clearly decreased – a response to the obvious arrogance and incompetence of those in power.

Diplomats and commentators viewed the bombing of Rome on 19 July 1943 as decisive for Mussolini's removal. The chronicle of the 310th Bombardment Group, which was involved in the horrible attacks on Naples on 17 July and Rome on 19 July, makes this connection plain. It is recalled therein as a point of honor for the group.[7] The bombings continued after the collapse of the regime, however, in order to force the government into total capitulation – although the will of most Italians to get out of the war one way or another was obvious. The attacks in August were among the most tragic of the entire war.

On 8 September 1943, after the dreadful attacks on Naples in July and August, the ambassador of the Holy See spoke for the Vatican when he wrote to the British Foreign Office: "The recent attacks on Naples, which took place without obvious reference to a military target, have once again had a terrible effect on the city. I was emphatically informed that such attacks in no way do service to our military goals, but rather serve only to weaken the strength of the Italians and to prevent them from liberating themselves from the Germans."[8]

It seems that more bombs fell after the collapse of the Fascist regime – entirely without necessity – on a demoralized population that had already been subject to indescribable suffering. It is legitimate to ask today whether these bombings were still essential with regard to military strategy.

Strategic and tactical bombardments

Along with "moral bombing," strategic bombardments were a fixture of the entire war and were intended to block the economic and military activity of the enemy, as were tactical attacks occurring in connection with the land and sea operations. The language used to explain this strategic and tactical bombardment differed from the explicit and terror-filled formulations outlined above to illustrate "moral bombing." Both the RAF and the USAAF (United States Army Air Forces) used various means to conceal the number of deaths through mystifying imagery. As an example, the rhetoric dealt with "surgical" bombardments and "collateral damage." Here civilian deaths were never intended; rather, they were an unwanted and debatable consequence of dropping bombs over clearly determined targets.[9] There was tacit acceptance of the fact that the majority of the targets were in the middle of densely populated city centers and that their destruction would inevitably increase the number of civilian victims. Numerous cities and villages suffered devastating attacks. Some places were leveled to the ground because they were located on the bank of a river or near a bridge of strategic importance, because they were considered junctions of an important railway or road, or because there were important industrial facilities in the vicinity. The fact is that the "precision" attacks during the day in most cases were in reality devastating bombardments, and it is no coincidence that collective memory also categorizes them as "terror" attacks.

Two kinds of "surgical" bombing raids should be distinguished. One was directed against the industrial facilities in the cities, was deployed at the beginning of the war, and from fall 1942 onward gave way to the bombing attacks intended to terrorize; the other accompanied the military landings on Sicily, at Salerno and Anzio, as well as the battles on main front in order to support the advance of the troops. In these strikes the targets were elements of infrastructure such as bridges or the road and railway network. In short, anything that could have enabled or facilitated the enemy's advance. This way, villages were affected that had no idea of their strategic locations. There are long lists of targets in the American and British documentation in order of their importance (first, second, third category) and provided with the most precise of observations. They include photos from reconnaissance missions and maps with indications of the objects within the target areas.[10] For the cities and villages that were targeted by the bombers, the result was just the same as in the cases of "terror attacks" on the cities.

The military map of Naples speaks for itself: the city area is littered with numbers that signify targets. If we consider that the American planes dropped their bombs from an altitude of 20,000 to 25,000 feet and professed to strike a strategic facility in the middle of the city, we can imagine the consequences for the inhabitants.

The reports of the flight crews make it possible to reconstruct the practice of the bombing raids. Almost all commands for the operations over Naples identify the port zone as the target area. In addition, the report specifies a primary target as well as one or two secondary ones. If the original object was obscured by clouds, there were incidents or other adverse conditions, the crew aimed at the secondary targets. The pilots often declared in their reports that they had dropped bombs without finding the precise position of the object because of bad weather conditions, and that they had let them drop without "careful targeting," as asserted by the commander of the RAF crew who bombed Torre del Greco, a small city near Naples, on 25 April 1943, killing some one-hundred people, among them a large number of children.[11] This information is certainly not based on the reports from the bomber pilots, but rather on the notes from the rescue crews who experienced the bombardment on the ground. A commander asserted on 13 March 1943 that he had not been able to "make out" the ports and had dropped the bombs "on an area south of the port." Another reported that he had dropped the bombs through cloud cover "on the city zone halfway there."[12] A crew stated that it had bombed the zone of a secondary target:

a village that remains nameless. Not a single report makes mention of the consequences of these actions for the inhabitants of the cities and villages. The war that the military was reporting on knows no civilian casualties; they are constantly denied. One comes across detailed descriptions of the damage done to facilities and goods, but there are never records of the people killed in the process – they belong to the unwritten chapter of the history of the war.

One apt example of this is the documents concerning the bombing raid on Sonnino, a small village in southern Lazio. There was talk of this case thanks to the intervention of the Holy See after protests from the bishop of Terracina. There were forty-five people killed in the air attack on 22 April 1944, "thirty-three innocent children" among them. Eighty-five people were severely injured. The bishop added in his letter that there had not been a single potential military object in the village, nor any German soldiers.[13] The staff commander who had been confronted first looked for a justification, finally resorting to the logic of air war as an explanation: "The village of Sonnino lies approximately halfway between the Anzio bridgehead and the main Italian front, and thus lies in the middle of the war zone. It was selected as an alternative target by a federation of American Boston Bombers,[14] who were supposed to attack Valmontone thirty miles to the north-west." He continued: "The attack on Valmontone could not take place due to bad weather, and six pilots dropped their bombs on Sonnino. We don't know why Sonnino was selected as an alternative target … The Italian civilian casualties are certainly to be regretted, but I'm afraid that similar cases could happen again if the tactical zones remain populated."[15]

There could be no consideration for the population at the front lines. Evacuation was the only solution. Inhabitants had been warned in advance; they knew the risk they were taking. If they did not want to be affected, they would have to abandon the zone of risk. It is impossible to completely remove populations from large areas. Where evacuations were necessary, they tended to take on the form of forced deportations, like in the case of many villages the German soldiers evacuated along the Gustav Line. People who were inside this line – behind which Sonnino lay – had great difficulty getting out. They abandoned their villages to spend the long winter of 1943/44 in the mountains, in huts, or in grottos, only to perish after all for the most part – whether through cannon fire or bombs that fell down on them from all sides, from exhaustion, hypothermia, and starvation, or as victims of violence from the occupying forces.[16] The number of dead in Cassino, Formia, Gaeta, Minturno, and many other surrounding villages was immense. Sonnino was thus no "tragic accident," but a rule of this war.

Death that fell from the sky: the role of fate

The term "fate" dominates in accounts of the bombing raids. In fact there was no possibility of rescue if one ended up in the middle of a war scenario. We need only consider how many people died in the small villages on the front lines after the evacuation of Naples – villages where they had sought refuge before 1943. Resigning oneself to one's fate is a psychological means of defense against something that cannot be prevented. Maria Mandato from Capua tells the story of her father, who was miraculously rescued during the bombing raid on Capua, managed to escape from the repressive measures of the Nazis in Bellona (sixty men and youths were arrested, the campaign was stopped at number fifty-four, and he was among the last six), but finally met his end in the powder keg of Carditello. The "fate" that he had escaped on the front lines caught up with him in the end. This idea of being caught by fate is also evident in the following comment from a woman of the period who remarks on the fate of another woman: "Well with one boy, an eighteen-year-old boy, she herself was forty-two, still young; she came back from America [to her village]. And she came back only to lose her life here."

This belief surfaces in numerous statements from contemporary witnesses, as if they wanted to say: We all live under one sky that brings misfortune upon us and each of us then has his or her own fate:

> One of my uncles had gone to Nola to go to the market. He took the train, which came under machine gun fire, and did not die. He went home to his own country, where his son was, and said to him: "Toto, I'm still alive … they shot at the train and nothing happened to me, thank God." Suddenly a plane flew overhead. They had no place to flee too, so they took shelter under the trees. The father said: "Come to me, Toto." And the son replied: "No, Papa, I have a good place here." And so it happened that the father was on one side and his son on the other. They dropped the bombs, and when the son got to his feet again, he could not see his father. He began to call to him: "Papa! Papa!" The son went to have a look, and his father was dead under the tree. And I had another uncle who had a cow that was pregnant with a calf. And, well, the shrapnel reached as far as there and hit the cow. They brought her into the house, but she died, and so did the calf. The shrapnel also hit my uncle's wife's sister, who was in the house, and she died too. That's how they died: the sister-in-law, the brother-in-law, and the cow with the calf. The worst thing is that because of the war, we couldn't have a funeral, and so they had to bring them to the cemetery in San Nicola.[17]

To escape from the bombs only to die moments later: it is a classic story that bespeaks the human condition. But it is also a way to say: We went on living; we had to go on living. This fatalism is the only weapon of people who became the targets of bomber pilots or the victims of counterstrikes from the enemy army: "We gave up hope; we resigned because we said: 'Who knows if we will still be alive tomorrow?' The bombings at that time were terrible ... and you could be dead in five minutes ... So there was great resignation because you were completely helpless and exposed to what was going on."[18] Another contemporary witness recounts: "We were in the middle of the bombing raids. We were waiting for the moment when we would die ... what were we to do?"[19]

The term "fate" was also used to describe the event of the bombing. The technical jargon of the war strategists was translated into everyday language and culture. In everyday language, a thing that came from the sky, such as the bombs, stood for something unforeseeable, for one's lurking fate. The bomb penetrated the language of the people, literally falling into their heads and destroying more than lives. In the accounts from contemporary witnesses, the bombardment is almost always represented as a rift, a crack of lightning smashing into daily life. As a rule, it is associated with something else they were doing at the time in their recollections. The moment when the bomb lands is an abrupt interruption of life at a specific moment. Examples of this include the recollections of a girl who was coming out of school, a woman who was taking a bath, friends who were going to buy a gift for the engagement party of a certain Salvatore, sisters on their way to the engagement party of a friend, and a young boy playing soccer.

In these stories, the falling bombs are not associated with the person who dropped them. The individual responsible for them remains invisible. For this reason, there is seldom antipathy toward the Americans for the death of a family member. Rather, the bombardment was experienced as an uncontrollable natural catastrophe. Incidentally, this bears some similarity to the way people coped with the memory of the atomic bomb dropped on Hiroshima, as Günter Anders established already in 1959.[20]

The stories of the violent crimes committed by the German occupiers and how people assess them differ fundamentally from his interpretation, however. In this case, there was a specific person who brought death: the guilty party had a face. Cause and effect were directly related. The Italians felt the German violence much more deeply than that of the Allies, because it was – as one of the contemporary witnesses would express it – carried out with malice, frequently face to face with the victim. Here the victims were condemned to death and often subjected to one final physical humiliation beforehand.

Those who are "killed before dying" are the most unfortunate of mortals. To think that a beloved person was killed in this direct way is still more painful, if not unbearable. The long, detailed recollections of the Nazi atrocities clearly reveal the announcement, the fear, the flight, the hate that builds up in direct relation to these events; the stories refer to soldiers with machine guns and helmets, to their shouting. In contrast, soldiers do not surface in memories of the bombing raids. The bombings in general and the individual experiences are kept separate. On one side we have the image of the Americans who dropped bombs by the ton; on the other, there is the part of town or one's own house where the bombs landed, where they destroyed the life of a beloved person. One side has the image of the Americans as liberators who passed out chocolate and cigarettes; the other has the bomber pilots who brought death.[21]

Particularly in public discourse, the bombing raid appears as an inevitable part of modern warfare. As a rule, its interpretation was strongly influenced by military jargon used to describe and justify the air war: as a virtual, technological war with military targets that concealed the actual target, human life. Those who established the targets did not consider how many civilians would be affected. The talk was of bridges, train stations, railroads, and factories, but the military leadership knew very well that civilians would be killed; indeed, they were explicitly a target. The accounts of contemporary witnesses are ambiguous in their indifference toward death. Although all of them recount incessant bombings, they were always searching for reasons for the attacks that shook their homes, the lives of their parents and neighbors, and often adopted the theory of the Americans in interpreting the bombardments a "precision attacks." Thus, an inhabitant of Vico Giganti in Naples believed that the bombers wanted to destroy a printing house used by the Germans, a farmer from Bellona whose mother and sister had been hit by bombs as they worked in the fields suspected that the pilots had mistaken their wheat fields for a military camp, and the residents of Teano thought that the bombs had mistaken the cage on a church steeple for a radio antenna.

These interpretations reflect different variations of the multitude of discourses about the war. They show the ambivalence, even inconsistency of the deadly war led by "liberators." The spectrum of interpretations ranges from a specific war ethos that implies that anything goes in war to a "normal" morality as determined by the Fifth Commandment: Thou shalt not kill. People had difficulty admitting to themselves that the acts of violence were committed consciously, to achieve the highest number of dead in accordance with the logic of terror attacks, and they looked for reasons why. In this respect, they internalized the language of the victors, even if contradictions can still be found in their recollections. The collective memory of the nation, on the other hand, has ignored the individual experiences of war in certain regions such as southern Italy, or even denied them.

The mass rapes on the Gustav Line

After Italy's surrender and the Allied landing south of Salerno on 9 September 1943, the German army successively withdrew to various defensive lines with the order to hold the Gustav Line at Cassino and thereby prevent the Allies from advancing to the capital. The Allied troops required quite a few months to break through this line, from November 1943 to May 1944, and clear the way to Rome. They tried to force back the German divisions in different waves, with extensive air attacks accompanying the troop movements.

Ongoing struggles developed on the ground in which the adversaries temporarily held their positions sometimes on one side of the front line, sometimes on the other. There were attempts to break through with close combat, constant shooting from both sides, air attacks, and forced evacuations. The situation was very similar to the one in which people had found themselves at the main battle lines of the First World War, but with substantially more artillery and bombing attacks deployed. Just like the fate suffered by the population in Trentino and Venetia during the First World War,[22] this aspect is hardly present in the collective memory of the nation. As it were, the destruction of the Monte Casino monastery is the only symbol for the war along the Gustav Line, yet there are a great number of diaries, memoirs, works of domestic history, and histories of individual social groups that testify to a deeply rooted local memory. These recollections impressively describe life at the front lines, the chain of violent acts carried out by the various sides, everyday life amid the bombs, and the attempts to defend against being at the mercy of wartime events and to escape death.

The people who lived along the Gustav Line found themselves in an extreme situation, shaped by the long duration of the battles from November 1943 to May 1944, the far-reaching destruction wrought by the Allied air attacks, the Germans' stubborn defense of the line (frequently at the expense of the civilian population), and finally by the violent assaults on Italian women by the troops of the French expedition corps. Some contemporary witnesses explicitly stress that they lived in a no man's land. Photographs of the time show troops and the local population, cities and ruins in the snow. National memory has established the destruction of the Monto Cassino Benedictine monastery, one of the oldest Christian monasteries, but few recall that this battle from 17 January to 18 May 1944 also reduced the city of Cassino to ashes and rubble, and that many other places between Gaeta and Cassino were almost completely destroyed. At the same time, the people who fled to the mountains and hid there were exposed to the wrath of the Germans, who for their part had to fend off the Allied attacks. When people finally wanted to celebrate "liberation" on 22 May 1944, many cities were plagued with lootings and rapes by the French troops.

The contribution of the French expedition corps, which surrounded the German troops in the Aurunci Mountains by a pincer movement, was decisive for the breakthrough at the front. The French mountain troops were essentially comprised of Moroccan auxiliary forces – the so called *Goumiers*. They were the main actors in this difficult battle, which ended on 27 May 1944 after thousands had been killed on both sides. General Alphonse Juin wrote to General de Gaulle that the French expedition corps had taken 4,400 prisoners, among them 110 officers, but had themselves lost 7,000 men, including 260 officers. This was an important military victory that the French were very proud of. Both the Allies and the Germans recognized the military achievement of the troops, 70 percent of whom came from North Africa. But those who had taken refuge in the mountains from the chaos of war did not necessarily experience these days as liberating.

The acts of violence took on unimaginable dimensions in the Aurunci Mountains, Ciociaria, and the back country of Frosinone. It is very difficult to establish an exact count of women who were raped because no serious research was conducted on this subject in the postwar era given the diverse limitations on access to the files. In point of fact, the rapes were lost in the long lists of suffering and damages people charged in thousands of reports in the hope of gaining compensation in one way or another. Against this backdrop, the problem was always swept under the rug.[23] An analysis of the sources indicates about six-thousand cases of rape. It is impossible to represent their stories in detail on the basis of the culprits' motives and the recollections of the victims. It should merely be mentioned that the rapes usually occurred immediately after the battles, that the French command did not intervene, and that entire villages suffered: girls were raped by several men, many women lost their lives, and many others did not manage to rebuild their lives after the war. In a society dominated by the concept of women's honor, the loss of virginity in the women who were raped had decisive effects on their futures. Moreover, the suffering of these women was not recognized at the legal level. The state only provided compensation for the violence suffered when physical traces were left behind. Individual experiences and recollections thus differ markedly from the national discourse on the war.

Mentioned here are some recently reconstructed cases from the two towns of Lenola and Campodimele.[24] Two of the women consulted had lost their mother in the hail of Allied bombs; another one had seen her infant daughter die from want and her husband march to war a few days later. They were raped in May 1944. Thus, first it was bombs, then gunfire, starvation, cold, deportations, and finally rape. Here are just a few passages from their recollections that reveal recurring themes: "The liberators have arrived, they said, the Americans, but the Moroccans came instead. I never celebrated the day of liberation, because these are memories that I will never forget ... What kind of liberation is this, anyway? To be liberated in this way! They had their way with us, as they wanted ... What do you think ... Some women lost their lives." Or: "I remember very well that they arrived on the 22nd, because it was on this very day that they came to us, but I don't remember exactly when they went away again ... they stayed nine to ten days, and in these long days they did what the Germans never did in six months." Or: "I remember very clearly that they came in May, and you couldn't call what they did a liberation – it was really a work of destruction." Or: "The Moroccans were scoundrels, but so were the Americans for allowing that rabble to do so many things. It should have been a liberation, not this."

The victors who were supposed to bring democracy appeared as criminals, first because of the unexpected bombardments that the inhabitants of a small town in the Apennine Mountains could hardly find a military explanation for, and then in the form of the Moroccan rapists. There is nothing more removed from the national discourse on the war than these personal recollections of it. What happens when the contrast between the public telling of the story and the individual experiences is so strong? A feeling of astonishment surfaces in these recollections. "We hid out of fear of the war. We expected liberators, and in fact my mother-in-law went out with the white flag ... we believed they would be liberators." This initial astonishment quickly turned to dismay, to a pain that cannot be expressed in words, that was kept silent over long years and was expressed less by refusal than by a conscious distancing from the public rhetoric. Experience had taught people that in wartime everyone is a potential killer, that people's motives for action often got mixed up, and that the real victims of the conflict are the people who live in an area of battle.

Forced evacuations, deportations, shelter in mountain grottos and huts, cold, starvation, and bombs – everything came together along the Gustav Line. The memory of the postwar era, when people returned to the small towns and villages that had been destroyed, coincides with the memory of a catastrophe that words cannot describe. In Italy, as in Germany, the rebuilding of the country whitewashed the memory of this catastrophe for a long time.

Memory in public discourse

In the immediate postwar era, the national discourse took up the nationalist rhetoric of the *Risorgimento*, emphasizing that the partisan guerrillas had fought for freedom against Fascism and the German invaders. In this context, the victims of the reprisals and massacres were equated with those killed in battle. Various historians have shown how the discourse adopted and reformulated religious images and symbolism, such as the rhetoric of "martyrdom," "sacrifice," and the "blood that renews the nation." The generation that employed this obviously "masculine" language had still grown up with mythical ideas of war and nation. They also had to live down the defeat and counter the image of a "feminine" Italy incapable of battle that had already spread among the Allied soldiers before 1943.

How did this discourse develop at the local level? In northern central Italy, where the national liberation committee (*Comitato di Liberazione Nazionale* – CLN) had organized the partisan battle and the left-wing parties and partisan organizations had more institutional weight, the *Resistenza* was placed at the center of collective memory through commemorations and festive rituals. New studies, meanwhile, point to a deeply rooted hostility toward the partisans and to differences in individual and local recollections that stand in stark contrast to public commemoration – a contradiction that was also publicly expressed. For example, when the speakers at a festivity in Civitella in Val di Chiana wished to commemorate the local men who had been murdered in a "retaliatory measure" (*Sühnemaßnahme*) by the Nazis, they were literally chased away from the lectern by the widows of the deceased men. These women objected to the public discourse and turned the model of interpretation on its head. For them, their husbands were not martyrs who had died for a just cause, but rather involuntary victims of a violence unleashed by irresponsible partisans. Each year, the survivors in Sant'Anna di Stazzema, Bardine di San Terenzio, and many other places demonstrate against the participation of the representatives of the National Resistance Fighters' Association (*Associazione Nazionale Partigiani d'Italia*, ANPI) in the commemoration ceremonies.

In southern and southern central Italy, the process of normalization that did not begin in the rest of Italy until 1946/47 started immediately after the Allies had landed. "Purges" were rare and the old state apparatus reorganized quickly. Here the public discourse rested less on the *Resistenza* and more on patriotic-military traditions. As a rule, on 4 November, the anniversary of the victory over Austria-Hungary, patriotic and military hymns were sung in remembrance of all the victims: the members of the military, the front fighters, and the civilians together – preventing true remembrance.

The religious language of the Church was the only way to express people's pain, especially in those places where the state was not capable of representing or defending them. This explains the strong position of the Church in certain regions. Sacred symbolism has an immediate power to express the suffering of the war's victims that is much stronger than political rhetoric. Religious symbols and representations that inflate and glorify the pain of men and women are anchored in tradition and folk culture. They provide expressive and comprehensible metaphors and prompt emotions. A range of sacred images appears in the stories of contemporary witnesses, including Our Lady of Sorrows, the Deposition of Christ on the Cross, the Stations of the Cross, and the scenes of the martyrs. Far more than the bombastic hymns, these representations provided a possibility to express the suffering felt by the weak and the conquered, who probably felt like anything but winners.

In the postwar era, it was frequently priests, Catholic organizations, informal district organizations, and citizen groups who took on the function of "secondary social groups" (Jay Winter and Emmanuel Sivan) in constructing memory.[25] Their sphere of activity seldom reached beyond the city, however, and they did not develop a discourse on the war. Nowadays there are stone memorials all over Italy that have been donated by a hamlet or by Catholic or district organizations. They testify to a deeply rooted piety among the people and to a desire to remember and commemorate neighbors and relatives killed in the air raids. The stones have short, simple inscriptions. It would have been impossible to fall back on public vocabulary here.

Conclusion

The following points should be emphasized when considering this complex subject, which really deserves a more detailed treatment. Personal recollections, which have affected people's lives for a long time and could thus far only be expressed in religious images, are now coming to light. They are gradually finding expression in Italian public discourse as the memory of the suffering at the time. There is a great desire for public recognition as well as medals and other decorations that reflect the endured sorrow. This process is unfolding in many small towns and villages in Campania and southern Lazio, for example, and is producing individual local cultures of remembrance. In some cases, books and brochures have been published that tell the story of the war from a local perspective. These always end with a list of the names of those considered victims of the war: fellow citizens who perished at the hands of the Germans or in the hail of Allied bombs, who died from illness contracted in the forced evacuations to the mountains or during the deportations, or who were killed by mine explosions in the postwar period. Public remembrance discourse has come to consider this suffering as well. A stone was unveiled in Lenola in recognition of the mass rapes and a memorial slate in Formia recalls the nine months in which the town's inhabitants were at the mercy of Allied bombs and German tyranny. Decorations are awarded for having endured a bitter ordeal (*aspro calvario*), a long martyrdom (*lungo martirio*), and immeasurable ruin (*immani rovine*), as well as to citizens defenseless and exhausted from hardship (*cittadini inermi e stremati dalle privazioni*). The community of Foggia, which had already received a gold Order of

Civil Merit, was recognized in 2006 with a gold Military Cross because of the tragic air raids it had suffered (*aver subito tragici bombardamenti*).

This evolution of the memory of the war in Italy has emerged from the crisis of the old national discourse and the opening up of the culture of memory, which has led to a critique of the traditional analytical categories and rhetoric on war. The recognition of people's suffering, however, goes hand in hand with the attempts by a political elite to consolidate and coordinate these recollections in the language of a new national *Risorgimento* discourse. In this way, the manifold individual memories of suffering that cannot be reduced to an overblown national discourse are being instrumentalized for an undifferentiated discourse on the war and displaced by a new rhetoric of patriotism.

Notes

1. This article is based on the systematic evaluation of interviews conducted among contemporary witnesses who experienced the Second World War; cf. in detail Gabriella Gribaudi, *Guerra totale: Tra bombe alleate e violenze naziste. Napoli e il fronte meridionale 1940–1944* (Turin et al., 2005) (Nuova cultura, 109).
2. Cf. Public Records Office (PRO) London (today National Archives), AIR 2/7197, Operations Against Italy by Bomber Sqdns. 3 May 1940. Note on Air Offensive against Italy.
3. PRO, FO 371/33228, War Cabinet, Position of Italy, Memorandum by the Secretary of State for Foreign Affairs, A.E., Foreign Office, 20 November 1942.
4. Cf. PRO, CAB, 120/292, letter from Charles Portal to the Prime Minister, 29 October 1942. Italy is given as a current primary target in another letter from 1 December 1942.
5. Archivio di Stato di Napoli (ASN), Prefettura, Gabinetto, dossier 1224/1st RAF leaflet, May 1943. The other leaflets cited here come from the same dossier.
6. Air Force Historical Research Agency, Maxwell/Alabama (AFHRA), Microfilm A 6013-21. Headquarters Northwest African Strategic Air Force. APO 520. 1 August 1943. *Psychological Bombing Operations with the Goal of Inducing Italian Surrender*. "It is firmly believed that now is the time for decisive blows to be dealt to the ragged nerves and crumbling morale of Mussolini's regime. This can be by properly displaying the devastating power of the Strategic Air Force. To make it even more impressive and terrifying, they should be given part of a list of especially selected Italian cities which are to be systematically isolated and totally destroyed. Operations against these cities should be periodic and spaced between other operations ... The enemy should know that they are coming, but other bombing operations should be done to such an extent that could not effectively move to meet a previously announced attack on a doomed city, but with full knowledge that their city might be next, would have a tremendous effect on their nerves as these operations progress. These operations should receive Axis-wide publicity through radio propaganda broadcasts and leaflets. They should describe in minute detail previous strategic bombing, the destruction caused and the extent of damage ... Knowing this will cause, when either friendly or hostile aircraft fly overhead, a far greater terrifying effect ... These cities should be carefully selected so that all of Italy will feel the tremendous effect of such a war. This list should contain

cities such as Rome, Naples, Florence, Genoa and Venice as these cities are nearest to the heart of the Italian people."
7. Lt. Robert R. Thorndike, *The Air Echelon from the U.S.A. to Iceland*, in AFHRA, Microfilm B 0229-1859.
8. PRO, AIR 20/5304, To: Foreign Office, from: Holy See, Sir Osborne, 8 September 1943.
9. C.C. Crane, *Bombs, Cities and Civilians: American Airpower Stategy in World War II* (Lawrence/KS, 1993), 1.
10. AFHRA, B 567-1457, First, Second, Third Priority List. Target Chart Production. 12th Air Force.
11. AFHRA, B 5665-1665, Sortie Report, 178th Sqdn.
12. AFHRA, B 5664-1448, Sortie Report, 514th Sqdn.
13. Telegram from 2 May 1944 from the British Ambassador to the Holy See to the War Cabinet, PRO, PREM, 3/14/3.
14. These are twin-motor bombers of the Douglas AJ 20 type.
15. Letter from the Air Staff Vice Commander, Sir Douglas C.S. Evill, 6 May 1944, PRO, PREM, 3/14/3.
16. The attempt to break through the German Gustav Line (Cassino – Minturno) began in November 1943 and lasted until late May 1944.
17. Statement from Pasqualina Lo Fabio (born 1930 in Scisciano, Naples), interview by Marisa Di Palma, 1997, cf. Gribaudi (see note 1), 603; for a list of interviews, cf. 639–44.
18. Statement from Annamaria Romano (born 1926 in Naples), interview by Daniela Costanzo, 1996, cf. Gribaudi, ibid., 604.
19. Statement from Vincenzina De Micco (born 1909 in Cancello Arnone), interview by Gabriella Gribaudi, 2004, cf. Gribaudi, ibid., 604.
20. Günther Anders, *Der Mann auf der Brücke. Tagebuch aus Hiroshima und Nagasaki* (East Berlin, 1965), 97–99: "Without exception, they speak of the catastrophe as one does of an earthquake, a flood or an exploding sun. The consistency with which they leave out those responsible, abstract the fact that the event was man-made, and do not bear the least grudge even though they are victims of the most enormous crime, is too much. There is something off about it ... As strange as it may sound, the victims have in no way *experienced* the catastrophe as such. Only the life that went on before the catastrophe, and the life or death that followed, without the bolt of lightning that came in between. It was too monstrous, too suddenly there and suddenly past for them to even recognize it for what it was ... They still stress today that the enemy was anonymous; this remains an inadequate characterization and is already obsolete. What is true, however, is that no enemy remains visible today, and that no enemy remained visible in the case of Hiroshima either. Thus, there could be no correspondence between the strike and those responsible for it, and this is why no such correspondence was attempted in the first place. And so there is no hate on the part of the victims either ..."
21. Anders, ibid., 100: "When the GIs came into the country after the surrender and slipped chocolate and bubble gum to the children, they remained unrecognizable as the 'perpetrators' to the Japanese. Certainly this was not only understandable, but in a certain sense also justified because to equate these boys with the men who had ordered the bomb to be dropped would have been morally askew. I am referring to something different: to the danger that, due to the invisibility of the guilty, guilt itself will become invisible."
22. Daniele Ceschin, "Gli esuli di Caporetto. I profughi italiani durante la Grande Guerra, 'L'estremo oltraggio': la violenza alle donne durante l'occupazione austro-germanica (1917–18). Studi, fonti, prospettive di ricerca," lecture given at the third Congresso della Società Italiana delle Discipline Storiche (panel *Violenze di guerra*), Florence, 14–16 November 2003.

23. Cf. the study recently published in France by a military historian who stresses the achievements of the French expedition corps: J.C. Notin, *La campagne d'Italie. Les victoires oubliées de la France 1943–45* (Paris, 2002).
24. Gribaudi (see note 1), especially 510–71 (chapter 10: Gli stupri di massa).
25. Jay Winter and Emmanuel Sivan, "Setting the framework," in Jay Winter and Emmanuel Sivan, eds., *War and Remembrance in the Twentieth Century* (Cambridge, 1999), 6–39.

Chapter 9

ITALY AS OCCUPIER IN THE BALKANS:
Remembrance and War Crimes after 1945

Filippo Focardi

For more than twenty-nine months, from April 1941 to September 1943, Fascist Italy governed most of Yugoslavia and Greece as a military occupation power. The Italian monarchy had already annexed and occupied Albania in April 1939.[1] After Yugoslavia had collapsed under the attack of the Axis powers, the Fascist regime furthermore annexed southern Slovenia and Dalmatia, and de facto came to control the vast territory of the Croatian state ruled by Ante Pavelić. It created a protectorate in Montenegro and incorporated Kosovo and certain parts of Macedonia into Albania, thereby creating the so called Greater Albania.[2] In Greece, which could only be conquered with German assistance after the failed Italian offensive in October 1940, Benito Mussolini appropriated about two-thirds of the country's territory, including Epirus, Thessaly, Peloponnesus, large parts of Attica, and the Greek islands.[3]

The expansion into the Balkans was one of Fascist Italy's greatest territorial conquests in the Second World War. The Italian army maintained a considerable number of troops in this region, numbering between six-hundred and six-hundred-fifty thousand soldiers. This totaled thirty to thirty-five divisions, which was approximately half of all the divisions the Italian leadership commanded at the time.[4] Thus, the Balkans was the region to which Mussolini's Italy dispatched the most troops.

In Yugoslavia as well as in Albania and Greece, the Italian military and police forces soon became embroiled in a fierce and bloody battle with local partisan formations.[5] In consequence, they enforced a wide range of repression measures against the civilian population: they tortured and abused opponents, shelled and burned down villages (also killing women

---

Notes for this chapter begin on page 142.

and children), randomly executed partisans, took hostages and executed them in retaliation, and deported thousands of civilians to concentration camps.[6] After the Second World War, Yugoslavia estimated the number of domestic victims of the Italian occupation at two-hundred-fifty thousand, with Greece at one-hundred thousand.[7] These figures appear to be slightly too high, however. Indeed, we only have reliable data for the relatively small territory of Italian-occupied Slovenia – as provided by the historian Tone Ferenc – which had three-hundred-forty thousand inhabitants at the time. He has accounted for about three-thousand victims of Italian repression, not including the partisans who died in battle.[8] Moreover, the figures of Yugoslavian civilians who were deported to Italian concentration camps are also reliable. Carlo Spartaco Capogreco estimates them at about one-hundred-ten thousand.[9] Several thousands of them, including women, elderly people, and children, died as a result of the harsh conditions of the internment. In the main camp for Slavic prisoners on the island Rab, the mortality rate was at 19 percent.[10]

Putting these figures aside, the Italian occupation forces committed terrible war crimes in the Balkans, which in many ways compare with the atrocities committed by their German "comrades" – excluding the systematic persecution of the Jews as well as the Sinte and Roma. In the words of Giorgio Rochat, the most prominent Italian military historian, the Italian occupation regime in the Balkans represents the "dark side" of the Italian war.[11] National collective memory, however, has completely blocked out this aspect and continues to uphold the glorification of the antifascist resistance[12] and the indulgent myth of the "good Italian,"[13] which served the purpose of self-acquittal after the fall of the Fascist regime. In this chapter, I will briefly outline the reasons for and modalities of this development, and identify its main architects and advocates.

Even before the end of the war, beginning in spring 1944, the governments of national unity that were formed on the basis of an agreement between the Italian monarchy and the antifascist movement embarked on the fabrication of a historical narrative that continues to shape official remembrance to this day. This narrative explicitly distinguishes between the war of the "Axis," which Italy had waged alongside the Third Reich between June 1940 and September 1943 on the one side, and the war of the Allies against the National Socialist occupiers and the Fascist "traitors" after the proclamation of the armistice on the other.[14] They portrayed the first war as having been forced on the Italians, who "had neither wanted it nor perceived it as their concern" – as Mussolini's war at the side of an insincere, feared, and despised ally: Hitler's Germany. The second war, in turn, had been the Italians' "true" war in which they were finally free to fight for their ideals against the German enemy and the Fascists: the betrayers of the nation.

Together, the different governments of national unity tried to underline the achievements of the resistance against the Germans, a resistance they described in epic words as a national war of liberation, a second *Risorgimento*. In contrast, a veil of silence was drawn over the more than three years of war alongside the Germans: in an obvious distortion of the facts, the Italians appeared as the victims even where they had actually been the aggressors – such as in the Balkans.

This image did not merely spring from the will of the antifascist leadership, which had been the main protagonist in the liberation battle. The national interests at stake also played an important role. With the signing of the dual armistice on 3 and 29 September 1943, Italy was in the position of the conquered enemy vis-à-vis the Allies.[15] The subsequent recognition of Italy as a power waging war alongside the Allies (*cobelligeranza*) after it had declared war on Germany on 13 October 1943 did not significantly change the country's status. There was the very real danger – which became apparent in the course of the peace negotiations – that Italy would be punished for Mussolini's war at the side of the Third Reich instead of being rewarded for its efforts at the side of the Allies. For this reason, it was paramount to highlight the achievements of Italians in the battle against the Germans and the Fascists while downplaying and covering up the grave war crimes committed in the Balkans during the occupation.

The most important means for the Italian leadership to achieve this end was to emphasize the differences in conduct between the Italian and German forces in the occupied territories. Hence, responsibility for the atrocities of the Axis powers was almost exclusively passed to the Germans.[16] The Italian soldier, whom Mussolini had sent to the foreign front insufficiently equipped and badly nourished, was stylized as a victim of the war and praised for his humanity toward the civilian population: for example regarding the cases in which Italians had protected Serbs on the run from the Croatian Ustasha or Jews on the run from the Croats and Germans. The magnanimity of the "good Italian" was thus contrasted with the savagery of the "bad German" who relentlessly killed the peoples he considered racially inferior. It was not entirely far-fetched that the Italians had offered their protection to Jews and Serbs on some occasions – although this was not the rule. Nevertheless, the juxtaposition of the "good Italian" and the "bad German" was a convenient alibi to veil the ugly fact that the Italians had also suppressed and tormented people in the occupied territories.

The foreign ministry and war ministry were the first to elaborate this flattering, unrealistic image of the Italians' conduct in the Balkans. The diplomats and members of the military who had played a prominent role in the occupation of Albania, Greece, and Yugoslavia, and in most cases weathered the subsequent "purges" (*epurazione*) within the Italian apparatuses without harm, now united not only in order to protect the country from the danger of a punitive peace, but also – and for more compelling reasons – in order to protect their own persons.[17]

Mario Luciolli expresses the foreign ministry's point of view in his book *Mussolini e l'Europa*, which appeared immediately after the end of the war.[18] The author, a former official at the Italian embassy in Berlin and future ambassador to Bonn, described the Italian soldiers in the Balkans as "defenders of the oppressed" who were always ready to protect the civilian population from abuse by the "cruel" German ally.[19] Luciolli concedes that some Italian soldiers had "once in a while committed petty thefts or played pranks," but that, irrespective of rank, it would never have occurred to them to "scientifically program the plundering of the civilian population or to organize their mistreatment" as the Germans had done.[20]

As the most important card to prove that their conduct had been entirely different from that of the Germans, the Italian diplomats played the rescue of Jews.[21] Already in October 1944, the case of about two thousand Jews who had been saved due to the efforts of Italian diplomats and the military authorities was made public in a newspaper article written by Roberto Ducci, a high-ranking official in the foreign ministry and one of the main protagonists in this episode.[22] On Ducci's initiative, the ministry compiled an extensive documentation of the rescue operations conducted by Italians in all the occupied territories, i.e., not only in the Balkans, but also in France. During the peace negotiations with the Allies, the Italian side repeatedly drew on this documentation in order to obtain material for a press campaign and to underline Italy's achievements on the diplomatic level, thus asserting the country's right to be treated benevolently.[23] In the immediate postwar years, even representatives of the Jewish communities in Italy propagated the role of the Italian authorities in the rescue of the Jews, as they were interested in a quick reintegration into national society.[24] International historiography has subsequently also come to portray the Italians as the "rescuers of the Jews" – without sufficiently taking into account that the Fascist regime never distanced itself from the National Socialist policy of annihilation. It has moreover generally ignored those cases in which the Italian authorities cooperated with the German perpetrators, or at least facilitated their actions.[25] Indeed, the Italian authorities did not always protect the Jews: the prefecture of Fiume, for example, refused entry to about eight hundred Croatian Jews at the border and thereby consciously exposed them to the Germans and thus fatal deportation.[26]

Certain memoirs by members of the Italian military published directly after the war were very important for the construction of this remembrance narrative of the war in the Balkans aiming at self-acquittal. One such memoir was written by General Mario Roatta,[27] the commander of the Second Italian Army, which was based in Slovenia, Croatia, and Dalmatia at the time. Moreover, there are the books by Chief of Staff Giacomo Zanussi[28] and Giuseppe Angelini,[29] who was honored as a war hero for his operations in Croatia. All three were on Yugoslavia's list of war criminals – in first place was Roatta, who had been the army's chief of staff from May to November 1943 under the government of Pietro Badoglio.

In their writings, the three officers[30] firmly defend the conduct of the Italian troops, whose "humanitarian mission" to the benefit of the civilian population they portray in the most idyllic colors. The primary aim of their writing was to defend the Italian soldiers against the Yugoslav government's accusations of the war crimes. In the process, they not only resorted to the image of the "good Italian" and "bad German," they also turned the tables on the Yugoslavs and accused them of having committed atrocities. Tito's savage partisans had allegedly committed inhuman crimes against the good Italians who, according to Zanussi, "rather tended to get slaughtered than to do any slaughtering themselves."[31] In Angelini's words, the Italians "never betrayed their long tradition of loyalty and humanity that is immanent to the Latin race."[32] At the most, he concedes the "theft of chickens or pigs" or deems it possible that a few houses from which Italian units had been shot at were set on fire. Roatta and Zanussi also admit sporadic violent responses by the Italians, which were, however, committed by the Fascist Blackshirts, not by members of the royal army. They, too, reject the Yugoslav allegations that the Italian troops had committed numerous crimes as "fantastic."[33] It is noteworthy that these authors' descriptions of the Balkan partisans as ferocious, bloodthirsty perpetrators and their insistence on the Italians' superior Latin culture is obviously a Fascist legacy which had served to promote radical anti-Slav racism among the troops during the occupation.[34]

The highlighting of the supposed humanitarian achievements of the Italians and the attempt to turn the accusation of war crimes around against the accusers were two important aspects of the defense strategy employed by various Italian administrations in order to avoid the extradition of war criminals.[35] According to the terms of the armistice of September 1943 and the peace treaty signed in February 1947, Italy was obliged to extradite its war criminals so that they could be put on trial in those countries where they had committed their crimes. Yugoslavia, Greece, and Albania were the main prosecutors. They demanded the extradition of about 1,000 Italian soldiers and civilians (Yugoslavia 750, Albania 140, Greece between 110 and 180).[36] Not a single person has been handed over to the authorities in these countries to this day. On the grounds of its participation in the war against Germany, Italy insisted on the right to try the alleged war criminals at home. A commission of inquiry was created for this purpose, which delivered about forty individuals (among them Roatta) to military courts. However, the authorities did not press charges against a single defendant, and in 1951 let the whole process come to nothing. The aim of insuring the war criminals' impunity was successful because Italy enjoyed the patronage of Great Britain and the United States, who wanted to protect certain high-ranking Italian officers.[37] Moreover, Yugoslavia, the most important accuser, lost the only influential supporter of its claims after the break between Tito and Stalin in June 1948.

The sparing of Italy's war criminals, who had committed the most serious crimes against the civilian populations of the countries occupied by the Fascist regime, contributed to establishing the image of the "good Italian" as a myth of national identification after the Second World War.[38]

One point in particular must be underlined: in order to be able to disprove Yugoslavia's accusations of war crimes, the Italian government commissioned a counter-documentation in November 1944. The intention was not to investigate the veracity of the other side's allegations, but rather to collect proof of the crimes committed by the Yugoslavs against the Italians.[39] On the one hand, this pertained to the captured Italian soldiers who had been abused and killed by Tito's partisans during the occupation years, on the other to the crimes perpetrated against Italian soldiers and civilians in Venezia Giulia after the armistice of September 1943, and especially during Tito's brief occupation of the region from the end of the war until June 1945. According to some estimates, about five thousand Italians died at the hands of Yugoslavs. Some were thrown into the deep sinkholes in the Karst mountains near the Slovenian and Croatian coast called *foiba* (hence the name "foibe massacres"), others died in concentration camps.[40] In short, this documentation was a counter-list of Yugoslav crimes, at the head of which stood Marshall Tito himself.[41] It was moreover intended to provide material for an aggressive press campaign in Italy that condemned the foibe massacres. Hence, the Italian public was very well informed about Yugoslav crimes, but knew next to nothing of the Italian atrocities that had preceded them.

The role played by the Italian antifascist Left, i.e., the Communists, Socialists, and the Action Party (*Partito d'Azione*) is quite illuminating in this context. After the liberation of Rome in 1944, the antifascist Left sincerely attempted to bring those responsible for Italian war crimes – particularly certain high-ranking military officers like Roatta – to justice in the framework of the "purges" within the military.[42] In order to achieve this, antifascist newspapers openly reported on the crimes the Italian occupiers had committed in the Balkans. After Yugoslavia's occupation of Venezia Giulia in spring 1945, which brought home the danger that a defeated Italy faced, this campaign was discontinued. Even the left-wing parties in government at the time saw the necessity to defend national interests and in consequence came to adopt a different stance regarding the question of war crimes. All reports about atrocities committed by the Italians disappeared from the press and documents of government authorities, and within the apparatuses the Left aligned itself with the official position, which was against the extradition of alleged war criminals. In any case, the accusations had only targeted the Blackshirts and the Fascist officers – certainly not simple Italian soldiers. Thus, Luigi Longo, one of the leading exponents of the Communist Party, wrote: "The infantrymen, the *Alpini* [mountain troops], and the Italian *Bersaglieri* [a special army corps] would never have followed orders to burn down a village or to kill women and children. These are deeds only the Germans or the Fascists could have accomplished."[43] Actually, it had been precisely the infantrymen, the *Alpini*, and the *Bersaglieri* who committed many of these crimes. Thus, even the Left drew a relatively indulgent image of the Italian soldiers, whose "innate feeling of humanity" they contrasted with the "cold mechanical brutality" of the "German machine" capable of every imaginable offense.[44] The Left's typical line of argumentation was that the Italian soldiers had turned "from occupiers into partisans" and that their solidarity with the people of the Balkans had prompted them to participate in local resistance movements.[45] This narrative served to emphasize the connection between the Italian *Resistenza* and the European resistance movements. However, it conceals the fact that only a minority of Italian soldiers consciously decided to join this movement at the time.

The state apparatus as well as the antifascist movement developed an interpretation of the Italian occupation regime in the Balkans that underlined the violence the Italians suffered as well as their humanitarian efforts, thereby masking the war crimes they had committed. This way, a solid but rather one-sided remembrance culture was created. The fact that veterans of the Second World War only produced a fairly meager memoir literature – which reveals a deep-seated unease in their personal memories[46] – demonstrates, with few exceptions,[47] the difficulty of recognizing one's own role as an aggressor and perpetrator, which has moreover been superseded by the figure of the "bad German." As a result of their painful memories of German war captivity directly after the armistice, many veterans simply blocked out the preceding experience of occupying the Balkans.[48]

In the past, the state apparatus has fiercely defended the image of the "good Italian," which, as already mentioned, served the purpose of self-acquittal. Let us briefly consider the case of the British documentary film *Fascist Legacy* about Italy's war crimes.[49] Its airing on the BBC in 1989 was followed by diplomatic protest from the Italian embassy. Later RAI, the Italian public broadcast, bought the film, but never aired it.[50] Public opinion in Great Britain and the United States has also contributed to establishing the image of the "good Italian." In this context, mention of the novel *Captain Corelli's Mandolin* and the subsequent film of the same name, which portrays the Italians stationed in Greece as incorrigible latin lovers on vacation, ought to suffice.[51] Last but not least, one should point out the great deficits of Italian historiography, which are not only to be attributed to language difficulties, but also to the problem of access to primary sources, particularly to documents stored in the military archives. Following the pioneering study of the 1960s by Enzo Collotti und Teodoro Sala,[52] a new generation of historians such as Davide Rodogno, Lidia Santarelli, Carlo Spartaco Capogreco, Costantino Di Sante, Brunello Mantelli, Eric Gobetti, and myself has only begun to investigate various aspects of the Italian occupation and to bring to light long-suppressed facts – such as the war crimes. This research has only recently come to be perceived by the Italian public after years in which only left-wing newspapers such as *L'Unita* or *Il Manifesto* reported on the topic and publicly condemned Italian crimes committed in the Balkans and in Africa.[53] However, two books (by Angelo Del Boca[54] and Gianni Oliva[55]) that destroy the myth of the "good Italian" and target a wide audience have since appeared. Taking into consideration the latest findings established by historical research, especially Oliva focuses on Italy's war crimes in the Balkans and the charges that were never pressed against the perpetrators. But there are also contradictory tendencies, as can be observed in the concentration on the Yugoslavian foibe massacres in public commemoration and television films.[56] Thus, much remains to be done for historians as well as all those who desire a truthful historical consciousness in the country and wish to see that justice is received by the victims of the Italian occupation regime in the Balkans.

Notes

1. On the Fascist-imperialist plans for the Mediterranean and Italian occupation policies in the Balkans and in France, cf. Davide Rodogno, *Il nuovo ordine mediterraneo. Le politiche di occupazione dell'Italia fascista in Europa (1940–1943)* (Turin, 2003).
2. Cf. Brunello Mantelli, ed., *L'Italia fascista potenza occupante: lo scacchiere balcanico*, special issue of *Qualestoria*, 30 (2002); H. James Burgwyn, *Mussolini's Conquest of Yugoslavia 1941–1943* (New York, 2005); Eric Gobetti, *L'occupatione allegria. Gli italiani in Jugoslavia (1941–1943)* (Rome, 2007).
3. Research has not yet exhausted the issue of Italian occupation policies in Greece. On the topic, cf. Giorgio Vaccarino, "L'occupazione italiana in Grecia," in: Pier Paolo Poggio and Bruna Micheletti, eds., *L'Italia in guerra 1940–45* (Brescia, 1992), 237–57; Enzo Collotti, "L'occupazione italiana in Grecia: problemi generali," in *Annali dell'Istituto milanese per la storia dell'età contemporanea*, 5 (Milan, 2000), 365–71 (now also in Enzo Collotti, *L'Europa nazista. Il progetto di un Nuovo ordine europeo 1939–1945* [Florence, 2002], 293–302); Rodogno (see note 1), 136–38, 286–88, 389–91; Lidia Santarelli, "Il sistema dell'occupazione italiana in Grecia. Aspetti e problemi di ricerca," in *Annali dell'Istituto milanese per la storia dell'età contemporanea, della resistenza e del movimento operaio*, 5 (Milan, 2000), 365–79; Id., "Fra coabitazione e conflitto: invasione italiana e popolazione civile nella Grecia occupata (primavera-estate 1941)," in Mantelli, ed. (see note 2), 143–55. For a comparison between Italian and German occupation policies, cf. Mark Mazower, *Inside Hitler's Greece* (New Haven, 1993).

4. Cf. Giorgio Rochat, *Le guerre italiane 1935–1943. Dall'impero d'Etiopia alla disfatta* (Turin, 2005), 363.
5. On repression measures in the Balkans, cf. Enzo Collotti, "Sulla politica di repressione italiana nei Balcani," in Lorenzo Paggi, ed., *La memoria del nazismo nell'Europa di oggi* (Florence, 1997), 181–208 (now also in Collotti [see note 3], 257–92); Rodogno (see note 1), 182–227 and 397–415. On repressions in Yugoslavia, cf. Burgwyn (see note 2); Teodoro Sala, "Guerra ed amministrazione in Jugoslavia 1941–1943: un'ipotesi coloniale," in Poggio/Micheletti, eds. (see note 3), 83–94; Costantino Di Sante, ed., *Italiani senza onore. I crimini in Jugoslavia e i processi negati (1941–1951)* (Verona, 2005). On Slovenia, cf. in particular Marco Cuzzi, *L'occupazione italiana della Slovenia 1941–1943* (Rome, 1998); Tone Ferenc, *La provincia "italiana" di Lubiana. Documenti 1941–1942* (Udine, 1994); Id., *"Si ammazza troppo poco". Condannati a morte-Ostaggi-Passati per le armi nella Provincia di Lubiana 1941–1943* (Ljubljana, 1999); Id., *Rab-arbe-Arbissima. Confinamenti-Rastrellamenti-Internamenti nella Provincia di Lubiana 1941–1943* (Ljubljana, 2000). On Greece, cf. Lidia Santarelli, "La violenza taciuta. I crimini degli italiani nella Grecia occupata," in Luca Baldissara and Paolo Pezzino, eds., *Crimini e memorie di guerra* (Naples, 2004), 271–91.
6. On the internment of civilians in the occupied territories, cf. Carlo Spartaco Capogreco, "Una storia rimossa dell'Italia fascista. L'internamento dei civili jugoslavi (1941–1943)," in *Studi Storici*, 42 (2001), 204–30; Id., *I campi del duce. L'internamento civile nell'Italia fascista (1940–1943)* (Turin, 2004); Rodogno (see note 1), 419–31.
7. Brunello Mantelli, "Die Italiener auf dem Balkan 1941–1943," in Christof Dipper, Lutz Klinkhammer and Alexander Nützenadel, eds., *Europäische Sozialgeschichte. Festschrift für Wolfgang Schieder zum 65. Geburtstag* (Berlin, 2000), 57–74, here 57–58.
8. Ferenc has documented the cases of 1,569 Slovenians who were executed by Italians (with or without a prior trial), while 1,376 Slovenians died in Italian concentration camps. Furthermore, according to his findings, Italian military courts tried 13,186 Slovenians in 8,337 trials during the Italian occupation. Cf. Ferenc (see note 5), 27.
9. Cf. Capogreco, "Una storia rimossa dell'Italia fascista" (see note 6).
10. Cf. Id., *I campi del duce* (see note 6), 270. We can assume that out of 7,541 prisoners, at least 1,435 died.
11. Cf. Rochat (see note 4), 360.
12. Cf. Jens Petersen, "Der Ort der Resistenza in Geschichte und Gegenwart Italiens," in *Quellen und Forschungen aus italienischen Archiven und Bibliotheken*, 72 (1992), 550–71; Filippo Focardi, *La guerra della memoria. La Resistenza nel dibattito politico italiano dal 1945 a oggi* (Rome, 2005).
13. Cf. Filippo Focardi, "'Bravo italiano' e 'cattivo tedesco': riflessioni sulla genesi di due immagini incrociate," in *Storia e Memoria*, V, no. 1 (first half-year 1996), 55–83; Id., "La memoria della guerra e il mito del 'bravo italiano': origine e affermazione di un autoritratto collettivo," in *Italia Contemporanea* (2000), no. 220–21 (September–December), 393–99.
14. Cf. Focardi (see note 12), 4–14; Id., "Gedenktage und politische Öffentlichkeit in Italien 1945–1995, " in Christoph Cornelißen, Lutz Klinkhammer and Wolfgang Schwentker, eds., *Erinnerungskulturen. Deutschland, Italien und Japan seit 1945* (Frankfurt/M., 2003), 210–21.
15. Cf. Elena Aga Rossi, *Una nazione alla sbando. L'armistizio italiano del settembre 1943 e le sue conseguenze*, new, expanded edition (Bologna, 2003), first edition 1993; Id., *L'inganno reciproco. L'armistizio tra l'Italia e gli angloamericani del settembre 1943* (Rome, 1993); includes extensive primary-source material.
16. Cf. Focardi, "'Bravo italiano' e 'cattivo tedesco'" (see note 13).
17. Cf. Filippo Focardi, "Criminali impuniti. Cause e responsabilità della mancata Norimberga italiana," in: Luigi Borgomaneri, ed., *Crimini di guerra. Il mito del bravo italiano tra repessione del ribellismo e guerre ai civili nei territori occupati* (Milan, 2006), 133–78.

18. Cf. Mario Donosti [alias Mario Luciolli], *Mussolini e l'Europa. La politica estera fascista* (Rome, 1945).
19. Ibid., 271.
20. Ibid., 97–98.
21. Cf. Guri Schwarz, *Ritrovare se stessi. Gli ebrei nell'Italia postfascista* (Rome, Bari, 2004), 129–40.
22. Cf. Verax, "Italiani ed ebrei in Jugoslavia," in *Politica Estera*, 1, no. 9 (1944), 21–29. Verax is a pseudonym for Roberto Ducci. During the war, he headed the Croatia department in the foreign ministry.
23. The initiative of Italian diplomacy culminated in the preparation of a volume entitled *Relazione sull'opera svolta dal Ministero degli Affari Esteri per la tutela delle comunità ebraiche (1938–1943)*, in which the entire documentation of the actions undertaken to rescue Jews was collected. In spring 1946, the Italian government sent this report to the representatives of the four powers who were preparing a draft of the peace treaty with Italy in Paris. Cf. Schwarz (see note 21), 139.
24. The Jewish communities thus themselves tended to draw a veil of oblivion over the persecution by the Italian Fascists from 1938 onward and to highlight the support they had received in the face of Nazi extermination policies. Cf. Schwarz (see note 21), 141–49; Enzo Collotti, "Il razzismo negato," in Ibid., ed., *Fascismo e antifascismo. Rimozioni, revisioni, negazioni* (Rome/Bari, 2000), 355–75.
25. Cf. Leon Poliakov and Jacques Sabille, *Gli ebrei sotto l'occupazione italiana* (Milan, 1956); Susan Zuccotti, *The Italians and the Holocaust: Persecution, Rescue and Survival* (New York, 1987); Jonathan Steinberg, *All or Nothing. The Axis and the Holocaust 1941–1943* (London, New York, 1990); Menachem Shelah, *Un debito di gratitudine. Storia dei rapporti tra l'Esercito italiano e gli ebrei in Dalmazia (1941–1943)* (Rome, 1991); Daniel Carpi, *Between Mussolini and Hitler: Jews and the Authorities in France and Tunisia* (Hanover, NH, 1994).
26. Cf. Rodogno (see note 1), 439–41 and Id., "Italiani brava gente? Fascist Italy's Policy Toward the Jews in the Balkans, April 1941–July 1943," in *European History Quarterly*, 35, no. 2 (2005), 213–40.
27. Cf. Mario Roatta, *Otto milioni di baionette* (Milan, 1946).
28. Cf. Giacomo Zanussi, *Guerra e catastrofe d'Italia*, 2 vols. (Rome, 1945–1946), vol. 1.
29. Cf. Giuseppe Angelini, *Fuochi di bivacco in Croazia* (Rome, 1946).
30. After the armistice, Mario Roatta was initially forced to resign his post as army chief of staff in November 1943 due to protests from Yugoslavia and Great Britain. Later, however, he was brought to trial in the framework of the "purges" and convicted to a life-sentence on account of crimes perpetrated against Italian antifascists he had been responsible for as head of the military secret service before the Second World War. However, Roatta successfully evaded his punishment by fleeing to Spain. Giacomo Zanussi was active in the military resistance after 8 September 1943, where he distinguished himself in the final phase of the liberation battle alongside the Allies as the commander of a large division of the Italian army. Giuseppe Angelini, finally, responsibly headed the official army organ *Rivista militare*.
31. Cf. Zanussi (see note 28), 222.
32. Cf. Angelini (see note 29), 319.
33. Cf. Roatta (see note 27), 178.
34. Cf. Enzo Collotti, "Sul razzismo antislavo," in Alberto Burgio, ed., *Nel nome della razza. Il razzismo nellastoria d'Italia 1870–1945* (Bologna, 1999), 33–61; Teodoro Sala, "Guerriglia e controguerriglia in Jugoslavia nella propaganda per le truppe occupantiitaliane (1941–1943)," in *Il Movimento di liberazione in Italia*, 108 (July–September 1972), 91–114.
35. On the punishment of Italian war criminals, cf. Filippo Focardi, "La questione della punizione dei criminali di guerra in Italia dopo la fine del secondo conflitto mondiale," in *Quellen und Forschungen aus italienischen Archiven und Bibliotheken*, 80 (2000), 543–624;

Filippo Focardi and Lutz Klinkhammer, "La questione dei 'criminali di guerra' italiani e una Commissione di inchiesta dimenticata," in *Contemporanea*, 4 (2001), 497–528; Filippo Focardi, "I mancati processi ai criminali di guerra italiani," in Luca Baldissara and Paolo Pezzino, eds., *Giudicare e punire* (Naples, 2005), 185–214; Id., "I crimini impuniti dei 'bravi italiani'", in *Contemporanea*, 7 (2005), 329–35; Di Sante, ed. (see note 5).

36. Besides these states, France, Ethiopia, and the Soviet Union demanded the extradition of alleged Italian war criminals who were accused of having committed crimes against the civilian population. France lodged thirty requests, the Soviet Union twelve, and Ethiopia ten, which later confined itself to the main defendants Pietro Badoglio and Rodolfo Graziani, however. Great Britain and the United States registered more than eight hundred Italians as potential perpetrators and witnesses with regard to the killing or abuse of prisoners of war at the responsible UN commission. Indeed, Great Britain and the United States arrested many Italian war criminals and tried them in Italy. In some cases, the pronounced death sentence was even carried out.

37. Cf. Effie G. H. Pedaliu,"Britain and the 'Hand-over' of Italian War Criminals to Yugoslavia, 1945–48," in *Journal of Contemporary History*, 39 (2004), 503–29. Pedaliu shows that the strongest support came from the United States. The British Labour government, on the other hand, initially tended to meet the obligations toward Yugoslavia that had been agreed to concerning the extradition of Italian war criminals. London only changed its position in the second half of 1946 and aligned itself with the position of the United States. The latter refused to extradite Italian war criminals in order not to weaken a country like Italy that was beginning to play a strategically important role in the Cold War.

38. Cf. Filippo Focardi, "L'Italia fascista come potenza occupante nel giudizio dell'opinione pubblica italiana: la questione dei criminali di guerra (1943–1948)," in *Qualestoria*, 1, June 2002, 157–83; Filippo Focardi and Lutz Klinkhammer, "The Question of Fascist Italy's War Crimes: the Construction of a Self-acquitting Myth (1943–1948)," in *Journal of Modern Italian Studies*, 9 (2004), 330–48.

39. Cf. Focardi, "I mancati processi ai criminali di guerra italiani" (see note 35), 188–89; Di Sante, ed. (see note 5), 17–26.

40. Cf. Raoul Pupo and Roberto Spazzali, *Foibe* (Milan, 2003); Raoul Pupo, *Il lungo esodo. Istria: le persecuzioni, le foibe, l'esilio* (Milan, 2005); Giampaolo Valdevit, ed., *Foibe. Il peso del passato. Venezia Giulia 1943–1945* (Venice, 1997).

41. Cf. Focardi, "I mancati processi ai criminali di guerra italiani" (see note 35), 199; Id., "Criminali impuniti. Cause e responsabilità della mancata Norimberga italiana" (see note 17).

42. Cf. Focardi, "L'Italia fascista come potenza occupante" (see note 38), 159–61.

43. Cf. Luigi Longo, *Un popolo alla macchia* (Milan, Verona, 1947), 66.

44. Cf. Salvemini, Gaetano/La Piana, Giorgio, *La sorte dell'Italia* (Rome et al., 1945), 55.

45. Cf. for example Chiesi, Marta/Bilenchi, Romano, "Italiani in Jugoslavia," in *Società* (1945), 182–251.

46. Cf. for example Giulio Bedeschi, *Fronte greco-albanese: c'ero anch'io* (Milan, 1977); Giulio Bedeschi, *Fronte greco-albanese: c'ero anch'io* (Milan, 1985, repr. 1999); Ugo Scialuga, "La memorialistica sulla campagna di Grecia," in: Poggio/Micheletti, eds. (see note 3), 269–87. How the Italian soldiers saw themselves is revealed in the important primary source collections compiled by Giulio Bedeschi: as victims of a war they did not feel emotionally connected to, which was moreover being conducted in a preposterous fashion by incompetent officers and only brought about suffering and sacrifices for the front-line soldiers. The main focus is on the painstaking war of conquest in 1940–41, whereas the subsequent occupation period, including the measures taken to retain control over the territory, is generally neglected.

47. Also of interest is the novel written by war veteran Ugo Pirro, *Le Soldatesse*, which takes place in Greece (published in 1956 by Feltrinelli), and Renzo Biasion's collected stories *Sagapò*, which also take place in Greece and were published in 1953 by Einaudi.
48. Cf. Angelo Bendotti, Mario Pelliccioli and Eugenia Valtulina, *Prigionieri in Germania. La memoria degli internati military* (Bergamo, 1990).
49. Cf. Ulrich Beutler, "Über den Dokumentarfilm 'Fascist Legacy' von Ken Kirby. Ein Beitrag zur längst fälligen Diskussion über die italienischen Kriegsverbrechen," in *Geschichte und Region/Storia e Regione*, XIII, no. 2 (2004), 175–88.
50. In Italy, this documentary film was only aired by private TV stations: in 2003 by LA7 and in 2005/06 on the History Channel of SkyTV.
51. *Captain Corelli's Mandolin* is a novel by the English writer Louis de Bernières which appeared in 1995 and was successfully made into a Hollywood film in 2001 by director John Madden with prominent actors such as Nicolas Cage und Penelope Cruz. It takes place on the Greek island of Caphalonia during the Italian occupation and tells the love story of the Italian captain Antonio Corelli and the young Greek woman Pelagia. The Italian ceasefire and the subsequent German massacre of the Division Acqui, to which Corelli belonged, destroy this private idyll.
52. Cf. Enzo Collotti, Teodoro Sala and Giorgio Vaccarino, *L'italia nell'Europa danubiana durante la seconda guerra mondiale* (Milan, 1967); Enzo Collotti and Teodoro Sala, *Le potenze dell'Asse e la Jugoslavia. Saggi e documenti 1941–1943* (Milan, 1974).
53. Cf. Focardi (see note 12), 88–90.
54. Angelo Del Boca, *Italiani brava gente? Un mito duro a morire* (Vicenza, 2005). The book by this greatest connoisseur of Italian colonialism deals with crimes Italy committed from the foundation of the centralized state onwards, whereby the author concentrates on the crimes committed in the colonies. One chapter is dedicated to Italian repressions in Slovenia during the Second World War.
55. Gianni Oliva, *"Si ammazza troppo poco." I crimini di guerra italiani 1940–43* (Milan, 2006).
56. Particularly the *Alleanza nazionale*, which emerged in 1995 from the *Movimento sociale italiano*, the neo-fascist party that was formed immediately after the end of the war, supported the cause of keeping the memory of the foibe massacres alive. Thanks to this party, which is also supported by other political parties in the center-right coalition, the Italian parliament instituted a *Giornata del ricordo* [commemoration day] in March 2004 in memory of the victims of the foibe massacres and the Italians who were expelled from Istria and Dalmatia. On the remembrance politics of the center-right coalition in Italy from the 1990s onwards, cf. Focardi, *La guerra della memoria* (see note 12), 61–76.

Chapter 10

BREST UNDER BOMBARDMENT (1940–1944):
Being in War

Pierre Le Goïc

What is the meaning of war experiences in the sense of "being in war"? Instead of a "culture of war," which is based on collective experiences, this chapter takes life in a bombarded city as the point of departure – the effects of the individual's experiences on his or her character development as well as on the wider community. At a later point in time, these experiences moreover play a significant role in shaping images of the past. But how can the immediate impression, which will invariably be altered by later experiences, be extracted from the torrent of time? In the following pages will be found arguments in favor of relying on written accounts rather than oral ones, as sources such as diaries have the advantage of capturing most closely the emotions and perceptions of the time.

Certainly this type of source is ambiguous – there should be no illusions about that. In order to serve as a means to construct an archeology of emotions of sorts, ideally the diary will have to have survived in its original form and not been intended for later publication. An example of this type is briefly introduced at the end of the analysis. From the two diaries presented here, the first one complies more closely with this criterion. The second one was in fact published – the circumstances of this publication will be described more closely – but this does not diminish its value in any way.[1] Apart from that, even if an author is primarily a witness of his or her own times and experiences, he or she is always also reflecting on the future. Without it, there would hardly be any point in writing at all. The categories once established by Reinhart Koselleck are thus very useful for this analysis.[2] Last but not least, diaries are also interpreted by their readers. If a reader never personally experienced war, images of Baghdad under bombardment, where cars are still jamming the streets, or Sarajevo,

---

Notes for this chapter begin on page 158.

where anyone who went out to see a friend faced the danger of sniper fire, seem strange and disconcerting. How can we explain that after four years of perpetual bombardment and shortly before its final destruction, there were still sixty thousand people living in Brest, a seaport and naval base on the Atlantic coast in Brittany in northwestern France?

This raises questions surrounding evasive strategies that helped people to face the fear, but also surrounding the internalization of certain norms. The appropriation of automatisms can also be the result of practice or at least an expression of corps spirit: soldiers, medical orderlies, and members of the civil defense generally do not reveal their emotions in their reports. In the case of civilians, however, the opposite is often true. Nonetheless, I will rely on the war diary of Erich Kuby, a German soldier stationed in Brest in 1944, as a counterexample to the diary of Suzanne Langlois, a civilian inhabitant of Brest with a physical disability. Throughout the war, Kuby, an anti-militarist and opponent of National Socialism, actually perceived himself as a civilian who had been drafted by force and never submitted to military discipline. He drew his boldness from sources other than his role as a soldier. Although it is not very original to approach a topic from its fringes, precisely because of the extreme situation they were in, these two marginal figures perhaps demonstrate most clearly how the majority of people felt at the time. Before I embark on an exploration of their diaries, however, I will provide a brief recapitulation of the preceding years of bombardment.

The bombardment of Brest, a German naval base

The city and the port of Brest were bombarded by the Royal Air Force from summer 1940 onwards, after it had been taken and occupied by German forces on 19 June.[3] The United States Army Air Forces joined the efforts in 1942. The old fortress town, which lay at the end of a sheltered sea road accessible from the Atlantic, had a large arsenal and numerous servicing docks. For the German navy, Brest was a strategically vital base throughout the war, particularly for the U-boat war and the maintenance of the German fleet. Since the chronology of the bombardment is more or less well known, only the most important phases will be briefly outlined.[4] While in 1940 the air strikes were still sporadic, in spring 1941 the RAF began to systematically bomb the port after the battle ships Scharnhorst and Gneisenau arrived for repairs and the Germans began to build a fortified U-boat base. The effects of the German anti-aircraft fire forced the British and later also the Americans to attack at night and from high altitude. Due to the evidently insufficient means of radio steering at the time, this primarily devastated the civilian parts of town and less so the port facilities. According to official figures, there were 428 victims among the civilian population, which may appear small in comparison to the loss of human lives the towns of Normandy suffered in June 1944 (which in turn bear no proportion to the extent of destruction in German cities). The municipal administration of Brest built numerous effective shelters and issued a first evacuation order in February 1943. However, in 1944, at the beginning of the German besiegement which lasted from 7 August to 18 September, there were still sixty thousand people out of a population of one-hundred-fifteen thousand (as counted in 1940) still living in the city. The battles claimed about ten thousand lives on both sides, among which there were few civilian victims, since the population was evacuated on 14 August 1944. After that, only about two thousand civilians, administrators, hospital staff, fire fighters, and members of the civil defense remained in the city. As a result of an explosion following an accident in a bunker, the number of civilian victims was almost doubled in the end with no direct connection to the bombardment: approximately four hundred Brestians and almost five hundred Germans died in this explosion. At the end of the siege, nothing remained of the old city center, which was completely devastated by napalm and phosphorus bombs, as well as the fires laid by the retreating German soldiers.

As already mentioned above, the strange resistance of many of Brest's inhabitants to the repeated evacuation orders is the point of departure for this investigation. Certainly only those who were dispensable as far as their professions are concerned – and who moreover had a place to go – could leave. In addition, it was often more dangerous to go out into the streets than to stay indoors. However, contemporary oral accounts convey the striking impression that people appear to have been indifferent to the danger, that despite all the damages inflicted on the city, there was even a sort of jubilation of the British and American efforts in the air over Brest. Suzanne Langlois's diary allows for a differentiation of this impression: her entries oscillate between expressions of a deeply rooted fear and moments of irony, which she shares with Erich Kuby. He, in turn, does not reveal any fear at all. This "comedy of war," which is obviously a strategy of evasion and survival, becomes even more interesting once the tone changes: after a certain level of violence had been reached, both the civilian inhabitant of Brest and the German soldier, who were so similar and yet so different, were powerfully overtaken by fear.

Suzanne Langlois, an intrepid disabled woman

Suzanne Langlois was a young disabled woman (*infirme*, as she describes herself) who could only move around in a wheelchair, probably with a chain drive worked by hand. She gave private French, Latin, and Greek lessons in her home. As a rather traditional, fervent Catholic, she spent her time in the company of her students, at church, and on long outings in the countryside, which she needed in order to expend her excess energy. She wrote in a somewhat flowery language, sometimes with a touch of "girl-scout cheerfulness" that could often be encountered in literature for young people at the time. Her diary, which was never published, is composed of two file folders containing five hundred pages each and an authentic school notebook, which deals with a later time period, however.[5] The two file folders comprise a transcript of the loose notes that she made at the time. The author sometimes refers to this circumstance, particularly when she does not remember the precise date of an event. However, it is not an edited version, but rather a clean copy of her sketches that she compiled with the aim of sorting and preserving her recollections. Some pages contain documents (often newspaper clippings) pasted onto the page. All indications are that this tremendous effort was only intended to serve private and personal aims. Its scope can be explained by the fact that Langlois had a lot of leisure time in the evenings and, as a young French teacher, simply enjoyed writing.

Suzanne Langlois lived in Brest under British bombardment for two years before she was finally evacuated. She lived in a very exposed quarter, only a few metres from the Saint-Martin church, which burned down on 3 May 1941. As an ardent admirer of Charles de Gaulle and a devout Catholic, she was filled with exuberant energy. When she uses the word "fear" at the beginning of her diary, she never refers to herself, but rather to political motives, for example on 17 June 1940, when the Germans were closing in on Brest: "The afternoon drags on. And, of course, no alarm! Alas! How this absence of alarms causes us anxiety, and with good reason." And on 1 November 1941: "But this fear (*angoisse*) of betraying England ... "[6]

Forgetting the danger

Most likely as a result of her faith, Langlois was initially indifferent toward the danger. On 17/18 August 1940, in reaction to the onset of British bombardment, she notes: "Mother and I looked over the rooms and laughed until we cried: My study is at the front, perfect for being hit by [German anti-aircraft] shells ending their trajectory just above the church. ... The same goes for my parents' bedroom. ... Only the back bedroom facing a little courtyard doesn't risk being hit – save by bombs. ... But the bombs![7] Either the front or the back!" On 3 March 1941: "The alarm has been booming for about an hour. I got dressed anyway to go to mass. ... I made a dash in the direction of the church. The noise was deafening. There was a shower of sparks above our heads like a swarm of golden insects and the shells flying by cast a pale glow against the church wall. ... I must have broken my own speed record!" On 14 April 1941, after a night of intense bombing that destroyed part of the center of town within the city walls, she writes: "I'm going out to the countryside – to forget, if I can."[8]

Langlois was aware of the fact that due to her handicap, she could not jump out of harm's way into the roadside ditches like other people, that she had to remain on the road in her wheelchair in plain view. Does this strategy of evasion by means of intense physical activity, which we also encounter in the case of Erich Kuby, border on recklessness? In January 1941, she took her eight-year-old nephew along on one of her escapades. Her father also accompanied her on this occasion. They got into an air raid and the father was able to save the child by pressing him against a slope only in the nick of time. Afterwards, they continued their walk, but without the child. After an uneventful walk in March 1941, Langlois writes: "This main road must be bad luck. We cannot cross it without being confronted by cannon fire, by machine guns. … The sudden click of machine guns, cannon fire, raining shrapnel – and the nearest house at least 500 meters away! I pedaled at full speed, my head tucked down between my shoulders."[9]

A further element in her strategy was to aestheticize the attacks. In another entry from March 1941, she describes an attack on her neighborhood: "the splendor of these fireworks – searchlights, tracer bullets of every hue, the small shells fired by the machine guns like golden bees raining down. There is a kind of beauty in this monstrous concert. … All of my students are mad about it and spend hours at the window."[10] Indeed, she was not the only one to brave the danger in this way.

Alacrity in Brest

Suzanne Langlois liked to sneer at those she considered to be cowards: her elderly neighbors, some of her younger friends who, admittedly, had to go out onto the streets in order to visit her – something she never really became aware of. For her, only the fact that they set off at a run on hearing the first alarm mattered. Nevertheless, her diary provides abundant evidence of a collective strategy that involved daring and laughter. January 1941: "6 PM – English airplanes. Father and I stay at the window, tortured by excitement and fear. Fear for the English, of course. The crowd [on the main square] was shouting and laughing in their agitation and excitement." In early July, two neighboring buildings were hit: "The whole corner of the house is destroyed, from top to bottom – and not a single person injured! Following the Brestian tradition of seeking out disaster spots, there is a crowd parading up and down rue Fautras. The inhabitants of the building – who wouldn't dream of moving – are very proud and contemplating the onlookers from their windows … The whole family, by the way, appears to be very happy, and although they lost everything, they're wiping tears of laughter from their cheeks: 'Sad, us? Oh, come on! We were incredibly lucky!'"[11] 14 July provided an opportunity for a patriotic game. The aim was to conquer the streets by all conceivable means by showing a combination of the three colors that could, in itself, not afford a justification for arrest: for example the combination of a white blouse, blue skirt, red lips, and white drawers hung out of the window. In retaliation, the Germans sounded the sirens all night. "The next day the laughter was unanimous. The Brestians made fun of each other with joyful vigor because everyone had been terrified ... And they laughed, laughed until they cried."[12]

However, these were as many poses. The more the city center is devastated and the higher the death toll rises in the course of the bombardment, the more often Langlois uses the word anxiety (*angoisse*) in reference to herself and her fellow citizens – and not only in order to express her sympathy for the British aviators. On 14 April 1941, on her solitary walk already mentioned above, the tone becomes dramatic: "The bombs are falling in the heart of the city ... Was the civilian hospital hit? ... The blast is so violent that at Saint-Martin it feels like the shutters are going to be torn off their hinges every time a bomb explodes." She notes that in the morning, "the Brestians' faces have changed: they are haggard, serious, hard."[13]

These were the very same people who would – ironically – demonstrate three months later, but the remainder of the diary is no longer written in the, until then, light-minded tone.

Erich Kuby – hedonistic resistance

Erich Kuby, a writer and journalist, was proud of the fact that he spent the entire war as a simple soldier awarded nothing higher than the Iron Cross (*Eisernes Kreuz*) second class. He never got promoted. He was an opponent of National Socialism, an anti-militarist, and a stubborn character. The sort of irony that was still cheerful in the case of Suzanne Langlois is much more pronounced in his writing. As punishment for a clash with an officer, he made the acquaintance of the eastern front, from which he was delivered by his transfer to Brest. At the end of the besiegement of the fortress, he was captured by American troops – to his own delight – and soon after the war returned to Germany, where he worked for the radio, among other things. In this context, he wrote a radio play for the Nordwestdeutscher Rundfunk (NWDR) on the besiegement of Brest,[14] in which he accuses Hermann Ramcke, the general of the German paratrooper unit stationed there, of being a fanatic National Socialist and of having prolonged the siege to absurdity before finally capitulating on 19 September 1944.

Ramcke, who had until then enjoyed a quiet and unchallenged retirement, filed a lawsuit against Kuby, which the latter won, however. These events prompted Kuby to publish his war diary.[15]

This case is thus different from that of Suzanne Langlois in the sense that we are dealing with a publication or, strictly speaking, a plea. Although there are unmistakable traces of editing – for example the integration of various days and episodes – the rare occasions on which this was done do not taint the authenticity of the work in its entirety. Moreover, Kuby explicitly points out details that he has forgotten. In this case also, the original version was written directly at the time. Formally, the diary is a collection of letters that Kuby wrote to his wife, of course without hoping that she would ever actually receive them since he came to Brest on 29 June 1944, when the situation had already dramatically escalated. He was thus actually writing more for himself at the time. This diary in the form of letters, if you will, which he generally wrote in the evenings after his day's work, is composed of narrations of the events of the day as well as personal reflections.

Kuby's job was to install and repair telephone lines between the various bunkers of the staff of command stationed on the outskirts of Brest. He was thus always outdoors and exposed to the battles on the ground that took place in his zone from August 1944 onwards, or to the air strikes. For the rest of the time, he was supposed to remain in a vast underground fortification that vertically delved into a high cliff and reached down to the ocean in close vicinity to the U-boat docks, which were especially targeted by enemy air strikes. He was not a combatant and even took pride in not wearing a proper uniform: "When I walk through the terrain looking for malfunctions, I wear really light things: canvas pants, a pair of sailor's shoes that a marine soldier traded for cigarettes, and a very light field coat. I carry my ammunition in the pockets of my pants and my rifle over my shoulders pointed downwards. Against all regulations, I push the steel helmet way back. The way I'm dressed – that's how I feel, that's how I move about."[16] Kuby had only one hope: to return home safe and sound as soon as possible. How did he face the permanent danger when even many of the soldiers in the bunker below did not dare to go outside?[17] Kuby employed two strategies: wild hatred of the other soldiers and the paradox pleasure of his excursions outdoors – even under the constant shelling and bombardment of this sunny summer 1944.

Kuby draws a merciless picture of his comrades in the bunker. On 6 August 1944, he writes: "Small amounts of alcoholic beverages bought from the sutler, probably augmented with 'organized' stocks, suffice to make certain corporals and sergeants dead drunk every evening … I wonder whether alcohol has to serve to overpower fear already."[18] On 22 August, "The next morning, they holler, rage, and fight amongst themselves, then sleep until evening and start all over again."[19]

Kuby, in contrast, was a real sportsman and mindful of his health. From an unknown soldier's letter to his sister Lene dated 9 August 1944, which he found in the dirt after a bomb attack, he cites: "I've made a human being of myself again, shaved, washed."[20] Shortly afterwards, Kuby himself writes: "I meet the insanity we have been forced to take part in with a sort of casual arrogance – this war comedy that is being played here with unbelievable sacrifices, more than a thousand kilometers away from the actual front, this shabby fear that fills the constantly drunken rabble down here in the bunker. Of course it's all pose. But it puts me in a good mood and helps me to master the situation with passable decency."[21] Because the bunker increasingly resembled a garbage dump and drowned in the wads of smoke emitted by the filed kitchens, Kuby made a habit of slipping away even when he did not have an assignment. He used the well maintained washing facilities of the marines as well as the swimming pool in the nearby École navale: "This is how I live, in some ways cheerful, while a world perishes – at least and for the time being our world here in Brest."[22]

A special day

Suzanne Langlois was determined to retain her mobility that was already limited due to her handicap. She was prepared to face the risk of enemy bombardment on her long walks outdoors that served her physical training. Kuby, the anti-militarist soldier, likewise carried out dangerous assignments, especially if they allowed him to escape the bunker for a little while. These short trips gave him the courage that he needed to keep his spirits up and protected him from being wounded or killed – or so he thought. He always returned unscathed even from the most dangerous missions as well as from his hedonistic and usually solitary escapades. On Sunday, 27 August 1944, he carried out an assignment with another soldier whom he did not particularly like. In the middle of the apocalypse, he nevertheless allowed himself a little relaxation:

> We made our way over the one-time "flirt beach" St. Anne, up- and downhill through narrow passes, through thorny bushes on poky paths, and millions of ripe blackberries seamed our path. Behind St. Anne, we reached a considerable height from which we could overlook the wide sea. In the dazzling August sunshine, the deep blue sea road and its connection to the ocean lay beneath us ... A few of our ships could still be seen on the blue mirror-surface. They were quite still and the shining silvery war-birds swooped down on them like hawks, spitting fire. The water around them was boiling with the sheaves of projectiles that did not hit their targets and the vessels went up in flames. Some of them floated along like great baskets of fire, others issued great columns of smoke that drifted along behind them ... We got the telephone stuff working

again, and then I bathed in the clear sea and washed afterwards with the bowl-sized reservoir of a sweet-water trickle that I built myself three weeks before for this purpose. Afterwards, walking naked along the bushes, I collected handfuls of blackberries.[23]

In these few lines, the true Kuby is revealed: he kept all of his senses keen in order to keep at bay the fear of the very real danger he is exposed to every day. As far as the aestheticization of the war is concerned, his tone would border on cynicism if all of this did not concern him personally. The deaths of those he does not consider his comrades are drawn like a portrait and the ocean in which he luxuriously bathes is actually a battlefield just a few kilometers away.

Suzanne Langlois and Erich Kuby, overtaken by fear at last

Langlois and Kuby are similar, and not only in the ways they negated the danger and evaded their fear, including their strategies for preserving their physical capabilities and their aestheticizing of the risk. They were both also suddenly confronted with their anxiety again. Both believed they had mastered this anxiety, but at a certain point it turned into the sheer fear of not surviving the war. From their diaries, we can discern the precise points in time when this abrupt rupture occurred in both cases.

In the case of Suzanne Langlois, from June 1941 onwards her language and her habits changed. The two battleships Scharnhorst and Gneisenau harbored in the port of Brest in March. Two historians have argued: "From that moment on, life in Brest became a nightmare for the population. Not a day passed without at least one air-raid warning. Armor-piercing bombs of 200 kilos – aimed at German battleships – destroyed houses from top to bottom."[24] The very first mention of a feeling of panic – after a year of occupation, bombings, and bravado! – surfaces in Suzanne Langlois's journal: "10 June. Night. A very violent and continuous … alarm. … Sometimes we huddle together anxiously. At one point I was alone and lay down, carefully spreading out my dress. Both legs nice and straight, feet at right angles. Rosary between my fingers, hands joined, I tried to doze in the horrifying racket."[25] Further on, she radically contradicts what she had repeatedly affirmed in the first pages of her journal: "Being for the English doesn't prevent fear (*angoisse*)!" July 1941: "I'm waiting for the first canon shot. Waiting – why am I waiting? I'm waiting regardless, with growing anxiety … The silence is total. Our throat is growing tighter and tighter."[26] In the night 3/4 August, her body no longer responded: "Horrible bursts of German anti-aircraft fire. I'm afraid, and this time I am no longer the master of my fear. I stay calm, of course, and don't say anything, but I shake violently when I dress." 19 September: "Last night

I was able to confirm the truth of Turenne's famous line: you tremble, old carcass ... At 2:30 AM, the sirens began wailing and went on for a long time. From the first note I started to tremble, really tremble! My whole body was trembling, so much so that the electric lamp above my head was nothing but a series of luminous lines. The funny part was that I was laughing at seeing myself quiver like that."[27] Two Suzannes encountered each other in the hail of bombs: one who continued to keep fear at bay through laughter and one whose undoubtedly all too rigid barriers were pierced by the terror of the bombardment.

Erich Kuby also changed the tenor of his writing at a certain point. From 5 September 1944 onwards, nothing remained of the hedonistic athlete's physical fitness. Kuby suddenly suffered from terrible abdominal pain and moaned about the risk of falling ill with scurvy due to the bland diet of potatoes and meat in the bunker. He had previously not been in the habit of complaining like this, as we have seen. A few days earlier, he had still considered himself lucky to have found some canned fruit in a ruined building and thus not to run the risk of vitamin deficiency anymore. Toward the end of the besiegement, however, he let himself get carried away by dejectedness and a new kind of fear: He, who had taken such good care of himself only in the hope of returning safe and sound to his young wife, became aware of the possibility that he might never return to Germany again. His diary becomes less anecdotal; he rather indulges in long reflections about the future of war and humanity, as well as his own future: "I do not think about it all the time, like many others, but at times I enjoy taking a deep breath and the certainty of the preservation of life ahead ... I cannot imagine that I should be able to enjoy my future so wholly and completely – equally I cannot imagine that I should not enjoy it."[28]

On the same day, he had the opportunity to perform guard duty and to see Brest go up in flames. From 10 September 1944 onwards, however, going outdoors became impossible in light of the American advance in the close vicinity of the bunker. He was forced to remain locked up in the overcrowded and reeking depths of the bunker. Kuby, the provocateur, was forced to make concessions. His personal defense strategy was in ruins. Eight days remained for him to endure being locked up before he was finally captured by the American forces, saw the light of day again, and found new hope.

Résumé

This attempt at reconstructing suppressed feelings is certainly debatable as far as its aims are concerned. But is there not the risk of transforming history into a simple psychological analysis as well as its methods? And what can an individualizing approach that relies on texts that were –

however slightly – edited after the events explain? We are at the very boundaries of a micro-history that can help to raise questions without the claim of providing conclusive answers. There certainly exist other evasive strategies than those employed by Suzanne Langlois and Erich Kuby. Likewise, there are various other forms of coping with danger, which go beyond the appropriation of automatisms, that were not addressed here. Kuby certainly relied on various strategies, since he survived despite his adventurous lifestyle. Perhaps he refused to acknowledge them due to his total rejection of discipline. These two cases are valid only with respect to themselves. However, they can help to read primary sources that might seem surprising, such as this simple little anonymous pocket calendar from the municipal archives in Brest, from which I quote, by way of example, the entries from Friday 4 July to Monday 7 July 1941 (the passages in square brackets are mine):

> 4 July: fishing with Hyacinthe from 7 AM to 7 PM. 47 fish each; washed and salted the fish in the Kerfautras garden [it goes without saying that this was not a pleasure fishing trip!].
>
> 5 July: the damages are enormous. The museum, the library, the American monument, etc. A tragic night – alarm from 12:45 AM to 3 AM. We saw an English plane go down in flames at 2:20 AM. Boussard Germain, his wife Yvonne, and his two sisters-in-law killed at the café located at 68 rue Victor Hugo. Little Robert (4 years old) injured. Cleared out cellars with Hyacinthe and others all afternoon.
>
> 6 July: Very hot – sun. Worked in the garden in the afternoon and organized the greenhouse at Kerfautras. Ate supper together in the shed. Saw *La marraine de Charley* [Charley's Godmother] at the Celtic [movie theater].
>
> 7 July: Very hot – sun. Horrible bombing from 1 to 2 AM. Bombs on Kérichen, Kérigonan, Kerhuon, near the two stations, etc. Numerous casualties and destroyed houses pretty much everywhere in Guelmeur, etc. Afternoon: swimming at Saint-Marc [main beach in Brest].[29]

The two individuals described were most likely two widowers who lived together or two pensioner bachelors. Virtually no comments are provided, but the concise passages convey the same interplay between scenes of war, work, and pastime activities that can be found in the diaries of Suzanne Langlois and Erich Kuby: an attempt at coping with the violence that surrounds them.

As marginal figures, Suzanne Langlois and Erich Kuby display similarities that point toward other possible strategies of suppressing one's fear. Indeed, neither Langlois due to her disability nor Kuby due to his military status (even if he regards himself as autonomous) had to provide for themselves, although Kuby preferred to go out and find his own food among the farmers of the region or in nature as long as this was still possible. However, this was his personal decision and not a result of necessity.[30] In contrast, there can be no doubt that in order to meet the needs of their families, many civilians in Brest were forced to go out onto the streets and face the danger again and again because they had no other option. Did they not also undergo changes comparable to those of Suzanne Langlois and Erich Kuby?

Notes

1. For details of the diary's publication, see note 15.
2. Reinhart Koselleck, *Vergangene Zukunft. Zur Semantik geschichtlicher Zeiten* (Frankfurt/M., 1989), 349–75.
3. The distinction between "Germans" and "Nazis," Kuby insists, would require a more detailed elaboration of the situation in Brest, where various troop segments and command units, especially paratroopers, were stationed alongside one another – not always peacefully. In the following, the two terms are not equated.
4. For more detailed treatments, see Jean-Yves Besselièvre, "Les bombardements de Brest, 1940–1944," in *Revue historique des armées*, 211 (1998), 97–108. See also the dissertation by Lars Hellwinkel, which was completed in 2006 in the framework of a cotutelle at the universities of Kiel and Brest, Lars Hellwinkel, *Der deutsche Kriegsmarinestützpunkt Brest 1940–1944. Aufbau, Entwicklung und Ende* (Bochum, 2010), (Kleine Schriftenreihe zur Militär- und Marinegeschichte,16).
5. Today, the diary is in the Archives municipales et communautaires de Brest. It was given to the archive by the clergyman of the retirement home in Ponchelet, where Suzanne Langlois lived until the end of her life. The following quotes are taken from this diary.
6. "L'après midi se traîne. Et pas d'alerte, bien sûr! Hélas! Ce manque d'alertes, comme il nous angoisse à juste raison." … "Mais cette angoisse: trahir l'Angleterre … ".
7. Suzanne Langlois is distinguishing between the risk of a volley of shrapnel penetrating into the apartment and that of being hit by a bomb, which, at this date, had already caused the collapse of buildings in her neighborhood.
8. "Maman et moi, nous visitons les pièces en riant aux larmes: mon bureau est sur le devant, juste à point pour recevoir les obus, terminant leur trajectoire juste au-dessus de l'église. … Idem pour la chambre des parents… Seule la chambre du fond, donnant sur une petite cour, ne risquait aucune trajectoire – hormis les bombes. … Mais les bombes! Chambre sur le devant ou le derrière!" … "L'alerte tonne depuis une heure à peu près. Je me suis habillée tout de même pour aller à la messe. … Je fonce, dans la direction de l'église. Grand fracas, gerbes de mouches d'or au-dessus de nos têtes et, sur le mur de l'église, lueurs pâles des obus qui filent. … Je dois avoir battu tous mes records de vitesse!" … "Je sors, vais à la campagne. Oublier, si possible."
9. "Cette grand route porte malheur, je crois! Nous ne pouvons y passer sans coups de canons, mitrailleuses. … Brusquement, déclic de mitrailleuses, coups de canons, éclats qui pleuvent! Pas de maison à moins de 500 mètres! Je pédalais à toute allure, la tête rentrée dans les épaules."

10. "…splendeur de ces feux d'artifice: projecteurs, balles traçantes de toutes couleurs, pluie d'abeilles d'or des petits obus que lancent les mitrailleuses! Il y a une beauté aussi dans ce monstrueux concert. … Tous mes élèves sont enthousiastes et passent des heures à leur fenêtre."
11. "6 h du soir – avions anglais. Papa et moi, nous restons à la fenêtre, torturés d'enthousiasme et de crainte. De crainte pour les Anglais, naturellement. [Sur la place principale] la foule criait et riait d'énervement et d'enthousiasme." … "Tout l'angle de la maison est détruit, de haut en bas: pas un blessé! Selon les traditions brestoises, la foule visite les endroits sinistrés et défile donc rue Fautras. Les habitants de la maison, qui ne songent pas à déménager, très fiers, à leurs fenêtres, contemplent les badauds … Toute la famille se montre d'ailleurs très gaie, et quoiqu'ils aient tout perdu dans l'aventure, ils en rient aux larmes: 'Tristes, nous? Ah, bien vrai! On a eu trop de veine!'"
12. "Le lendemain, rires unanimes. Les Brestois se moquent les uns des autres avec une joyeuse vigueur, car l'épouvante fut générale … Et l'on rit, rit aux larmes."
13. "Les bombes tombent en plein coeur de la ville … L'hôpital civil est-il bombardé? … Le souffle est tellement violent qu'à Saint-Martin, on a l'impression que les volets s'arrachent à chaque éclatement de bombe." … "les visages des Brestois ont changé: têtes tirées, visages graves, durs."
14. The radio play was aired in spring 1954 and the text of the diary cited below was published five years later.
15. Erich Kuby, *Nur noch rauchende Trümmer. Das Ende der Festung Brest. Tagebuch des Soldaten Erich Kuby mit Text des Hörbildes, Plädoyer des Staatsanwalts, Begründung des Urteils* (Hamburg, 1959).
16. "Wenn ich jetzt auf Störungssuche durchs Gelände gehe, trage ich ganz leichtes Zeug, eine Drillichhose, ein Paar Bordschuhe, die mir ein Marinesoldat gegen Zigaretten gegeben hat, einen ganz leichten Feldrock. Die Patronen trage ich in der Hosentasche, die Flinte hängt mir mit dem Lauf nach unten über der Schulter. Den Stahlhelm schiebe ich ganz gegen die Vorschrift weit aus der Stirn. So wie ich angezogen bin, so fühle ich mich auch, so bewege ich mich." Ibid., entry on 27 August 1944, 75.
17. From August 1944 onwards, only the sailors, marines, and soldiers in the city center are fully operational.
18. "Geringe Mengen alkoholischer Marketenderwaren, wahrscheinlich vermehrt durch organisierte Bestände, genügen, allabendlich einige Unteroffiziere und Feldwebel stockbetrunken zu machen … Ich frage mich, ob der Alkohol schon jetzt dazu dienen muss, Angstgefühle Niederzukämpfen." Kuby (see note 15), entry on 16 August 1944, 65.
19. "Sie brüllen, toben, streiten sich am anderen Tag untereinander, schlafen dann bis zum Abend und beginnen von neuem." Ibid., entry on 22 August 1944, 70.
20. "Ich habe mich auch wieder einmal menschlich gemacht, rasiert, gewaschen." Ibid., entry on 16 August 1944, 69.
21. "Dem Irrsinn, in den wir hier hineingezwungen werden, dieser Kriegskomödie, die hier mit ungeheuren Opfern gespielt wird, mehr als tausend Kilometer von der eigentlichen Kriegsfront entfernt, der schäbigen Furcht, von der dieses stets betrunkene Gesindel im Bunker erfüllt ist, setze ich eine gewissermaßen sportive Arroganz entgegen. Natürlich ist das Pose. Aber diese Pose versetzt mich in gute Laune und hilft mir, die Situation mit leidlichem Anstand zu bestehen." Ibid., entry on 27 August 1944, 74.
22. "So lebe ich, heiter auf mancherlei Weise erheitert dahin, indes eine Welt zugrundegeht, zum mindesten und fürs erste unsere Brester Welt." Ibid., entry on 30 August 1944, 80.
23. "Wir nahmen unseren Weg über den ehemaligen Flirtstrand St. Anne, hügelauf und hügelab durch Hohlwege, quer durch das Stachelgebüsch auf wildschlupfengen Pfaden, und Millionen reifer Brombeeren wuchsen uns entgegen. Wir erreichten hinter St. Anne eine bedeutende Höhe, von der aus das offene Meer weit hinaus zu sehen war. Im strahlendsten Augustsonnenlicht lagen die tiefblaue Reede und ihre Verbindung

zum Ozean unter uns ... Auf dem blauen Spiegel schwammen noch einige unserer Schiffe. Sie lagen still, und aus dem blauen Himmel stürzten sich silberglänzend die Bombenvögel gleich Habichten feuerspeiend auf sie herab. Das Meer rings um die Schiffe kochte von den Geschossgarben, die ihr Ziel nicht erreichten, und die Schiffe gingen in Flammen auf. Einige fuhren wie große Feuerkörbe auf dem blauen Spiegel dahin, andere zogen gewaltige Rauchsäulen hinter sich her ... – Wir erledigten den Telefonkram, und ich badete im klaren Meer und wusch mich dann mit Süßwasser an der schüsselgroßen Rinnsalstauung, die ich selbst vor drei Wochen zu diesem Zweck gebaut habe, und pflückte nackt an den Hecken entlang gehend Hände voll Brombeeren." Ibid., entry on 27 August 1944, 76–77.

24. "A partir de ce moment, la vie à Brest devint un cauchemar pour la population. Pas un jour ne se passa sans – au moins – une alerte aérienne. Les bombes perforantes de 200 kilos – destinées aux cuirassés allemands – effondraient les maisons, des combles aux caves." Alain Boulaire and Adolphe-Auguste Lepotier, *Brest, Porte océane* (Paris, 1968), 353.

25. Suzanne Langlois is adopting the attitude of preparing for death, which she no doubt learned as a young girl.

26. As a Latinist, Suzanne Langlois was certainly aware of the etymology of the word *angoisse* (anxiety/fear), which is related to tightness. Her last sentence is an intensification of her expression of anxiety and stands in stark contrast to the beginning of the journal.

27. "10 juin. Nuit. Alerte ... très violente et continue. ... Nous nous groupons parfois, angoissés. A un certain moment, seule, je me suis bien allongée, en étendant soigneusement ma robe. Les deux jambes bien droite, les pieds en équerre. Le chapelet aux doigts, mains jointes, je tâchais de sommeiller, dans l'effroyable tapage." ... "Etre pour les Anglais n'empêche pas l'angoisse!" ... "J'attends le premier coup de canon. Attendre? Cette fois-ci, pourquoi? J'attends tout de même, dans l'angoisse qui monte ... Le silence est total. Notre gorge se serre de plus en plus" ... "Il y a de terribles rafales de DCA. J'ai peur, et cette fois-ci, je ne domine plus ma peur. Je reste calme, bien sûr, et je ne dis rien, mais je tremble fortement en m'habillant." ... "Pu, hier soir, vérifier la véracité du fameux mot de Turenne: tu trembles, vieille carcasse ... Or, à 2 h 30, longs hurlements de sirène. Dès la première note, je me suis mis à trembler, mais à trembler! De tout le corps, et si fort que la lampe électrique au-dessus de ma tête n'était qu'une série de traits lumineux. Le comique était que je riais moi-même de me voir grelotter ainsi."

28. "Sie ist mir nicht Denkmittelpunkt wie vielen, aber zuweilen genieße ich das tiefe Atemholen und die Sicherheit der Lebenserhaltung voraus ... Ich kann mir nicht vorstellen, dass ich sie so heil und ganz soll genießen können, ebenso wenig wie ich mir vorstellen kann, dass ich sie nicht genießen soll." Kuby (see note 15), entry on 9 September 1944, 93.

29. 4 juillet: à la pêche avec Hyacinthe de 7h à 19h. 47 poissons à chacun, nettoyé et salé les poissons au jardin de Kerfautras [il va de soi qu'il ne s'agit pas d'une pêche de loisir!] ... 5 juillet: les dégâts sont énormes. Le Musée, la bibliothèque, le monument américain etc. Nuit tragique: alerte de minuit 45 à 3h du matin. A 2h20 nous voyions tomber un avion anglais en feu. Au café sis 68 rue Victor Hugo, tués: Boussard Germain, sa femme Yvonne et ses 2 belles-soeurs. Le petit Robert blessé (4 ans). Déblayé les caves avec Hyacinthe et autres toute l'après-midi. ... 6 juillet: Très chaud – soleil. L'après-midi travaillé au jardin et arrangé la serre à Kerfautras. Soupé tous les deux dans la cabane. Au Celtic [cinéma]: La marraine de Charley. ... 7 juillet: Très chaud – soleil. Terrible bombardement de 1h à 2h du matin. Bombes sur Kérichen, Kérigonan, Kerhuon, les alentours des deux gares, etc. Nombreuses victimes et maisons détruites un peu partout au Guelmeur etc. Après-midi: bains à Saint-Marc [principale grève de Brest].

30. The two men in the small pocket calendar resemble Kuby in this regard: they succeed at being self-sufficient – at least more or less.

Chapter 11

EXPERIENCES OF WAR, MEMORIES OF WAR, AND POLITICAL BEHAVIOR:
The Example of the French Communist Party

Philippe Buton

Is the memory of war fundamental to the experience of war? This chapter will examine this question by using the statistics on local support for political parties, which historiography generally considers to be resistant to trends in the field. Indeed, the French sociologist André Siegfried, in his essential book from 1913, went so far as to make the mildly provocative assertion that the map was the deciding factor, determining the most important borders and delivering a geographical overview of voting behavior in advance: "Limestone or granite: that is the great distinction to be made."[1] I will test Siegfried's idea of the permanence of "political temperament" against the level of support for the Communist electorate,[2] questioning whether the experience of war substantially changed the forms of political engagement in France. If the answer is yes, which experiences of war had this effect, and what role does memory play in these possible changes?

Let us begin by looking at the structure of the Communist electorate from its first appearance until the Second World War. There were four major elections (see Maps 1 through 4) during this time, and the four maps suggest that the structure of the Communist vote remained the same. As Annie Kriegel established almost four decades ago, the geographical extent of the French Communist Party (*Parti communiste français*, or PCF) can be visualized as a "fungus," rather than an octopus. Although its strength may vary according to circumstances, rapidly growing or declining in power, the affected area remains the same.[3]

Notes for this chapter begin on page 179.

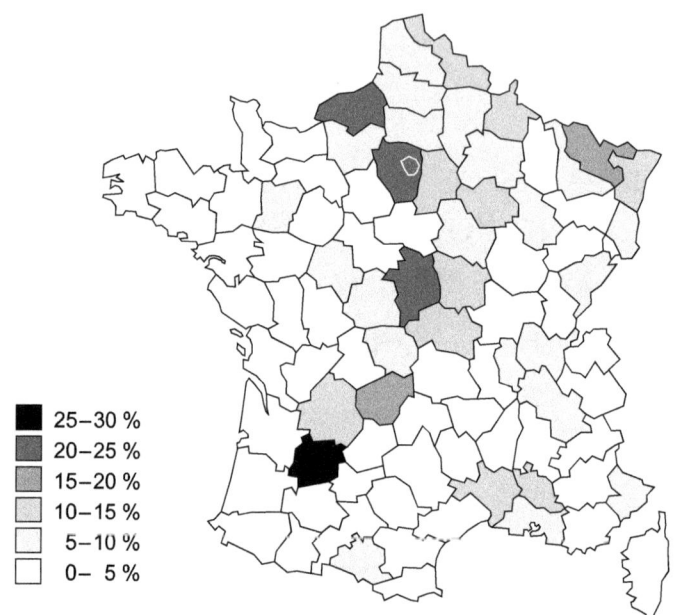

Map 1: Election results for the PCF in 1924
© MGFA 05716-03

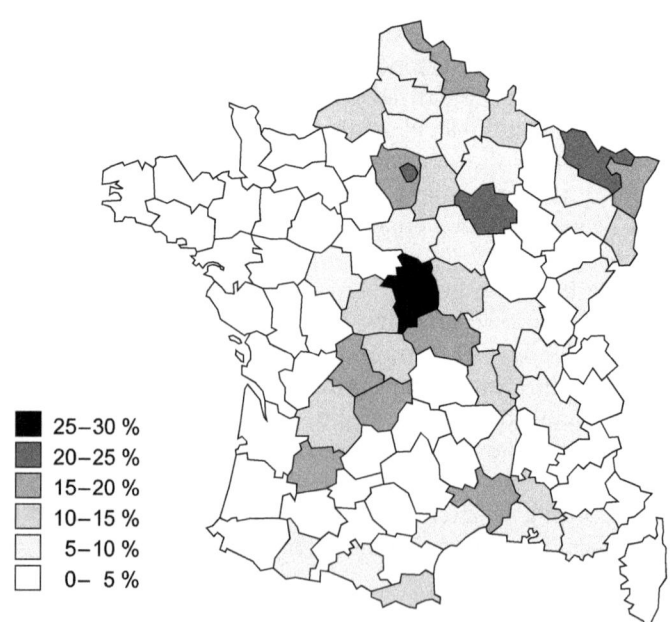

Map 2: Election results for the PCF in 1928
© MGFA 05717-03

The Example of the French Communist Party | 163

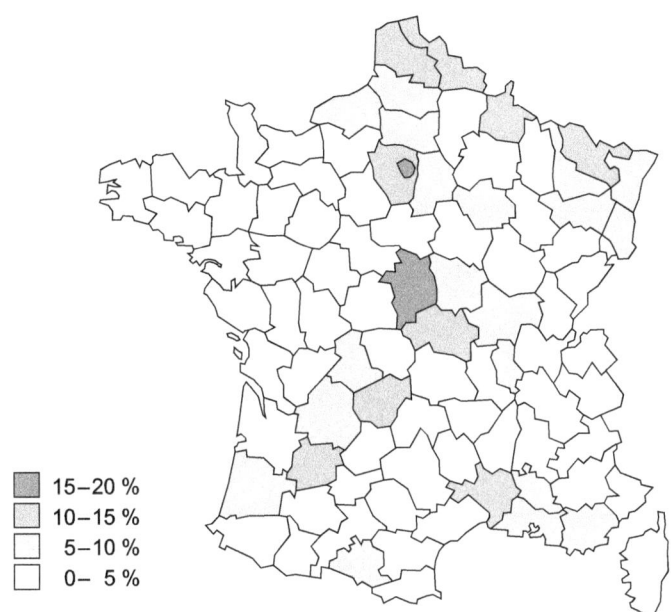

Map 3: Election results for the PCF in 1932
© MGFA 05718-04

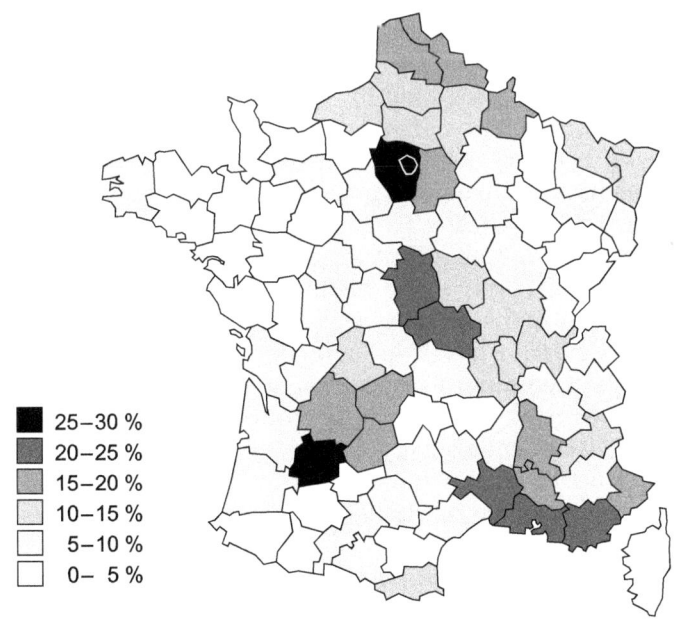

Map 4: Election results for the PCF in 1936
© MGFA 05719-03

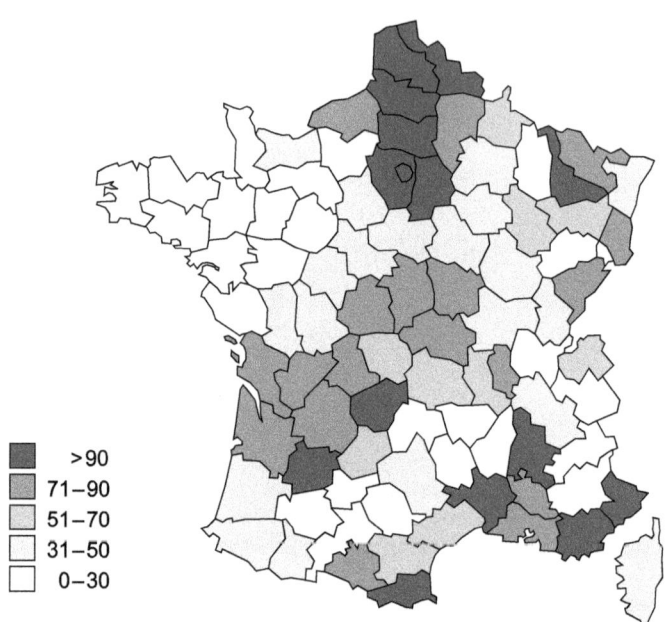

Map 5: Distribution of PCF members in 1937 by *département* (per 10,000 inhabitants)
© MGFA 05720-04

This structure of the electorate is all the more constant when it coincides with the distribution of the party adherents – in other words, with the "Communist density" (see Map 5). This is an uncomplicated model of local support for the party. There are no subtle gradations, but rather a clear contrast between the Communist strongholds and those areas in which voters have yet to be won over. Strong Communist support unites the northern parts of Greater Paris, the Picardy and the Seine Maritime, the Nord- and Pas-de-Calais *départements* in the north, the iron and steel industry region in Lorraine, the Mediterranean coast and its extension toward the Rhône in the south, as well as the western and northern edge of the Massif Central, which aligns with the north of the Aquitaine basin. In contrast, the Communist presence is weak in the west and south of France, the inner Alps, the south of the Aquitaine basin, and the southern and eastern Massif Central.

Did this structure remain the same during the liberation? Maps 5 and 7 show a comparison of the PCF in 1936 and 1945. The comparison identifies continuities, but also fractures. The main continuity is that the most important Communist bastions were retained: the whole region of greater Paris, the Nord-Pas-de-Calais region, the Picardy and the Mediterranean coast, as well as the western and northern Massif Central. But there were changes too.

The Example of the French Communist Party | 165

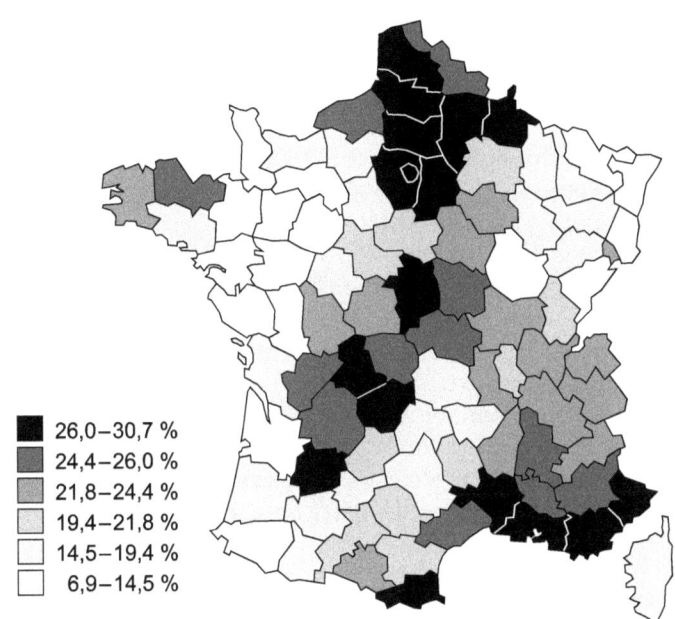

Map 6: Election results for the PCF in 1946
© MGFA 05721-03

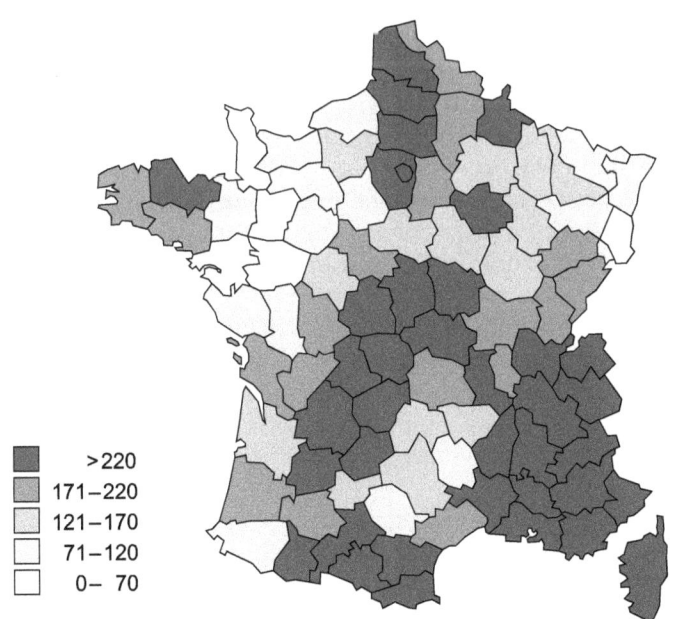

Map 7: Distribution of PCF members in 1946 by *département* (per 10,000 inhabitants)
© MGFA 05722-03

If we take members of the Communist Party rather than the voters for the Communist Party as a criterion, we first notice some weak points in certain industrial areas such as the Seine-Maritime, the Lorraine, and the Paris region, whose relative weights decline. The importance lies not in these weak points, however, but in the strength of the local support for the Communists. Between 1936 and 1946, we can see a dual advance: on the one hand a general Communist Party increase (as shown by the shading on the maps), and on the other – for the first time – a substantial change in its territorial foundation. Until 1946, the party actually took root in the rural regions – the inner Alps, the Languedoc, the coastal regions in Brittany and in Corsica – in terms of both voters and party members. If the development between the two world wars resembled a fungus, to return to the aforementioned metaphor, it was now closer to an octopus that was taking hold of rural and southern France. Once again, this change can be observed more clearly in regards to the distribution of Communist Party members than that of Communist Party voters.[4]

Was this a short interim phase, or a structural fracture? If we consider the distribution of the Communist Party members (see Maps 8 and 9), we see quickly that a structural change occured following the liberation of France. The map illustrating local support for active PCF members during the Cold War shows that although the newly-established bastions grew weaker after the war, they did not disappear. This is the case in western Brittany, in the center of the Aquitaine basin, in the inner Alps, and in Corsica. There is a further similarity in that bastions that were lost after the war were not reestablished. The core area of the Paris region and the Nord-Pas-de-Calais/Picardy slowly dissolved as well. These conclusions show up again in the map for 1979 (Map 9), which was the golden age for active PCF sympathizers.

If we look at the voters, the ratios are not much different (see Maps 10 to 16). The consistency of the voting patterns by area is astonishing: for fifty years, the areas in which the PCF was strongest and weakest remained the same. The octopus turns back into a fungus.

We can draw one conclusion from this first expansion: for eighty years, local support for Communism had only two different faces. The voting pattern of Communist voters and sympathizers achieved at the beginning of the 1920s remained stable until the Second World War. Following this experience of war, a new voting pattern developed that likewise remained stable for five decades.

How then should we understand the revolution produced by the war, a revolution that had such long-term effects on the local support for the Communists in France? In order to address this question, we must take a closer look at the areas that were affected by these political changes at the end of the war.

The Example of the French Communist Party | 167

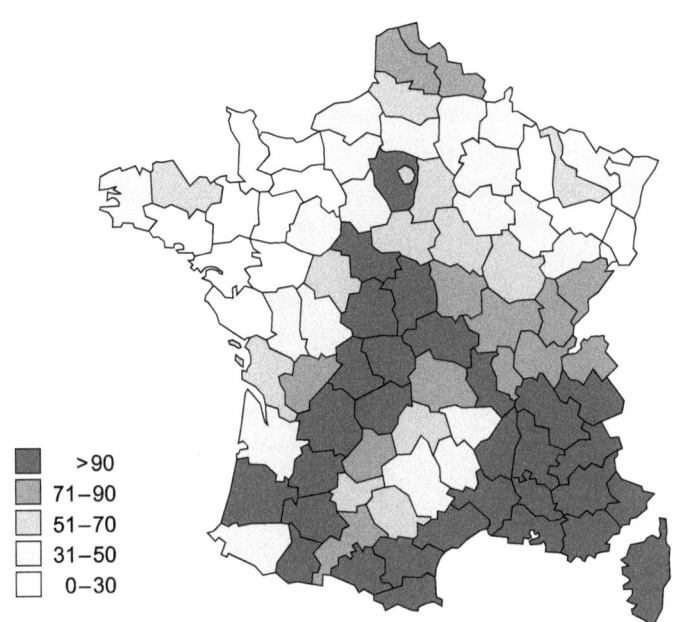

Map 8: Distribution of PCF members in 1952 by *département* (per 10,000 inhabitants)
© MGFA 05723-03

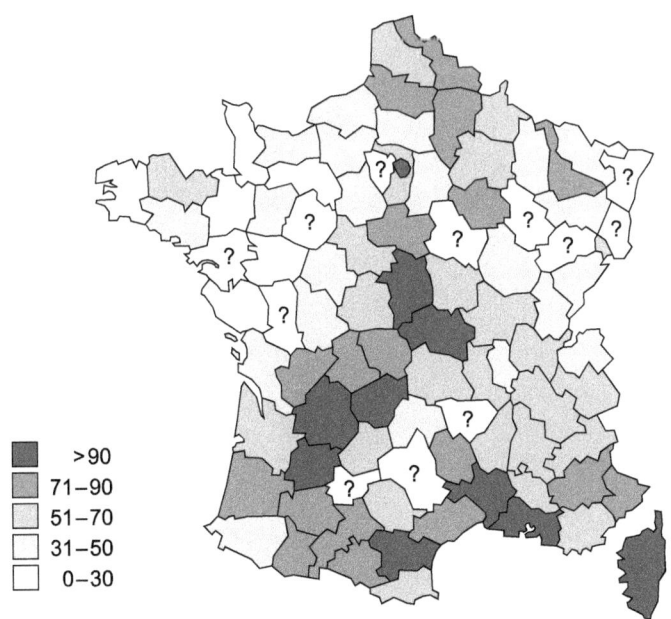

Map 9: Distribution of PCF members in 1979 by *département* (per 10,000 inhabitants)
© MGFA 05724-06

168 | Philippe Buton

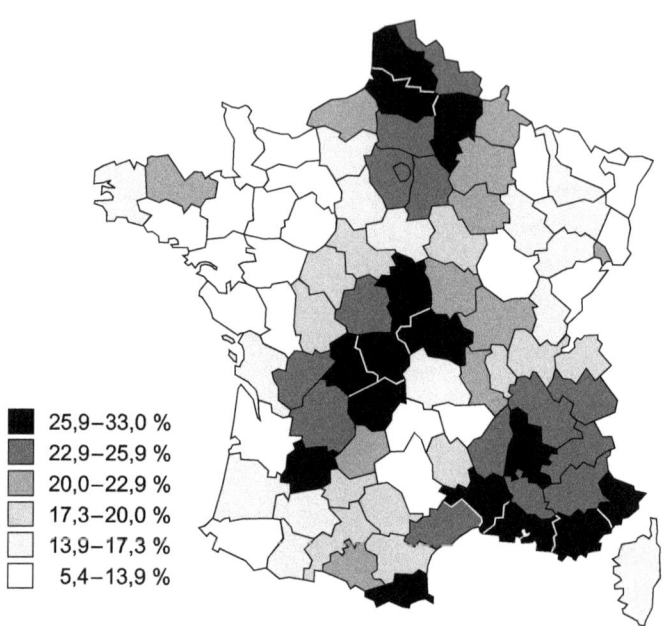

Map 10: Election results for the PCF in 1951
© MGFA 05725-03

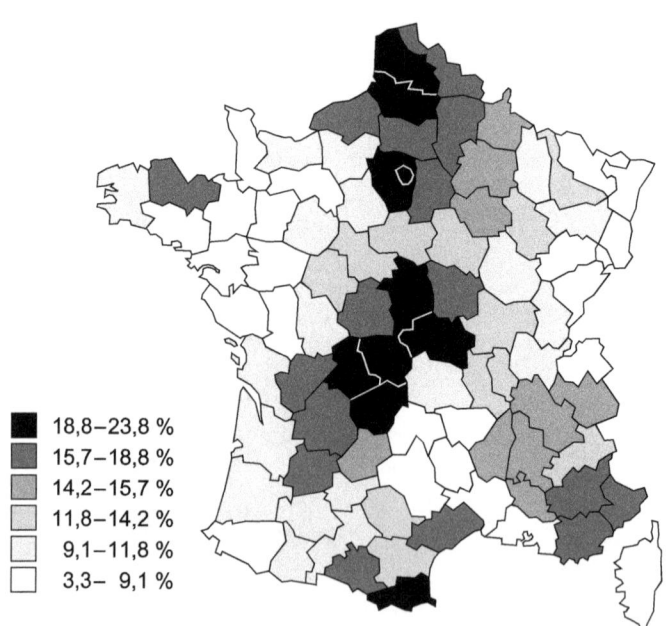

Map 11: Election results for the PCF in 1958
© MGFA 05726-03

The Example of the French Communist Party | 169

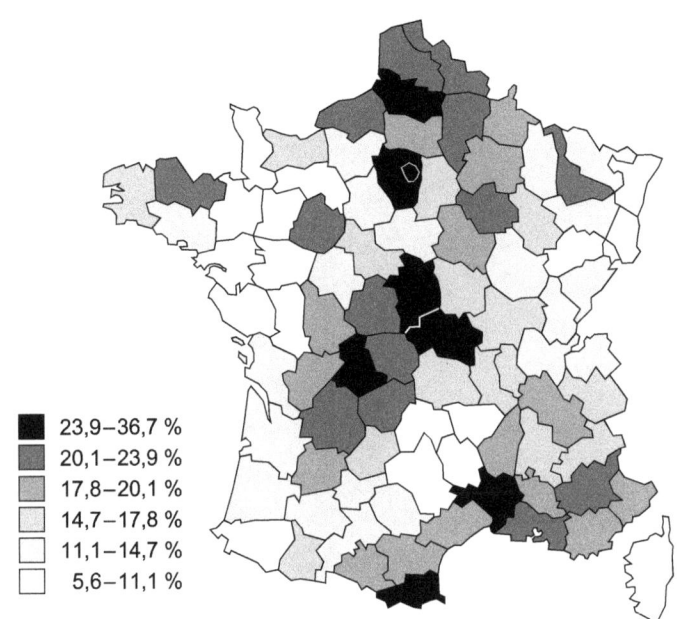

Map 12: Election results for the PCF in 1967
© MGFA 05727-03

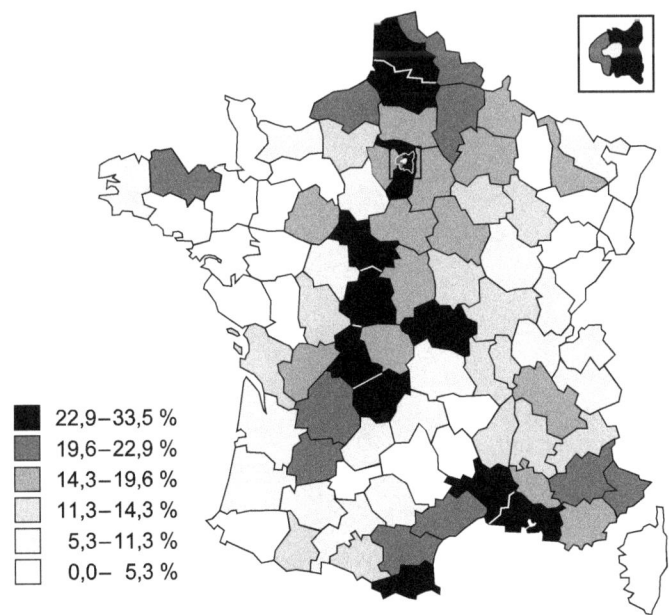

Map 13: Election results for the PCF in 1973
© MGFA 05728-04

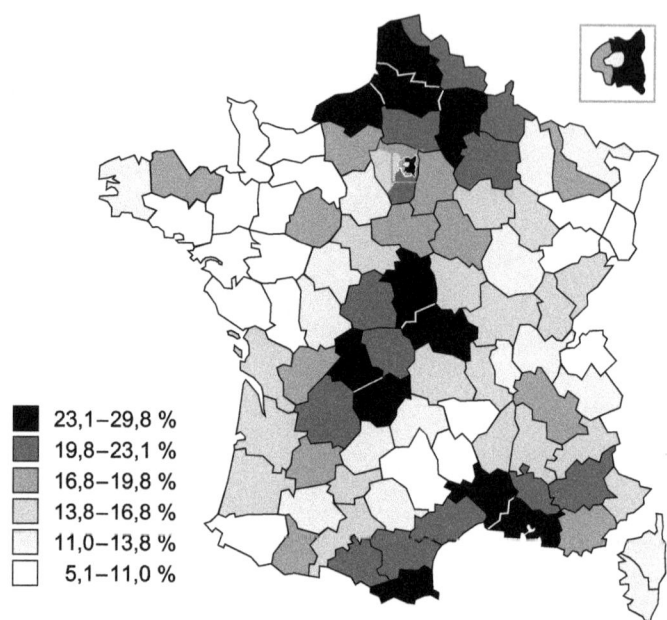

Map 14: Election results for the PCF in 1978
© MGFA 05729-03

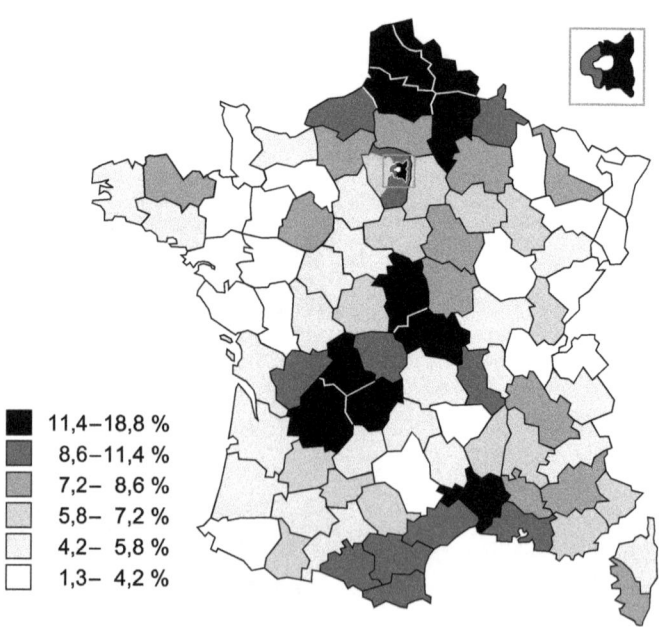

Map 15: Election results for the PCF in 1988
© MGFA 05730-04

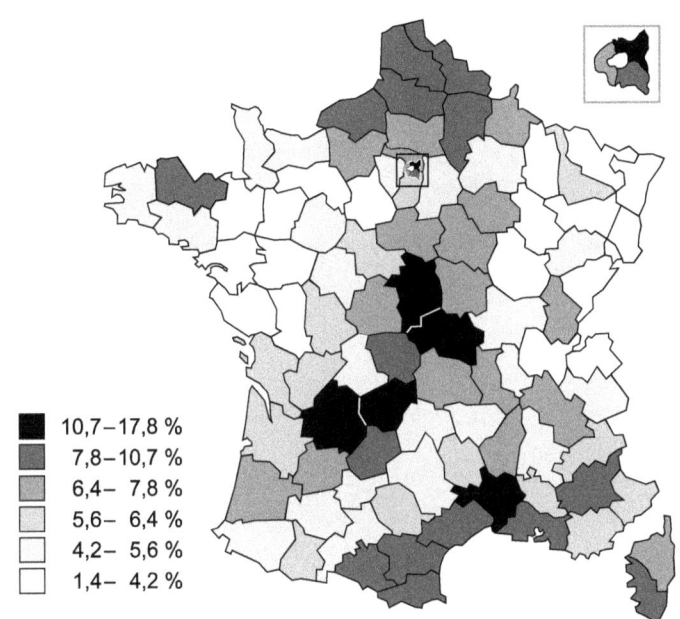

Map 16: Election results for the PCF in 1997
© MGFA 05731-04

Map 17 is a comparison of the growth in Communist density that occured in the French *départements* in the pre- and postwar era. In view of the Communist expansion that occurred, it is worth rendering these areas more precisely for the geographical correlation.

The first hypothesis we can test relates to the French resistance movements: did the PCF have the greatest growth where the *Résistance* was the strongest? We have a source that allows us to establish the strongholds of the *Résistance*: the geographical distribution of the membership cards that were issued to the "voluntary combatants of the resistance" (*Combattants volontaires de la Résistance*, CVR) (see Map 18). If we analyze the distribution, we can see two distinct lines. There is one broad stripe that runs clearly from the north to the south, connecting a large part of the French mountain regions via Corsica, the Alps, the Jura mountains, and the Vosges; and there is another line that runs from the southwest to the northeast going out from the Pyrenees, which moves through the western and northern Massif Central and finally ends up in the first area. Besides these two large interconnected areas, there are two further bastions of the resistance marking the northern part of France: the western and central Brittany region, northern France from Pas-de-Calais to the Ardennes, plus the occasional islands, above all the *départements* of the Seine, Aube, Yonne, and a part of upper Normandy (*Haute Normandie*).

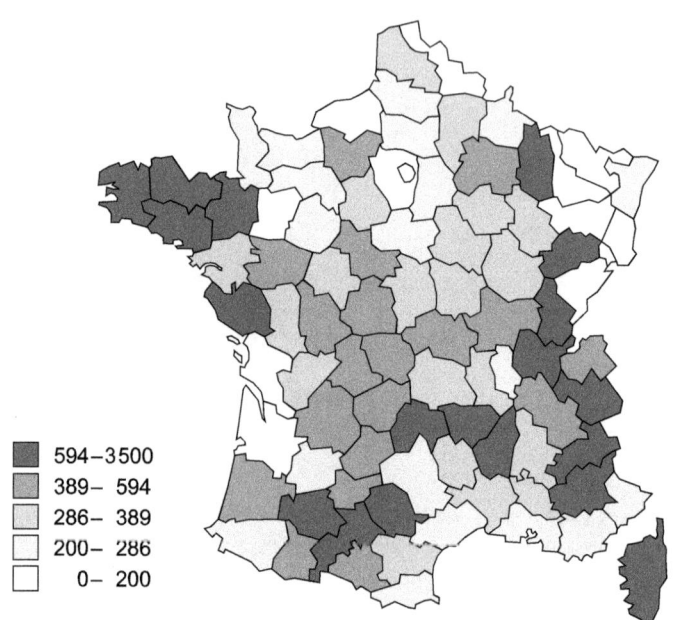

Map 17: Comparison in the growth of the PCF, 1937–1945
© MGFA 05732-04

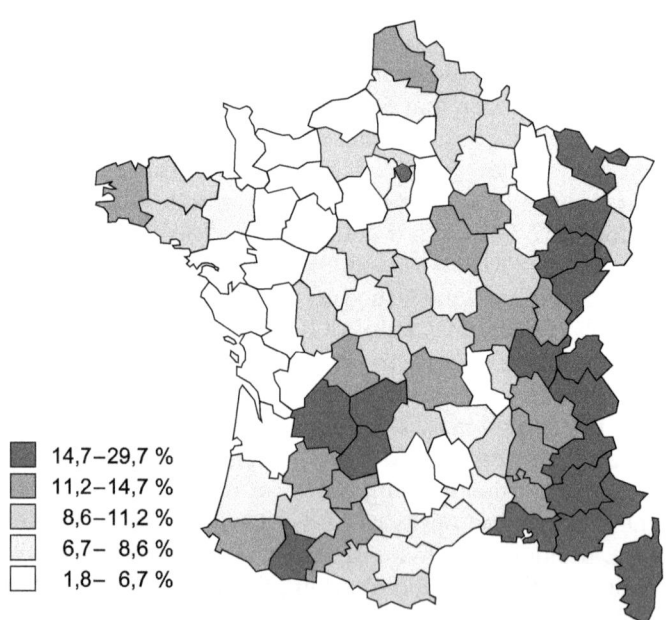

Map 18: Distribution of volunteer *Résistance* fighters in 1944 by *département*
© MGFA 05733-04

There are two methodological problems with these statistics on card-carrying members of the CVR, however. A first problem is that the data collected after the war reveals the place of residence of resistance members at the time that the membership cards were issued, not the location of their resistance activities. As a result, these documents give excess weight to the *départements* in the south and allow for no inferences to be made about Alsace and Lorraine, since the population and *Résistance* members from the three relevant *départments* were particularly affected by the temporary migration phenomenon associated with the war. If we exclude the areas of Alsace and Lorraine, we cannot deny a certain relationship between the strength of the Communists and the appearance of the *Résistance* (cf. Map 19). But what does this causal connection look like? Did the Communist presence before the war encourage the resistance during the war, or was it the *Résistance* that fostered the Communist expansion after the war? The two phenomena seem to have worked in tandem. The map of the Communist density before the war does in fact resemble the map of the resistance presence, but the map of the Communist expansion exhibits the strongest similarity. This leads us to the conclusion that this experience of resistance during the war is what changed the geographical pattern of French Communism.

Using the CVR cards as a source also poses a second methodological problem. Civil resistance for cultural reasons was less and less noticeable after the war, so that the CVR mapping is more of a depiction of the armed resistance fighters than of all members of the resistance. In view of the equal weight of the Gaullist *Forces françaises libres* (FFL) and the internal French *Forces françaises de l'intérieur* (FFI), the CVR cards to a large extent are consistent with the distribution of the FFI over the French territory, with the exception of the territories of Alsace and Lorraine. This gives rise to a second hypothesis: rather than correlating Communist influence with the appearance of the resistance, we should correlate the Communist influence with the start of armed confrontation, the form of violence that permeated France during the liberation phase. Indeed, the presence of the FFI may have slightly increased the tendency for violent campaigns. Since it took time for the concept of immediate armed conflict to take root, the French resistance fighters in the forests and mountains (the *maquis*) and those belonging to underground organizations in the cities no longer served as reserve armies waiting for the Allies to land. Instead, they represented armed groups who carried out acts of sabotage and attacks on German soldiers or collaborators, which in turn resulted in counterstrikes, acts of vengeance, and carnage. If we emphasize the FFI presence on the map, we are saying broadly that France itself carried out a large part of the violent acts that accompanied the liberation of the country.

The direct or indirect consequences of the FFI presence were not the only forms of violence in the struggle for liberation, of course. During

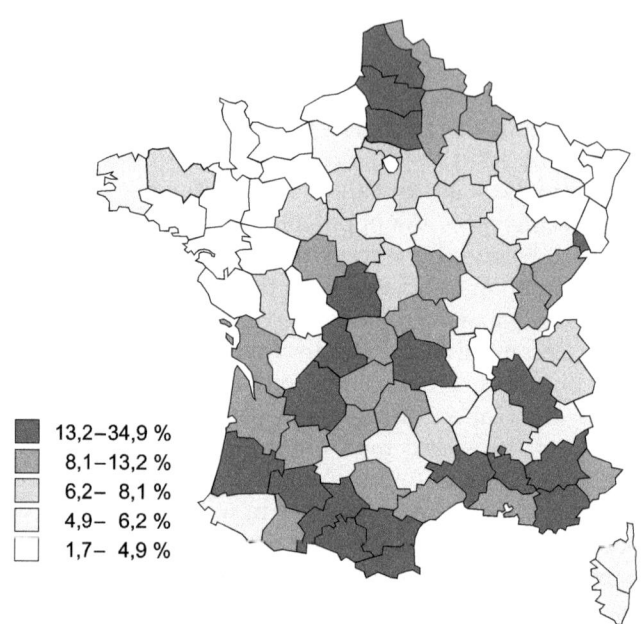

Map 19: Distribution of PCF members in 1945 by *département*
© MGFA 05734-05

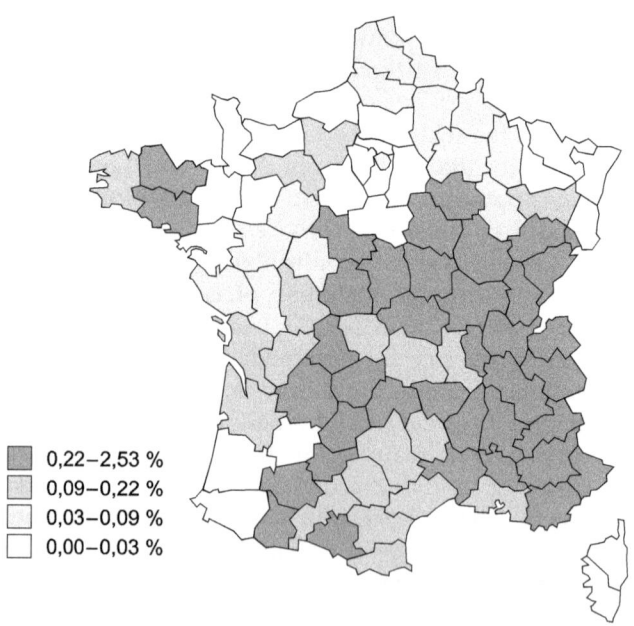

Map 20: Summary executions per inhabitant during the liberation
© MGFA 05735-05

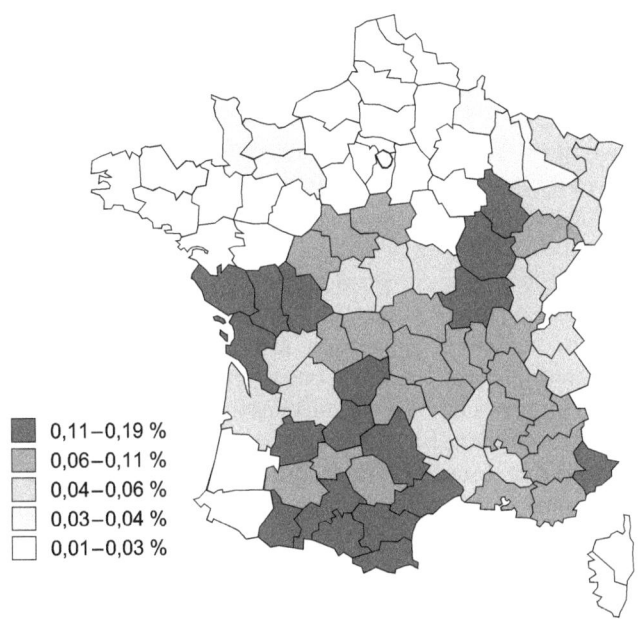

Map 21: Death sentences during the liberation
© MGFA 05736-03

the last six decades, most of the confrontations were met by summary executions, some 10,000 of them.[5] The geographical distribution of these executions (see Map 20) shows a striking similarity with map 18 depicting the presence of the FFI. In both cases, the south of the country dominates, with an attenuation occuring on the Atlantic coast. We find the same thing in the northern foothills of inner Normandy, northern France, and above all in western Brittany, as well as on the northern edges of the Massif Central, where it continues in a northerly direction up to the Yonne and Aube *départements* and in a northeasterly direction including the Franche-Comté. This geographical correlation seems to allude strongly to the unsurprising connection between the FFI presence and the *maquis*, on the one hand, and the summary executions on the other. The very appearance of a *maquis*, which could easily lead to denunciations, battles, and acts of repression, created a suitable environment for acts of revenge. This was because the summary executions were not, for the most part, arbitrarily enforced, even though constitutional law was seldom followed – more seldom, at any rate, than was the case in the framework of the ensuing legal purge (*Épuration*).

This legal purge is the third form of violence that must be considered when looking at the question of the change in political behavior. Mapping the legal purge is not without its problems, however. We must first decide which indicator to choose. There is an abundance of numerical data available to us: the death sentences pronounced by the courts (7,055), the death sentences announced only in the presence of the accused (2,861), and the death sentences that were actually carried out (791). In the ideal case, those sentences pronounced in civil jurisdictions would be complemented by those from military courts. In fact, it is known that there were about 900 executions pronounced by the French military courts.[6] But since the distribution across *départements* is still missing, we can merely check which sentences were pronounced by the civil courts. The first established piece of information, the total number of those sentenced to death, seems inconclusive. The people knew very well that the sentences were largely symbolic in character, because if the person who had been sentenced was imprisoned, they would have a new day in court. A second indicator is more meaningful: the announcement of the verdict had a big impression on public opinion. The frequent pardons, pronounced first by the Commissioners of the Republic, and then by General de Gaulle, would later alleviate the initial public shock, without eradicating it completely.

The selection of suitable indicators is not the only methodological difficulty. Unfortunately, the only statistics available at present use the regional jurisdiction as a territorial unit rather than the *département*; more research is pending. These regional averages blur the differences between the individual *départements*. The effect is the worst for the Paris jurisdiction, though by no means limited to it. The Paris district at the time comprised no fewer than seven *départements*, so that in this case repression inequalities were considerably obscured.

What do the maps tell us? For almost thirty years, since the appearance of Jean-Pierre Rioux's essay in the journal *L'Histoire*,[7] it has been repeatedly stressed that mapping the legal purge shows it to be the opposite of any sort of wild cleansing (*Épuration sauvage*), which led to the hypothesis of a relatively uniform distribution of repression within France. If we look at the maps published here, however, a different picture emerges.

Despite the weak points of this source, it is clear that maps 20 and 21, which represent the legal death sentence pronouncements, do not show the opposite of the overview of the summary executions.[8] Neither do they completely agree, as shown by the examples from Brittany and the north. All in all, however, the map depicting the legal executions is more similar to any of the maps showing summary executions than it is their adverse. In other words, if the most serious proceedings were most likely concluded with summary executions, it is also very likely that enough cases still remained for the legal courts; the repression was cumulative rather than compensatory.

If we look at the three mappings of liberation-era tyranny – the FFI, the summary executions, and the legal death sentences – in relation to one another, they show large areas of geographical agreement that lead to the confrontation of one France against the other: the France of the *maquis*, the battles, the carnage, the summary court martials, the corpses at daybreak, and the state-sanctioned death sentences; and the France that could hardly have had less of a civil war. In the first France, the deaths were primarily those of political opponents and their neighbors – deaths as occur in the common representations of civil war.[9] In the second France, death often came from the sky (in the form of Allied bombs) and was a consequence of the war and of geographical chance. In short, the first France embodies war and vengeance, the second France embodies guilt and grief.

These two elements had a lasting effect on how the collective memory was structured. The first France was persuaded by collective memory to liberate itself or to allow the FFI to liberate it. The second France, on the other hand, knew that without the English and the Americans, the Germans would have remained in the country longer. The first France put a face on those responsible for this accident of fate: the traitors, or "fifth column," the members of the militia, and the followers of Fascist collaborator Jacques Doriot. Hate strengthened believers tenfold and relieved the traumatic experience of war. The second France, however, seemed more fatalistic, because the concepts responsible were far away: war, Hitler, Germany. There was only one thing left to do: to see to their wounds and turn the page.

In closing, we must ask why this frontline experience of violence encouraged Communism. The French Communists were not the only ones who participated in the *Résistance*. Neither were they the only ones alert to preserving its memory. Nevertheless, the geographical correlations show that Communism came out of the violence in France in 1944 and 1945 as the biggest winner.

The Communist Party experienced particularly strong development in those areas of France which were most strongly affected by the brutality. The connection between experience of violence and political rise is less pronounced in the case of the Socialists, to say nothing of other political forces, for which there is no statistical correlation. This is all the more interesting because the Communism of the liberation developed a discourse that, paradoxically, is hardly a pronounced rhetoric of class struggle – as if the French on the other side of the discourse had noticed that the PCF was a party like no other.

There are elements in the political culture of the Communists that can clarify the link between an atmosphere of violence and Communist engagement (the correlation in the category of "Communist adherents" is more strongly pronounced than in the category of "Communist voters"). Of particular importance is the element of connection to revolt, political activism, and armed struggle. The *Résistance* was naturally a national conflict. It was also an individual revolt against a certain established order that for a long time had possessed all the attributes of legality. Communism masterfully embodied this tradition of permanent revolt, an obvious bridge to contact with the new dissidents. This contact also encouraged the connection to political activism. What defined a Communist in this era? Above all, a Communist was someone who was serious, brave, and disciplined. These were precisely the qualities that strengthened the underground struggle. This must have been what had seduced the brave and fresh-faced youths to join the FFI. After the war, these same qualities turned into weaknesses to some extent. Of all the members of the *Résistance*, it was largely the PCF that retained the logic of the *miles*, the activists, the party soldiers, until the end. From the end of the First World War, the PCF had supported a violent form of political struggle that French Socialism had turned its back on. Communism was the doctrine that had originally been founded upon the necessity of civil war. It had certainly been some time since Lenin had proclaimed the militarization of the political arena, and we cannot overlook the political crisis of 1934 that resolved in favor of the *Front populaire*. But something remained of that Bolshevik legacy and had penetrated the Communist political culture. The strength of the Communist Party at the time of the liberation came from its ability to give political expression to this culture of conflict, to these partial or imaginary signs of civil war.

The transition between a traumatizing experience of war and a durable political restructuring, however, did not take place spontaneously in any sense of the word. The process had much more to do with a constantly curated collective memory. The Communist collective memory of war has always dominated, whether during the struggles in the 1940s over the memory of liberation and the competition between Gaullist and Communist collective memory, the protest in the 1950s against the European Defense Community (EDC) and German rearmament, or the reactivation of Communist collective memory in the 1960s, competing first against the Gaullist, then against the leftist collective memory discourse.[10] This collective memory was sometimes in accord with the Gaullist variants and sometimes in opposition to them, but constantly in service of that myth of resistance, of victimization and heroism (*Résistancialisme*). This perspective in many ways keeps a memory alive that has shaped and informed an equally vibrant political culture, which in turn nourished a microclimate that was conducive to Communist involvement. Thus one conclusion of political scientists is again confirmed: belonging to the French Left is less about social class or socioeconomic factors than it is about engagement in a political culture that rests on active and well-directed collective memory, in which specific recollections of the experience of liberation and the end of the war play an important role.

Notes

1. André Siegfried, *Tableau politique de la France de l'Ouest* (1913) (Paris, 1995), 69f.
2. First elements and some additional considerations on the subject were first set out in Philippe Buton, *La Joie douloureuse. La Libération de la France* (Brussels, 2004).
3. Annie Kriegel, "Le Parti communiste français sous la IIIe République (1920–1939): mouvement des effectifs et structures d'organisation," in *Le Pain et les roses jalons pour une histoire des socialismes* (1968), new edition (Paris, 1973), 277–390. See also Annie Kriegel, *Les communistes français: dans leur premier demi-siècle 1920–1970*, edited and expanded new edition (Paris, 1985).
4. This radical change in local support for the Communist Party is thoroughly analyzed in Philippe Buton, *Les lendemains qui déchantent. Le Parti communiste français à la Libération* (Paris, 1993).
5. This phenomenon has since become known thanks to the work of the Comité d'histoire de la Deuxième Guerre mondiale, which was continued by the Institut d'histoire du temps présent (IHTP). Some two thousand five hundred executions occurred before the summer of 1944, five thousand during the summer and one thousand six hundred after the liberation.
6. Henry Rousso, "L'épuration en France, une histoire inachevée," in *Vingtième siècle*, 33 (1992), 78–105, and in Henry Rousso, *Vichy, L'événement, la mémoire, l'histoire* (Paris, 2001), 489–552.
7. Jean-Pierre Rioux, "L'épuration en France, 1944–1945," in *L'Histoire*, 5 (1978), 24–32; Jean-Pierre Rioux, *La France de la Quatrième République*, 2 vols., vol 1: *L'ardeur et la nécessité, 1944–1952* (Paris, 1980), 49–50.
8. Cf. Rousso, *Vichy* (see note 6), 496–97. One source of error is the comparison between the mapping of absolute data points (the number of summary executions) and relative data points (the criminal prosecutions). Another is the comparison of the summary executions with the total number of criminal prosecutions (about 150,000), rather than simply with the death sentences (2,861).
9. This refers to the representation of civil war, rather than the reality of the war itself, because France did not experience any true fratricidal war upon liberation; cf. Philippe Buton, "La Francia della Liberazione e la guerra civile," in *Memoria e ricerca*, 21 (2006), 101–11.
10. For further thoughts cf. Buton, *La Joie douloureuse* (see note 2) and Buton, "La memoria collettiva francese della seconda guerra mondiale, crisi d'identità e consolidamento democratico," in *Ventunesimo Secolo*, 7 (2005), 61–81.

Chapter 12

THE AIR WAR, THE PUBLIC, AND CYCLES OF MEMORY

Dietmar Süß

I.

Memory is a contested good: it is valuable and vulnerable, it transforms and deforms itself, it can adapt to new conditions, become blurred or experience unimagined upswings – as did memory of the air war. Since the 1990s, and especially since Jörg Friedrich's bestseller "The Fire: The Bombing of Germany, 1940–1945,"[1] practically no other topic has left a stronger mark on the public landscape of memory in Germany than the debate about the Allied air raids on German cities.[2] The lines of tension between individual experiences of the war and collective memory of the war came to the fore distinctly, showing how strongly the interpretation of the Second World War has shaped, and will continue to shape, the political culture of divided and now unified Germany. Some of these connecting lines will be at the center of this chapter, which explores the semantics of the air war, its public presence and codification, as well as the different narratives that connect the war years with the postwar period. For this reason, the first step will be to discuss the meaning of the air war for the public during the dictatorship, and attention will be focused on propaganda and National Socialist perception of the crisis. Finally, in a second step, the different narratives that structured the cycles of the culture of memory of the air war after 1945, and that tied the war years and the postwar period together, will be examined.

Notes for this chapter begin on page 193.

II.

For National Socialist propaganda and communications policy, the air war was one of the central challenges.[3] The Allied bombs made the war into an event that was public in every respect in the Reich and whose risks were difficult for the regime to assess. In addition to state-controlled spaces and forms of public exercise of power, informal forums emerged for gathering and exchanging information, expressing opinions, and forming rumors about the air war that were less subject to tight control. The bunker could be such a place, as well as the trains with evacuees on the long journey from Westphalia to Upper Bavaria, the homes to which children from the city were evacuated, but also the cemeteries and burial ceremonies, or the lines of people waiting in front of the War Damage Agencies where the regime and the general public negotiated about the amount of compensation.

When we speak of "the public sphere" in the dictatorship, it seems to be a contradiction at first glance; after all, the concept of "the public sphere" belongs to the normatively connoted core elements of a civil, bourgeois, enlightened society – nothing less than the opposite of the National Socialist reign of terror against freedom of opinion. But even in dictatorships such as National Socialism, there were spaces and (partly) public spheres beyond the reach of the Party's instructions to the press and staged mass rallies. In particular the air war created such new zones within which there were struggles about power and representation and which were of decisive importance for the stability of the regime. In this respect, propaganda was not a one-way street, but also a response and a reaction to changing needs and moods.

For this reason, generating "trust" and reducing the distance within the vertical relationship between leadership and the general public were major goals of National Socialist policy. Both together were responses to the increasing pressure to legitimize the air war, unknown up until then, and its destructive effects. From the regime's point of view, "trust" had a dual meaning. Firstly, the regime aimed to achieve the public's subordination under the trusteeship of the political leadership: the public was to place itself in the leadership's custody and to submit to its unconditional authority.[4] "Trust in the responsible authorities"[5] – that was what the regime demanded during the air war. Questions were unwelcome, as was neighborly, horizontal exchange about what people had seen or heard, and any exchange was to take place only with the authorities responsible for it, with public notices informing people what the agencies' responsibilities were. Whoever did not develop trust in the power of the regime's air defense, whoever did not follow the instructions of the air-raid wardens or did not want to muster the publicly practiced and practically declared belief in the leadership was part of the "society of mistrust" (Jan C. Behrends) on which the National Socialist state had declared war.

From the regime's perspective, soliciting trust appeared to be a necessary precondition for the "stability of the home front."[6] This included, for example, publications disseminating detailed information about rescue plans and above all about the policy of compensation, and which emphasized that although the regime did demand sacrifices, it also spread the burdens and wanted to ensure material compensation. In addition to the propagandistic orchestration of high-ranking officials' visits to areas endangered by the air war, the practice of insurance against damages in the event of attacks was an important element of generating trust.[7] At the same time, and this was the second part of the policy of trust, the regime responded to the air raids with a sweeping expansion of societal monitoring and control agencies to observe the public mood, thereby creating a basis for decisions regarding sanctions or priorities for propaganda in the air war. In the eyes of the National Socialist leadership and following the estimation of the *Sicherheitsdienst* (SD, security services), this was necessary because the first bombing raids upset the public considerably and engendered substantial loss of trust, although they had caused only minor material damages. There was talk of an "atmosphere of panic,"[8] of the public's "anxiety psychosis," and its "wearing down in mind and body" in the affected areas in the west and north of the Reich. In total, there was said to be a drop in the "joy of working"[9] and higher production losses of up to 30 to 45 percent in some businesses. The workers were overtired, resulting in accidents, as the observers of the SD noted.[10] When the anticipated successes in the air offensive against England had not materialized, the SD registered an increasing loss of trust in the leadership of the *Luftwaffe*.[11] In particular Hermann Göring's grandiose proclamations, even just before the war, that the Ruhr area would not be subject to even a single bomb from enemy airplanes,[12] were still vivid in people's memories in the affected areas when the first air-raid sirens sounded and the bombings began.[13] There was a distinct discrepancy between people's experiences and their expectations – even if this was a local phenomenon at first. Where air raids took place, false alarms, delayed signals, a lack of protection, and difficulties in coordinating local authorities quickly caused a loss of respect, as the SD noted with alarm in the summer of 1940. The people had responded to a raid on northern and western Germany with displeasure and "criticism" precisely because there had been no public air-raid warnings and the anti-aircraft guns had responded much too late. There was also talk of "bitterness" and a lack of discipline which would arise in the event that the administrative failure of government and military authorities became obvious and – as in the case of blue-collar workers in Aachen – could even lead them to threaten to go on strike if the air defenses did not work more efficiently.[14]

III.

Rumors, which the Nazi leadership increasingly picked up since the beginning of the war, were a clear indication of disturbances in the relationships of trust in the eyes of the regime. In this respect, the air war was still a local event in early 1940. After all, stories about it circulated mostly in narrowly delimited spaces, in places where, as in Wilhelmshaven, initial raids had taken place, but where the regional press had not reported about them at all or in an obviously grossly falsifying way. Since early summer of 1940, after Allied aircraft had flown over cities almost on a daily basis and had also conducted the first air raids by day, reports about damages and impending losses became more frequent in the Rhineland and Westphalia. For example, the SD reported from Dortmund and Münster, where people had talked excitedly about possible future British bombings, that five thousand airplanes were rumored to be available to bomb the Ruhr area. But not only that: gas, too, was to be employed. "These rumors," the SD's analysis read, "are ... extraordinarily widespread and are repeated everywhere in the streetcars, trains, in stores, and in the street."[15]

Rumors of this type, which were began spreading in the autumn of 1940 and kept gaining importance until 1942, and whose reach gradually grew beyond the confines of a local area, displayed five characteristics: [16] firstly, the rumors predicted the next raid; secondly, they named a possible date for the bombing; thirdly, time and again, they named British leaflets or "enemy radio" as their source of information; fourthly, they used signal words such as "major offensive" or the precise number of enemy bombers to describe the dimensions of what was to come, and fifthly, they included direct or indirect references to the shortcomings of air-raid protection – a problem which became evident not least regarding the issue of evacuating children to the country. The regime's plan to evacuate all children between three and fourteen years of age from Berlin and other cities threatened by the air war had triggered a kind of shock wave,[17] resulting in the wildest stories (about impending poison-gas attacks and mass raids) getting out of control and causing "practically the strongest alarm on the part of Berlin's population since the beginning of the war."[18]

The rumors reflected the attempts of the general public to grasp the future in their discourse. In the stories and exaggerations about air raids, people struggled for a language and terms to describe what was to come, which diverged so much from what they had known before the war. At the same time, these rumors served to create a form of prognostic security by fitting the future bombing raids into the system of coordinates of what could be conceived of and uttered, including the description of future targets which, like Augsburg and Munich, did not yet belong to the British bomber pilots' regular points of attack in 1941.[19] While these rumors were about the future, others attempted to describe the past. This referred above all to estimates and interpretations of raids that had already taken place, the size of the bomber squadrons or the figures referring to damages and casualties.[20] The attempt to structure events of the past after the fact and to adapt them to people's expectations fulfilled at least two functions in this way. Firstly, retrospectively giving the problem a dimension established a connection between the past and the future of the air war. Quantifying it produced a yardstick for people's experiences of the violence and simultaneously opened up the horizon for what was yet to come. Secondly, the quest for the effects of the air raids was also a response to the shortcomings of the regime's communications and its media "restraint" following bombings. Goebbels had rightly recognized the dangers of the "policy of silence" when he noted after an air raid on Berlin in September 1941: "I will ensure that we will now regularly provide the population with a clear overview of the damages sustained and especially of the numbers of deaths on the day after every air raid. That is necessary to prevent opening the floodgates for untenable rumors; and as is generally known, the rumors always go beyond the facts."[21]

In fact, the magnitude and reach of the rumors increased markedly since the first carpet bombings began in 1942, with the raids on Lübeck, Rostock, and Cologne, the day raid on Augsburg, and the first heavy bombings of Hamburg, Saarbrücken, and Nuremberg. After the raid on Lübeck in late March 1942, which had primarily destroyed numerous residential areas, SD informants reported not only about the "great dismay" on the part of the general public. They also observed rumors going around about enormous losses of an "unprecedented"[22] magnitude which had, as they said, triggered "great unease" in large parts of the Reich. The SD also noted a similar development after the "1000 bomber raid" on Cologne in late May. Estimates about its aftermath – above all about the number of deaths – were circulating which, as the SD believed, had nothing to do with the real figures.[23] The number of bombers that had been shot down served as the basis for estimating the number of British pilots, resulting in a basis for forecasting future raids.[24] As the air raids increased, it was obviously even more important to develop communication-based coping strategies, which, however, threatened to lag behind the events, thereby developing a dynamic of their own. This explains the increase of rumors oriented towards future events, which were ever more difficult for the regime to get under control and which starkly revealed the tension between the supply of and the demand for information. The more difficult it was to get an overview of the course of the war in light of the publicly reglemented and propagandistically loaded generation of information, the more the paths of informal communication broadened. The National Socialist regime attempted to employ intensive propaganda to counter these developments which were dangerous from its point of view. Goebbels was able to celebrate his, if you will, greatest and also his last victory by spinning Dresden as a "catastrophe."[25] In January 1945, the Ministry of Propaganda initiated another attempt to put "the Allies' strategic air war" on the international agenda via the German diplomatic missions. Germany was to appear as the victim of long-term plans of the Allies to annihilate the country, whose response in defense was merely appropriate to its own plight. This interpretation was also accompanied by another motive that had been used more and more frequently ever since the beginning of the war: the air war as a symbol of cultural barbarism which at its core amounted to the destruction of European and occidental values. Even as the diplomatic missions were beginning to place these messages in the European countries, the Allies bombed Dresden in a large-scale air offensive on the night of 13 February 1945. Just one day later, on 15 February – news of the dramatic aftermath of the raid on the metropolis on the Elbe River which had caused around twenty-five thousand deaths had by then reached the Reich's public authorities in Berlin – the *Deutsches Nachrichtenbüro* (the official press agency of the Third Reich) disseminated the National Socialist interpretation of the raid, acting on behalf of the Ministry of Propaganda. The pattern of argument determined the guidelines for the last months of the war.[26] The terror attack against the European art metropolis Dresden was the latest piece of evidence proving that the Allies were in the end concerned only with annihilating and eradicating the Germans, but not with achieving military goals. Mustering its last ounce of strength, the propaganda machinery appealed to the inner strength of the *Volksgemeinschaft* (community of the people) and the public's will to persevere; after all, if this war were lost, then in the final analysis that could only mean the irrevocable demise of the nation. In the reports that were issued directly following Dresden, the forms of language with which the regime attempted to determine the framework for interpretation and speaking changed. This applied less to the agitation against the "Allied air gangsters" than to the reports about the air raid itself.

Not least because of international reporting, Dresden had become the symbol of the destructive force and the technical precision of Allied air raids within a very short period of time. In fact, the raid had not been planned as an exemplary annihilation strike,[27] but nonetheless, the commentaries and reports in Europe and overseas reinforced Dresden's outstanding position for Allied warfare within a few days.[28] It was above all the neutral Swedish press, also guided by the German censorship agencies, that published news providing information about the extent of the destruction. There was talk of "tremendous sacrifice[s] of human lives," of the tragedy of a city, of the plight of the refugees who had been in the city at the time of the air raid, and of a seemingly infinite number of deaths. Citing confidential sources, the newspaper *Svenska Morgenbladet* reported on 17

February 1945 of one hundred thousand deaths out of the approximately 2.5 million people who had allegedly been in the city. Other newspapers, including American ones, took up these figures and discussed more and more often the unimaginable force of destruction, and the uniqueness of an Allied raid that had reduced a European city to rubble. Now, the air raid on Dresden no longer appeared to be a military strike among many, but rather as the epitome of the catastrophe of war. While the military and strategic motives were given less and less prominence in the reports, the focus was now above all on the aspect of destruction. Shortly thereafter, the *Svenska Dagbladet* finally reported the newest estimates of the numbers of deaths in Dresden: almost two hundred thousand victims.[29] That figure was in the public realm from that point on, probably based not least on the reports of interested German propaganda authorities, and from there, it was disseminated further as evidence of the Allied air raids being acts of terror. Finally, the Allies themselves played into Goebbels's hands: a report by the AP news agency on 16 February that had not been stopped by the censorship authorities discussed a press conference in the headquarters of the Allied expeditionary forces during which there was talk of a change in strategy on the part of the Allied air force command following the air raid on Dresden. The "intentional terrorist bombing of German population centers" was supposedly at the center of the new approach as well as the uncompromising use of all means available.[30] While the Allies did attempt to stop and deny the report, once it was in the public realm, it seemed to confirm precisely what Goebbels had emphasized before time and again.

In contrast, neither the number of victims nor the large flows of refugees were mentioned at this point in time in German radio and press communications. Instead, they focused more on vague allusions to the extent of the destruction which were soon breached by informal communication networks, refugees, and evacuees, just as had occurred after the air raids on Hamburg. Up until the spring of 1945, those official accounts of the air war that appealed most of all to the Germans' thirst for revenge, their willingness to make sacrifices, and the unbroken solidarity of the *Volksgemeinschaft* predominated. Robert Ley's outburst of fury in a foaming commentary in the *Angriff* took the same line.[31] The air war, begun by "mercenaries of the Jews," had made "half the nation penniless" and destroyed one of the "most valuable jewel[s]," the artistic and peaceful Dresden. Similar to Hitler before him, Ley attempted to reinterpret the aftermath of the bombing war as a part of the National Socialist revolution that was, in the final analysis, useful – anti-Semitic agitation and bloody rhetoric of perseverance going hand in hand.

Goebbels considered this type of publicly propounded cynicism propagandistically devastating in light of the catastrophic situation. In contrast, his response, and that of the Ministry of Propaganda, tried to emphasize other points that diverged substantially from the previous wordings of the accounts of the bombing war. They tried to take up the advantages they had gained from the international reporting about the destruction of the cultural metropolis on the Elbe. On 4 March, a contribution by Rudolf Sparing appeared in the *Reich*, titled "The Death of Dresden,"[32] which in an unusually open manner analyzed the large-scale Allied air raid and differed from previous reporting in many ways. The article took up what had been circulating for quite some time in the foreign press, namely the assumption that the destruction of Dresden had been unique, something that differed in its effect from other bombings and therefore merited special attention. For this reason, Sparing made no secret about the "Dresden catastrophe" in his account – on the contrary, he strove to report in a largely "realistic," at least understandable and credible way. This included using language that differed from Ley's acrid tirade not least by the fact that it presented criticism of the Allies without foaming at the mouth. Sparing's portrayals of the air raid were so detailed that everyone, even those who had heard only rumors about the destruction, could imagine it – without panicking, but at the same time with a feel for the vehemence of the bombing and the extent of suffering that the civilian population had to endure. In this case, different strategies were to help compensate for the otherwise so very serious lack of credibility and trust of National Socialist propaganda: this included quantifying the number of refugees and inhabitants, put together, at approximately one million people, which by no means seemed exaggerated. But it also included talking about death in the "firestorm," about the anonymous mass graves and the large number of corpses which could not be identified. However, in contrast to the propaganda disseminated abroad, domestic propaganda in the Reich succeeded in conveying the unique qualities of the event without stating concrete numbers of victims. Sparing did not place heroic death at the center of his description, as National Socialist propaganda had attempted to do so obtrusively and for so long, but rather individual death, neighborly helpfulness, the sighted lending helping hands to the blind, the "civilian population's power of self-assertion." The home front held up – that was the message, even if it was conveyed much more subtly than before.

Taking in the entire situation, Sparing noted the things his readers themselves experienced on a daily basis: "For millions, going down to the basement is part of the daily routine, being bombed out has become an episode of the war or of its coolly deliberated contingencies." And still, he implied, the Allied raid on Dresden had been different from all previous ones. For it showed what would happen if "occidental culture [was] surrendered self-destructively." He drew a direct line from the Allies' strategy of avoiding outlawing air raids at the level of international law to the orgy of annihilating culture. "An urban silhouette displaying perfect harmony has been erased from the sky over Europe." Dresden, the symbol of European culture, the "trustee of occidental common property," had been annihilated and fallen victim to Anglo-American cynicism and the air war's spiral of violence. Within a few weeks, it was as if Dresden had become a codeword for the senselessness of war and the dissolution of any boundaries on war in National Socialist propaganda; the symbol of a unique catastrophe, of a gargantuan, lightning-like, technical explosion of what was feasible, a senseless destruction of occidental civilization that was by no means justifiable militarily;[33] a moral bargaining chip which the regime likely wanted to use to its own benefit not only in the last months of agony, but also during the postwar period and the discussion to be expected then regarding the responsibility for starting the war as well as war crimes. At the same time, the Wehrmacht's propaganda initiated a final attempt to stigmatize the Allies as cowardly sadists because of the air raid, as the city had become a huge refugee camp after the advance of the Red Army and bombing the innocent people had become an "eternal monument for this valiant deed of a chivalrous American officer and man of honor."[34] The longer the war had lasted, the more difficult it had become for the National Socialist regime to conduct the struggle for the general public's support in the dictatorship with means other than violence and agitation. Nonetheless, the orchestration of the Dresden catastrophe was the regime's last, perhaps also one of its most effective successes – so effective that in the postwar period, central narrative structures of the air war could be traced back to its leitmotifs with their substantial interpretive power, and they are still powerful in their effects down to the present day.

IV.

Especially in the debate about Jörg Friedrich's book mentioned at the outset, it was possible to recognize the seminal influence and explosive power of these narratives concerning the culture of memory. At first, it was the book's clever presentation in the media as a breaker of taboos which caught the public's attention. Friedrich's book was – at least, this was how large segments of the population interpreted it – a kind of psychosocial exoneration of the repressed German subconscious. The trauma of the bombing war had allegedly needed an incubation period of almost sixty years until it could be articulated in public, no longer only in the war generation's narrations at home. Filling this "blank space" and writing about the air war in the passive – i.e., victims' – voice, for the first time after many a long year – that was what it was all about for Friedrich, as he said himself, and for which he received so much applause.

However, it rapidly became apparent that the air war was certainly no "taboo" of German history, on the contrary: the "air war as a taboo" itself was part of a cycle of the culture of memory and a movement seeking a culture of memory. For example, recent research has examined very precisely how elastically the memory of the air war in Hamburg and Kassel could be adapted to the present – and not only in secret or in private, but definitely also in the public sphere. In Hamburg, for example, memory of the "Operation Gomorrah," the air raids in late July 1943 which cost about forty thousand people their lives, was made into an important propagandistic tool for integration even during the war. This memory was supposed to help conceal the upheavals and fault lines within a society among the ruins. The "narrative of the persevering community,"[35] as Malte Thießen described it, was a central leitmotif from 1945 into the 1960s in the city governed by Social Democrats. The main emphasis of the commemoration ceremonies was to underline that the people of Hamburg had not lost their courage and their will to resist in the nights of terror of the Allied bombing raids. On the contrary, they had braved the catastrophe and had joined forces with one another in solidarity, transcending class boundaries, to overcome adversity – just as was to be done now: people standing together after 1945, dedicated to reconstruction, rolling up their sleeves and removing the ruins of the war. "The survivors did not give up," the newspaper *Harburger Anzeiger* stated ceremoniously in 1963, praising the "unbroken Hanseatic will to live."[36] In the same vein, the daily *Hamburger Morgenpost* concluded a multi-week series about the air war with the defiant statement that the Allies had "not achieved any of their goals": "Neither did the German people rise up against the Nazi government nor did [the Allies] succeed in shattering production."[37]

In this interpretation, the air war was considered a symbol of modern warfare and of what modern societies were capable of doing – an idea that was anything but reassuring in light of the Cold War. In the final analysis, the raids had proven only that all wars were senseless and bound to fail due to the strength of the people's will to persevere – this message was also to be heard in speeches by the mayors of other major German cities.[38] Since the 1950s, numerous city chronicles and memoirs had documented the image of the Germans as a people with a common destiny, fighting in solidarity and making sacrifices. Even early on in appeals printed in newspapers, the goal was to create a space for personal stories of loss and suffering and for the reports about individual cases of destruction, death, and pain, and about experiences of nights spent in air-raid shelters. There was an additional motive which also found expression in numerous later publications on the history of the air war: the heroic defensive struggle of local functionaries against the external threat.[39] Using the example of the jointly experienced proverbial baptism by fire in the struggle against the incendiary bombs, it was shown that the municipal authorities had done everything in their power to prevent worse things from happening. This was a source of a certain kind of self-confidence, even pride in people's joint achievement which was now continued in reconstruction.[40] At the same time, this story about the heroism of the defensive struggle permitted people to distance themselves offensively from National Socialism. After all, in the end it was National Socialism that had been responsible for the problems and shortcomings of civil defense, at least if one believes the municipal functionaries' carefully ordered reports up until today. In general, however, National Socialism played at most a marginal role in the "documents of German war damages" and in other publications of the 1970s and 1980s – and if it was mentioned at all, then only as the cause of administrative chaos or as a point of reference from which one desired to distance oneself. In doing so, the "German people" are on one side and Hitler, at times Goebbels as well, on the other. The lines of continuity of this self-victimization all the way to Jörg Friedrich and other local memoirs, which were thrown on the market in the boom running up to the sixtieth anniversary of the bombing of Dresden, are particularly striking.[41] These lines are: the exclusion of the air war from the history of the National Socialist regime; the reduction of the relationship between municipality and party to just a history of conflict; the dominance of the history of victims and losses; and the perception of the air war as a fundamentally barbarian, failed, Anglo-American act of transgression in the "total war's" battle of annihilation – an understanding that determined the perception and official models of interpretation of the GDR, albeit based on somewhat different premises.[42]

In West Germany, at least two further narratives overlapped. Firstly, this refers to the connection between the histories of the destruction and the reconstruction of the city and "homeland."[43] The individual stories of suffering often were upstaged in favor of a history of urban redesign on the ruins of the bombed homeland. The histories of the downfall and the West German success story often melded to create a new narrative of the rebirth of the "old city" as a symbol of progress and renewal.[44] The "old city" was the innocent, so to speak, urban landscape before its destruction from the air; that was medieval alleys, lively marketplaces, and tall church spires, scenic idylls and social order that had defied the centuries and had gone down only because of the vehemence of the Allied destruction. Therefore, "reconstruction" had two meanings. On the one hand, it was a symbol of the power of resistance on the part of the local people's community with a common destiny, a processing of "death," and part of the handing down of local – not necessarily National Socialist – identity beyond the caesura of the year 1945. On the other hand, it was also possible for the narration of urban reconstruction to be a positive point of reference for a new urban search for meaning which sought to integrate the heritage of the war and the material loss into the present. In Munich, one could observe this process not least in the fact that the new symbol of West German openness was built on the ruins of the bombing war: the site of the 1972 Olympic

Games. A cross commemorated the fact that the new had emerged from the ruins of the bombed city of Munich, and at the same time, it enjoined people to promote peace and reconciliation in the present – the memory and the consequences of the bombing war had thereby become part of an active policy of peace in the context of the East-West conflict.[45]

Secondly, beginning in the mid 1980s, a new interpretation gained the upper hand, following Richard von Weizsäcker's famous speech on the occasion of the fortieth anniversary of the end of the war and placing the motive of the end of the war as "liberation" at the center. The bombing war appeared to become nothing less than the prerequisite for the "liberation of Germany." In Hamburg, on the occasion of the 1993 speech to commemorate "Operation Gomorrah," First Mayor Henning Voscherau emphasized the necessity of the air raids, which he now presented as the precondition for the new beginning in 1945, no longer as the burden to be borne by it. He asked the rhetorical question, "If the Allies had not found the courage and the determination to counter National Socialist violence with violence, to fight down the 'Third Reich' with many sacrifices, would liberation, would renewal and a free, democratic future have been possible?"[46]

As early as the 1990s, the motif of the air war as a "taboo" of German history had emerged – a rhetorical figure which itself was an expression of a cycle of the culture of memory. Even before Jörg Friedrich, literary scholar W.G. Sebald had initiated the debate. His provocative thesis on the history of the effects of the bombing war was:[47] German postwar literature had "never really come to grips with"[48] the destructions of the Allied carpet bombings and had contributed to the fact that "the images of this gruesome chapter of our history had never really stepped across the threshold of the national consciousness."[49] Sebald called the repression of the horrors a "scandalous shortcoming"[50] for which not only the writers of the young Federal Republic were to blame, but also serious historical scholarship. Both disciplines had been unable "to sound out the depths of traumatization in the souls of those who came from the epicenters of the catastrophe."[51]

There is much to be said for the idea that the "taboo motif" was not least the response of the war generation to its dwindling place in the public realm.[52] It was often the memoirs of the war children, masses of which were published, that gave the debate momentum. The quickly compiled collections of individual stories about nights of bombings, evacuations, and the fates of anti-aircraft helpers, which had been encouraged above all by newspaper editors, were often designed in a very similar way, bundling and stringing together the most varied fragments of memories without comment.[53] The descriptions range from people's experiences in the air-raid shelters and their deep traumatization which can still be sensed more than sixty years later and which led the people to the verge of breaking down, to memories of people buried by collapsing buildings, losses of family members, the bombing war as a youthful "adventure," and to precise descriptions of the racial exclusion and the hierarchization of life in the air-raid shelters. The contributions are far from being methodically reflected oral history. Most of these eyewitness reports should therefore be read as attempts to give things meaning at the local level, where the urban catastrophe appears as a part of the Allied violence of war which was becoming more radicalized – without, however, also integrating the character and impulse of the German war of annihilation and the radicalizing forms of exclusion in the city's memory.[54] It fits well with this that new "heroic epics" of survival were placed alongside the narratives of victims and horrors, epics that praised above all the struggle against the fire and the havoc that the "party" had wrought when quenching the flames.[55] However, pointing to the generational change of the bearers of memory and the transition from communicative to collective memory should explain just one, albeit an important, part of the transformation of the culture of memory.

When one asks why this topic concerned the general public and not only the small circle of intellectuals, at least two more reasons surely play a role: firstly, the return of war. Since the early 1990s, reunified Germany has had to concern itself with the question of participating in a war not just once, but several times. The apparently so silent and accurate "clean war" waged from the air played an important role, as did the criticism of American military doctrine and its attempts to mislead the public about the success or failure of its strategy. Secondly, the way the media conveyed the "breaking of the taboo," the spiral of how it was orchestrated publicly, and the competitions of images and television stations spurred the debate in very significant ways and determined the rules of the debate. This includes above all a combination of scandalization and voyeurism for which the bombing war with its suffering and mass deaths provided an outstanding sounding board, thus lending itself as a topic to be conveyed to younger viewers via their viewing habits.

V.

It should have become clear that the memory of the air war and the history of its reception after 1945 are a mirror and a catalyst of cycles of the culture of memory which provide a precise image of the Germans' ways of dealing with National Socialist history. This includes very different and overlapping narratives, ranging, for example, from "downfall" and "reconstruction," "homeland" and "people with a common destiny," "destruction of culture," and admonition for peace in the context of the Cold War, to the interpretation of the air war as a prerequisite for the liberation of Germany from National Socialism, which has gained currency since the late 1980s and early 1990s. At the same time, one should not take the easy way out regarding the narrative of the air war as a "taboo" of German history, at least where it is not about obviously new myths of victimhood. It makes a lot of sense to take the "privatization of the consequences of war"[56] seriously as an important branch in the history of the aftermath of National Socialism and to ask questions about actually unspoken wartime experiences with which people "have not come to terms." After all, we still know very little about which forms of traumatization people suffered in the air-raid shelters, with the constant wailing of sirens, people buried beneath collapsing buildings, and the sight of corpses and people burned to death, and which long-term psychological consequences these experiences brought about. Some of those harmed by the air war suffered permanent harm that was never recognized as such, much less was compensated for – and whose diagnosis was often made by the same physicians who during the National Socialist period had either deemed them "capable of fighting" for the *Volksgemeinschaft* in spite of their illnesses or had labeled them "antisocial" and "feeble."[57] In particular the connection between traumatization, medical diagnosis, and familial communication should prove to be a broad area for future research. This holds all the more for the attempt to view the air war as part of a transnational, global history of violence in the twentieth century.[58] How the experience of war and the memory of war can appropriately be related to one another when taking such a perspective is still an open question, as is the one as to the extent to which the concept of "total war" can carry weight.[59] Can it really make the different national variants of the socialization of violence, the processes of inclusion and exclusion, the glorification and technicization of the practice of violence, and the indifference vis-à-vis the victims' suffering associated with these phenomena understandable?[60] And how can we succeed in integrating killing and dying as well as the fear of losing life and property in a history of "total war"? A history of the air war, expanded to include these questions and that does not cling tightly to 1945 as the end of the epoch, thereby combining the histories of war experiences and war memories marked by violence with one another, has every opportunity of giving new impetus to the debate about the future of the social and cultural history of the war.[61]

Notes

1. Jörg Friedrich, *Der Brand. Deutschland im Bombenkrieg 1940–1945* (Munich, 2002), in English translation: *The Fire: The Bombing of Germany, 1940–1945* (New York, 2006), c.f.

for example Dietmar Süß, *Tod aus der Luft: Gewalt, militärische Eskalation und die Kulturen des Krieges im 20. Jahrhundert* (in print).
2. Cf. Jörg Arnold, Dietmar Süß and Malte Thießen, eds., *Luftkrieg. Erinnerungen in Deutschland und Europa* (Göttingen, 2009)
3. A differently accentuated way of accessing the history of propaganda in the National Socialist state is chosen in the contributions by Aristotle Kallis, Jeffrey Herf, and Birthe Kundrus in *Die deutsche Kriegsgesellschaft 1939 bis 1945. Ausbeutung, Deutungen, Ausgrenzung*, commissioned by the Militärgeschichtliches Forschungsamt, ed. Jörg Echternkamp (Munich, 2005) (= Das Deutsche Reich und der Zweite Weltkrieg, 9/2).
4. On this, and regarding the communist dictatorships, cf. esp. Jan C. Behrends, "Soll und Haben. Freundschaftsdiskurs und Vertrauensressourcen in der staatssozialistischen Diktatur," in *Vertrauen. Historische Annäherungen*, ed. Ute Frevert (Göttingen, 2003), 338–66.
5. *National-Zeitung* of 17 May 1940, "Herr Meier meint: Da klappt was nicht!"
6. President of the *Oberlandesgericht* (higher regional court) Bamberg to *Reichsjustizministerium* (ministry of justice of the *Reich*), 28 October 1942, in Archive of the Institut für Zeitgeschichte, MA-430/1.
7. Cf. Dietmar Süß, "Nationalsozialistische Deutungen des Luftkrieges," in *Deutschland im Luftkrieg. Geschichte und Erinnerung*, ed. Dietmar Süß (Munich, 2007), 99–110.
8. *Meldungen aus dem Reich*, 8 July 1940, vol. 5, 1354.
9. *Meldungen aus dem Reich*, 4 July 1940, vol. 5, 1335.
10. *Meldungen aus dem Reich*, 11 July 1940, vol. 5, 1365.
11. *Meldungen aus dem Reich*, 20 July 1940, vol. 4, 1152.
12. Archiv der Gegenwart, 1939–1940, 4166; Olaf Groehler, *Der Bombenkrieg gegen Deutschland* (Berlin, 1990), 240–41.
13. *Meldungen aus dem Reich*, 4 July 1940, vol. 5, 1339.
14. *Meldungen aus dem Reich*, 10 June 1940, vol. 4, 1236; cf. Jörg Arnold, *Bombenkrieg und Kriegsmoral. Die Auswirkungen der alliierten Luftangriffe auf die Stimmung und Haltung der deutschen Zivilbevölkerung im Spiegel vertraulicher Berichte und privater Aufzeichnungen* (Zulassungsarbeit zum 1. Staatsexamen), Heidelberg University 2001, 37.
15. *Meldungen aus dem Reich*, 27 May 1940, vol. 4, 1176.
16. Following Franz Dröge, *Der zerredete Widerstand. Zur Soziologie und Publizistik des Gerüchts im 2. Weltkrieg* (Düsseldorf, 1970), 127.
17. Cf. Katja Klee, *Im "Luftschutzkeller des Reiches". Evakuierte in Bayern 1939–1953: Politik, soziale Lage, Erfahrungen* (Munich, 1999), 44–70; Gerhard Kock, *"Der Führer sorgt für unsere Kinder". Die Kinderlandverschickung im Zweiten Weltkrieg* (Paderborn et al., 1997).
18. *Meldungen aus dem Reich*, 30 September 1940, vol. 5, 1622.
19. Dröge (see note 16), 127; cf., among other sources, *Meldungen aus dem Reich*, vol. 7, 13 November 1941, 2963.
20. *Meldungen aus dem Reich*, 6 March 1941, vol. 6, 2075.
21. *Die Tagebücher von Joseph Goebbels*, ed. by Elke Fröhlich, 15 vols. (Munich, 1993 et seq.): part II, vol. 1 (Munich 1996): 3 September 1941, 364.
22. *Meldungen aus dem Reich*, 2 April 1942, vol. 10, 3567.
23. *Meldungen aus dem Reich*, 4 June 1942, vol. 10, 3787–88.
24. Cf., among other sources, *Meldungen aus dem Reich*, 30 July 1942, vol. 10, 4016.
25. Following Matthias Neutzner, "Vom Alltäglichen zum Exemplarischen," in *Das rote Leuchten. Dresden und der Bombenkrieg*, eds. Oliver Reinhard, Matthias Neutzner, and Wolfgang Hesse (Dresden, 2005), 12–14; extensively also Frederick Taylor, *Dresden. Dienstag, 13 Februar 1945: militärische Logik oder blanker Terror?* (Munich, 2004); Götz Bergander, "Vom Gerücht zur Legende. Der Luftkrieg über Deutschland im Spiegel von Tatsachen, Erlebter Geschichte, Erinnerung, Erinnerungsverzerrung" in *Geschichtsbilder. Festschrift für Michael Saleswki zum 65. Geburtstag*, eds. Thomas Stamm-Kuhlmann,

Jürgen Elvert, Birgit Aschmann, and Jens Hohensee (Stuttgart, 2003), 591–616, here 605–7.
26. "Deutsches Nachrichten Büro," 15 February 1945, in *Archiv des Instituts für Zeitgeschichte*, Z. 2095.
27. Extensively on Dresden, cf. Götz Bergander, *Dresden im Luftkrieg*, second, revised, and expanded edition (Weimar, 1994); Götz Bergander, "Vom unattraktiven zum besonders lohnenden Ziel," in Reinhard, Neutzner, and Hesse (see note 25), 44–57.
28. *New York Times*, 15 February 1945: "Ten Cities Bombed"; *The Times*, 18 February: "Bombing Policy Stated"; *Washington Star*, 19 February 1945: "Terror Bombing".
29. *Svenska Dagblatt*, 25 February 1945, quoted in: *Dokumente deutscher Kriegsschäden*, 2 Beiheft 469.
30. Michael S. Sherry, *The Rise of American Air Power* (New Haven, 1987), 261–63; Ronald Schaffer, *Wings of Judgment* (New York, 1985), 95–103; Tami Davids Biddle, "Wartime Reaction," in *Firestorm. The Bombing of Dresden, 1945*, eds. Paul Addison and Jeremy A. Crang (London, 2006), 96–122, here 106–8.
31. *Der Angriff*, 3 March 1943.
32. *Das Reich*, 4 March 1945.
33. Cf. Neutzner (see note 25), 126–27.
34. Quoted in ibid., 124.
35. Malte Thießen, "Gedenken an die 'Operation Gomorrha'. Hamburgs Erinnerungskultur und städtische Identität," in Süß (see note 7), 121–31, 123–25; The following also ibid. Cf. Malte Thießen, *Eingebrannt im Gedächtnis. Hamburgs Gedenken an Luftkrieg und Kriegsende 1943–2005* (Munich, 2007).
36. *Harburger Anzeiger und Nachrichten* on 27 July 1963: "Vor 20 Jahren sank Hamburg unter dem Bombenhagel in Schutt und Asche," quoted in Thießen, Gedenken (see note 35), 124.
37. *Hamburger Morgenpost*: "Als der Himmel brannte" (ninetenth part of the series), 10 June 1963, quote in ibid.
38. Convincing, esp. for the example of Kassel, Jörg Arnold, "'Krieg kann nur der Wahnsinn der Menschheit sein!' Zur Deutungsgeschichte des Luftangriffs vom 22. Oktober 1943 in Kassel," in Süß (see note 7), 135–49.
39. Cf. Erich Hampe, *Der zivile Luftschutz im Zweiten Weltkrieg. Dokumentation und Erfahrungsberichte über Aufbau und Einsatz* (Frankfurt/M., 1963); Georg Wolfgang Schramm, *Der zivile Luftschutz in Nürnberg 1933–1945*, 2 vols. (Nuremberg, 1983); Hans Brunswig, *Feuersturm über Hamburg. Die Luftangriffe auf Hamburg im 2. Weltkrieg und ihre Folgen* (Stuttgart, 2003).
40. Regarding the term, cf. Thomas Kühne, "Die Viktimisierungsfalle. Wehrmachtsverbrechen, Geschichtswissenschaft und symbolische Ordnung des Militärs," in *Der Krieg in der Nachkriegszeit. Der Zweite Weltkrieg in Politik und Gesellschaft der Bundesrepublik*, eds. Michael Th. Greven and Oliver von Wrochem (Opladen, 2000), 183–96.
41. An overview is given by Jörg Arnold, "Sammelrezension Bombenkrieg," *Historische Literatur*, 2 (2004): 17–38 (http://hsozkult.geschichte.hu-berlin.de/rezension/ 2004-2-062).
42. Cf., among others, Gilad Margalit, "Der Luftangriff auf Dresden. Seine Bedeutung für die Erinnerungspolitik der DDR und für die Herauskristallisierung einer historischen Kriegserinnerung im Westen," in *Narrative der Shoah. Repräsentationen der Vergangenheit in Historiographie, Kunst und Politik*, eds. Susanne Düwell and Matthias Schmidt (Paderborn et al., 2002), 189–207.
43. Cf. esp. Arnold (see note 38), 140–42.
44. Ibid.

45. Cf. on Munich esp. the work by Gabriel D. Rosenfeld, *Munich and Memory: Architecture, Monuments, and the Legacy of the Third Reich* (Berkeley, 2000).
46. Quoted in Thießen (see note 35), 127.
47. Cf. on this issue Stephan Braese, "Bombenkrieg und literarische Gegenwart: zu W.G. Sebald und Dieter Forte," *Mittelweg 36*, 11, no. 1 (2002/03): 4–24.
48. Winfried G. Sebald, *Luftkrieg und Literatur. Mit einem Essay zu Alfred Andersch* (Munich/Vienna, 1999), 18.
49. Ibid., 19.
50. Ibid., 82.
51. After being accepted initially, this interpretation was also criticized sharply, cf. esp. Volker Hage, *Zeugen der Zerstörung. Die Literaten und der Luftkrieg* (Frankfurt/M., 2003), 113–31.
52. This is the convincing interpretation of Malte Thießen and Jörg Arnold.
53. Sven Felix Kellerhoff and Wieland Giebel, eds., *Als die Tage zu Nächten wurden. Berliner Schicksale im Luftkrieg* (Berlin, 2003); Nina Grotzki, Gerd Niewerth, and Rolf Potthoff, *Als die Steine Feuer fingen. Der Bombenkrieg im Ruhrgebiet* (Essen, 2003).
54. This applies especially to Egbert A. Hoffmann, *Als der Feuertod vom Himmel stürzte. Hamburg Sommer 1943* (Gudensberg-Gleichen, 2003).
55. Hans Brunswig, *Feuersturm über Hamburg* (Stuttgart, 2003).
56. Vera Neumann, *Nicht der Rede wert. Die Privatisierung der Kriegsfolgen in der frühen Bundesrepublik. Lebensgeschichtliche Erinnerungen* (Münster, 1999).
57. Especially Svenja Goltermann, *Die Gesellschaft der Überlebenden. Deutsche Kriegsheimkehrer und ihre Gewalterfahrungen im Zweiten Weltkrieg* (Stuttgart, 2009).
58. A new, interdisciplinary project is running at the Forschungsstelle für Zeitgeschichte in Hamburg.
59. Regarding a convincing implementation of the concept, see esp. Jörg Echternkamp, "Im Kampf an der inneren und äußeren Front. Grundzüge der deutschen Gesellschaft im Zweiten Weltkrieg," in *Die deutsche Kriegsgesellschaft 1939–1945. Politisierung, Vernichtung, Überleben*, commissioned by the Militärgeschichtliches Forschungsamt, ed. Jörg Echternkamp (Munich, 2004), 1–92 (= Das Deutsche Reich und der Zweite Weltkrieg, 9/1).
60. On this perspective, cf. esp. Heinrich Popitz, *Phänomene der Macht. Autorität, Herrschaft, Gewalt und Technik* (Tübingen, 1986).
61. For an overview, cf., among others, Jeremy Black, *Rethinking Military History* (London, 2004).

Chapter 13

THE LONG SHADOWS OF THE SECOND WORLD WAR:
The Impact of Experiences and Memories of War on West German Society

Axel Schildt

The Federal Republic of Germany is not past history; rather, in the unified Germany of post-1990, which retained the name Federal Republic with good reason, the history of the previous Bonn state remains of great interest and, given the country's search for a better future, as a point of orientation. This history has to be told to Germany's new citizens: the people of the former GDR and the many new migrants from different cultures. West Germans, in turn, must become aware of the histories of these new citizens, their new neighbours. In the process, it will be important to appreciate that West Germany has a historiography which discovered late, but not by chance, just how significant the experiences and memories of the Second World War have been in shaping its history. The recognition of these influences, which emerged from behind the processes of modernizing, liberalizing, and Westernizing the Federal Republic, especially since the late 1950s, add an important facet to our understanding of Germany's postwar history. For the history of the Federal Republic of Germany can only be understood fully if it is primarily seen as the history of a society that is trying to come to terms with its critical role in one of the worst wars humanity has ever experienced.

Ever since contemporary historians started to look systematically at German history after the Second World War,[1] the question of how the relationship between continuity and change in 1945 should be portrayed has been a major focus of interest. Tied up with this is the precise definition of the influence of the war on civil society in the postwar period. Until well into the 1970s a popular view of history prevailed in the Federal

---

Notes for this chapter begin on page 208.

Republic that was largely independent of historical research, and was determined by the political strategies of the Cold War. According to this view, Germany "collapsed" in 1945 and the Western part was then able, by the efforts of its own inhabitants but also with the help of the Western Allies, to rise like a phoenix from the ashes to the heady heights of democracy and prosperity. This master narrative of public memory did not sit comfortably with the topic of continuities: for instance, the fact that members of the elite from the period before 1945 lived on keeping their social status in the new era. It was not until the final phase of the "old" Federal Republic, when the Cold War had lost its dramatic character and new generations, who no longer had first-hand experience of the Third Reich, had taken the stage, that West German society was able to approach its own history with some sort of composure. And this meant talking about continuities without denying the abrupt break represented by 1945 in political terms. In an important volume of essays on the social history of the Federal Republic, published in 1983, whose subtitle (contributions to the problem of continuity) suggests a new perspective, the historian Werner Conze said that despite the deep political caesura at the end of the war, the "continuity of settlement (*Siedlungskontinuität*) formed the crucial bridge between past and present."[2] To put it more simply, although the political situation had changed radically, the people were still the same and had brought their biographies with them into the new era. This generational factor must always be taken into account when looking at postwar German society. Anyone who was a 65-year-old pensioner in 1950 had grown up in the Kaiserreich. Many of the men had already started their family life before the First World War and had gone on to fight in it. The middle phase of their lives was the interwar period. This generation of *Wilhelminer* played an important political part – one only has to think of Adenauer – because the next generation, those born around the turn of the century, were far more heavily tainted by their involvement with Nazism in the Third Reich.[3] Below the level of state leadership, however, this generation also played a major part in reconstruction after 1945. And amongst historians there is a broad consensus that an even younger generation clearly set the tone if we look at the history of the Federal Republic over a longer period, namely, the generation of the Hitler Youth, also known as the *Flakhelfer-Generation*. This refers to those born around 1930, who grew up under the Nazi regime and who, in the fanatical final battle at the end of the Second World War, were called to arms. Dirk Moses has labelled this generation the Forty-Fivers,[4] because completely new career opportunities opened up for its members in 1945, indeed, new perspectives for the whole structure of their lives. Politicians such as Helmut Kohl (born in 1930), philosophers such as Jürgen Habermas (also 1930), sociologists and historians such as Ralf Dahrendorf (1929) and Hans-Ulrich Wehler (1930), writers such as Hans Magnus Enzensberger

(1929) and Günter Grass (1927) all belong to this generation. Of course, the generational dimension does not explain everything because there are no homogeneous generations as active subjects, but their experiences must be taken into account as an important factor in the long shadow the war cast over the civilian society of the postwar period.[5] In any case, the discovery and discussion of biographical continuities was the prelude to professional contemporary historical research and offered a new approach to embedding the history of the Federal Republic into the history of the twentieth century.[6]

Contemporary historiography thus recognized something that the people had long known from their own experience. In the early 1960s Heinrich Böll (born in 1917) stated in an essay that the West Germans distinguished between the "bad" times and the "good" times, and did not see the turning point as 8 May 1945, but 20 June 1948, the day of the currency reform in West Germany.[7] In retrospect, for a large section of the population this day seemed to mark the end of the bad times, which included the end of the war and the early postwar years, in other words, the end of the period marked by suffering and the immediate consequences of the war.

In public memory, and, indeed, to a large extent in private memory too, 1945 was seen as a humiliating collapse, as Germany's darkest hour, and in the words of Friedrich Meinecke, the "German catastrophe," which, in turn, was followed by another dark period. A public opinion poll commissioned by the German federal government and conducted by the Institut für Demoskopie in Allensbach in 1951 asked: "When, do you feel, was Germany's best time in this century?" Forty-four percent of respondents replied that the Third Reich was Germany's best time, forty-three percent the Kaiserreich before the First World War, and only seven percent the Weimar Republic. Even further behind, with only two percent, was the "period after 1945." In fact, eighty percent named the postwar period as Germany's worst time, presumably thinking of what had happened to them personally.[8] In the popular view this was bound up with diverse memories of crises during the interwar period related to the bourgeois democracy of the 1920s and certainly not to the Nazi regime. During the phase of rapid armament before the Second World War, many had been able to keep their jobs, and new opportunities for advancement had opened up, especially for the young, all of which seemed to have been cut off abruptly by the outcome of the war. Admittedly, this view could be accompanied by a posthumous positive transfiguration of the Third Reich, but at its center was a private perspective from which the 1930s and 1950s soon came to be perceived as equally peaceful, happy times.[9] In 1985 Richard von Weizsäcker, the President of the Federal Republic, in a speech commemorating the end of the war, said for the first time that, without denying the feeling of collapse, Germany had also been liberated. This break with the traditional rules of speech in official memorial culture, especially as he also paid tribute for the first time to the Communist resistance and hitherto unmentioned victims of Nazism, gave rise to considerable public criticism at the time. Since then, however, it has largely been accepted in the differentiated form he put forward there.[10]

It is easy to see why the majority of contemporaries recalled the end of the war as a catastrophic collapse rather than a liberation. This does not apply, of course, to those released from prisons and concentration camps – Jews, those imprisoned for ideological reasons, and political prisoners – nor to those few who had worked for the end of the Nazi regime through illegal resistance or internal opposition to it. But at the end of the war the overriding emotion for most of the population was relief, often overlaid with apathy and fear, either specific or more abstract. Germany had lost the war. Nazi propaganda, which to the last had promised "final victory" and which many had believed in for a long time if not to the very end, had clearly been exposed as lies. National hubris was followed by a mood of moral depression. But all the same, at least the risk of dying a completely pointless soldier's death at the very end had gone. Of the more than 4 million German *Wehrmacht* soldiers killed, half had died in the last year of the war, and almost a quarter of them actually in the final battles of the last months. Families back home no longer had to fear that just before the end of the war they would see in the newspaper that their husband, brother, or father had died a hero's death for "Führer, Volk und Vaterland." Those born between 1906 and 1927 paid the highest price; among soldiers born in 1920, the death rate was 41.1 percent.[11]

Women, children, and old people in towns and cities who, since 1942–43, had spent countless nights in cellars and bunkers sheltering from Allied air raids, could breathe freely again. It has been estimated that Allied bombing raids killed up to half a million people; about 3 million people were wandering around rootless as evacuees; and about a quarter of the housing stock of the Western zones (in some of the major cities as much as three-quarters), including schools and hospitals, had been destroyed.[12] Simply not having to lie in bed fully clothed with emergency supplies for the air raid shelter close to hand, but being able to go to sleep without fear – this is described as a deeply felt relief in many personal testimonies.

The widespread apathy, confirmed by many observers, and the emotional paralysis of the German people which accompanied the relief can easily be traced back to the enormous stress of the war which, to the end, was conducted with brutal ruthlessness. The main feature of the final Nazi weekly newsreel was women being raped by Red Army soldiers and children being killed in East Prussia. They presaged the fate of the Germans after defeat. "Enjoy the war, peace will be dreadful," was the message whispered everywhere, one which the Nazi leadership used to try to take the whole population with them into the abyss of a final battle they could never win. Those who hung the white flag from their windows prematurely, or said that there was no longer any point in the war, risked being hanged from the nearest tree by units of the field police or the Gestapo, with a placard round their necks calling them "traitors." The last deserter was shot "according to orders" as late as 11 May 1945 in Flensburg at the command of the government that succeeded Hitler under Admiral Karl Dönitz and Lutz Graf Schwerin von Krosigk – by which time British troops were already in the town.[13]

Widespread fears amongst the people were initially caused by anticipation of draconian punishment, which even those who had not been embroiled in the crimes of the regime feared would come their way. It soon became clear, however, that the Allies were not going to impose "collective punishment" in their zones of occupation. Even the plans concocted during the second half of the war by Lord Robert Vansittart in Britain and Henry Morgenthau Jr. in the USA to transform Germany from an industrial society into a largely agricultural one as a measure against the danger of Prussian militarism, had, by the end of the war, already been consigned to the files by their respective governments.[14]

The families of the POWs were extremely concerned. After the inhumane treatment of Soviet prisoners in Germany in particular – at first they were left to starve, and then in the second half of the war they were exploited quite brutally as forced laborers – many expected a similar fate for the German POWs, 1.7 million of whom had survived the war. After the capitulation the number catapulted up to nine million, though all but two million of them had been released by the spring of 1947. Most of the remaining POWs were released by 1950. The gap between their conscription at the outbreak of war and their return to an uncertain future at home might have been as long as a decade.[15] Very often husbands and wives had become alienated; during the first five years after the war the divorce rate was extremely high. People often found it difficult to get close to their own children, and, if it happened at all, it was a very gradual process.

Another concern was the punishment of former Nazis. At the end of the war the Nazi Party had some 6 million members; the organization as a whole, including branches and associations, had many more. Condemnation of the "major war criminals" at the Nuremberg trials was largely accepted. After all, these were the prominent functionaries of the Third Reich. But the denazification undertaken by the Western Allies was highly unpopular with the people, partly because it was done so bureaucratically and disadvantaged the unimportant members and fellow-travelers (*Mitläufer*) who were dealt with first. The cases of the higher functionaries were generally decided later, and often dealt with leniently, with the result that there was talk of a "factory of fellow-travelers."[16] What is more, there was a widely held view that the victors, who had conducted the air war against the German civilian population, had no right to sit in judgement on Germans. This view, nowadays held only by those on the extreme Right, was that of the majority in the postwar years and was vigorously supported by prominent clergymen of both the major Christian denominations, in particular, Protestant bishops. In fact, however, considering the number of punishments, the degree of denazification was very modest. Out of a total of about 3.6 million trials, initially in Allied denazification courts and then in courts run by Germans, 1,667 people were given prison sentences or severe fines as "major criminals" and 23,000 as criminals, while 15,000 got away with small fines as minor accessories. The remaining ninety-five percent of the trials ended with the defendant either being classed as a "fellow-traveler" or exonerated, or else they were halted prematurely by amnesties. The Bundestag put a stop to it all for a decade with one of its first laws passed at the end of 1949, which meant that even serious Nazi criminals, including those who had committed manslaughter, could no longer be pursued by the courts.[17]

However, to assess denazification as a failure would be very superficial. The elites guilty of Nazi involvement saw the postwar period, when many were held in Allied internment camps for months or even years on "automatic arrest," as a life crisis. At the end of it came social integration, with roughly the same status as before the war, but it was understood as a warning not to get involved with the extreme Right again.[18] This corresponded to the main thrust of what Norbert Frei has called West German *Vergangenheitspolitik*. Offers of far-reaching social integration were combined with official stigmatization of the expression of Nazi or anti-Semitic views. The process of learning and assimilating was not difficult in the 1950s because personal social integration went along with the stabilization of parliamentary democracy as a model for success, economic recovery, and growing prosperity. But in 1945 this could not yet be foreseen.

In the immediate postwar period fears concerning collective punishment were combined with worries about survival in a situation of extreme hardship. It would, of course, be a total exaggeration to say that the Germans never lived as well as during the Second World War.[19] But the regime, by ruthlessly plundering the occupied territories, made sure that there was plenty of food on the Home Front, unlike in the First World War. At the beginning of the war, around 2,700 calories per day were given out to the German population and by the spring of 1945 it was still officially 2,100, though in many places supplies had dried up.

In the first year after the war the Allies imposed a ration of 1,500 calories per day for "normal consumers." No one could live on this in the long run, but meals for schoolchildren made possible by foreign aid in the Western zones at least, vegetables grown in community gardens, foraging trips by urban dwellers into the countryside to exchange jewelery, clothes, and other desirable items for food, or risky deals on the Black Market which, though obviously illegal, was tolerated, it was just about enough to survive on. The situation became dramatically more critical when, in the spring of 1946, rations in the US zone were reduced to 1,330 calories, in the British zone to 1,050 calories, and in the French zone to 900 calories per day. This was only about a third to a half of pre-war levels. Admittedly, there were no great plagues or epidemics as there had been after the First World War, largely because of the vaccinations immediately provided by the Allies. But the lack of adequate food, clothing, and shoes led to a general decline in the ability to work and an increased susceptibility to illness. The deterioration in the population's general health could also be attributed to the second great problem of the early postwar period, that is, a lack of fuel and lengthy electricity supply cuts during the very long and cold winters, especially in 1946–47, when hundreds of people froze to death.[20] At the time these hundreds of people left a deeper mark on the memory than the millions who died in the war.

It was, indeed, a characteristic of what Christoph Klessman has called "a society in collapse" (*Zusammenbruchsgesellschaft*) that the social inequalities that continued to exist and the new ones that were added were thus covered over. Because no general overview of the situation was possible, the description of a society totally engulfed by poverty that we encounter in many contemporary publications ignored the fact that social status made a great difference. The experience of a working-class family which had been bombed out in a city and was now wandering around without any means of support was not the same as that of the bourgeois owner of a villa in a still-intact suburb whose life might, at times, be disrupted by being forced to take in tenants, but who was allowed to keep his property. At the latest the currency reform of June 1948, which virtually impoverished normal savers when they exchanged their Reichmark for the new DM, while property owners saw the value of their property increase enormously, brought the social inequalities sharply into focus again.

The erosion of the "national community"(*Volksgemeinschaft*) during the final phase of the war and the immediate postwar years, as detected by historical research, was reflected in the degree to which the people empathized with the various victims of the war, as revealed in contemporary demoscopic surveys. Top of the list, of course, were members of one's own family, relations, and friends, including work colleagues and neighbors. Then came those whose fates people could imagine – victims of the war and those who had been bombed out. On the other hand, those who had been liberated from prisons and concentration camps, many of them Jews, and were now waiting as Displaced Persons (DPs) to be repatriated to their European homelands or to emigrate overseas, were largely regarded with mistrust and suspicion. The fact that they were, for a time, given preferential treatment by the authorities in terms of food and accommodation, caused great annoyance, though this was hardly reflected in the media.[21]

The largest group of people affected particularly severely by the war, but whom the indigenous population was far from willing to help, were the refugees and expellees.[22] They also represented the largest number of war victims amongst the civilian population: according to semi-official estimates, there were two million of them. They died when, on their treks, they were caught between the fronts of the final battle, froze to death, or simply could not survive the hardships of being on the run. The "refugee" as a vernacular generic term – it is far more differentiated in official statistics – for those who left, or had to leave, their homeland because of the war, was elevated in contemporary sociology into a "figure of the changing times," a symbol of humanity per se.[23]

The first census held in the Federal Republic in 1950 registered 7.9 million refugees. This figure comprised Germans who were living in the eastern areas of the German Reich when war broke out and no longer counted as Germans, and 1.5 million who had immigrated from the Soviet zone/GDR. Most were initially settled in predominantly agricultural regions of Schleswig-Holstein (the expellees and refugees made up 33.2 percent of the population in September 1950), Lower Saxony (27.3 percent), Bavaria (21.2 percent), and Hesse (16.6 percent) where in some regions they actually constituted a majority of the population. Members of the former minority German group in Czechoslovakia (Sudeten Germans) mainly settled in Bavaria.

The integration of refugees and expellees into village communities was not without its problems. Many farmers did not regard them as citizens with equal rights, but as foreigners, at best as welcome cheap labor to replace the forced laborers who had left after the war. Rapid integration was also hindered by the fact that refugees and expellees who were looking for their families kept changing their place of work and residence. The main points of conflict arose from the fact that farmers were forced to provide them with accommodation, and were then disappointed when those they had taken in turned out not to be skilled laborers because they had previously done quite different jobs. In addition, the arrival of the expellees often caused a split in communities that had previously been of one denomination, and this could certainly cause conflict. Nonetheless, the Catholic and Protestant communities set great store by integrating the new citizens from outside.[24]

The political situation gradually stabilized. There was a relatively high turnout for the elections to the regional parliaments in the Western zones, in which the Christian Democrats as a new supradenominational union and other bourgeois parties gained a majority.[25] A new constitution, the Basic Law, was promulgated with elements of traditional German democracy and Western influences, and the Federal Republic was founded.

But below the surface of a new "normality," the catastrophe of the war remained ever-present in various diverse dimensions. Initially the image – literally – of postwar society was strongly influenced for many years by those disabled in the Second World War (and, indeed, there were still some veterans left from the First World War). Between 1.5 and two million disabled people, both soldiers and civilians, were living in the Federal Republic in 1950. To integrate this group of people into society was seen as an important political task.[26] It was a common experience for pupils in the 1950s to be instructed by someone who had been disabled in the war. It became part of the German vernacular that people would go on about their "Stalingrad experiences," and even today, this still means boring listeners with tales of heroic deeds in the war. And, of course, war experiences were constantly disseminated not only in classrooms but also in pubs and popular literature, of which there was plenty. Subjective descriptions of what happened during the war obviously met a widespread need, and contradicted the thesis often put forward that Nazism and the war were "suppressed" by the public, although "suppression," as a psychoanalytical concept, should not be equated here with not talking about it.[27] In fact, the war was never talked about more than in the 1950s. The question is, how was it remembered? The answer is: by excluding or "suppressing" the Holocaust and always holding up *Wehrmacht* soldiers and, indeed, wives on the home front, as positive heroes.[28]

To a large degree memory of the war was also kept alive by social policy formalized in the *Bundesversorgungsgesetz* (Federal Support Law) passed at the end of 1950. In the first year it applied to about 3.9 million people entitled to financial support. In addition to the "warwounded," this included about 900,000 widows and 1.3 million orphans. The number of those receiving state support rose slightly towards the middle of the 1950s but after that it gradually declined. However, in the last year of the "old" Federal Republic it was still 1.4 million, half of them war invalids – a clear sign of the long-term social burdens imposed by the Second World War.[29]

Although, as has already been mentioned, almost all the POWs had returned by the time the Federal Republic was founded, the media kept this topic alive. Every day the Red Cross ran missing-persons announcements in the newspapers and virtually every hour after the news on the radio. This upset many people during the early years of the Federal Republic and ensured that memory of the war did not fade away. The last POWs, some of them rightly condemned as war criminals, returned from Siberia after Konrad Adenauer's visit to Moscow in 1955. To this day, a wave of films and books deals with their return, although this group was by no means representative of the whole group of POWs, but particularly well suited to tales of national sacrifice.[30]

In addition, in a differentiated political culture, the expellees' associations flourished, headed by a number of functionaries with Nazi pasts. The Sunday speeches of the expellee functionaries, who were often not free of Nazi taint, especially at the Whitsun meetings of the regional groups, constantly referred to the crime of driving people from their homeland and the end of the war and the postwar period as a catastrophe. It was not until the expellees were gradually integrated into the society of the Federal Republic, given state accommodation, and incorporated into the booming economy, that this particular culture of war memory gradually started to fade.[31]

Given the lack of an army and militarism, the society of the early Federal Republic was literally a civilian society. The clear subordination of the military to the primacy of politics after the *Bundeswehr* was founded guaranteed this clear discontinuity compared to the interwar period. Nonetheless, in the first half of the 1950s the social status of the military was discernibly upgraded and former professional soldiers were rehabilitated. This manifested itself in a self-confident veterans' culture among former members of the *Wehrmacht* and the *Waffen-SS*, which the political parties also acknowledged. At this time a strict distinction was drawn between a "clean *Wehrmacht*" and "dirty SS" in popular films, for instance, although members of the *Waffen-SS*, who also guarded concentration camps in rotation, were numbered among the soldiers without taint. High-ranking politicians and church leaders even spoke up for the war criminals in Allied prisons, and large sections of the press sympathized with them as "condemned by war."[32]

Thus there were a number of factors that allowed the war to influence the civilian society of the Federal Republic. The war was so strongly present that it was not necessary to recall it. An additional factor was that on the front between the two world systems, fear of war was especially rife. The majority of West Germans expected the Third World War to break out in the near future, imagining themselves to be in a brief period of respite between two world wars. During the Korean War in the early 1950s there was stockpiling of food supplies, and in the town-planners' debates about high-rise flats, which had not existed in Germany before 1945, a point against them was that they would be easily identifiable enemy targets in the next war.[33] The end of the Second World War, therefore, did not mean the end of the fear of war, but introduced a phase in which this fear could be communicated in a restructured public sphere.[34] What still needs to be analyzed, however, is which war experiences could be discussed in public and in what form – and which ones could not. As we know, the Holocaust was largely excluded for nearly two decades,[35] and many war crimes received no official attention. The violence done to women by soldiers was taboo in many families and remained so until very recently. The whole dimension of a society traumatized by war still leaves much to be examined.[36]

Work on West German rearmament up to the formation of the *Bundeswehr* in 1956 has shown that the motives for rejecting it were so mixed up that they are difficult to distinguish. Nationalism, anti-Westernism, and national neutralism were overlaid by more everyday emotions ("Ohne mich");[37] it was not so much a question here of an abstract fear of war, rather a fear of the Russians. Using political posters the German Federal Government headed by Konrad Adenauer successfully functionalized the enemy image of the Bolshevik, designated as Asiatic, as an argument in favor of creating an army that was integrated into the Western alliance. The engineering of a culture of fear,[38] and the organization of propaganda strategies are, nowadays, presented in different ways by historians.[39]

Nonetheless, it would not have been possible to keep enemy images and fears alive if they had not been rooted in experience and disseminated a million times in public media. One small episode shows how deep-seated was the expectation that one day "the Russian" would come. A contemporary witness recalls a childhood scene from the early 1950s. A neighbor had built two rooms onto his house. When the witness's father went to have a look, our witness overheard him ask quietly, "And where is the hollow space?" The neighbor immediately knew what he meant, and just pointed with his finger to a spot under the staircase. When the witness asked his father that evening what it meant, his father replied, "That's where you put important papers and jewelry when Ivan comes."[40] Fear of Communism, or, as contemporaries mostly called it, "Bolshevism," constituted one of the most powerful lines of continuity from the Second World War to the newly constructed society of the Federal Republic. The arsenal of the ideologically hegemonic Western apotheosis in the first half of the 1950s included the construction of a metaphysical opposition between freedom (in the sense not of "liberal," but of a Christian ideology) in the West and the collectivist East that offers great scope for political analogies.[41] After the 1950s, a decade of overcoming the immediate material consequences of war, discussion of German war victims, and abatement of the real fear of war, the interest of the public gradually became less intense. Although this cannot easily be presented in statistics, however, deep-seated individual and family problems remained that continued to leave their mark on society. Families torn apart, the death of close relatives or friends, alienation between husbands and wives after the separation of the war years, youngsters growing up without fathers, the trauma of air raids, flight and expulsion, and rape by Allied soldiers – all these continued to have an impact beneath the surface of successful reconstruction, but were discussed very little within the family.[42] In public, on the other hand, from the 1960s onwards, Nazi mass crimes against the Jews, and, indeed, against other "forgotten victims" who were not part of the *Volksgemeinschaft* were constantly unearthed: gypsies, homosexuals, and, finally, also the millions of foreign forced laborers.[43] Then in the 1990s came heated discussions about the crimes of the German *Wehrmacht*, when the fiction of a large, clean *Wehrmacht* was called into question.[44]

Finally, in recent years there has been a revival of the discourses of self-victimization, supposedly under the auspices of breaking taboos, even though they have since become part of the mainstream of popular memory culture. The end of the East–West divide has created a new mass-media forum for previously internalized memories of private experiences, and not only in Germany.[45] This applies above all to discussions about the victims of air raids, flight, and expulsion. What is more, the generation of war children has grown older; they have come to the end of their careers and want to sum up their lives. This generation, which was largely "mute" as regards their own experiences, but who played a crucial part in the controversies about German history, are now starting to articulate their own traumatization in the war and immediate postwar period, often in literary form, and have attracted considerable interest from the media.[46] The current debate about Günter Grass's book, *Beim Häuten der Zwiebel* (2006), in which, aged 78, he mentions for the first time that at the age of 17 he belonged to the *Waffen-SS*, is symptomatic of the fact that German society has by no means dealt with the subject of the war and shows how difficult it is for those who went through it to lay it to rest.[47]

Looking back over the last ten or twenty years, it is clear that incidents giving rise to debates on Nazism, the war, and mass crimes have been following one another in ever more rapid succession. They range from the *Historikerstreit* in the second half of the 1980s,[48] to the discussion about compensation for forced laborers,[49] the books by Goldhagen and Aly,[50] the erection of the Holocaust Memorial in Berlin,[51] the planned center against expulsion,[52] and the biography of Günter Grass, to give just a few striking examples. Historians should take this as a challenge to present the so-called second history of Nazism, that is, the history of the repercussions of the Third Reich and the Second World War and how it was dealt with, in a differentiated way at a level beneath the spectacular cases. Without this dimension it is impossible, even today, to understand the history of the Federal Republic as the history of a postwar society under the very long shadows of the Second Word War.[53]

Notes

1. A methodologically aware synthesis is Edgar Wolfrum, *Geglückte Demokratie: Die Geschichte der Bundesrepublik Deutschland von ihren Anfängen bis zur Gegenwart* (Stuttgart, 2006); on the state of research see Axel Schildt, *Die Sozialgeschichte der Bundesrepublik Deutschland bis 1989/90* (Munich, 2007).

2. Werner Conze, 'Staats- und Nationalpolitik: Kontinuitätsbruch und Neubeginn', in id. and M. Rainer Lepsius (eds.), *Sozialgeschichte der Bundesrepublik Deutschland: Beiträge zum Kontinuitätsproblem* (Stuttgart, 1983), 441–67, at 442; for a critical voice on this see Lutz Niethammer, 'Zum Wandel der Kontinuitätsdiskussion', in Ludolf Herbst (ed.), *Westdeutschland 1945–1955: Unterwerfung, Kontrolle, Integration* (Munich, 1986), 65–83; Paul Nolte, *Die Ordnung der deutschen Gesellschaft: Selbstentwurf und Selbstbeschreibung im 20. Jahrhundert* (Munich, 2000), 212–14.
3. See Volker Depkat, *Lebenswenden und Zeitenwenden: Deutsche Politiker und die Erfahrungen des 20. Jahrhunderts* (Munich, 2007); in his *Habilitation* thesis for the University of Greifswald, Depkat describes addressing the turning point of 1945 as an "awareness of a zero point pushing towards the reorientation of an autobiographical awareness of periodization in the Federal Republic of Germany" (ibid. 186).
4. Dirk Moses, "The Forty-Fivers: A Generation between Fascism and Democracy, *German Politics and Society*," 17 (1999), 105–27.
5. See numerous references to the research in Jürgen Reulecke, *Generationalität und Lebensgeschichte im 20. Jahrhundert* (Munich, 2003).
6. Axel Schildt, "Nachkriegszeit: Möglichkeiten und Probleme einer Periodisierung der westdeutschen Geschichte nach dem Zweiten Weltkrieg und ihrer Einordnung in die Geschichte des 20. Jahrhunderts," *Geschichte in Wissenschaft und Unterricht*, 44 (1993), 567–84; for the European dimension see Ulrich Herbert and Axel Schildt (eds.), *Kriegsende in Europa: Vom Beginn des deutschen Machtzerfalls bis zur Stabilisierung der Nachkriegsordnung 1944–1948* (Essen, 1998).
7. Heinrich Böll, "Hierzulande," *Gewerkschaftliche Monatshefte*, 12 (1961), 129–34.
8. See Axel Schildt, *Moderne Zeiten: Freizeit, Massenmedien und "Zeitgeist" in der Bundesrepublik der 50er Jahre* (Hamburg, 1995), 306–8; in this data the Third Reich was, quite naturally, it seems, conceptually separated from the Second World War.
9. See Ulrich Herbert, "Die guten und die schlechten Zeiten," in Lutz Niethammer (ed.), *"Die Jahre weiß man nicht, wo man die heute hinsetzen soll": Faschismuserfahrung im Ruhrgebiet* (Berlin, 1983), 67–96; Ulrich Herbert. "Zur Entwicklung der Ruhrarbeiterschaft 1930 bis 1960 aus erfahrungsgeschichtlicher Perspektive," in Lutz Niethammer and Alexander von Plato (eds.), *"Wir kriegen jetzt andere Zeiten": Auf der Suche nach der Erfahrung des Volkes in nachfaschistischen Ländern* (Berlin, 1985), 19–51.
10. Speech quoted from Richard von Weizsäcker, *Von Deutschland aus: Reden eines Bundespräsidenten* (Munich, 1985); see Peter Reichel, *Politik mit der Erinnerung: Gedächtnisorte im Streit um die nationalsozialistische Vergangenheit* (Munich, 1995), 290–92; Jan-Holger Kirsch, *"Wir haben aus der Geschichte gelernt": Der 8. Mai als politischer Gedenktag in Deutschland* (Cologne, 1999), 96–98; in general also Burkhart Asmuss et al. (eds.), *Der Krieg und seine Folgen: 1945. Kriegsende und Erinnerungspolitik in Deutschland* (Berlin, 2005).
11. Details in Rüdiger Overmans, *Deutsche militärische Verluste im Zweiten Weltkrieg* (Munich, 1999).
12. See Olaf Groehler, *Bombenkrieg gegen Deutschland* (Berlin, 1990); Michael Krause, *Flucht vor dem Bombenkrieg: "Umquartierungen" im Zweiten Weltkrieg und die Wiedereingliederung der Evakuierten in Deutschland 1943–1963* (Düsseldorf,1997).
13. See Wolfram Wette, Ricarda Bremer, and Detlef Vogel (eds.), *Das letzte halbe Jahr: Stimmungsberichte der Wehrmachtpropaganda 1944/45* (Essen, 2001); Jörg Hillmann and John Zimmermann (eds.), *Kriegsende 1945 in Deutschland* (Munich, 2002); Bernd-A. Rusinek (ed.), *Kriegsende 1945: Verbrechen, Katastrophen, Befreiungen in nationaler und internationaler Perspektive* (Göttingen, 2004).
14. Bernd Greiner, *Die Morgenthau-Legende: Zur Geschichte eines umstrittenen Plans* (Hamburg, 1995); Jörg Später, *Vansittart: Britische Debatten über Deutsche und Nazis 1902–1945* (Göttingen, 2003).

15. See Albrecht Lehmann, *Gefangenschaft und Heimkehr: Deutsche Kriegsgefangenschaft in der Sowjetunion* (Munich, 1986); Arthur L. Smith, *Die "vermisste" Million: Zum Schicksal deutscher Kriegsgefangener nach dem Zweiten Weltkrieg* (Munich, 1992); Klaus-Dieter Müller et al. (eds.), *Die Tragödie der Gefangenschaft in Deutschland und der Sowjetunion 1941–1956* (Cologne, 1998); Rüdiger Overmans, *Soldaten hinter Stacheldraht: Deutsche Kriegsgefangene des Zweiten Weltkriegs* (Berlin, 2000).
16. Lutz Niethammer, *Die Mitläuferfabrik: Die Entnazifizierung am Beispiel Bayerns* (Berlin, 1982). See also the regional studies by Rainer Möhler, *Entnazifizierung in Rheinland-Pfalz und im Saarland unter französischer Besatzung von 1945–1952* (Mainz, 1992); and Armin Schuster, *Die Entnazifizierung in Hessen 1945–1954: Vergangenheitspolitik in der Nachkriegszeit* (Wiesbaden, 1999).
17. See Jörg Friedrich, *Die kalte Amnestie: NS-Täter in der Bundesrepublik* (Frankfurt/M., 1984); Clemens Vollnhals (with Thomas Schlemmer), *Entnazifizierung, politische Säuberung und Rehabilitierung in den vier Besatzungszonen 1945–1949* (Munich, 1991); Cornelia Rauh-Kühne, "Die Entnazifizierung und die deutsche Gesellschaft," *Archiv für Sozialgeschichte*, 35 (1995), 35–70; Norbert Frei, *Vergangenheitspolitik: Die Anfänge der Bundesrepublik und die NS-Vergangenheit* (Munich, 1996).
18. See Axel Schildt, 'NS-Eliten in der Bundesrepublik Deutschland', *Geschichte, Politik und ihre Didaktik*, 24 (1996), 20–32; Ulrich Herbert, "Deutsche Eliten nach Hitler," *Mittelweg 36*, 8 (1999), 66–82; Norbert Frei, *Karrieren im Zwielicht: Hitlers Eliten nach 1945* (Frankfurt/M., 2001).
19. This is the impression created by Götz Aly's recently widely discussed book, *Hitlers Volksstaat: Raub, Rassenkrieg und nationaler Sozialismus* (Frankfurt/M., 2005); cf., by contrast, the more balanced account in Jörg Echternkamp (ed.), *Die deutsche Kriegsgesellschaft 1939 bis 1945*, Das Deutsche Reich und der Zweite Weltkrieg, 9, vol. 2 (Munich, 2005).
20. On the social misery of the postwar period, especially the lack of food, see Karl-Heinz Rothenberger, *Die Hungerjahre nach dem Zweiten Weltkrieg: Ernährungs- und Landwirtschaft in Rheinland-Pfalz 1945–1950* (Boppard, 1980); Gabriele Stüber, *Der Kampf gegen den Hunger 1945–1950: Die Ernährungslage in der britischen Zone Deutschlands, insbesondere in Schleswig-Holstein und Hamburg* (Neumünster, 1984); Michael Wildt, *Der Traum vom Sattwerden: Hunger und Protest, Schwarzmarkt und Selbsthilfe* (Hamburg, 1986); Willi A. Boelke, *Der Schwarzmarkt 1945–1948: Vom Überleben nach dem Kriege* (Brunswick, 1986); Paul Erker, *Ernährungskrise und Nachkriegsgesellschaft: Bauern und Arbeiterschaft in Bayern 1945–1953* (Stuttgart: 1990); Günter J. Trittel, *Hunger und Politik: Die Ernährungskrise in der Bizone (1945–1949)* (Frankfurt/M., 1990); and Rainer Gries, *Die Rationen-Gesellschaft. Versorgungskampf und Vergleichsmentalität: Leipzig, München und Köln nach dem Kriege* (Münster 1991).
21. See Wolfgang Jacobmeyer, *Vom Zwangsarbeiter zum heimatlosen Ausländer: Die Displaced Persons in Westdeutschland 1945–1951* (Göttingen, 1985); Patrick Wagner, *Displaced Persons in Hamburg: Stationen einer halbherzigen Integration 1945–1958* (Hamburg, 1997); Angelika Eder, "Displaced Persons/ ,Heimatlose Ausländer' als Arbeitskräfte in Westdeutschland," *Archiv für Sozialgeschichte*, 42 (2002), 1–17; Sonja von Behrens, *Die Zeit der "Polendörfer"* (Petershagen, 2005).
22. The contemporary standard work is Eugen Lemberg and Friedrich Edding (eds.), *Die Vertriebenen in Westdeutschland: Ihre Eingliederung und ihr Einfluß auf Gesellschaft, Wirtschaft, Politik und Geistesleben*, 3 vols. (Kiel, 1959); the voluminous research literature includes Wolfgang Benz (ed.), *Die Vertreibung der Deutschen aus dem Osten: Ursachen, Ereignisse, Folgen* (Frankfurt/M., 1985); Marion Frantzioch, *Die Vertriebenen: Hemmnisse, Antriebskräfte und Wege ihrer Integration in der Bundesrepublik Deutschland* (Berlin, 1987); Rainer Schulze et al. (eds.), *Flüchtlinge und Vertriebene in der westdeutschen Nachkriegsgeschichte: Bilanzierung der Forschung und Perspektiven für*

die künftige Forschungsarbeit (Hildesheim, 1987); R. Endres (ed.), *Bayerns vierter Stamm: Die Integration der Flüchtlinge und Heimatvertriebenen nach 1945* (Cologne, 1998); and Dieter Hoffmann et al. (eds.), *Vertriebene in Deutschland: Interdisziplinäre Ergebnisse und Forschungsperspektiven* (Munich, 2000).

23. Elisabeth Pfeil, *Der Flüchtling: Gestalt einer Zeitenwende* (Hamburg, 1948).
24. Hartmut Rudolph, Evangelische Kirche und Vertriebene 1945 bis 1972, 2 vols. (Göttingen 1984–85); Michael Hirschfeld, Katholisches Milieu und Vertriebene: Eine Fallstudie am Beispiel des Oldenburger Landes (Cologne, 2002); Rainer Bendel, Aufbruch aus dem Glauben? Katholische Heimatvertriebene in den gesellschaftlichen Transformationen der Nachkriegszeit 1945–1965 (Cologne, 2003).
25. For a detailed account see Gerhard A. Ritter and Merith Niehuss, *Wahlen in Deutschland 1946–1991: Ein Handbuch* (Munich, 1991), 121–23.
26. James M. Diehl, *The Thanks of the Fatherland: German Veterans after the Second World War* (Chapel Hill, NC, 1998).
27. Manfred Kittel, *Die Legende von der "zweiten Schuld": Vergangenheitsbewältigung in der Ära Adenauer* (Berlin, 1993), for instance, makes this simplistic equation.
28. Axel Schildt, "Der Umgang mit der NS-Vergangenheit in der Öffentlichkeit der Nachkriegszeit," in Wilfried Loth and Bernd-A. Rusinek (eds.), *Verwandlungspolitik: NS Eliten in der westdeutschen Nachkriegsgesellschaft* (Frankfurt/M., 1998), 19–54.
29. Lutz Wiegand, "Kriegsfolgengesetzgebung in der Bundesrepublik Deutschland," *Archiv für Sozialgeschichte*, 35 (1995), 71–90.
30. See Robert G. Moeller, *War Stories: The Search for a Usable Past in the Federal Republic of Germany* (Berkeley, 2001), 88–90.
31. See, for different evaluations, Samuel Salzborn, *Grenzenlose Heimat: Geschichte, Gegenwart und Zukunft der Vertriebenenverbände* (Berlin, 2000); Matthias Stickler, *"Ostdeutsch heißt Gesamtdeutsch:" Organisation, Selbstverständnis und heimatpolitische Zielsetzungen der deutschen Vertriebenenverbände 1949–1972* (Düsseldorf, 2004).
32. See Bernd-Oliver Manig, *Die Politik der Ehre: Die Rehabilitierung der Berufssoldaten in der frühen Bundesrepublik* (Göttingen, 2004).
33. See Axel Schildt, *Die Grindelhochhäuser: Eine Sozialgeschichte der ersten deutschen Wohnhochhausanlage. Hamburg-Grindelberg 1945–1956* (Hamburg, 1988), 147; see id., "Die Atombombe und der Wiederaufbau: Luftschutz, Stadtplanungskonzepte und Wohnungsbau 1950–1956," *1999: Zeitschrift für Sozialgeschichte des 20. und 21. Jahrhunderts*, 2/4 (1987), 52–67.
34. In this context, a comparison between the postwar periods of the First World War and Second World War would be of interest; see Gottfried Niedhart and Dieter Riesenberger (eds.), *Lernen aus dem Krieg? Deutsche Nachkriegszeiten 1918 und 1945* (Munich, 1992).
35. See Peter Reichel, *Vergangenheitsbewältigung in Deutschland: Die Auseinandersetzung mit der NS-Diktatur von 1945 bis heute* (Munich, 2001); Volkhard Knigge and Norbert Frei (eds.), *Verbrechen erinnern: Die Auseinandersetzung mit Holocaust und Völkermord* (Munich, 2002).
36. Regina Mühlhäuser, "Vergewaltigungen in Deutschland 1945: Nationaler Opferdiskurs und individuelles Erinnern betroffener Frauen," in Klaus Naumann (ed.), *Nachkrieg in Deutschland* (Hamburg, 2001), 384–408; see Richard Bessel and Dirk Schumann (eds.), *Life After Death: Approaches to a Cultural and Social History of Europe During the 1940s and 1950s* (Cambridge, 2003).
37. See Michael Geyer, "Der Kalte Krieg, die Deutschen und die Angst: Die westdeutsche Opposition gegen Wiederbewaffnung und Kernwaffen," in Naumann (ed.), *Nachkrieg in Deutschland*, 267–318.
38. Bernd Greiner, "Zwischen 'Totalem Krieg' und 'Kleinen Kriegen:' Überlegungen zum historischen Ort des Kalten Krieges," *Mittelweg 36*, 12/2(2003), 3–20; see Axel Schildt, "'German Angst': Überlegungen zur Mentalitätsgeschichte der Bundesrepublik," in

Daniela Münkel and Jutta Schwarzkopf (eds.), *Geschichte als Experiment: Studien zu Politik, Kultur und Alltag im 19. und 20. Jahrhundert. Festschrift für Adelheid von Saldern* (Frankfurt/M., 2004), 87–97; Eckart Conze, "Security as a Culture: Reflections on a 'Modern Political History' of the Federal Republic of Germany," *Bulletin of the German Historical Institute London*, 28/1 (May 2006), 5–34.

39. See esp. the pioneering work by Bernd Stöver, *Die Befreiung vom Kommunismus: Amerikanische Liberation Policy im Kalten Krieg 1947–1991* (Cologne, 2002); Thomas Lindenberger (ed.), *Massenmedien im Kalten Krieg: Akteure, Bilder, Resonanzen* (Cologne, 2006).
40. Reported by Harm Mögenburg, *Kalter Krieg und Wirtschaftswunder: Die Fünfziger Jahre im geteilten Deutschland* (Frankfurt/M., 1993), 99.
41. See Axel Schildt, *Zwischen Abendland und Amerika: Studien zur westdeutschen Ideenlandschaft der 50er Jahre* (Munich, 1999), 21–23.
42. See Vera Neumann, *Nicht der Rede wert: Die Privatisierung von Kriegsfolgen in der frühen Bundesrepublik. Lebensgeschichtliche Erinnerungen* (Münster, 1999); Harald Welzer et al., *"Opa war kein Nazi:" Nationalsozialismus und Holocaust im Familiengedächtnis* (Frankfurt/M., 2002); Volker Ackermann, "Das Schweigen der Flüchtlingskinder: Psychische Folgen von Krieg, Flucht und Vertreibung bei den Deutschen," *Geschichte und Gesellschaft*, 30 (2004), 434–64.
43. On the 1960s see some of the essays in Axel Schildt et al. (eds.), *Dynamische Zeiten: Die 60er Jahre in den beiden deutschen Gesellschaften* (Hamburg, 2000; 2nd edn. 2003).
44. Dozens of books have been published on this; see some of the essays in Michael T. Greven and Oliver von Wrochem (eds.), *Der Krieg in der Nachkriegszeit: Der Zweite Weltkrieg in Politik und Gesellschaft der Bundesrepublik* (Opladen, 2000); most recently Hannes Heer, *Hitler war's: Die Befreiung der Deutschen von ihrer Vergangenheit* (Berlin, 2005).
45. See, out of an enormous amount of literature, Christopher R. Browning, *Holocaust History and Postwar Testimony* (Madison, Wis., 2003); and Wulf Kansteiner, *In Pursuit of German Memory: History, Television, and Politics after Auschwitz* (Athens, OH, 2006).
46. Martin Sabrow, Ralph Jessen, and Klaus Große Kracht (eds.), *Zeitgeschichte als Streitgeschichte: Große Kontroversen seit 1945* (Munich, 2003); id., *Die zankende Zunft: Historische Kontroversen in Deutschland nach 1945* (Göttingen, 2005).
47. Günter Grass, *Beim Häuten der Zwiebel* (Göttingen, 2006); on the discussion see Manfred Bissinger (ed.), *Die Springer-Kontroverse: Ein Streitgespräch* (Göttingen, 2006); Willi Gorzny (ed.), *Die Grass-Debatte: Berichte, Stellungnahmen, Kommentare, Interviews, Leserbriefe. Bibliographie und Pressespiegel (12.8.– 31.8.2006)* (Pullach, 2006); on the background see Harro Zimmermann, *Günter Grass und die Deutschen: Chronik eines Verhältnisses* (Göttingen, 2006).
48. See *"Historikerstreit": Die Dokumentation der Kontroverse um die Einzigartigkeit der nationalsozialistischen Judenvernichtung. Texte von Rudolf Augstein u.a.* (Munich, 1987; 9th edn., 1995); Richard Evans, *Im Schatten Hitlers? Historikerstreit und Vergangenheitsbewältigung in der Bundesrepublik* (Frankfurt/M., 1991); Alfred D. Low, *The Third Reich and the Holocaust in German Historiography: Toward the Historikerstreit of the mid-1980s* (New York, 1994); Jürgen Peter, *Der Historikerstreit und die Suche nach einer nationalen Identität in den achtziger Jahren* (Frankfurt/M., 1995); Charles S. Maier, *The Unmasterable Past: History, Holocaust, and German National Identity* (Cambridge, Mass., 1997); Wolfgang Wippermann, *Wessen Schuld? Vom Historikerstreit zur Goldhagen-Kontroverse* (Berlin, 1997); Steffen Kalitz, *Die politische Deutungskultur im Spiegel des "Historikerstreits": What's right? What's left?* (Wiesbaden, 2001).
49. Since the 1980s dozens of local studies and studies of individual businesses have been published; for an overview see Mark Spoerer, *Zwangsarbeiter unter dem Hakenkreuz: Ausländische Zivilarbeiter, Kriegsgefangene und Häftlinge im Deutschen Reich und im*

besetzten Europa 1939–1945 (Stuttgart, 2001); on the compensation debate see Susanne-Sophia Spiliotis, *Verantwortung und Rechtsfrieden: Die Stiftungsinititiative der deutschen Wirtschaft* (Frankfurt/M., 2003).

50. The controversy about Daniel Jonah Goldhagen's book, *Hitlers willige Vollstrecker: Ganz gewöhnliche Deutsche und der Holocaust* (Berlin, 1996; German edition), is outlined by Michael Schneider, "Die 'Goldhagen-Debatte:' Ein Historikerstreit in der Mediengesellschaft," *Archiv für Sozialgeschichte*, 37 (1997), 460–81; ten years later, the book by Aly, *Hitlers Volksstaat*, had a similar but shorter-lived resonance. In both cases experts in the field were devastating in their criticism – see numerous contributions to the internet journal *Sehepunkte*, 5 (2005) and the journal *Sozial.Geschichte: Zeitschrift für historische Analyse*, 20/3 (2005). But the experts' judgements contrasted with the positive response on the part of the general public with an interest in history, which used these books as a screen on which to project its own need to deal with the topic.

51. Lea Rosh, *"Die Juden, das sind doch die anderen:" Der Streit um ein deutsches Denkmal* (Berlin, 1999); Michael S. Cullen (ed.), *Das Holocaust-Mahnmal: Dokumentation einer Debatte* (Zurich, 1999); Jan-Holger Kirsch, *Nationaler Mythos oder historische Trauer? Der Streit um ein zentrales "Holocaust-Mahnmal" für die Berliner Republik* (Cologne, 2003); Claus Leggewie and Erik Meyer, *"Ein Ort, an den man gerne geht:" Das Holocaust-Mahnmal und die deutsche Geschichtspolitik nach 1989* (Munich, 2005).

52. Samuel Salzborn, "Geschichtspolitik in den Medien: Die Kontroverse über ein 'Zentrum gegen Vertreibungen'," *Zeitschrift für Geschichtswissenschaft*, 51 (2003), 1120–30; Piotr Madajczyk, "The Centre against Expulsions vs. Polish–German Relations," *Polish Foreign Affairs Digest*, Warsaw, 4/2 (2004), 43–78; Bernd Faulenbach (ed.), *Zwangsmigration in Europa: Zur wissenschaftlichen und politischen Auseinandersetzung um die Vertreibung der Deutschen aus dem Osten* (Essen, 2005); Jan M. Piskorski, *Vertreibung und deutsch-polnische Geschichte: Eine Streitschrift* (Osnabrück, 2005).

53. Beyond this, it is interesting that this theme relating to German or West German society has also become one of the most important focal points for contemporary history with a transnational orientation; see, most recently, Bernd Faulenbach and Franz-Josef Jelich (eds.), *"Transformationen" der Erinnerungskulturen in Europa nach 1989* (Essen, 2006).

Chapter 14

THE WAR IN POSTWAR SOCIETY:
The Role of the Second World War in Public and Private Spheres in the Soviet Occupation Zone and Early GDR

Dorothee Wierling

I.

Contrary to some expectations, memories of the Second World War are quite heterogeneous – not only across Europe, but also within the various European states that were involved in the war. These memories are determined by the regional, social, and political affiliations of the individuals or entities in question, to name only the most obvious factors.[1] The term "collective memory" will therefore be avoided in this chapter, not only because the benchmark it most often refers to – the nation – is actually composed of various such "collectives," but also because the relationship between individual and public memory is always tense, as the example of East Germany will illustrate. In contrast to other European states in the postwar era, the situation in postwar Germany was special in the sense that the political systems of the German Democratic Republic and Federal Republic of Germany, which belonged to two opposing blocs, shaped two diverging models of memory and remembrance.

When first conducting oral history interviews in the GDR with Lutz Niethammer and Alexander von Plato among the reconstruction generation in 1987, one of our interviewees coined the following catchy phrase in reference to the history of the German interpretation of the Second World War, "We lost the war; you (West Germans) won the war."[2] If I remember correctly, despite our surprise this interpretation intuitively made sense to us at the time. Even toward the end of the GDR, the extraneous circumstances – the cities, the political situation, and everyday culture – in many ways called to mind that it had indeed "Risen from

---

Notes for this chapter begin on page 226.

the Ruins," as the national anthem intimates.³ We also observed a strong concentration on the war in our interviewees' spontaneous personal memories in the course of our work – particularly as they were faced with West German interviewers, it appeared. After the shared history of war and National Socialism, there was a feeling of having pulled the blank out of a lottery wheel with only two tickets in it and to have left the jackpot for the West Germans. In any case, in contrast to the West, where most people soon – and certainly after the building of the Berlin Wall – stopped bothering about what had become of their fellow countrymen in the Soviet Occupation Zone (SOZ), in East Germany there was a clear awareness of a shared history up to that point.⁴

It seems that there are indeed two different histories of historical interpretation. In the following, I will outline the early phase of this development in the GDR. I will show that there were also areas of common ground between the two German states and similar ways of coping with the past. However, these commonalities were adapted to the two different – even opposing – political and economic frameworks, i.e., the lived history of the postwar era, and in the process underwent changes that resulted in two specific and in some ways contrary narratives. At the same time, the two "strands of interpretation" remained closely interconnected and in some ways even developed as a furtive dialogue – or rather conflict. My analysis encompasses three steps. First, I will outline the military, material, and political backdrop of the specific interpretation of the war in the SOZ/GDR. In a second step, I will address the former war opponents and their roles in this interpretation. In conclusion, I will explore the public and private war narratives in the SOZ/GDR, including their mutual interdependencies and interplay.

II.

The war's end in "Middle Germany" at the time was marked by a particularly high degree of violence. Berlin and Dresden had been the targets of the last great Allied bombardments, claiming the lives of many civilians. The advance of the Red Army, their crossing of the River Oder, and the capture of Berlin entailed intensive battles on the ground and in the streets of the German "Core Empire." The traces of these battles are visible to this day, especially in East Berlin, in the form of bullet-holes and patched facades – something that is taken for granted by most Berliners but sensational for foreign visitors. In West Berlin, the ruin of the Kaiser-Wilhelm-Gedächtniskirche recalled the war's destructiveness, and in Dresden, the ruin of the Frauenkirche similarly served as a memorial. However, while the ruined church in West Berlin was augmented by a modern church building in 1961, the Frauenkirche was reconstructed as a brand-new, faithful copy on the same spot in 2006. Only its freshness and cleanness betrays that a war memory was overbuilt here. In the GDR, there were no cemeteries that recalled the Germans who died in the fierce final battles, for example on the Seelow Heights on the west side of the River Oder. The graves and the monument on this spot only commemorated the Red Army soldiers who died in the battles.[5]

Even before the actual arrival of the Soviet troops, millions of refugees from the former eastern territories of the German Empire had announced their advance and given accounts of the accompanying violence and their consequent flight. It has often been stressed that these accounts were like an *a posteriori* vindication of National Socialist propaganda concerning the "Slavic *Untermensch*." They were subsequently employed to ensure the perseverance of the civilian population in the last months and weeks of the war. At the same time, these accounts fuelled the Germans' fear of brutal retaliation by the "Russians," as they were aware of the German warfare at the eastern front. Indeed, the occupation of the Red Army was accompanied by a wave of unregulated, extra-military violence, in particular sexual violence. Theft and plundering, as well as the constant threat of violence in the intoxication of conquest (and alcohol) were quite common in the first weeks of the occupation.[6] After this initial phase, a regulated occupation administration (*kommandatura*) put an end to this violence by means of strict control and draconic punishments. Nevertheless, this experience of the early occupation phase in the SOZ shaped the core of people's perceptions of the war's end, which persisted for a very long time although at least officially it was hushed up. We cannot be sure of the extent to which these experiences were talked about and passed on within families during the Soviet occupation and later under the GDR's dictate of silence, however. The first postwar generation, at least, grew up with family narratives that highlighted the suffering of their parents during the war and in the immediate postwar years. Among these were accounts of personal experiences of violence on the run from the Red Army, during the early occupation phase, and in war captivity.[7]

III.

What we consider the postwar era in the stricter sense, i.e., the material and psychological presence of the war, lasted considerably longer in the SOZ/GDR than in West Germany. The traces of destruction in the West, particularly in the industrial cities, were eliminated and whitewashed more quickly and thoroughly in the course of the so-called reconstruction.[8] The SOZ bore the first and the heaviest burden of the stream of refugees from the east. Although these refugees were overproportionately represented among those who later fled to the FRG, over four million people had to be permanently accommodated in the Soviet Occupation Zone – a zone in which living space and infrastructure could only slowly be rebuilt. In 1950, the GDR decided to strike the category of "resettlers," as they were officially called, from the statistics. However, the social problems remained, including integrating this group into society and providing for them. In the early 1950s, people from this group were very likely to become dependent on social welfare services.[9]

The SOZ moreover carried the weight of an occupation power whose material and human losses by far surpassed those of the other war opponents. The Soviets lacked not only the will to help their own occupation zone back onto its feet, but also the material resources and (most likely) the technological know-how. Instead, they attempted to compensate their own domestic losses by means that were oftentimes misguided in economic terms, for example the wild transfer of infrastructure and industrial plants – sometimes including the respective workforces. Later on, they pursued a policy of extracting a certain proportion of the goods produced by the rebuilt industry. However, the most important firms on the territory of the SOZ/GDR attained the legal status of a Soviet corporation and thus produced directly for the Soviet Union.[10] The Wismut-AG, which was responsible for uranium mining and was only officially returned to the GDR in 1953, occupied a special position in this system.[11]

The extreme shortages in the provision of basic supplies for the people in the GDR regarding food, clothing, and living space were not only characteristic of the late 1940s, but also the early 1950s. The monetary reform of 1948 and the simultaneous establishment of state HO-shops (*Handels-Organisation*, i.e., trade organization shops) supplemented food rationing, which was in place until the end of the 1950s, and the subsidization of basic goods through freely purchasable but extremely expensive goods.[12]

Beyond the provision of the most necessary items, the 1950s were an era of economic crisis and low-quality products. Besides the war as a cause for this suffering, another point of reference was soon found: the West, where at least the visible effects of the war soon disappeared. This was not only a result of the various comparisons that GDR citizens were able to make on their visits to West-German relatives or on the visits of these relatives to the GDR. In 1958, the year in which the rationing of basic foodstuffs was officially ended, Walter Ulbricht, the Chairman of the Council of State of the GDR, began to tackle the challenge head-on by proclaiming that the GDR would "surpass [the West] without catching up" in the area of consumption. With this statement, he laid a claim to attaining not only quantitative, but also qualitative superiority over the Federal Republic in the near future.[13] The failure of this endeavor soon forced the GDR government to revise the current five-year-plan and finally to close the border with West Germany in order to stabilize the GDR economically on the one hand, and to keep the country's citizens from defecting to the prosperous West on the other. Indeed, the building of the Berlin Wall initially achieved the aim of economically stabilizing the country and thus constitutes an important caesura that heralded the end of the postwar era in the GDR.

IV.

The political situation in East Germany also remained influenced by the war more directly and for longer than in the West. The Soviet occupants initially played the part of the punitive victors: the duration and conditions of internment for convicted National Socialists by far surpassed what was usual in the occupation zones of the Western allies. The fact that former concentration camps such as Buchenwald and Sachsenhausen were transformed into "special camps" until 1950 amplified the feeling of a continuity of repression under the new system. This was particularly the case as an indeterminate number of prisoners were convicted of anti-Soviet or anti-Stalinist activities – often simply on the grounds of mere suspicions and unconfirmed denunciations. In the early phase, there were generally no interrogations. Transparent and due trials were never conducted.[14]

In contrast to West Germany, there was a sweeping elite exchange in the SOZ, which also entailed the removal of former NSDAP members as well as Nazi activists and functionaries from their positions. In the course of the land reform, "large landowners" were expropriated early on. Many entrepreneurs whose companies were transferred into Soviet ownership or whose production was classified as strategic lost their property and generally left for the FRG. Some, however, accepted the position of company director in the firm they had previously owned. Although these measures were formally part of the process of "antifascist democratization," they paved the way for the systematic destruction of the bourgeoisie as a social class. The Socialist Unity Party of Germany (*Sozialistische Einheitspartei Deutschlands* – SED) had evolved from the Communist Party, which forced the Social Democratic Party into this "unity." The SED was considered the enforcer of the occupation power by a large segment of the population, or simply the "Russian party." What it lacked in legitimacy it replaced with the backing of the Red Army. This perception, which was confirmed by its response to the East German workers' uprising in 1953, was only dispersed in the course of Gorbachev's reforms in the Soviet Union. The so called "block parties," i.e., the Christian Democratic Union, the Liberal Democratic Party, the Democratic Farmers' Party, and the National Democratic Party were supposed to ensure the political attachment of various social groups such as Christians, shopkeepers, farmers, and former

National Socialists. Last but not least, new political mass organizations such as the Free Federation of German Trade Unions, the Free German Youth and its children's section *Junge Pioniere*, the Democratic Women's Association of Germany, and the Cultural Association were founded from 1946 onwards. Although officially nonpartisan, these organizations were also intended to politically control and mobilize various segments of society.[15] Even if the desired political capture of the entire population was mostly oriented toward the future, it also had a close connection to the past in the sense that it aimed to reeducate people in the spirit of antifascism. At the same time, the means by which this aim was pursued in many ways mirrored the rituals of National Socialist mass mobilization and thus appeared as a significant element of continuity.[16]

V.

Images of "the Russians" in the GDR were ambivalent from the very beginning. In people's accounts of the war's end, they recur as poor wretches with nothing but rags tied around their feet who ride in horse wagons, or as soldiers who fry bacon over an open fire. Many people perceived the fact that this sort of troop had defeated Germany as particularly insulting. Moreover, in accordance with a long tradition of images of Russia and the Russians, they were portrayed as unpredictable and brutal drinkers who were, however, kind to children and animals and open to a bargain. Russians also often appeared as highly educated connoisseurs of German culture, as modernizers and doers, however. Finally, they were perceived as cruel despots, as little Stalins.[17]

For most people, they were simply the occupiers one had to come to terms with. All aspects of material and social life, especially the reestablishment of political structures, depended on the authorization, the support, and the guidelines of the Soviet occupation power. This encompassed official as well as unofficial arrangements. The Russian heads of the "Soviet corporations" were notorious for their insatiable hunger for statistics, while a large proportion of the black market was in the hands of members of the occupation troops.

A minority of people in East Germany indeed perceived the Soviets as liberators. First and foremost, this pertained to the forced laborers from the Soviet Union, whose later fates in the Gulag after their repatriation remain shrouded in mystery.[18] It also pertained to the inmates of Nazi prisons and concentration camps, including the Jews who survived. Last but not least, it pertained to a minority of German exiles, leftists, and liberals, to those weary of war (or with a guilty conscience) who truly believed in the possibility of a fresh start under the banner of antifascism. A tragic note was added to the GDR's founding myth in that this antifascism was discredited by Stalinism from the very beginning and could thus not unfold its liberating potential – in the military victory over Nazi Germany as well as in the reconstruction efforts in the SOZ. The Society for the Study of the Soviet Union (later renamed German-Soviet Friendship Society) was soon founded as a surrogate for the lack of legitimacy the "Russians" and the "Russian party" possessed. Toward the end of the GDR, however, the notion of the Soviet "friends" only had a subversive, ironic connotation. The image of the Russian soldier moreover soon lost its terror. Instead, a feeling of pity, which had been an important element in this image from the start, came to dominate. People knew or suspected that the Soviet troops stationed in the GDR, and particularly the simple soldiers, lived in pitiful material and social circumstances. The physical violence that pervaded the troop, including the shooting of deserters on the spot, was an inherent aspect of the repertoire of rumors and stories in the GDR.

VI.

The slogan that was created in the course of the founding of the German-Soviet Friendship Society, "to learn from the Soviet Union means to learn victory," refers to two strategies of converting the former war enemy into an ally, including Soviet claims to being a role model and leader. For one thing, the transformation of the political realm, the economy, and society was highly dependent on the Soviet Union's historical experiences and visions, although the tradition of the socialist labor movement in Germany also played a certain role. The speed of many developments and their direct impacts on the country indeed led to a superficial Sovietization. However it would appear that it never unfolded the same potential for cultural transformation as the Americanization of Western Europe did.[19] The authoritative character of the Soviet example was sometimes even involuntarily funny, as is demonstrated by the teaching manual for pioneer leader training in the early 1950s, which was a direct translation of its Russian counterpart: therein, the nascent pioneer leaders were instructed to take children on field trips to battle sites of the "Great Patriotic War."[20] Certainly less comical was the obligatory reading for the first generation of young comrades in the SED, the *History of the Communist Party of the Soviet Union (Bolsheviks). Short Course*, in which the chapter on Stalin's political opponents polemicizes in blatantly social-racist terms.[21]

The second reference of the victory slogan cited above appears to concern a deeper and more long-term effect. In the post–1945 era, it was an invitation especially to the young generation to make amends for the shameful defeat, the loss of the National Socialist leader, and the disorientation that followed in the wake of the breakdown of Nazi

Germany and its racial ideology through repoliticization. This went far beyond the early amnesty of the members of the Hitler Youth. The aim was to explain to the disturbed and insulted, in many cases even traumatized adolescents that they had been seduced and cheated, but that those who were responsible for the defeat had themselves been defeated by somebody who was wiser, better, and stronger, among other things due to the fact that he was in possession of the right, the only true worldview. This new leader was furthermore the spearhead of an international movement that had history, and thus also the future, on its side. With this hermetic model of interpretation, the occupiers succeeded in politically, but also emotionally capturing a large proportion – albeit a minority – of the Hitler Youth generation in the SOZ/GDR. Particularly young people from lower-middle-class and working-class backgrounds readily accepted this offer of a new ideology, hierarchy, and leader. In a moment of biographical weakness, the victorious aggressor reached out and offered the hand of ideological identification – and at the same time the promise of social and political integration. This group would soon become the recruiting base for a new socialist-based elite that remained in place until the demise of the GDR. It filled the ranks of the mid- and upper-level leadership of state administrations, the school system, the universities, the judicial system, the socialist economy, the new political parties, the mass organizations, and the cultural elites, which had been decimated by the war, subsequent denazification, and defection to the West.[22]

VII.

Official propaganda attempted to draw a connection between people's war experiences, the military defeat, and the material and human losses on the one hand and places where the other war opponents, i.e., Great Britain and especially the USA, had caused fear, pain, and death on the other. One such place was Dresden, which the "Anglo-American terror attacks," as was the official phrase in the GDR – incidentally adopted from Nazi terminology – had devastated. The ruin of the Frauenkirche became the inner-city monument for a war the Soviets had no part in: the destruction of industrial plants, residential buildings, and cities, the victims among the civilian population, and the suffering at home. This war had targeted women, children, and the elderly – all in all unarmed civilians. From the propaganda perspective, this fact discredited the opponent responsible for the bombardments, and its victims were hence rendered innocent.[23] In any case, the bombardment war was the only field in which historians of the Second World War could unambiguously pose and answer the question surrounding the violence suffered by the Germans.

The Russians, on the other hand, could (justifiably) argue that their country had been attacked, that they had been forced to defend themselves, that their opponents had been soldiers, and that the German war against the Soviet Union had been planned and implemented as a racially motivated war of annihilation from the very beginning. The non-military violence they had perpetrated against the civilian population in the course of the capture and occupation of Germany was covered up and denied with the aim of erasing this aspect from the memory of the war.

This aim was never fully realized despite extensive propaganda campaigns and taboos. However, "the Americans" came to occupy the place of the ultimate enemy in the minds of the war generation. Many moreover readily accepted the broader suggestion to regard West Germany as a territory permanently occupied by the USA[24] and to interpret American imperialism as a form of fascism. The Korean War at the beginning of the 1950s, shortly after the end of the Second World War, seemed to prove to the postwar generation the USA's inherent military aggressiveness. The Vietnam War – which was extensively dealt with in the GDR's media like no other war – again impressed this image upon the next generation. Once again, the figure of the bomber pilot who killed without facing battle himself and who targeted the innocent civilian population, became the prototype of the American enemy. We must also note, however, that this image enjoyed similar popularity in West Germany. But the GDR explicitly propagated and reasserted this image with films such as *Piloten im Pyjama* (Pilots in Pajamas) from 1967.[25] The oppositional peace movement of the 1980s in the GDR also referred to Dresden in its protests, and the city retained its symbolic significance even after the end of the GDR. In 2003, at a demonstration against the Iraq War, an elderly man held up a self-painted banner that read: "My father died in Dresden."

VIII.

Under the political circumstances in the GDR, public debates, official representations, and scholarly publications were ideologically homogenous. Although they addressed different audiences, they were hardly distinguishable in terms of language and content. This makes an outline of the official models of interpretation and memory in the GDR relatively easy. The question of how people received these interpretation offers and in how far they accepted them, i.e., interwove with their own personal memories and interpretations, is more difficult to answer however.

In official representations, the Second World War was never a "normal" war. Its role as a war of annihilation, especially in Eastern Europe, was never questioned. The myth concerning the Wehrmacht's innocence moreover never took hold in the GDR as it did in West Germany. Rather, the Wehrmacht was generally supplemented with the adjective "fascist." Of course this meant that even the simple soldiers who had been forced to take part in the war against their will had also been infected with the army's fascist character and warfare. The Soviet Union was portrayed not only as the victor, but also as the greatest victim – and it had made the greatest sacrifices in order to defeat fascism in Germany. In this sense, the Soviet soldiers were the comrades of the German antifascists, a term that stood for the communist resistance fighters. The Soviet prisoners of war and forced laborers were at the center of the commemoration of war victims. They came to inhabit the same place in the GDR's public commemoration as the Holocaust and the Jews in the FRG – as an expression of the Nazis' extra-military destructiveness. The national memorials site in the grounds and in the close vicinity of the former concentration camp Buchenwald is exemplary for this official model of interpreting National Socialism and the Second World War. Accordingly, the communists imprisoned in the concentration camp continued the struggle against the Nazis together with the foreign prisoners and were victorious in the end. In the official version, the camp liberated itself through the actions of a military arm under the command of an international communist camp committee.[26]

However, discourse on the fascist war went far beyond characterizations of the aggressors and the heroization of the resistance. Although German victims and losses could not be publicly mourned – with the exception of the victims of Allied bombardment – they were by no means denied, particularly in the early phase of the GDR. The suffering of the Germans was rather the price they had had to pay for their own or their parents' hesitance in fighting fascism, or because as women, children, or powerless workers, they had become objects of fascist politics and seduction. Thus, there was a latent blame that even those Germans who had been passive or apolitical under National Socialism bore. At the same time, according to Georgy Dimitrov's famous formulation of 1935, fascism was a political instrument of the most aggressive segments of finance capital, an instrument employed in its struggle with the working class and its organizers.[27] The fact that there had been a mass movement in Germany and that broad support for the Nazis had continued well into the war is not accounted for in this interpretation. Through indirect membership in the working class and under the premise of this Stalinist definition of fascism, people in the GDR could thus also define themselves as victims and feel victimized – at least in an abstract way – even if they had supported the Nazis, profited from their reign for many years, or at least not been accosted by them. The war as the great fascist producer of misery was the link that connected everyone. In the end, they had all been victims of the war – if only due to the fact that Germany had been defeated.

IX.

Not only in the GDR did people make use of these sorts of elements provided by official models of interpretation that promised exoneration, belonging, and credibility in their private recollections and interpretations – as a form of self-assurance as well as in their self-presentations within their families and in public. In recent years, research has come to focus precisely on these sorts of bonds and mutual influences between narratives of the past in the private and public sphere.[28]

Private recollections of the war are most vividly reflected in family narratives. In all likelihood, family narratives define personal memories, or rather individual interpretations even of past events not personally experienced, much more strongly than, for example, history lessons in school.[29] This was certainly more so the case in East Germany than in West Germany, as official historical interpretations were wholly placed in the service of the regime in the GDR. However, the party line enjoyed little credibility among the population – not only with regard to this question. Like in the West, people's personal histories of victimization and loss were central to family war narratives in the SOZ/GDR. Most likely, this was developed even more strongly due to the fact that the history of victimization continued in the immediate postwar era with its material destitution, Soviet occupation, and the continuous insult of state patronization. All things considered, the self-victimization also of the children's generation was more credible than in the West. Their parents, who could generally produce neither economic success nor political power, remained the victims, the conquered, the laden fighters at the front of managing everyday life. This way, they were spared critical questions from their children. In the GDR, there was never a generation conflict within families on the topic of the war and National Socialism.[30] Mitigating the discrepancies between official interpretations and family narratives must have been much more of a balancing act than in the West and required complicated mechanisms.

For those who were already adults in the National Socialist era, the official interpretation model surrounding the fascist war is attractive in the sense that it provided a link to another element of the antifascist narrative: the "Victim of Fascism." This honorary title, which was topped only by the title "Fighter against Fascism" in the GDR, connected with the fact that even those Germans who had not actively opposed the Nazi regime were regarded as victims. Since National Socialism was not thematized as a popular mass movement in the GDR, it became possible to evade this aspect in private narratives as well.[31]

Particularly for the former members of the Hitler Youth, who, as indicated above, were quite successful in the GDR, it was comfortable to take up these official suggestions concerning their own victimhood. It was conceded that they had been seducible at the time and had been betrayed. Indeed, personal narratives among this group circle around a deep personal crisis in 1945, when they were disappointed and disillusioned, but also disoriented. Subsequently, they were enlightened about the true character of the seducer by the real victims of fascism and accepted into the community of those who received the chance to atone for their guilt by contributing to the building of socialism. The moment of conversion becomes the center of their biographical constructions, however tied this generation remained to the sins of their youth – internally as well as externally. The SED's motto, "the party forgives, but it does not forget," ensured that these "reeducated" individuals could never entirely feel safe. However, family narratives bordering on taboos, frank talk at the *Stammtisch*, and outbursts of neo-Nazi discourse, rituals, and violence, which accompanied the history of the SOZ/GDR from the very beginning, showed that there were uncontrolled spaces in the GDR that the intricate official models of interpretation were never able to conquer.[32]

The official and public interpretations of the war soon came to play a legitimating role in the Cold War. Likewise, expressions of the lost or won war – depending on one's perspective – which I outlined at the beginning of my analysis, have a prehistory of progressing disassociation and alienation. This prehistory can be traced in the development of family relations and friendships on both sides of the German-German border as documented in countless letters. These correspondences often began between families who were separated by the borders of the occupation zones. They also developed between former war comrades and their families who had sought and found each other after 1945. The shared war experience was initially in the foreground of these exchanges. Soon, however, the realization dawned on people that their postwar experiences diverged considerably. For reasons that do not require further elucidation here, this division was perceived more acutely in the East than in the West. Moreover, the war's legacy remained more tangible in the GDR – in the concrete everyday experience of its aftermath and in the fear of a new war.[33]

Since the fall of the GDR and German reunification, we can as yet discern little unification in the public and private cultures of memory and remembrance beyond the preexisting commonalities. Certainly this is an unconcluded and inconclusive field of research. Shared war experiences, diverging and contradictory postwar experiences, as well as different intergenerational dynamics ensure that nothing is in a hurry to "grow together," because it does not "belong together" quite so readily.[34]

Notes

1. Cf. the other contributions in this volume.
2. This project is documented in Lutz Niethammer, Alexander von Plato, and Dorothee Wierling, *Die volkseigene Erfahrung. Eine Archäologie des Lebens in der Industrieprovinz der DDR* (Berlin, 1991).
3. The first line of the GDR's national anthem was: "Risen from the ruins and looking toward the future." However, in the late 1980s, hardly anyone appeared to be "looking toward the future" anymore.
4. Not only do the comprehensive surveys conducted by opinion research institutes confirm this trend, but also oral history projects with comparable samples conducted in the Federal Republic of Germany. Cf. Lutz Niethammer and Alexander von Plato, eds., *Lebensgeschichte und Sozialkultur im Ruhrgebiet*, 3 vols. (Berlin et al., 1983–85).
5. Alf Lüdtke, "Lebende und ihre Toten. Augen-Blicke bei einem Ausflug in das Oderbruch," *Geschichtswerkstatt*, 16 (1988): 24–28.
6. Norman Naimark, *The Russians in Germany: A History of the Soviet Zone of Occupation, 1945–1949* (Cambridge, 1995) particularly chapter two: Soviet Soldiers, German Women, and the Problem of Rape. On the topic of sexual violence, cf. also the controversial documentary film by Helke Sander: *Befreier und Befreite* (1991/92) as well as the film's companion volume: Helke Sander and Barbara Johr, eds., *Befreier und Befreite* (Munich, 1992). For a critical discussion, see Gertrud Koch, "Blut, Sperma, Tränen," *Frauen und Film* (1994): 54–55, and Atina Grossmann, "A Question of Silence: The Rape of German Women by Occupation Soldiers," *October*, 72 (1995): 43–65.
7. There are many examples of this in Dorothee Wierling, *Geboren im Jahr Eins. Der Geburtsjahrgang 1949 in der DDR, Versuch einer Kollektivbiographie* (Berlin, 2002), especially in chapter 1.1: Familiengeschichten und der Platz in der Geschichte, 24–26.
8. Cf. the contribution by Axel Schildt in this volume.
9. Alexander von Plato and Wolfgang Meinecke, *Alte Heimat – Neue Zeit: Flüchtlinge, Umgesiedelte, Vertriebene in der Sowjetischen Besatzungszone und in der DDR* (Berlin, 1991); Manfred Wille, ed., *Sie hatten alles verloren: Flüchtlinge und Vertriebene in der sowjetischen Besatzungszone Deutschlands* (Wiesbaden, 1993). On the relationship between refugee status and dependence on social welfare, see Marcel Boldorf, *Sozialfürsorge in der SBZ/DDR 1945–1953: Ursachen, Ausmaß und Bewältigung der Nachkriegsarmut* (Stuttgart, 1998), 23–25.
10. Rainer Karlsch, *Allein bezahlt? Die Reparationsleistungen der SBZ/DDR 1945–1953* (Berlin, 1993).
11. Rainer Karlsch and Harm Schröter, eds., *Studien zur Geschichte des Uranbergbaus der Wismut* (St. Katharinen, 1996).
12. On the immediate postwar years, see Rainer Gries, *Die Rationengesellschaft. Versorgungskampf und Vergleichsmentalität. Leipzig, München und Köln nach dem Kriege* (Münster, 1991), 41–145; a good overview is provided in Annette Kaminsky, *Wohlstand, Schönheit, Glück. Kleine Konsumgeschichte der DDR* (Munich, 2001).
13. Ina Merkel, *Utopie und Bedürfnis. Die Geschichte der Konsumkultur in der DDR* (Cologne et al., 1999), 310–12, distinguishes between three phases of consumer culture in the GDR: the "society that meets basic needs" (*Bedarfsdeckungsgesellschaft*) until 1958, the "posterior satisfaction of desires" (*nachholende Bedürfnisbefriedigung*) until 1970, and "farewell to utopia" (*Abschied von der Utopie*) until 1989. The utopia of GDR consumer society was characterized by the attempt not to simply "catch up" with the West – thus to measure up to it – but rather to create one's own, socialist consumer culture. It is disputed, however, in how far this endeavor ever succeeded.
14. Peter Reif-Spirek and Bodo Ritscher, eds., *Speziallager in der SBZ. Gedenkstätten mit "doppelter Vergangenheit"* (Berlin, 1999).

15. On the establishment of a Stalinist party system, cf. Naimark (see note 6), chapter five: The Soviets and the German Left. There are detailed studies on the early histories of some of these new mass organizations: Magdalena Heider, *Politik – Kultur – Kulturbund. Zur Gründungs- und Frühgeschichte des Kulturbundes zur demokratischen Erneuerung Deutschlands 1945–1954 in der SBZ/DDR* (Cologne, 1993); Ulrich Mählert, *Die Freie Deutsche Jugend 1945–1949: von den "Antifaschistischen Jugendausschüssen" zur SED-Massenorganisation. Die Erfassung der Jugend in der Sowjetischen Besatzungszone* (Paderborn, 1995); Leonore Ansorg, *Kinder im Klassenkampf: die Geschichte der Pionierorganisation von 1948 bis Ende der Fünfziger Jahre* (Berlin, 1997).
16. Numerous interviewees in 1987 testified to this fact when they repeatedly mixed up the National Socialist and GDR mass organizations in their narratives. Certainly this does not provide grounds to judge actual or supposed similarities between both systems; it only offers insights into the prevalence of the subjective perception of such similarities among members of the older generations in the GDR.
17. Cf. Niethammer et al. (see note 2), 577. The interviewee, who was a young girl at the time, describes the Soviet soldiers as a "totally worn out and dead tired troop," while a man of the same generation remembers the Russians as "tough, really really tough," ibid., 591.
18. According to the latest estimates, about 25% of the Soviet prisoners of war and forced laborers the Red Army encountered in Germany at the end of the war were directly sent to Soviet labor camps, since their survival was interpreted as betrayal and collaboration with the enemy. Cf. Ulrike Goeken-Haidl, *Der Weg zurück. Die Repatriierung sowjetischer Kriegsgefangener und Zwangsarbeiter während und nach dem Zweiten Weltkrieg* (Essen, 2006).
19. Konrad Jarausch and Hannes Siegrist, *Amerikanisierung und Sowjetisierung in Deutschland 1945–1970* (Frankfurt/M., New York, 1997). See especially the editors' introduction, 11–46.
20. The *Handbuch des Pionierleiters* (Berlin, 1952) was in use until 1961.
21. Commission of the Central Committee of the CPSU, ed., *History of the Communist Party of the Soviet Union (Bolsheviks). Short Course* (New York, 1939).
22. On the Hitler Youth generation as a generation of upward mobility, see Dorothee Wierling, "The Hitler Youth Generation in the GDR: Insecurities, Ambitions and Dilemmas," in *Dictatorship as Experience*, ed. Konrad Jarausch (New York, Oxford, 1999), 307–24.
23. The standard work for the GDR is Olaf Groehler, *Bombenkrieg gegen Deutschland* (Berlin, 1990), which includes an afterword written after the *Wende*. The memory of "Dresden" is a particularly interesting case of "memory battles" and certainly warrants further research. In this context, the recently produced German TV-film *Dresden*, which tells the love story of a German-British couple, provides a fascinating object of investigation. Moreover, there is a touching, righteous, but controversial striving among historians to provide the exact death toll of the bombardment of Dresden and to anchor these numbers in private memory and public remembrance. Cf. the conference report by Thomas Widera on a conference conducted by the Hannah-Arendt-Institute in Dresden: "Quellen zum 13. Februar 1945. Arbeitsmethoden der Historiker." Apparently, this conference did not primarily address the numbers themselves, but rather the possibility of their attainment. This quest was guided by the desire to expose the numbers established in the GDR as anti-imperialist propaganda – an agenda the audience quickly recognized and accordingly met with "personal and political statements," as the reporter, himself a speaker at the conference, critically remarks (see H-SOZ-KULT, 20 July 2006). The discussions that have unfolded in recent years concerning the military and moral dimensions of the bombardment of German cities in the Second World War were prompted by: Jörg Friedrich, *Der Brand. Bombenkrieg gegen Deutschland 1940–1945* (Munich, 2002).

24. Cf. for example the geography textbook *Lehrbuch der Erdkunde* for the fifth grade (Berlin, 1960), which portrays West Germany as a territory occupied by British and American troops on page 17.
25. The documentary film duo of the GDR, Walter Heynowski and Gerhard Scheumann, produced this documentary on the basis of interviews conducted with ten US pilots shot down over North Vietnam and held captive there.
26. Although official representations during the entire existence of the GDR insisted on the version of self-liberation, the various available accounts also allow for varying interpretations, especially concerning the chronology of events, which imply that there was only a small time window of less than one hour between the flight of the SS troops and the appearance of the American troops – a time window in which the militarily organized prisoners would have had to occupy the strategic and symbolical points of the concentrations camp, such as the observation towers and the entrance gate. Notwithstanding these inconsistencies, the story of Buchenwald's self-liberation is at the heart of the antifascist prehistory of the GDR. It was molded in an exemplary and immensely popular novel: Bruno Apitz, *Nackt unter Wölfen* (Berlin, 1960). For a critical treatment of the resistance in Buchenwald and its posthistory in the GDR, see Lutz Niethammer, *Der "gesäuberte" Antifaschismus. Die SED und die roten Kapos von Buchenwald* (Berlin, 1994).
27. Dimitrov proclaimed this powerful formulation on 2 August 1935 at the Seventh World Congress of the Communist International: "[Fascism is] *the open terrorist dictatorship of the most reactionary, most chauvinistic and most imperialist elements of finance capital*," http://www.marxists.org/reference/archive/dimitrov/works/1935/08_02.htm.
28. On public interpretations, using the example of Hamburg, see Malte Thießen, "Gedenken an 'Operation Gomorrha'. Zur Erinnerungskultur des Bombenkrieges von 1945 bis heute," *Zeitschrift für Geschichtswissenschaft*, 53 (2005): 46–61.
29. Harald Welzer, Sabine Moller, and Karoline Tschugnall, *"Opa war kein Nazi!" Nationalsozialismus und Holocaust im Familiengedächtnis* (Frankfurt/M., 2002).
30. This finding is not only confirmed by my own, but also by other studies on the history of generations in the GDR. Dorothee Wierling, "Nationalsozialismus und Krieg in den Lebens-Geschichten der ersten Nachkriegsgeneration der DDR," in *Eine offene Geschichte. Zur kommunikativen Tradierung der nationalsozialistischen Vergangenheit*, ed. Elisabeth Domansky and Harald Welzer (Tübingen, 1999), 35–56. On generations and intergenerational relationships in the GDR, see the recent study: Annegret Schüle, Thomas Ahbe, and Rainer Gries, eds., *Die DDR aus generationengeschichtlicher Perspektive. Eine Inventur* (Leipzig, 2006), especially Sabine Moller and Nina Leonhard's treatment of National Socialism in intergenerational relationships.
31. The postwar generation's recollections and answers to the question: "What did your parents tell you about National Socialism" illustrate this point well. See Wierling (see note 7), chapter. 1.1.
32. In general, the literature on the topic only refers to developments of the 1980s. As yet, there is no systematic treatment of the entire history of right-wing radicalism in the GDR. Secluded cases are treated in Wierling (see note 7), 260–62.
33. Ina Dietzsch, *Grenzen überschreiben? Deutsch-deutsche Briefwechsel 1948–1989* (Cologne et al., 2004).
34. This is a reference to former German chancellor Willy Brandt's optimistic diagnosis at the time of the *Wende* in 1989/90: "Now grows together what belongs together."

Chapter 15

VIOLENCE AND VICTIMHOOD:
Looking Back at the World Wars in Europe

Richard Bessel

In January 1946, schoolchildren in the district of Prenzlauer Berg in the Soviet sector of Berlin were assigned the task of writing short essays about their memories of the Battle of Berlin during the previous spring. Among these were the observations of 10-year-old Winfried Schubarth, who wrote:

> Finally the time is past where we (no longer) have to live in the cellar. When the sirens sounded, we always were afraid. In November 1944 fifteen firebombs fell on our building. The men from our building, however, were at their posts, for they quickly discovered the fires and put them out. When the Russians came we all naturally were very afraid. We were also afraid for our mummy, because she always went out shopping during the shelling and cooked in the flat. A grenade fragment also flew through our double window and remained lodged in the wall. When the Russians arrived, the word was, out with the white flags or the building will be blown up! So we quickly and happily helped to raise white flags. Today we are all content and happy that it is all over and that the evil war has come to an end. And we want nothing more to do with it.[1]

At almost exactly the same time, Erich Dethleffsen, who had been named Chef der Führungsgruppe im Generalstab des Heeres in late March 1945 and thus became a visitor to the "Führerbunker" in Berlin during the last days of the Third Reich, was sitting in a prisoner-of-war camp in Allendorf, Kreis Marburg, and drafting personal memoirs. He began with the following observation:

> Only gradually, with dismay and reluctance, are we [i.e., we Germans] awakening from the agony of recent years and recognising ourselves and our situation. We are seeking exoneration, in order to avoid responsibility for

---

Notes for this chapter begin on page 242.

everything that led to the war now lying behind us, its ghastly casualties and terrible consequences. We feel we have been made fools of, seduced, misused.[2]

There is nothing particularly remarkable about either of these reflections in and of themselves. On the one hand, hundreds of thousands, perhaps millions of children could have expressed themselves in a fashion similar to Winfried Schubarth in 1946, describing their fear during war and their relief and happiness that the war had ended; on the other hand, the view expressed by Erich Dethleffsen, that the soldiers of the Wehrmacht "have [...] acted according to our best knowledge and conscience and have known little or nothing about all the dreadful crimes" ("nach bestem Wissen und Gewissen gehandelt und von all den scheusslichen Verbrechen wenig oder nichts gewusst [...] haben"), became common currency in postwar West Germany. Yet these reflections nevertheless are noteworthy precisely because they are unexceptional – in that they reflect the ways in which countless Europeans framed their experiences and memories of the Second World War. For millions of people, their experiences of war were remembered in terms of fear and agony, of sacrifice and of the terrible consequences of conflict, of being the objects of the horrors of war, of having behaved as best they could in terrible situations forced upon them, of having been betrayed – in short, remembered in terms of violence and victimhood.

Indeed, this became characteristic of the ways in which war in Europe came to be understood in the twentieth century – a consequence of the experiences of the two world wars and the ways in which Europeans remembered those experiences. If there has been one major change in mentalities that the world wars brought about in twentieth-century Europe, it is a turn away from the glorification of war. People came to be seen – and to see themselves – as passive victims of, not as active participants in violence. In the wake of the Second World War a popular and political consensus emerged across Europe that war was something terrible, something barbarous and something to be avoided if at all possible. Ministries of War became Ministries of Defence; military alliances – both NATO and the Warsaw Pact – proclaimed their aims to be defensive and their mission to be securing peace; political leaders, even when preparing for war, professed their commitment to peace; exhibitions devoted to the history of the world wars – for example, at the Imperial War Museum in London, the Historiale de la Grande Guerre at Péronne or the present-day museum at Berlin-Karlshorst at the site where Field Marshal Wilhelm Keitel signed the surrender document presented to him by Soviet Marshal Gregory Zhukov on 8 May 1945 – stress the pain, sacrifice and brutality of warfare.

Of course this postwar European conviction that war was to be avoided at all costs needs to be seen in its broader historical context. It also was a product of the Cold War, in which the dark cloud of possible nuclear annihilation hung heavy over European populations. Nightmares arising from past world wars joined fears of a future nuclear war. In the Federal Republic of Germany, protests against rearmament and possible "atomic death" brought hundreds of thousands of demonstrators out onto the streets in 1957 and 1958; in the German Democratic Republic as well, fears about a new, atomic war were widespread during the Korean crisis and as the East German state established its new socialist armed forces.[3] At the same time, it also should not be forgotten that, for all their horror at war, Europeans nevertheless fought numerous wars around the world after 1945 – from the Dutch East Indies, French Indochina and Malaya to Kenya, Korea and Algeria. But these wars generally were far away, and the civilians killed and maimed in them were not in the main Europeans.

The public consensus that war is hell was paralleled by the growing attention paid by historians over the past few decades to the victims of war: to the combatants who were killed in military conflict;[4] to the front soldiers caught in murderous battle and forced to endure dreadful conditions whether in the trenches of northern France or in the ruins of Stalingrad and Berlin; to the refugees made homeless by war; to the widows and orphans whose families were shattered by war; to the war wounded and war invalids who would bear their scars for the rest of their lives; to those bombed out of their dwellings; to the victims of rape which so often has accompanied war; to those (particularly the women) who faced the shortages, the malnutrition, the harsh working conditions on the home front "behind the lines."[5] Of course, there remains an ever-growing, obsessive popular literature about armies, battles, and military hardware; those who are fascinated by soldiers, uniforms, military equipment, and the minutiae of battle probably always will be with us. However, the trend in recent historical research, like that in the public sphere, has been to view war in terms of the violence it embodies and the destruction, both mental and physical, that it leaves in its wake. The history of war in Europe has become, in large measure, a history of its victims – and just about everyone has come to be counted among the victims of war.

This was not always so. Before the First World War, Europe's wars, and the soldiers who gave their lives in those wars, were celebrated with victory arches and victory columns.[6] Death in battle was remembered in terms of heroic sacrifice, which sanctified the ground on which the battle had taken place.[7] The readiness to frame experiences of war in terms of heroism and noble sacrifice was profoundly shaken and undermined through the mass slaughter which overwhelmed Europe between 1914 and 1945. The change did not happen at once or uniformly across the continent, and in some countries it would take two world wars rather than one to establish suffering and victimhood at the center of the ways in which Europeans remembered their wars. In many respects the French and the British were in the vanguard of this development. The 9-year-old French schoolgirl who, after being taken to see antiwar films in the summer of 1937, wrote that "war is a horror," was both a representative of the society and culture in which she was raised and a harbinger of things to come.[8] The sombre, funereal atmosphere of the ossuary at Douaumont (with its interior walls bearing inscriptions from the survivors of military units to the memory of their fallen comrades), the empty tomb of the Cenotaph in Whitehall and the gigantic memorial designed by Edward Lutyens at Thiepval for "The Missing of the Somme," reflect the attitudes of "the thousands of veterans who fervently commemorated war in order not to inflict it on their children."[9] As Eugen Weber has pointed out for interwar France:

> Armistice Day, November 11, provided annual reminders that the hecatomb it recapitulated should be the last. After 1919 the anniversary of the victory in 1918 became not a celebration of triumph but a remembrance of death. Anchored in that gloomy November day, the cult of the dead that loomed so large throughout the twenties and thirties became an annual reminder that repetition of recent horrors should be avoided at all costs.[10]

Although the British and French pacifism of the interwar years sat uneasily with the challenges posed by the military build-up of the Nazi regime, in many respects the ways in which the French and British looked back at the First World War – for both nations the greatest bloodletting in their histories – became the modern (European) face of war remembrance in the twentieth century. The experience of war was of violence and suffering; the memory of war was of victimhood and loss.

In Germany a parallel development did not really take hold until after the Second World War, when there too it was the human losses and material ruins left behind by war which came to provide the public focus for how people conceived of their war experiences and framed their war memories. Immediately after the war, when in any case an anti-war consensus dominated German society, the ways in which Germans could commemorate their war were circumscribed. Even had they wanted to do so, Germans would not have been able publicly to look back on their war as an expression of glory and heroism. The Allied occupation powers proscribed public commemoration of the German war dead; with the Allied Control Council's Directive No. 30 of 13 May 1946, the planning or building of any monuments which might glorify war and militarism were prohibited and existing monuments which did so were to be destroyed. In the early years of the Federal Republic, the Second World War tended to be remembered publicly in terms of violence and victimhood. On 18 February 1951 the Bundestag observed an hour of commemoration not just for fallen German soldiers but for all victims of war, including those who had died in the bombings, in the expulsions and in the concentration camps; instead of the "Heldengedenktag" ("Heroes' Remembrance Day") instituted by the Nazis in 1934 (and held in the spring), in 1952 the practice of the "Volkstrauertag" ("People's Day of Mourning"), instituted initially in 1919, was resuscitated and shifted back to November, the traditional month of mourning; memorials to the civilian victims of war – in keeping with the Allied directive – were erected across the country, usually employing religious imagery (mourning angels, crosses, *pietas*) to commemorate the violence and suffering of the victims of bombing and expulsion and usually erected in churchyards or other secluded places; and during the early 1950s POW memorials were created, in part as a call for the repatriation of those still in captivity.[11] The common inscription on the memorials was "For the victims of war and violence."

This motif has remained prominent and powerful, as evidenced in the choice by Helmut Kohl of an enlarged replica of Käthe Kollwitz's *pieta* to commemorate (and, controversially, to conflate) the victims of "war and the rule of violence" inside the Neue Wache on Berlin's Unter den Linden. Such a motif has been characteristic of the ways in which Europeans have looked back at the world wars and, as a result, at war in general. The emphasis is on the suffering and loss caused by the violence of war. It found clear expression in the most prominent public reminders of the war in postwar Germany: the preserved ruins of the Kaiser-Wilhelm Gedächtniskirche in (West) Berlin; the fragments of the Dresden Frauenkirche which were left as a ruin throughout the life of the German Democratic Republic and which served, in the words of the (last) official photo essay commemorating forty years of the GDR, to "remind of the destruction of the Elbe metropolis;"[12] and the former victory arch in Munich, which neatly encapsulates the transition from remembering war as victorious heroism to remembering war as a tragic destruction. The inscription on the Munich victory arch – "Dem Sieg geweiht, vom Krieg zerstört, zum Frieden mahnend" ("Consecrated for victory, destroyed by war, admonishing for peace") – may be seen as representative of how war came to be remembered in postwar West Germany.

Whether it is due to the unprecedented scale of the defeat suffered in 1945 or to the delay in the shift from lauding patriotic sacrifice to lamenting wartime suffering relative to France or Britain, in postwar Germany the tendency to view the experience of war in terms of victimhood has been particularly strong. This stands in stark contrast to the prevalence (but not monopoly) of a war-affirming "myth of the war experience" which (in the widely applauded view of George Mosse) served after the First World War to prepare the cultural and political ground for embarking on the next conflict.[13] The shift in German consciousness in 1945 was profound, as the German experiences of the Second World War left no room for a repeat of the war-affirming revanchism which followed the First. In this respect Hitler was proved right when he declared before the assembled Reichstag on 1 September 1939 that "a November 1918 will never be repeated in German history" ("ein November 1918 wird sich niemals mehr in der deutschen Geschchte wiederholen")[14] – but not at all in the way he had envisaged. In the last days of the Reich, Hitler and some of his more fanatical followers may have hoped that to continue the militarily hopeless, suicidal conflict would inspire future generations again to take up the struggle.[15] However, the total defeat which the Third Reich bequeathed to the German people in fact achieved just the opposite. It converted a nation once renowned for its reverence of the military into a nation which took what Konrad Jarausch has described as a fundamental turn to pacifism.[16] In this regard popular mentalities in the postwar Federal Republic of Germany, in which, according to public-opinion polls in the autumn of 1951, nearly half the population – and more than half of former Wehrmacht soldiers – now supported conscientious objection,[17] had come to resemble those of interwar France. War was seen not as a glorious crusade but as a terrible cataclysm which created only victims and was to be avoided at all costs.

More than that, war was not viewed solely or primarily as a male experience. Women too were regarded as participants in the conflict. However, their participation was largely as passive victims rather than as active protagonists. In her perceptive study of German women in the wake of the Second World War, Elizabeth Heinemann has observed that women's recollections of the war "focus on the events which most dramatically affected their lives: bombing raids, evacuation, flight, widowhood, rape and hunger."[18] This palette of war memories did not leave much room for glorifying war or the military. Instead, war experience and memories of war were framed in terms of loss, suffering, passivity, victimhood.

In order to understand this remarkable transformation of German mentalities, we need to remember that the final months of the war were by far the most violent, the most bloody for the Germans. The carnage of the last months of the Second World War gave the Germans a profound shock, even greater than the shock that the Battle of the Somme had given to the British almost three decades previously. For the Germans – who were the first nation in the history of the modern world to achieve total defeat – it was the experiences of the last months of the war and the first months of the "peace" in 1945 which burned most deeply into their memories. Half of the German casualties of the entire war occurred during the last year of the conflict, and the single month in which the Wehrmacht suffered its greatest losses was January 1945 (with the vast Soviet offensive which began on 12 January and effectively broke the back of the Wehrmacht);[19] and at the same time as German military losses were at their highest and the fighting on the ground reached German territory, the Allied bombing also reached its peak (as the entire Reich was within reach of Allied bombers and the Luftwaffe no longer was able to resist Allied incursions into German air space).[20] The violence of war was visited upon Germans to an unprecedented extent and with unprecedented intensity.

The catalog of suffering was vast. Millions lost their relatives, their limbs, their health, their possessions, their homes, their lives. Roughly eight million Germans were either bombed out of their dwellings or evacuated from cities to escape the bombing, and altogether some twelve million lost their homes in the provinces to the east of the Oder-Neiße and in the "Sudetenland." The catastrophic conditions faced by Germans in the last months of the war and the first months after the surrender overshadowed all that had come before – with the result that when Germans emerged from war in 1945 their memories of war were dominated by their terrible experiences at its end. In this way the earlier phases of the war – when the Wehrmacht was laying waste to much of the European continent and the German population had profited from a racist war of plunder – receded into the background. Instead, memories of the war tended to focus on the last months, when Germans themselves increasingly were the objects of the violence of war. Consequently, they emerged preoccupied with their own fate, their own victimhood.

This preoccupation was extreme among the millions of Germans who had lost their homes in the last months of the war and in the immediate aftermath, when the vast offensive by the Red Army in January 1945 precipitated the flight from their homes of millions of Germans, desperate to flee ahead of the advancing Soviet troops. The accounts of the flight and expulsions were given considerable publicity during the early years of the Federal Republic,[21] and during the postwar years occupied a central place in the German memory of the Second World War. For the millions of refugees, the shock of being cut off from established social networks and the infrastructure of modern industrial society and of being thrown back on their own resources in order to cope with the desperate day-to-day struggle to get food and shelter, could hardly have been greater. They had lost control of their lives; the communities in which they had lived were displaced and destroyed; the infrastructure which had sustained them and allowed for their wider social existence had been swept away. It is hardly surprising that they emerged with a profound sense of their own victimhood.

No less powerful was the sense of victimhood among the German soldiers who who found themselves as prisoners of war. This holds particularly true for those in Soviet camps. Their return provided constant reminders of the suffering caused by the war for a decade after the conflict had ended. The poor physical and mental condition of prisoners returning from Soviet captivity – the consequence of malnutrition, harsh treatment and hard labor – provided continuing evidence of the awful consequences of war. Men who returned in the late 1940s often were diagnosed as suffering from a specific "returnee disease" (*Heimkehrerkrankheit*), the symptoms of which included apathy, depression and a tendency to become easily agitated; throughout the 1950s studies continued to be made, and concern continued to be expressed, about the "long-term consequences" and the "permanent damage" caused by time spent in Soviet captivity.[22] These men attracted much public attention in the early postwar years and, rather than being regarded as active participants in Nazi Germany's wars, were regarded as its unfortunate victims.

The transformation of German memories of war experiences into memories of violence and victimhood – into memories which bore some resemblance to those which had emerged in France and Britain after the First World War – reflects the fact that the exposure of the crimes of the Nazi regime, the total defeat, and the enormous scale of the resulting suffering had emptied the war of any other meaning. The crimes of Nazism and the horrors of the war left no room for a celebration of heroism. Sabine Behrenbeck has observed the ways in which West Germans looked back from the late 1940s at their war, noting that "the heroes of war disappeared with the Nazis. Only war victims remained. The effects of war suffering were foregrounded instead of its causes." It was impossible to celebrate the cause for which the German population had suffered and for which the German war dead had died. As Behrenbeck has written: "Precisely because the war was emptied of any larger meaning, the fallen served to admonish the survivors about the need for peace."[23] The parallels with French and British perceptions after the First World War are striking in this regard: war was perceived as something senseless, devoid of meaning. The point of remembering the sacrifice of those who fell in battle or suffered due to war is to ensure that such senseless violence and slaughter does not recur. Like the veterans of the trenches who played dead soldiers returning home to judge the living in Abel Gance's film *J'accuse*, the victims of war admonish their successors to learn from catastrophe.[24] The sentiment inscribed on the First World War memorial at Gentioux, with a statue of a boy (presumably a war orphan) in the foreground calling attention to the inscription – "Maudite soit la guerre" ("cursed be war")[25] – became, if not universal, then at least pan-European.

It was not only among the losers – the civilians who lost members of their families and were bombed out or removed from their homes, the soldiers who languished for years and lost their health in prisoner-of-war camps, the Germans who emerged from the horrors of the last months of the war into a land which had achieved total defeat – that the experiences of the Second World War were viewed retrospectively through the prism of victimhood. The same sometimes even has occurred among the victors. For her recent exploration of the experience of the ordinary soldier of the Red Army, Catherine Merridale interviewed veterans six decades after their great victories over the Wehrmacht. Their narratives contained little reference to the "glory" that Soviet propaganda ritually had ascribed to the veterans of the "Great Patriotic War." Instead:

The war gave veterans very little. ... I asked every veteran I met if their army service had improved their lives, and most told me about the things that they had lost. The list included youth, years of freedom, health, and then the scores of people: comrades, parents, families. True, many soldiers received useful training, but most believe (correctly or not) that their skills could more easily have been acquired in peacetime. As for the loot, the feather pillows and the children's shoes, they were poor compensation for material loss and scant comfort for veterans' families in the lean years after the war. ... The only gain that significant numbers of the old soldiers did acknowledge was that the misery of war itself had made them value their survival more.[26]

One may argue that this is merely a (perhaps belated) recognition of reality – of the fact that misery and loss are what war has been about – or that it is a reflection of the demise of the Soviet Union and the end of a postwar period in which public glorification of the "Great Patriotic War" provided legitimation for the Soviet state. However, it also reflects a coming into line with what has become the dominant way in which people look back at the two world wars in Europe: war as violence and victimhood.

Why did this perspective become more widely accepted in Europe after the Second World War than after the First? One reason may lie in the contrasting nature of the two wars. As a result of the world wars, millions of people, civilians as well as soldiers, had experienced the violence of war at first hand across the European continent. However, unlike the First World War, at least in the West, the Second World War was a war of movement, which laid waste to vast tracts of the European continent and resulted in the deaths of at least as many civilians as it did of soldiers. In this, it perhaps resembled the Revolutionary and Napoleonic Wars a century and a half earlier more than it did the First World War; it was a global conflict, and it was fought from one side of the European continent to the other.

Nevertheless, unlike the Revolutionary and Napoleonic Wars but like the First World War, the story of the Second World War has revolved around the experience of violence and the memory of victimhood. Heroism provided an important motif for the ways in which the victorious superpowers remembered their Second World War – most prominently the massive Soviet war memorials built in the 1960s and 1970s at Volgograd (Stalingrad), at the fortress of Brest and at Vitebsk (where, according to a Soviet commentator in 1980 the "Breakthrough" complex with its giant statue of a partisan holding an automatic weapon "appealed for manliness").[27] (An American parallel is the monument in Arlington Virginia commemorating the raising of the flag on Iwo Jima with its inscription "uncommon valor was a common virtue," although, to my knowledge, no comparable memorial commemorates the American combat experience in Europe.) However, it has not done so elsewhere in

Europe. Here the war is looked back upon as a time of suffering, violence, death. In the wake of the world wars in Europe, combat has tended to be viewed from the perspective of those on the receiving end of the violence rather than those who delivered it. And now, more than sixty years after the end of the Second World War, European attempts to memorialize heroism in stone often seem peculiarly inappropriate – indeed, they can appear as strange abandoned iconography washed up from a bygone age.

In Western Europe, austere monuments to wartime experience already began to appear out of place in the less disciplined and more prosperous consumer societies which had taken hold by the 1960s.[28] There "the decay of patriotic memory" (Pieter Lagrou)[29] set in during the late 1960s and, especially, the 1970s – at the time when the first postwar generation was coming of age. More recently, the collapse of the Soviet Union has given a particular twist to the erosion of heroic war memories, as massive monuments to a heroic "Great Patriotic War" look out over landscapes culturally rather distant from those in which they were built. Among the most striking examples of this are the Soviet war memorials celebrating the liberation of places (such as Sevastopol and Kiev) which now lie outside of Russia, where liberation meant the transfer from Nazi barbarism to Stalinist tyranny, and in Berlin-Treptow, where the giant figure of a Red Army soldier holding a child while standing on a smashed swastika and where quotations from Stalin on shiny stone walls (erected between 1946 and 1948 and handed over to the Berlin city government in September 1949) have little connection to life in the capital of a reunited Germany. Catherine Merridale has observed that "there is, in fact, no political home anywhere for the patriotism that these buildings commemorate."[30] They are increasingly strange traces of a bygone age.

Among the most powerful reinforcements for remembering the world wars in terms of violence, destruction, suffering and victimhood were the landscapes of destruction which the wars left in their wake. The application of new technologies by mass armed forces led to destruction on an unprecedented scale. The most famous of such landscapes stemming from the First World War was the devastation left behind from the North Sea to Champagne by the fighting in northern France – a gigantic zone of destruction, the recovery and reconstruction of which was among the largest building projects undertaken anywhere on earth during the interwar years; the reconstruction project was not completed officially until 1931, and even during the 1930s a tenth of dwellings and factories in the zone had not been rebuilt.[31] After the Second World War, the landscapes of destruction left behind were far more extensive. The war of movement and aerial bombing vastly increased the extent of physical destruction across the European continent. From Coventry and Rotterdam to Warsaw and Minsk, from Brest and Hamburg to Dresden and Kiev, urban landscapes across Europe bore the scars of the conflict for decades. Enormously destructive land battles, from Monte Cassino to Stalingrad, from the Ardennes to Halbe, left large swathes of the European countryside a wasteland. For a generation after the Second World War, Europeans inhabited an environment which contained daily reminders of war: bombed-out and charred ruins, buildings pock-marked with bullet holes, piles of rubble. The desperate housing shortages left in the wake of the war – roughly one quarter of the German population was homeless at the end of the conflict – meant that for years millions of Europeans were compelled to live many to a room in cellars, bombed-out buildings, and camps. War – or, more precisely, the damage and suffering caused by war – remained a physical reality for decades.

The violence of war affected not just the built environment but also human bodies. During the postwar years there were millions of Europeans who bore the scars of war. The fact that so many people had experienced combat, either as soldiers or as civilians caught up in the fighting or suffering beneath the bombs, meant that the extent of war-related injuries in post-1945 Europe was enormous. As after the First World War, after the Second World War men without arms or legs were a common sight in the former combatant countries, men who became war's "living memorials."[32] In the Federal Republic of Germany, there were more than 1.5 million registered war-disabled in January 1952, and as late as 1957 over half of all the physically disabled in the country were disabled because of the war.[33] Inside the bodies of countless men across the European continent lay splinters of shrapnel; millions of people physically bore the mark of war. They were an enduring and visible reminder that war meant suffering, that war created victims.

The presence of war victims – of the hundreds of thousands of war disabled, war widows, war orphans, war refugees, people bombed out of their homes – reinforced the perception of war in terms of violence and victimhood in another way: it created huge reservoirs of people who became dependent upon state aid and private charity, and whose modest material welfare depended upon their status as war victims. In West Germany alone there were nearly a million registered war widows in 1952.[34] The world wars created a massive demand for state-sponsored social services and welfare programs; indeed, it is hardly an accident that the welfare state in Europe – whether in its liberal-democratic, social-market-economy form or in its state-socialist form – developed in the wake of the world wars. The victims of the world wars were among the main clients of the postwar welfare states. Economically dependent upon their status as war victims, they had a material interest in stressing the degree to which they had suffered as a result of war.

However, that now largely has receded into the past. Almost all the veterans of the First World War now have died; the veterans (and widows) of the Second World War are leaving the scene as well. European welfare rolls today are filled with single-parent families in societies where divorce has been liberalized, not with "mutilés de guerre" or with war widows. The landscapes of destruction left by the two world wars have largely disappeared, been paved over or submerged under new building. The traveler speeding through northern France on the TGV or the autoroute would need considerable imagination to realize that some of the areas seen out of the window once were described as a moonscape. The pedestrian walking through the centre of Berlin or Hamburg can be forgiven for failing to realize that these were scenes of utter destruction sixty years ago. Where battle-scarred buildings remain, they are now preserved, museum-like; the scars of war no longer form part of Europeans' everyday lives. In this regard, Pierre Nora is right: "sites of memory" (*lieux de mémoire*) have replaced memory.

In his fine study of the German disabled victims of the First World War, Robert Weldon Whalen concluded:

> The war victims seem almost contemporary. This is preeminently the century of the survivor; the survivor of Hiroshima, the survivor of Auschwitz. The victims of the Great War were the first generation of survivors. They are our ancestors. Their experience is our own.[35]

But these words were written more than two decades ago. "This century" no longer is our century. The war victims no longer seem almost contemporary; they may be our ancestors, but their experience no longer is our own. It therefore may be mistaken to assume that we now have arrived at a point whereby, thanks to the terrible experiences of the two world wars, enlightened Europeans finally have come to appreciate the true nature of war, and that this perception of war has become permanently fixed in European political culture and popular mentalities. The idea that the Second World War and the mass murder of European Jews inextricably linked to that war formed "a common historical foundation of Europe"[36] may have gained broad acceptance over the past few decades. But times are changing. We now live in a Europe millions of whose residents – with their origins in Africa both north and south of the Sahara, in Turkey, in India and Pakistan, in Indonesia and China – do not share this foundation for their historical consciousness. The experience and memory of the world wars either are not necessarily central to their historical consciousness or, if they are, may figure in ways quite different than in hitherto dominant European narratives of the world wars and their aftermaths. To note only one example: 1945 may signify something quite different to people who identify with Algeria, for whom the end of the Second World War was hardly a liberation, from what it does for people who identify with metropolitan France.

Furthermore, the problem is not simply that an increasingly multicultural Europe may be breaking up a sense of common historical heritage and memory stemming from the Second World War, or that those who experienced at first hand the world wars are dying out. The importance of the war in the consciousness of those born subsequently – of people for whom (as Dorothee Wierling has noted of those whose birth coincided with the founding of the GDR) "the past sufferings of their parents not only determine their entire pre-history but become their own experience, part of their own history"[37] – also is generation-specific. Thus the historians of the Second World War who were born and raised in a postwar world do not necessarily share the perspectives of their students, many of whom are too young even to remember when that postwar world came to its end in Europe between 1989 (with the fall of the Berlin Wall) and 1991 (with the fall of the Soviet Union). For them, as for the younger public generally, it is increasingly questionable whether the Second World War continues to provide a "common historical foundation."

Let me close with some personal observations. My mother's family perished in the Second World War. My father fought in the Second World War. The Second World War cast a long shadow throughout my childhood and adolescence. Although I did not experience the Second World War at first hand, it never was out of my consciousness. My historical points of reference were located in the Second World War. Many of my older relatives had lived through it; they had suffered as a result of it, and it had shaped their lives. The war was a frequent topic of conversation, and loomed in the background even when it was not mentioned explicitly. When as a child visiting relatives in Lorraine, very near the German border and only a few kilometres away from the largest American military cemetery in Europe at St. Avold, I was confronted constantly by physical and human fragments of the Second World War: the bullet holes in the houses, the warnings not to explore nearby forests as they might be mined, the story of my aged aunt who spent the war years in the French interior. I lived in a postwar world, and carry these memories with me today.

This is not true for my students or for my children. They are products not of a postwar world but of a post-postwar world. They did not grow up with war-scarred landscapes; their parents had not suffered at first hand from the war; they did not grow up listening to the war stories of those who had participated in the conflict; they have not had contact with people who lost their relatives or their limbs in war; they do not live in countries ruled by men who had fought in the world wars (such as Harold Macmillan, Charles de Gaulle, Leonid Brezhnev, John Kennedy and Helmut Schmidt). Their points of historical reference are not located in the Second World War, to say nothing of the First. For them the history of the Second World signifies something quite different, insofar as it figures at all. Either it is a historical event in the distant past, or else it has been lifted almost out of history as the incarnation of absolute evil in the form of the Nazi programs of genocide. There is, therefore, a significant gulf in historical consciousness which is opening up between the historians of the world wars and their publics.

What we have in common, however, is a language of war as violence and victimhood, of war as suffering and loss. This is a legacy of the world wars which has become part of our culture in Europe. Yet historical consciousness always changes, and the ways in which Europeans look back on the world wars also are located in a particular time, place and historical context. The second half of the twentieth century witnessed the development in Europe of a remarkable consensus about how one looks back on war, as a consequence of the incredibly violent history of the first half of that century. But that too may change.

Notes

1. Fascimilie reproduced in Bengt von zur Mühlen (ed.), *Der Todeskampf der Reichshauptstadt* (Berlin-Kleinmachnow, 1994), 398:

    Endlich ist die Zeit vorüber wo wir (nicht mehr) im Keller hausen müssen. Wenn die Sirenen ertönten, hatten wir schon immer vorher Angst. Im November 1944 fielen auf unser Haus fünfzehn Brandbomben. Unsere Männer aus dem Hause waren aber sehr auf dem Posten, denn sie haben die Brände bald entdeckt und gelöscht. Als die Russen kamen hatten wir natürlich große Angst. Um unsere Mutti hatten wir auch Angst, denn sie ist immer während des Beschüsses einkaufen gegangen und in der Wohnung hat sie gekocht. Durch unsere Doppelfenster ist auch ein Granatsplitter geflogen und ist an der Wand stecken geblieben. Als die Russen kamen, da hieß es, weiße Fahnen heraus oder das Haus wird in der Luft gesprengt! Da waren wir schnell und freudig dabei, die weiße Fahne zu hissen. Heute sind wir alle zufrieden und glücklich , daß alles vorbei ist und der böse Krieg ein Ende hat. Und wir wollen auch gar nichts mehr davon wissen.

2. Bundesarchiv-Militärarchiv Freiburg, N 648/1: Dethleffsen Erinnerungen:

    Erst langsam, erschreckend und widerstrebend erwachen wir [d.h. wir Deutschen] aus der Agonie der letzten Jahre und erkennen wir uns selbst und unsere Situation. Wir suchen nach Entlastung, um uns der Verantwortung an all dem, was zu dem hinter uns liegenden Krieg, seinen grausigen Opfern und furchtbaren Folgen geführt hat, zu entziehen. Wir glauben uns genarrt, verführt, missbraucht.

3. For the Federal Republic, see Michael Geyer, "Cold War Angst: The Case of West-German Opposition to Rearmament and Nuclear Weapons," in Hanna Schissler (ed.), *The Miracle Years. A Cultural History of West Germany, 1949–1968* (Princeton and Oxford, 2001), pp. 376–408. For the GDR, see the reports of the Volkspolizei on popular opinion about the establishment of a "People's Army" in mid-1952, in Mecklenburgisches Landeshauptarchiv Schwerin, Kreistag/Rat des Kreises Uekermünde/Pasewalk, Nr. 118.

4. Joanna Bourke notes in the introduction to her *An Intimate History of Killing. Face-to-Face Killing in Twentieth-Century Warfare* (London, 1999), 2, that "readers of military history books might be excused for believing that combatants found in war zones were really there to *be* killed, rather than to kill."
5. E.g., Margaret Randolph Higonnet, Jane Jenson, Sonya Michel and Margaret Collins Weitz (eds.), *Behind the Lines. Gender and the Two Wold Wars* (New Haven and London, 1987).
6. See, for example, Kai Kruse and Wolfgang Kruse, "Kriegerdenkmäler in Bielefeld. Ein lokalhistorischer Beitrag zur Entwicklungsanalyse des deutschen Gefallenenkultes im 19. und 20. Jahrhundert," in Reinhart Koselleck and Michael Jeismann (eds.), *Der politische Totenkult. Kriegerdenkmäler in der Moderne* (Munich, 1994), 91–105.
7. For example, in the keynote speech by Clemens Thieme (the Chairman of the "Deutscher Patriotenbund") at the unveiling of the Leipzig "Völkerschlachtdenkmal" ("Battle of the Nations Monument") in 1913. See Stefan-Ludwig Hoffmann, "Sakraler Monumentalismus um 1900. Das Leipziger Völkerschlachtdenkmal," in Koselleck and Jeismann (eds.), *Der politische Totenkult*, 276–77.
8. *Marie-Claire*, supplement *Nos enfants* (July 1937). Quoted in Eugen Weber, *The Hollow Years. France in the 1930s* (London, 1995), 21.
9. Jay Winter and Antoine Prost, *The Great War in History. Debates and Controversies, 1914 to the Present* (Cambridge, 2005), 181.
10. Eugen Weber, *The Hollow Years. France in the 1930s* (London, 1995), 16.
11. See Sabine Behrenbeck, "Between Pain and Silence. Remembering the Victims of Violence in Germany after 1949," in Richard Bessel and Dirk Schumann (eds.), *Life after Death. Approaches to a Cultural and Social History of Europe During the 1940s and 1950s* (Cambridge and New York, 2003), 37–64.
12. Klaus Ullrich, Peter Seifert, Brigitte Müller and Horst Sauer (eds.), *Deutsche Demokratische Republik* (Leipzig [1989]), 102: "Die Ruine der im zweiten Weltkrieg zerstörten Frauenkirche von Dresden – mahnt an die Zerstörung der Elbcmetropole." See also Rudy Koshar, *Germany's Transcient Pasts. Preservation and National Memory in the Twentieth Century* (Chapel Hill, 1998), 255–56.
13. George L. Mosse, *Fallen Soldiers. Reshaping the Memory of World Wars* (New York and Oxford, 1990).
14. Reichstagsrede vom 1. September 1939, in Erhard Klöss (ed.), *Reden des Führers. Politik und Propaganda Adolf Hitlers 1922–1945* (Munich, 1967), 215.
15. See Bernd Wegner, "Hitler, der Zweite Weltkrieg und die Choreographie des Untergangs," *Geschichte und Gesellschaft*, vol. xxvi (2000), no. 3, 492–518. See also Sabine Behrenbeck, *Der Kult um die toten Helden. Nationalsozialistische Mythen, Riten und Symbole* (Vierow bei Greifswald, 1996), 580–91.
16. Konrad H. Jarausch, "1945 and the Continuities of German History: Reflections on Memory, Historiography, and Politics," in Geoffrey J. Giles (ed.), *Stunde Null: The End and the Beginning Fifty Years Ago* (Washington, 1997), 18.
17. Michael Geyer, "Cold War Angst," 386–87.
18. Elizabeth D. Heinemann, *What Difference Does a Husband Make? Women and Marital Status in Nazi and Postwar Germany* (Berkeley, Los Angeles and London, 1999), 79.
19. Rüdiger Overmans, *Deutsche militärische Verluste im Zweiten Weltkrieg* (Munich, 1999), 265–66.
20. Over half the total tonnage of bombs dropped by the Allies on Germany during the war were dropped in 1944, and one quarter were dropped from January through April 1945. See Bundesminister für Vertriebene, Flüchtlinge und Kriegsbeschädigte (ed.), *Dokumente Deutscher Kriegsschäden. Evakuierte – Kriegsgeschädigte – Währungsgeschädigte. Die geschichtliche und rechtliche Entwicklung*, vol. 1 (Bonn, 1958), 46.

21. The most important effort in this regard is the three-volume documentation of the expulsion of Germans from east of the Oder-Neiße, collected by a commission headed by Theodor Schieder and published by the German Federal Ministry for Expellees, Refugees and War Invalids in 1954: Bundesministerium für Vertriebene, Flüchtlinge und Kriegsgeschädigte (ed.), *Die Vertreibung der deutschen Bevölkerung aus den Gebieten östlich der Oder-Neiße* (Bonn, 1954; reprinted Augsburg, 1993).
22. Frank Biess, "Men of Reconstruction – The Reconstruction of Men. Returning POWs in East and West Germany, 1945–1955," in Karen Hagemann and Stefanie Schüler Springorum (eds.), *Home/Front. The Military, War and Gender in Twentieth-Century Germany* (Oxford and New York, 2002), 338.
23. Sabine Behrenbeck, "The Transformation of Sacrifice: German Identity between Heroic Narrative and Economic Success," in Paul Betts and Greg Eghigian (eds.), *Pain and Prosperity. Reconsidering Twentieth-Century German History* (Stanford, 2003), 134–35.
24. Jay Winter, *Sites of Memory, Sites of Mourning. The Great War in European Cultural History* (Cambridge and New York, 1995), 15–22.
25. A photograph of the memorial may be found in Antoine Prost, *Les anciens combattants et la société française*, vol. 3, *Mentalités et ideologies* (Paris, 1977), monuments aux morts, no. 56.
26. Catherine Merridale, *Ivan's War. The Red Army 1939–45* (London, 2005), 334.
27. Frank Kämpfer, "Vom Massengrab zum Heroen-Hügel. Akkulturationsfunktionen sowjetischer Kriegsdenkmäler," in Koselleck and Jeismann (eds.), *Der politische Totenkult*, 327–49, quotation ("Der Memorialkomplex 'Durchbruch' ruft zur Mannhaftigkeit auf.") from 334. See also Sabine Rosemarie Arnold, "'Das Beispiel der Heldenstadt wird ewig die Herzen der Völker erfüllen!' Gedanken zum sowjetischen Totenkult am Beispiel des Gedenkkomplexes in Volgograd," in the same volume, 351–74.
28. Pieter Lagrou cites the interesting case of the Dutch national monument on the Damplein in Amsterdam, which became a famous place for youths to gather in the late 1960s. See Pieter Lagrou, *The Legacy of Nazi Occupation. Patriotic Memory and National Recovery in Western Europe, 1945–1964* (Cambridge, 2000), 295.
29. Lagrou, *The Legacy of Nazi Occupation*, 15.
30. Merridale, *Ivan's War*, 324.
31. See Hugh D. Clout, *After the Ruins: Restoring the Countryside in Northern France after the Great War* (Exeter University Press, 1996); Weber, *The Hollow Years*, 15–17.
32. The phrase comes from Deborah Cohen's excellent study of the war-disabled in Britain and Germany after the First World War, *The War Come Home. Disabled Veterans in Britain and Germany, 1914–1939* (Berkeley, Los Angeles and London, 2001), 102.
33. Vera Neumann, *Nicht der Rede wert. Die Privatisierung der Kriegsfolgen in der frühen Bundesrepublik. Lebensgeschichtliche Erinnerungen* (Münster, 1999), 22, 137.
34. Neumann, *Nicht der Rede wert*, 22, 137.
35. Robert Weldon Whalen, *Bitter Wounds. German Victims of the Great War, 1914–1939* (Ithaca and London, 1984), 192.
36. Thus the position paper offered by the organizers of the conference for which this article originally was prepared: "Der Zweite Weltkrieg und der mit ihm untrennbar verbundene Massenmord an den europäischen Juden ist – wenngleich auf ganz unterschiedliche Weise – ein gemeinsames historisches Fundament Europas."
37. Dorothee Wierling, *Geboren im Jahr Eins. Der Jahrgang 1949 in der DDR. Versuch einer Kollektivbiographie* (Berlin, 2002), 48: "Die vergangenen Leiden der Eltern bestimmen nicht nur die ganze Vorgeschichte, sondern werden zum eigenen Erlebnis, zum Teil der eigenen Geschichte."

Chapter 16

THE MEANINGS OF THE SECOND WORLD WAR IN CONTEMPORARY EUROPEAN HISTORY

Jörg Echternkamp and Stefan Martens

How tangible the past is does not depend on how far back it dates. Even events that are increasingly regarded as belonging to a different era can attain a new significance when the public's sensitivity increases, when fundamental conditions of memory and remembrance change (such as in 1989/90), or when historians discover and develop new aspects that enhance the complexity of the research topic. This appears to be particularly true for the Second World War and its aftermath – considering the Europe-wide "remembrance-boom" surrounding the commemoration of the sixtieth anniversary of 8 May 1945. By the beginning of the 1990s, at the latest, the history of the war was reestablished as a central topic in the humanities. For some time now – and not just within the "guild" itself – we can observe an increased interest in a multi-perspective military history that encompasses social and cultural aspects as well.

The Second World War ended in 1945; after that, a new chapter of history began. For decades, this was the manner in which the recent European past was conveniently classified. This chronological order can no longer be taken for granted, however, just as the concurrent complementary division of labor among historians is no longer self-evident. At least since 1989/90, the multilayered, mid- to long-term, in part still virulent effects of this "total" war in Western and Eastern Europe have become a focal point of public and academic interest. We have long come to realize how necessary and fruitful it is to break with the historiographical logic of the Cold War and its predetermined patterns of recognition and to – not least of all – examine the war's persistence in the postwar era more closely. This does not merely pertain to the material destruction. After victory or capitulation, farther reaching effects of the war prevented postwar

---

Notes for this chapter begin on page 263.

societies from settling down: the demographic shifts, especially those brought about by flight and expulsion, but also the – sometimes forced – repatriation of displaced persons, the reintegration of the returning, sometimes invalid soldiers, and the resulting exacerbated problem of social assimilation – all these aspects play an important role. In addition, the new political order established in the rough climate of the East–West antagonism ensured that the Hot War was quickly succeeded by a Cold War.

Rather than in retrospect constituting a *pre*history to something new, the postwar period should primarily be regarded in this light, i.e., as a time that was decisively molded by the war's multifaceted effects. This period following the war is succinctly denoted by the concepts postwar era, *Nachkrieg*, *l'après-guerre* – terms whose semantics simultaneously allude to the war and its legacy. This reflects the seemingly paradoxical circumstance that the war did not end with the end of the war. The caesura of 8 May 1945 begins to lose its poignancy already when considering the developments in a single country more closely. Extending the vantage point to incorporate the historical experiences and perceptions of more than one country, it can even be quite misleading. The war ended at different points in time and its effects reached far beyond its end. The years of extreme passive and active experiences of violence threw long shadows, some of which even reach into the present.

The postwar era was not least of all shaped by the manner in which the wartime was conveyed or hushed up. The tension between remembering and forgetting, the competition of different inclinations toward action and interpretation as consequences of the war, the possible discrepancy between personal, private recollections and official versions, especially in dictatorships – this is the conflict-laden presence of the past to which the wordplay "the war in the postwar era" alludes. This way of approaching the issue bears witness to the increased interest in the social, cultural, and military dynamics of the transformation phase between war and postwar era, as – for example – studied in France under the caption *sorties de guerre*.[1]

A snapshot of the Belgian village Houffalize near Gouvy illustrates certain aspects of this transition (see photo). Houffalize is one of those places whose destruction marks the beginning of the end of the war. On 6 January 1945, it was leveled to the ground: 310 of its 345 houses were destroyed and 200 of its 1450 inhabitants fell victim to the attack. This occurred during the last great battle on the ground, in which over one million soldiers were involved, the Ardennes Offensive, or the Battle of the Bulge, as the Americans call it owing to the indentation the Wehrmacht briefly struck into the frontlines in this eastern and northeastern part of Belgium as well as in parts of Luxembourg. The black and white photograph[2] depicts the deep, tangible traces of the battles – both the ground battles as well as the Allied bombardments – that eventually forced the Wehrmacht's Commander-in-Chief West, Field Marshal Gerd von Rundstedt, to retreat. The small village resembles a wasteland of ruins and debris. In the foreground of the photograph, a German *Panther V* tank reminds the observer of the source of the disaster. The tank had been employed by the 116th armored division to guard a bridge and had fallen into the Ourthe River. In the background, the steeple of the Church of St. Katharina, built in the twelfth and thirteenth centuries, still stands. The photograph was not taken during the war, but shortly after its end in June 1945. The battles are over; it is as if one "hears" the deathly silence after the uproar of war. Upon closer inspection, one discovers four elderly men toward the right and in the center of the picture who still disbelievingly look upon the remainders of their existence. From the bridge, two men observe another man who is manipulating the tank. However, the photograph does not simply depict the destruction. It also documents first attempts at reconstruction. The debris has already been moved aside, the street has been cleared and a temporary bridge with a wooden handrail leads across the little river. The photograph is an impressive snapshot of the transition period between the war and the postwar era with its allusion to the years before and after 1945. To this day, the tank, which now stands on a pedestal, serves as a monument to the end of the war in Houffalize.[3]

Photo 1: Battle of the Bulge, Houffalize/Belgium 1945; CEGES (Brussels), picture no. 13037

Although there are recent studies in the research on the World Wars focusing on national history which, in addition to the strategic, operational, and tactical processes as well as political and diplomatic developments, to varying degrees also allow room for social history, history of mentalities, and history of experiences with respect to the war. There also exist comprehensive studies that explore the World War as a *world* war from a global historical perspective[4] instead of ultimately resorting to a national history approach that traces the events as seen through "nationally-tinted" glasses – sometimes the conception betrays the semantics. Lastly, in the history of memory and remembrance there are – in addition to analyses informed by national history – a few scattered international comparisons of the multiple "cultures of remembrance" with respect to the war.[5] But despite the historical and contemporary significance of the Second World War, there is to this day a lack of convincing studies whose methodological approach reaches further and accomplishes both: first, to relate war experiences and war memories to one another in a way that transcends the approach limited to the "caesura" of 1945, assuming that one's own respective "experiences" shape an inclination toward specific, culturally codified memories; and second, to study this process of the interpretative treatment of the war era before and after 1945 in a European, if not global, context.

I. European history, history in Europe, and the war

It seems paradoxical: historical nationalism research has studied the complex process of nation building over the past years, among other things closely examining the relationship between war and "nation,"[6] and exposed traditional myths that surround the founding of the nation state. But, by choosing the "nation" as the historiographical frame of reference, this area of research in a way implicitly reinforced the importance of nations and national histories as entities of world history. In this perspective, the important European nexus was frequently neglected while the development of national identities, for example, always stood in the foreground.

The beginnings of this nexus often dated to the 1950s and its causes are mainly attributed to the experiences of violence between 1939 and 1945. Especially from a political history perspective, (national) history appears to have reached a qualitatively new level as a result of the European unification process.[7] If, instead, we define the term "Europeanization" more broadly as an increase in interaction and communication, our viewpoint transcends the perceived caesura of the war's end and reaches well into the eighteenth century. In this case, "Europe" has less to do with cultural and geographical factors than with the – non-judgmental

– dynamic category of experiencing interaction and with "uneven and asymmetric relations, and competitive, often violent encounters."[8] The guiding question of such a Europeanized historiography would then target the respective manifestations of transnational experiences, contingent on certain times and places, for men and women belonging to a specific generation or class.

The border-transcending character of the war, especially of its destructive dimension, is obvious. The "total war," totalitarian ideologies, and ethnic tensions in twentieth-century Europe led to an exceptional dynamic of violence,[9] although even the totality of this total war had its boundaries.[10] In general, evidently any assessment of twentieth-century war violence crucially depends on whether one focuses on the modern European–North American history of war or on the epoch-spanning violence of war in antiquity.[11] Although they were rarely studied as such, wars and their aftermaths are undoubtedly inter- and transnational phenomena *par excellence*.[12] Regardless of whether in public, media-conveyed memory or in historiographical representation: to this day, the field of vision within which "the war" appears is frequently constricted (if not distorted) by national history perspectives. These national accounts of the war center around the life and death of one's "own" population, while even in retrospect the "others" are often left unconsidered. On the one hand, this is understandable if one considers the magnitude of the losses suffered, the immediate "affectedness" – which in itself, of course, is partially constructed beyond the actual affectedness through national memory in the first place.

On the other hand, national accounts of the war are certainly related to the fact that experiences and memories played (or again play) an immensely important role for the definition of national identities. The Second World War was a deep break in the continuity of existence for individuals and social groups. Memory work was and continues to be an effective way to come to terms with these experiences. A fitting interpretation of the supposedly shared (war) past therefore plays a special role in the construction and reconstruction of collective, of national identities – especially when considering the problems of social integration all postwar societies are confronted with. For some time now, ever since the "cultural turn," the construction of these sorts of images of the past that generate meaning as well as models of interpretation and reasoning has been a preferred object of historical research. "Myths of the Nation" (*Mythen der Nation*) was hence the fitting title of an exhibition at the German Historical Museum in Berlin dealing with constructions of history rooted in the war, with the founding myths of "national rebirth" from a history of perception and history of memory perspective. Here, the stereotypical icons of the Second World War that constantly resurface in the "memory of images" were at the center of attention – those well known from postcards, stamps, or medals.[13]

In this sense, there is a lack of modern comprehensive accounts. The partially similar, partially divergent events and experiences in Europe are thus far less known to the general public than those in the home country. This is particularly true for those places where the national view has until now dominated for reasons related to the close connection between the memory of the war and "coming to terms" with one's own (National Socialist or Fascist) past, or collaboration.[14] The debates on the significance of the Second World War in different European societies are likely to be even less well known, as these are often widely branched historiographical, hence academically specialized discussions. Nonetheless, the core of these discussions may well be of interest to those unfamiliar with the discourse as they elucidate the dependence of historical images on political changes – especially since the end of the Cold War.

Not just the political justification, but also the scholarly benefit of a historical treatment of Europe is undisputed – particularly in those cases where historiography goes beyond the mere juxtaposing of national histories and recognizes new issues, raises new questions,[15] transcends conventional historiography, and enhances the attractiveness of European history (or histories) again. Wherever there is talk of Europe and history, two approaches can generally be distinguished: history in Europe and European history. The history in Europe approach usually amounts to a more or less heterogeneous compilation of historical processes in different European countries. The in this sense uniqueness of the European case is not of primary interest here. Not least of all, a comparison with a non-European example would be required in order to recognize Europe's specifics. European histories, in turn, primarily rely on structural–historical developments, usually addressing questions of convergence and divergence. In conclusion by analogy, for example, they infer the eventual convergence of countries from similarities in social structure, political institutions, or bureaucracy. Frequently, the nation state also plays a role here.[16]

In this context, an analysis of those construction processes in which Europe appears as an object of reference is also of interest, more so than the basically essentialist ascriptions and normative notions of what Europe is and should be.[17] It is about perceptions of oneself and the other, about the "idea Europe" in historical perspective – for the development of which the beginning of the Second World War played a central role. The Europe-discourse of German expatriates, for example, changed fundamentally in 1938/39. Until then, the experiences of the Weimar Republic had shaped rather vague notions of "Europe." The Munich Agreement, the Hitler–Stalin Pact, and last but not least the World War as well as precursors to a bipolar world order led to a systematic discourse on Europe which distanced itself from the National Socialist ideas of a racially determined continent.[18] After the end of the war, this discourse would have continuing effects on the ideology of the "occident."[19]

The European historiography that conceives Europe as a whole and depicts culture and progress as intrinsic values of a European culture, was time and again directly related to experiences of extreme crisis: during the First World War, the 1930s, and finally the Second World War. In 1944/45, the title of Lucien Febvre's inauguration speech at the recently liberated Collège de France was "L'Europe. Genèse d'une civilization."[20] Moreover, European works of history were part of the ideological battle of Western democracies against National Socialism and Fascism, first and foremost *The Unity of European History*, which John Bowle had written in large parts during the war.[21] In the postwar era, especially after the founding of European institutions, European histories were written with teleological intent. They were supposed to bear witness to the path toward European unity, which had already been laid out and traveled in the past. Entirely in the narrative style of the older national histories, the historical roots of a collective (national or European) identity were to be laid bare, and the lines of continuity purportedly dating back centuries drawn into the present. This is understandable in the sense that the intent was primarily to unmask the nationalistic myths that had led to such catastrophic consequences in the war.

During the Cold War, a strategic, selective memory of the war on both sides of the Iron Curtain ensured that the status quo was firmly established.[22] Selective does not mean wrong, however. Rather, an excerpt of the past was generalized in such a way that other memories were blocked out in favor of a positive self-image. Those who focused on official versions, which emphasized victimhood, were able to forget personal digressions, or at least to push these into the background along with the victimization of others, especially the Jews. The way in which the war was remembered reflected the political constellation and ideological competition of the Cold War. The smallest common denominator was the conviction that the Germans carried the responsibility for the war, the suffering, and the crimes. Independent of its plausibility, this consensus had the advantage of blocking out other, less "suitable" memories of the war and the immediate postwar years.[23] With the exception of Germany and Italy, the European states considered themselves victims (as in the case of Austria) or referred to national resistance movements (as in the case of France).

Since the 1980s, these static war memories increasingly lost their persuasive powers in Western Europe. The myth of the *Résistance* cracked in France in view of the collaboration of the Vichy regime, and in Austria the cliché of having been Hitler's first victim dissolved. In allegedly neutral Switzerland, nagging questions about the country's immigration policy and the role of the banks surfaced. Historians confronted the public with new facets of the past and drew a more differentiated picture reflecting the latest historical findings. In Eastern Europe as well, the end of the Cold War caused official versions of the war's history to fade. Certainly the experiences of two dictatorships in these countries entailed complex memories in which perpetration and victimhood blended. As a result, new myths developed, or at least a new strategically selective memory emerged.[24] In Poland, the feeling of one's own victimhood complicates the recognition of the Jewish victims and prevents the thematization of Catholic anti-Semitism. In Hungary, self-perception is primarily shaped by the feeling of having been a victim of communist, National Socialist, and Habsburg oppression. In Russia, a heroic winner-mentality claims exclusive validity, according to which the Red Army liberated Europe and led it toward a bright future in the "Great Patriotic War." In this view, there is neither room for the victims of Stalinism or of the Winter War between the Soviet Union and Finland, nor for Soviet involvement in the division of Poland, as the beginning of their war is dated 22 June 1941 – the day the Wehrmacht attacked the Soviet Union.

That this tense dual memory of liberation and occupation is not just an academic matter is illustrated by an event that occurred in Estonia in the spring of 2007, which also made headlines in Western Europe and demonstrated the otherness and complexity of the memories of the Second World War in Eastern Europe: the relocation of the main Soviet war memorial commemorating the Red Army's victims from the center of Tallinn to a war cemetery became an international political issue and a cause for violent protests. On the anniversary of the end of the war, the police in Estonia were put on high alert, and authorities issued a prohibition of assembly and even banned the selling of alcohol. This was due to the fact that there had been major riots when members of the Russian minority in Estonia had protested against the relocation of the war memorial in Tallinn at the end of April 2007. Already a year earlier, on 9 May 2006, the conflict between Estonia and Russia had escalated to a political crisis when demonstrators waving red flags in front of the bronze statue of the soldier allegedly tore down an Estonian flag. To many Estonians, this represented a glorification of the former Soviet occupation power. Behind this conflict over symbols stand two opposing, irreconcilable interpretations of the recent past, which Estonian President Toomas Hendrik Ilves and Prime Minister Andrus Ansip succinctly captured in a joint statement: "For many, the end of the Second World War represents the victory of freedom over tyranny, and for many it represents the replacement of one violent regime by another."[25] Hence there are two commemoration days: the official one on May 8 and the second for the Russian minority on May 9 – the day on which Russia also celebrates the victory over Fascism. After the relocation of the war memorial, then President Vladimir Putin proclaimed from Moscow that those who defame memorials of war heroes sow "hostility and mistrust between nations and people."

Those interested in the significance of the Second World War in Europe can therefore no longer disregard the Eastern European account and will inevitably arrive at a less optimistic image of Europe in the twentieth century which also takes the downsides and dead ends of its development into consideration.[26] This, in turn, has ramifications for a "European" historical consciousness and a European identity.

II. European historical consciousness, European identity, and the War

European integration is not least of all a reaction to the Second World War. The European Union perceives itself as, and aspires to be, more than a common market for producers and consumers. A "European identity" is supposed to increase the acceptance and legitimacy of the Union and to contribute to overcoming nationalism and racism in Europe. The agreement reached at the European Cultural Convention in 1954 and the Declaration on European Identity of 1973 bear witness to this objective.[27] For a considerable amount of time now, politicians, historians, and museologists have been working on a common European history that is to be conveyed through symbols, school textbooks, and commemorative ceremonies. European research groups, which are in part funded by the European Science Foundation, are defining key European events.[28]

Nevertheless, even after the Maastricht Treaty, the Union is still "a far cry away from [offering] a comprehensive and final point of reference for the development of a collective identity."[29] The artificially created European rituals and symbols lack a common cognitive and emotional system of reference that would make a homogenous interpretation possible in the first place and turn Europe into a reference point for its inhabitants' actions and orientations. European identities continue to be nationally and regionally fragmented. Apart from the fact that the idea of "Europe" cannot be reduced to the European Union and that these two things should be viewed separately, we cannot in the future aim for a supranational homogenization of cultural identities, as the maximalist position advocates. Rather, European identity can be understood more meaningfully – instead of teleologically – as a continuous process of interaction which does not merely comprehend "unity in diversity" as a European specific, but also the interdependence of this diversity: the "encounter of differences, antagonisms, competitions, and complementarities."[30] Not the homogenization of cultural identities, but rather the "mediation of the value relations between individual national cultures" can be the goal at present. In this sense, European cultural politics are politics of mediation.

Against this backdrop, shaped among other things by cultural politics, the Europeanization of contemporary history and World War research attains its trend-setting significance. The question of a European identity, and hence the extent to which people in Europe consider themselves European, inevitably leads to the question concerning the role of history and a (partially) shared understanding of the past. Historical orientation[31] and a historically founded European identity are necessary not despite, but because of the rapid process of globalization in order to counteract alienation and to ensure freedom and security in Europe on the basis of mutual understanding – this is the key argument. Any contribution to history in Europe is in this sense part of the cultural dimension of the European unification process, which invariably raises the question regarding the historical identity of the member states. If there is a need for a "cultural euro" (Jörn Rüsen) – a common cultural currency to reduce the discrepancy between political–institutional and economic unification on the one hand and cultural identity on the other[32] – the Second World War attains a special status as a still distinctive, if not significant point of reference. The basic research question concerning a European historical consciousness, i.e., the degree of "common patterns in the ways in which populations in Europe relate to history,"[33] can therefore focus on the important empirical test case of the Second World War.

Skeptics, in turn, associate Europe not just with the daunting bureaucracy of Brussels, but also point to a eurocentrism that leads some Europeans to look down upon the "other" Europeans as less "European" – a variation of the normative asymmetric pattern according to which the otherness of others is considered negative per se. To the extent that the perceived differences are rooted in the past of the Second World War as well as in the cultivated, partially imposed official historical representations, explanations of the social, political, and cultural conditions of the evolution and development of Europe as well as the various functions of legitimation should also pave the way for the common acceptance of the different memories. In contrast to a nationalist conception of the world and of history, this requires the acceptance of cultural differences, to not reject the "other" because of his/her otherness, and the avoidance, if not prevention, of historical myths.

A Europeanization of the historical image must therefore take the shape of a *compositum mixtum*, which can only develop momentum and form identity if the mechanisms of inclusion and exclusion – established at the latest since the rise of nationalism in the nineteenth century – can largely be suspended. Before this backdrop also, European world war research can make a contribution – not as a legitimizing science for the "project Europe," but as a reservoir of historical knowledge from which contemporary European history[34] can draw, among other things in the practice of history teaching[35] and in museological methods.[36] The logic of accepting different traditions naturally implies that this cannot succeed if a universal curriculum is applied. Rather, specific topoi that facilitate identity formation can be treated.

Jörn Rüsen, for instance, has rightly emphasized that this incorporates not only events and developments in European history associated with positive values, hence primarily those events and developments that do not devaluate the experience and the interpretation of different ways of life and acknowledge them as enriching, but also the negative experiences, in particular the World Wars and the Holocaust, which are so closely linked to the evolution of the European idea and which – just like Stalinism and communism – shaped the unification process.[37] "Such negative historical experiences have to be kept alive along with the need to support the power of mediation in Europe that has been at work to transform those conflicts into a peaceful coexistence. ... The memory of the experience of terror in European history muffles the ethnocentric element in historical thinking."[38] By conveying historical consciousness, the ethnocentric tensions and confrontations that are rooted in the logic of historical differentiation between the self and the other can be overcome.

According to this view, the visualization of the Second World War in Europe can – indeed hopefully – promote a European historical consciousness by undermining the ideal-typical structures of every ethnocentric, nationalist world view: the Manichean comparison between the good history of one's own nation and the bad history of the others; the teleological delusion of its intact, bright development from the past into the future; and finally the assumption that one's own position is at the center of world history, which accordingly marginalizes the "others." A European aware of the violence that occurred during the war in Europe, Rüsen argues, will not as easily buy into a retrospective teleology of Europe, but rather will be more aware of the historical contingency and the ruptures in the history of Europe and hence more open-minded toward the future. Wherever barbarity is present as part of one's own past, this attribute is no longer suited to be ascribed to non-Europeans in an insider-outsider relationship. Only when negative experiences, particularly those of the Second World War, take their place in European historical consciousness will the kind of ambivalence of historical orientation prevail that sensitizes for cultural difference.

This sort of approach is also not easily compatible with a linear master narrative. Unusually, here the war does not stand at the center of a meaningful "success story" of European integration that spans from the sweeping destruction of the continent via cooperation to unification, blocking out the interdependence of many actions and their constraints – even if the master narrative, entirely in the spirit of a self-fulfilling prophecy, serves as an ideological catalyst for the unification process on a political level. Analytically more fruitful and appropriate for the task at hand are, as Jost Dülffer has recently emphasized with regard to a conception of European contemporary history, "research perspectives that capture inverse movements, dialectic contradictions, and multiple interactions and which envision a Europe of coexistence and pluralism, of voluntary and forced ambitions for unification as well as counteracting forces."[39] World War research could make a contribution in various areas of European contemporary historiography, for example regarding the "criteria for the construction" of Europe according to certain features of inclusion and exclusion (What was defined as European, when and where?), issues of "internal differentiation" (Where were *the* Balkans?; what was considered the center of Europe, what the fringe?), or the perceived geographical categories of demarcation beyond the allegedly natural borders. Another area could be mental maps (How was space perceived?) in the course of the violent expansion of the National Socialist regime, but also the peace settlements after the end of the war.[40]

Not least of all, this pertains to the question concerning a "European culture of remembrance." The project of national–historical *lieux de mémoire*,[41] which was initiated in France but has since spread to many Western European countries, at least raises the question of transnational, European places of remembrance.[42] A glance at World War research in Europe and the question surrounding the significance of the World War for European historical consciousness demonstrates, by way of example, not just the "asynchronous character of European historiography,"[43] but also the current unlikelihood of a European historical consciousness and thus of a shared European memory culture that goes beyond the shared experiences of active and passive war violence in the "age of extremes." The end of the Second World War continues to be remembered primarily in *national* contexts. Where commemoration takes on an international character, for example when foreign guests and speakers are invited, it nevertheless targets a national audience. In fact, commemoration cultures in Europe have remained mostly national and their Europeanization is, as Dülffer suspects, a project for future generations.[44]

An exception to this is perhaps the transnational veterans' culture: the experiences of active and passive violence as combatants led to communication across borders early on, in part already during the war. The basis of this communication, as illustrated by the contacts of former Wehrmacht soldiers to other European countries, was apparently a minimal degree of solidarity based on the shared status as soldiers – a highly ambivalent case of "Europeanization" through war.[45] The fact that in various countries propaganda counteracted this development, simultaneously conveying specific images of other European countries, is another story. Even if the memory of war events was usually employed for a subsequent dissociation from former opponents, it is certain that the negative character of most war experiences does not necessarily stand in the way of a positive, unifying memory of the war. The European movement and European politics since the 1950s are also an example of this.

Is the search for historical vanishing points after the end of the war even necessary? Does not the Holocaust, as Dan Diner holds, already offer the point of reference for a European historiography, the starting point for the construction of a European identity? Indeed there are efforts to institutionalize a transnational commemoration of the Holocaust as the nucleus of a European memory. Since the mid 1990s (not earlier), the universal memory of the genocide of the European Jews, which contemporary World War research has quite strongly emphasized as a central feature of the war, cannot be overlooked. This past is moved to the foreground of memory culture through official commemoration days, exhibitions, and memorials – usually employing the mode of commemoration.[46] On 27 January 2000 – fifty-five years after the liberation of Auschwitz – representatives of sixteen nations agreed in Stockholm that the genocide of six million European Jews should have a central place in future collective memory, not least of all in order to signal the joint striving toward mutual understanding and justice.[47] Almost five years later, the United Nations commemorated the Shoah for the first time during a special session.

The memory of this genocide is no longer a specifically European one.[48] The Holocaust has become a blueprint for the way in which other genocides and traumas are perceived and thematized worldwide. In contrast to, for example, the United States, the memory of the Holocaust in Europe is inseparably linked to the memory of the Second World War, which affected all European countries, albeit it in different ways. Here, a common European memory therefore encounters, and sometimes clashes with, a wide range of national memories. Where these different historical constellations are not taken into account, European memory will invariably remain abstract.[49] Only the differentiation between perpetrators and victims cannot be allowed to become blurry. The differentiated insight that perpetrators can at the same time be victims and victims at the same time perpetrators does not change this.

Finally, we must raise the question whether European integration in the cultural sphere can ultimately only be accomplished by forgetting. Could only "closure" – to transfer a metaphor from German remembrance discourse to Europe – enable European unification? The tremendous degree of violence and its traumatic consequences, some of which only fully surfaced in recent years, would argue against this. In order to nevertheless reach an understanding based on a shared memory instead of a collective memory loss, Aleida Assmann has suggested the following standards for the peaceful coexistence of European memories: separating political argument and collective memory, as the former is not inherent in the latter; refraining from a summation of victims, as if personal guilt could be minimized in a zero-sum game; abandoning a competition of victimhood, which, in a hierarchy of suffering, will marginalize allegedly less dreadful experiences; the opening of collective memory for the benefit of complexity; an emphatic acknowledgement of the victims' memories; the contextualization of one's own experiences and memories, which is only possible in retrospect and counteracts an "irreconcilable solipsism;" and last the framing of multiple memories with values and goals that will form identity, restrain destructive potential, and enable integration.[50]

III. European war histories

In order not to step blindly into the trap of the respective dominant national narratives of the past – the master narratives[51] – in this endeavor and, referring back to the secondary literature of other European states, not to get caught up in the logic of national historiographies, two things were necessary in the framework of the conference. On the one side, it was agreed that the topic would be addressed not in a mere reception of the pertaining literature, but in a *discussion* with the participating experts from various countries. On the other side, in the examination of the historical research object "World War," it was also imperative to designate its place in historiography critically, and thus also one's own position in the development of national–historical discourse over the past decades. Not least of all on the basis of this reflection on the respective historiographical foundations, it quickly became clear that every national history has its own tendencies, focus points, and development trends – contingent on its specific history of historiography.[52] This insight prevented a short circuit of national histories in a European history of the Second World War, but allowed for a fruitful discussion simultaneously on both levels. For example, it was tested in how far a predominantly socio– and cultural–historical approach to the war *and* the postwar era opens up a perspective that can transcend the bias of national history as well as the predominance of Western Europe.

In addition, with the two terms "experience" and "memory," two established concepts were selected as guidelines that, due to their pervasiveness in the various national historical discourses, offer many points of intersection as heuristic categories of a military history that emphasizes social and cultural aspects as well. Just to call to mind an important point: of course this does not imply a one-to-one depiction of experiences – as if that were possible. It implies the "portending appropriation of the war's reality by those who were affected by it, as well as the ascertainment of actual war experiences and the way they shaped postwar society." War experience is thus "the respective contemporary practice during the war and serves – in a sedimentary form of sorts – as a model of sense-making and interpretation in communication and interaction processes outside of war times." This definition allows, even compels us to reconnect individual war experiences with societal structures in time and space.⁵³ Although "experience" and "memory" have their equivalents in other languages, the semantic problem of a multilingual debate on the topic is not to be underestimated. It presumes an awareness of the different meanings and connotations the key terms possess in the different languages and, what is more, that a term in one language corresponds to various terms in another: for example, *Erinnerung*, *Gedächtnis/memory/remembrance* and *Volk, Nation/nation/nation*.

As a rule, portrayals of nineteenth- and twentieth-century European history tend to focus on Western Europe. France, Germany, and Great Britain are generally at the center of attention while smaller countries at the northern, western, and southern periphery, as well as Eastern European states, are not, or only marginally accounted for. Often, the at times explicit, at times implicit underlying assumption is that in the course of European history, the focus of political, economic, and cultural development shifted toward the West and that the benchmark of a Western modernization model, according to which certain states played a less important role in history, is to be applied.⁵⁴ Were the perspective reversed – which is rarely the case – and directed from the fringes toward the center, the benchmark of normality would also shift. (This would particularly be the case if one regarded Europe from a non-European standpoint.) The predominance of Western Europe in histories of Europe thus entails another methodical deficit. Wherever the West sets the agenda because it is supposedly home to the decisive development trends that led toward the present, the specific logic of the histories of certain other societies is hardly captured. Alternative developments are excluded.

That is why besides the Netherlands, Belgium, and Luxembourg, Poland and Russia are also included in this volume. Another criterion was the country's role during the war and the "mode" of memory and remembrance. Hence, Great Britain and France are represented along with the former "Axis Powers" Italy and Germany. The memories of "victors" as well as "losers" (Ute Frevert) on both sides of the Iron Curtain can thus be scrutinized. The volume is European in its orientation also due to the fact that the German case is not central to the analysis – be it only as an implicit reference point or benchmark of comparison. Only the double-state status after 1949 justifies the treatment of the diverging developments in East and West Germany in two separate contributions – besides an article directly addressing the county's wartime experience. It is not our goal to emphasize Germany's special role in the sense of a particularly fervent "coming-to-terms" with the past in comparison with other "non-German" states. Certainly it would be desirable to also take the Asian and American experiences into account. But the intended added value of this conference was, for the time being, to go beyond bilateral comparisons between two, or a synopsis of a few selected states – hence to take a first step. One could also have envisioned a thematic structure, or selected topics such as war crimes and their judicial persecution, elite continuity, or the war's historiography as a framework. Or one could have selected the functioning of the media as a guideline and thus explored the war in film, school textbooks, or in literature.[55] However, it appeared sensible to let the experts from the respective countries freely choose their own focus points – within the conceptional framework outlined above – in order not to overly predetermine the depiction of national–historical development.

In the context of the preliminary considerations outlined above, and as a result of our debate, the authors of this volume do not aim to write a European master narrative composed of the various national histories and to merge them in a narrative of the war's European dimension. The aim is rather to regard the Second World War from specific viewpoints as outlined by contemporary research and, in close connection with this aspect, to trace the position it inhabits in the "historical consciousness" of selected European societies. If the specific portrayals focus on specific nation states, this reflects on the one hand the pervasive boundaries of research, and on the other the state of the art in research: as yet, there are no cross-border historical comparisons on the European level or, for example, analyses of transnational images of the war.[56] Thus, it is not the individual contributions that transcend borders, but the volume as a whole. Through the conveyance of knowledge on the various discourses, it is, however, certainly intended to contribute to the formulation of systematic questions.

In order to facilitate the building of bridges between the contributions, the authors were asked to take specific problems into account, provided that they were pertinent to their selected topics. Among them are notably the pre-structuring significance of the First World War for the experience and memory of the Second World War, civilians' experiences of violence, especially the bombardments, the "mode" of memory and remembrance (private; public/official) in combination with a media-history perspective, the periodization of memory, and the selected scope of historical treatment (individual, local/regional, national, European). These guidelines were not specified a priori, but rather resulted from intense debates, in the course of which they crystallized as recurring parameters of World War discourse.[57] In light of the thematic breadth, it does not appear sensible to take into consideration *all* these dimensions in every individual case. At the same time, the sum of the contributions demonstrates that there are central elements in the visualization of Europe's war past.

The volume also bears witness to the authors' interest in what the French historian Jacques Revel has termed *jeux d'échelles*: the switching between the micro and the macro level.[58] Accordingly, the spectrum of specific sources is wide. They range from documents on political debates, judicial procedures, and scholarly treatments of the war via documents on popular culture, memoirs, art, literature, and television to so called ego-documents, be they diaries of people who lived "under bombardment"[59] or contemporary witness interviews conducted decades later.[60] Wherever the contributions address dominant forms of memory and remembrance, they profit from emphasizing counternarratives, the generally small-scale memory cultures that go against the grain, thus accounting for the fundamentally conflictual character inherent in all memory work – despite all the identity-forming and integrative accomplishments of World War myths.[61] This certainly presupposes a multi-perspective approach that goes beyond the level of state (and military) without losing itself in culturalistic heights.

Moreover, in most cases we see that the authors share basic historical assumptions despite the diversity of their selected topics. Among them is particularly the conviction that the history of dealing with the Second World War past demonstrates three things: first, how it is constructed based on the selection of certain topics and the accentuation of certain aspects; second, the political, social, and cultural contexts in which this takes place; and third, that there are cycles in memory contingent on changes in these contexts. Exploring these cycles as a historical phenomenon, in turn, serves a central function of historical orientation: to illustrate the temporal dimension of the lifeworld using the example of the temporality of collective memory itself.

The contributions in this volume on the one hand underline this diversity; on the other they also exhibit commonalities. The question concerning the contemporary significance of the World Wars for example demonstrates that the Second World War is admittedly inconceivable without the First, but that the significance of the latter is quite differently assessed in the various European countries. For the British, Belgians, and French, "The Great War" or "La Grande Guerre" is omnipresent to this day. In German memory and remembrance, on the other hand, the First World War is overshadowed by the events and crimes of the Second – in some ways even entirely buried beneath them. Despite highly symbolic gestures at historical sites such as the handshake in Verdun between François Mitterrand and Helmut Kohl in 1984, today not only the war theaters in Africa, Asia, and the Near East, but also the events at the Eastern Front have largely faded into oblivion.[62] In the academic as well as public realms of Western countries, up to the fall of the Berlin Wall, the First World War was often described as the "great seminal catastrophe." In contrast, perceptions in Eastern Europe differed drastically. Not only Poland, but also a number of other countries attained their independence thanks to the defeat of the Central Powers and their allies. While memory of the First World War was outright eradicated in the Soviet Union over the course of many decades under Stalin's rule, the breakdown of the Communist regime in 1991 has entailed the recollection of this historical epoch in some of the successor states.

We can infer that the mediation of historians is more strongly needed than ever. The multi-perspective approach allows for – even gives preference to – a heterogeneous image of Europe at war. It profits from the insight of historical nationalism research into the workings of the nation, which was never the homogenous unit nationalists simultaneously asserted and imagined.[63] This does not mean that we must dispense with conceptions of European history, but rather that we must conceive it as less homogenous and more heterogeneous, construing this heterogeneity as an inherent trait, not as a deficit or as proof of the futility of historiographical attempts at grasping Europe. The breadth of experiences in the Second World War thus on the one hand exhibit common, integrating points of contact – in particular active and passive violence – but also "common" demarcations. After all, it was about a military conflict in which the participants defined one another as "others," abominated each other as foes, or attempted to turn yesterday's enemies into tomorrow's friends, e.g., when leaflets were dropped in order to break the resistance of the Italians. The historian's perspective on Europe in the Second World War and the postwar era is by nature particularly apposite to demonstrate this diversity of the historical simultaneity of integration and exclusion. If the dynamic of violence was characteristic of Europe or an expression of the general problems of an ambivalent modernity,[64] seeking "order" and perfection is another, open question that recalls the world history context into which European contemporary history is embedded.

Individual national memories are certainly locked in a tense mutual relationship. "To the extent, however, that seeing beyond national borders becomes a European habit of thought, the self-serving nature of national myths will become more and more untenable."[65] Thus, the issue at hand is to contribute to European knowledge of the war past and to a differentiated European historical consciousness that goes beyond the history of political relations. This will not obliviate individual national memories, but rather integrate them into a common European frame in which differences can be thematized without instrumentalizing them for purposes of political legitimation in a manner reminiscent of the Prussian historian Heinrich von Treitschke.[66] The Europeanization of memory cannot and should not result in the denationalization of the respective political memory cultures. Recollections of the war will continue to be tied into various national memory discourses. Their diversity will rather increase through competing local and regional accounts. This minimizes the risk that the multitude of voices in national memory might be obliviated for the sake of the smallest common denominator in the political aim of creating a new, European construction of identity – on the part of the perpetrators possibly with apologetic intent (Didn't everyone suffer under *the* war?).

However, memories of the Second World War in Europe are inevitably intertwined. Transforming these strands of memory into shared memories

– which is not the same thing as an imposed shared European memory as would be expounded, for example, in a European school textbook – means creating a common historical consciousness of events and their causal connections. This way, taking up a recurring theme in many contributions to this volume, knowledge about one another and the recognition of the suffering of civilians in the war could attenuate the destructive, divisive power of national memories.[67] In this sense, the World War serves as a landmark of European contemporary history: not a new master narrative, but rather a universally acknowledged frame necessary to convey disparate national memories. World War research should Europeanize its central questions, which in particular cases allows for different geographical focuses in the framework of the analysis of specific developments and problems. In this sense, the historicity of perceptions and memories of the war that shape actions is a useful example. Here lies the heuristic added value for a European military history.[68]

Notes

1. For France, cf. the working group (*Groupe de travail*) "Sorties de guerre des deux conflits mondiaux," which was directed by Guillaume Piketty and Bruno Cabanes at the Institut d'Études Politiques in Paris (Sciences Po) and at Yale University. In Germany, the project "Kriegsenden, Nachkriegsordnungen, Folgekonflikte im 19. und 20. Jahrhundert im Vergleich" at the Military History Reasearch Institute in Potsdam was dedicated to an analysis of the transformation phase across various epochs: http://www.mgfa-potsdam.de/html/forschung_fb_keno.php.
2. The editors would like to thank the Centre d'Études et de Documentation Guerre et Sociétés Contemporaines (CEGES) in Brussels, particularly Chantal Kesteloot and Rudi Van Doorslaer, for the permission to use the photograph.
3. See the photograph at http://www.ftlb.be/de/attractions/fiche.php?avi_id=945.
4. Cf. for example Gerald L. Weinberg, *A World at Arms. A Global History of World War II* (Cambridge, 1994).
5. Christoph Cornelißen, Lutz Klinkhammer and Wolfgang Schwenke (eds.), *Erinnerungskulturen: Deutschland, Italien und Japan seit 1945* (Frankfurt/M., 2003), 11; Astrid Erll, *Kollektives Gedächtnis und Erinnerungskulturen* (Stuttgart, 2005); Fabienne Bock, *Les sociétés, la guerre, la paix, 1911–1946* (Paris, 2003); Bruno Cabanes and Édouard Husson (eds.), *Les sociétés en guerre 1911–1946* (Paris, 2003); Philippe Chassaigne et al. (eds.), *Les sociétés, la guerre, la paix, 1911–1946* (Paris, 2003); *Les sociétés, la guerre, la paix: 1911 à 1946, Europe, Russie puis URSS, Japan, États-Unis*, ed. by Michel Margairaz, Jacques Portes and Danielle Tartakowski (Paris, 2003); Antoine Prost, *Guerres, paix et sociétés, 1911–1946* (Paris, 2003).
6. For the German case, cf. Jörg Echternkamp and Sven Oliver Müller (eds.), *Die Politik der Nation. Deutscher Nationalismus in Krieg und Krisen 1760–1960* (Munich, 2002); Nikolaus Buschmann and Dieter Langewiesche (eds.), *Der Krieg in den Gründungsmythen europäischer Nationen und der USA* (Frankfurt/M., 2003).
7. Cf. Gerhard Brunn, *Die europäische Einigung von 1945 bis heute* (Stuttgart, 2002).

8. Cf. Ute Frevert, "Europeanizing German History," Eighteenth Annual Lecture of the GHI Washington, 18 November 2004, in *GHI Bulletin*, no. 36 (spring 2005): 9–31, 12. Cf. Ute Frevert, *Eurovisionen. Ansichten guter Europäer im 19. und 20. Jahrhundert* (Frankfurt/M., 2003).
9. Cf. John Horne, "War and Conflict in Contemporary European History, 1914–2004," in *Zeithistorische Forschungen/Studies in Contemporary History*, Online-Edition, 1 (2004), 3, at http://www.zeithistorische-forschungen.de/16126041-Horne-3-2004.
10. Cf. the publication of the conference series: Stig Förster and Jörg Nagler (eds.), *On the Road to Total War. The American Civil War and the German Wars of Unification, 1861–1871* (Cambridge, 1997); Manfred F. Boemeke (ed.), *Anticipating Total War. The German and American Experiences, 1871–1914* (Cambridge, 1999); Roger Chickering and Stig Förster (eds.), *Great War, Total War. Combat and Mobilization on the Western Front, 1914–1918* (Cambridge, 2000); Roger Chickering and Stig Förster (eds.), *The Shadows of Total War. Europe, East Asia and the United States, 1919–1939* (Cambridge, 2003); Roger Chickering, Stig Förster, and Bernd Greiner (eds.), *A World at Total War. Global Conflict and the Politics of Destruction, 1937–1945* (Cambridge, 2005).
11. Cf. Dieter Langewiesche, "Eskalierte die Kriegsgewalt im Laufe der Geschichte?" in *Moderne Zeiten? Krieg, Revolution und Gewalt im 20. Jahrhundert*, ed. Jörg Baberowski (Göttingen, 2006), 12–29. In an epoch-spanning review, Langewiesche shows that the First World War only represents a return to the unchecked violence of war that had existed outside of Europe also in the nineteenth century if the view is limited to Europe (and, in this sense, is contemporary). Measured in terms of the rate of societal mobilization (the proportion of soldiers among the overall population) or the rate of loss (the proportion of killed or injured soldiers among the population), the wars of the modern era can hardly be distinguished from those of Greek and Roman antiquity.
12. For Germany, cf. for example the series *Germany and the Second World War*, which has been published by the Military History Research Institute since 1979. For an emphasis on the military aspects, cf. Rolf-Dieter Müller, *Der Zweite Weltkrieg*, 10th, new and revised edition (Stuttgart, 2004) (= Gebhardt, *Handbuch der deutschen Geschichte*, 21); Rolf-Dieter Müller, *Der letzte deutsche Krieg 1939–1945* (Stuttgart, 2005); Michael Salewski, *Deutschland und der Zweite Weltkrieg* (Paderborn, 2005). For France, cf. Jean-Pierre Azéma, *De Munich à la Libération (1938–1944)* (Paris, 2002); Jean-François Muracciole, *La France et les Français pendant la Seconde Guerre mondiale* (Paris, 2004); Jean-Pierre Azéma and François Bédarida (eds.), *1938–1948. Les années de tourmente: De Munich à Prague. Dictionnaire critique* (Paris, 1995); Marc Ferro, *Questions sur la Seconde Guerre mondiale* (Paris, 2007); Pierre Grosser, *Pourquoi la Deuxième Guerre mondiale* (Brussels, 1999); André Kaspi, *La Deuxième Guerre mondiale. Chronologie commentée* (Brussels, 1995).
13. Cf. Monika Flacke (ed.), *Mythen der Nationen: Ein europäisches Panorama. Eine Ausstellung des Deutschen Historischen Museums*, supplementary volume to the exhibition from 20 May to 9 June 1998 (Berlin, 1998).
14. Cf. for example George L. Mosse, *Fallen Soldiers: Reshaping the Memory of the World Wars* (New York, 1991); Jay Winter and Emmanuel Sivan (eds.), *War and Remembrance in the Twentieth Century* (Cambridge, 2000); Jay Winter, *Sites of Memory, Sites of Mourning. The Great War in European Cultural History* (Cambridge, 1995).
15. Cf. Stuart Woolf, "Europe and its Historians," in *Contemporary European History*, 12, no. 3 (2003), 323–37. A German example of a European history as the history of nation states is *Propyläen Geschichte Europas*, 7 vols. (Berlin, 1975–78).
16. Heinz-Gerhard Haupt, "Auf der Suche nach der europäischen Geschichte," in *Archiv für Sozialgeschichte*, 42 (2002), 544–56, 554; Herfried Münkler, *Reich, Nation, Europa. Modelle der politischen Ordnung* (Weinheim, 1997); Alan S. Milward, *The European Rescue of the Nation State* (London, 1992).

17. For a history of ideas on Europe, cf. Réme Brague, *Europa. Eine exzentrische Identität* (Frankfurt/M., 1993); Heiner Timmermann (ed.), *Die Idee Europa in Geschichte, Politik und Wirtschaft* (Berlin, 1998); René Girault (ed.), *Identité et conscience européene au XXe siècle* (Paris, 1994); Luisa Passerini (ed.), *L'identità culturale europea. Idee, sentimenti, relazione* (Scandicci, 1998); Heikki Mikkeli, *Europe as an Idea and an Identity* (Basingstoke, 1998); Kevin Wilson and Willem Johannis Van Der Dussen (eds.), *The History of the Idea of Europe* (London, 1993); Hartmut Kaelble, *Europäer über Europa. Die Entstehung des europäischen Selbstverständnisses im 19. und 20. Jahrhundert* (Frankfurt/M., 2001); Vanessa Conze, *Das Europa der Deutschen. Ideen von Europa in Deutschland zwischen Reichstradition und Westorientierung (1920–1970)* (Munich, 2005). Cf. also the exhibition catalog of the German Historical Museum in Berlin: *Idee Europa – Entwürfe zum "Ewigen Frieden": Ordnungen und Utopien für die Gestaltung Europas von der pax romana zur Europäischen Union (25. Mai – 25. August 2003)* (Berlin, 2003); Boris Schilmar, *Europadiskurs im deutschen Exil 1933–1945* (Munich, 2004) (= *Pariser Historische Studien*, 67).
18. This is Schilmar's thesis in *Europadiskurs* (see note 17).
19. Heinz Hürten, "Der Topos vom christlichen Abendland in Literatur und Publizistik nach den beiden Weltkriegen," in Albert Langner, ed., *Katholizismus, nationaler Gedanke und Europa seit 1800* (Paderborn, 1985), 131–54; Dagmar von der Brelie-Lewien, "Abendland und Sozialismus," in Detlef Lehnert and Klaus Megerle, eds., *Politische Teilkulturen zwischen Integration und Polarisierung* (Opladen, 1990), 188–219; Axel Schildt, *Zwischen Abendland und Amerika* (Munich, 1999).
20. Lucien Febvre, *L'Europe. Genèse d'une civilization. Cours professé au Collège de France 1944–1945* (Paris, 1999).
21. Cf. Woolf (see note 15), 327; John Bowle, *The Unity of European History. A Political and Cultural Survey* (London, 1948), revised and extended edition (London, 1970).
22. For a detailed treatment, cf. Étienne François, "Meistererzählungen und Dammbrüche. Die Erinnerung an den Zweiten Weltkrieg zwischen Nationalisierung und Universalisierung," in Monika Flacke, ed., *Mythen der Nationen, 1945 – Arena der Erinnerungen*, vol. 1 (Mainz, 2004) 13–28; Bernd Faulenbach, ed., *"Transformationen" der Erinnerungskulturen in Europa nach 1989* (Essen, 2006); Christoph Cornelißen (ed.), *Diktatur – Krieg – Vertreibung. Erinnerungskulturen in Tschechien, der Slowakei und Deutschland seit 1945* (Essen, 2005); Stefan Samerski, ed., *Die Renaissance der Nationalpatrone. Erinnerungskulturen in Ostmitteleuropa im 20./21. Jahrhundert* (Cologne, 2007).
23. Tony Judt, *Postwar: A History of Europe since 1945* (New York, 2005); Tony Judt, "The Past is Another Country: Myth and Memory in Postwar Europe," in István Jan Deák, T. Gross and Tony Judt, eds., *The Politics of Retribution in Europe. World War II and Its Aftermath* (Princeton, 2000), 293–323; Richard Ned Lebow, Wulf Kansteiner, and Claudio Fogu, eds., *The Politics of Memory in Postwar Europe* (Durham, 2006). Cf. also *Transit – Europäische Revue*, no. 15 (1998): *Vom Neuschreiben der Geschichte. Erinnerungspolitik nach 1945 und 1989*. This publication is a collection of contributions resulting from the project "Rethinking Postwar Europe," which was jointly carried out by the Institute for Human Sciences and the Remarque Institute at New York University from 1993 to 1998.
24. Cf. the contributions on Poland and Russia in this volume. On the following, see Aleida Assmann, "Europe: A Community of Memory?" Twentieth Annual Lecture of the GHI Washington, in *GHI Washington Bulletin*, no. 40 (spring 2007): 11–25, 14, as well as the commentary by Peter Novick and Assmann's response to it: ibid., 27–38. Cf. Aleida Assmann, *Der lange Schatten der Vergangenheit. Erinnerungskultur und Geschichtspolitik* (Munich, 2006).
25. Quoted in Claudia von Salzen, "Geteiltes Gedenken," in *Potsdamer Neueste Nachrichten* (10 May 2007): 6.

26. For an emphasis on the problems of democracy, cf. Mark Mazower, *Dark Continent: Europe's Twentieth Century* (London, 1998).
27. Frank Pfetsch, *Die Europäische Union. Eine Einführung* (Munich, 2001).
28. Cf. the agenda of the Ludwig Boltzmann Institute for European History and Public Spheres, http://ehp.lbg.ac.at.
29. Rainer M. Lepsius, "Die Europäische Union. Ökonomisch-politische Integration und kulturelle Pluralität," in Reinhold Viehoff and Rien T. Segers, eds., *Kultur, Identität, Europa* (Frankfurt/M., 1999), 201–23, 201 (authors' translation).
30. Wolfgang Lipp, "Europa als Kulturprozess," in Wolfgang Lipp, *Drama Kultur* (Berlin, 1994), 609–26, 622 (authors' translation).
31. Cf. Karl-Ernst Jeismann, *Geschichte als Horizont der Gegenwart. Über den Zusammenhang von Vergangenheitsdeutung, Gegenwartsverständnis und Zukunftsperspektive* (Paderborn, 1985); Jörn Rüsen, *Historische Orientierung. Über die Arbeit des Geschichtsbewußtseins, sich in der Zeit zurechtzufinden* (Cologne, 1994).
32. Jörn Rüsen, "'Cultural Currency'. The Nature of Historical Consciousness in Europe," in Sharon MacDonald, ed., *Approaches to European Historical Consciousness: Reflections and Provocations* (Hamburg, 2000), 75–86.
33. Sharon MacDonald and Katja Fausser, "Towards European Historical Consciousness," in MacDonald (see note 32), 9–40.
34. Cf. Norman Davies, *Europe. A History* (Oxford, 1996). Older literature on this topic includes: Werner Weidenfeld, ed., *Die Identität Europas* (Munich, 1985). Cf. also Hartmut Kaelble, *Auf dem Weg zu einer europäischen Gesellschaft. Eine Sozialgeschichte Westeuropas, 1880–1980* (Munich, 1987); Rudolf Speth, "Europäische Geschichtsbilder heute," in Petra Bock and Edgar Wolfrum, eds., *Umkämpfte Vergangenheit* (Göttingen, 1999), 159–75. Wolfgang Schmale, *Geschichte Europas* (Vienna, 2000); Michael Salewski, *Geschichte Europas. Staaten und Nationen von der Antike bis zur Gegenwart* (Munich, 2000); Gunther Mai, *Europa 1918–1939. Mentalitäten, Lebensweisen, Politik zwischen den Weltkriegen* (Stuttgart, Berlin, Cologne, 2001); Walther L. Bernecker, *Europa zwischen den Weltkriegen 1914–1945* (Stuttgart, 2002); Helmut Altrichter and Walther L. Bernecker, *Geschichte Europas im 20. Jahrhundert* (Stuttgart, 2004); Harold James, *Geschichte Europas im 20. Jahrhundert* (Munich, 2004). For the historiographical problem, cf. the conference "Thinking Europe. Towards a Europeanization of Contemporary Histories," conducted by the Center for Research on Contemporary History (ZZF) in collaboration with EurHistXX – The Network of European Contemporary History, 6–8 May 2004 in Berlin/Potsdam; cf. the review of the conference at http://www.h-net.msu.edu/reviews/showrev.cgi?path=745. The network can be accessed at http://www.eurhistxx.de.
35. Cf. Bodo von Borries, "Narrating European History," in MacDonald (see note 32), 152–62; Bodo von Borries, *Jugend und Geschichte. Ein europäischer Kulturvergleich aus deutscher Sicht* (Opladen, 1999). See also Falk Pingel, ed., *Macht Europa Schule? Die Darstellung Europas in Schulbüchern der europäischen Gemeinschaft* (Frankfurt/M., 1995); Falk Pingel, "Europa im Geschichtsbuch," in Stiftung Haus der Geschichte der Bundesrepublik, ed., *The Culture of European History in the 21st Century* (Bonn, 1999), 215–37.
36. Museum für Völkerkunde, ed., *Das gemeinsame Haus Europa. Handbuch zur europäischen Kulturgeschichte* (Munich, 1999); Flacke, *Mythen der Nationen: Ein europäisches Panorama* (see note 13).
37. Cf. for example Paul-Michael Lützeler, *Plädoyers für Europa. Stellungnahmen deutschsprachiger Schriftsteller 1915–1949* (Frankfurt/M., 1987).
38. Rüsen, "Cultural Currency" (see note 32), 79–83. Thereafter the following.
39. Jost Dülffer, "Europäische Zeitgeschichte – Narrative und historiographische Perspektiven," in *Zeithistorische Forschungen/Studies in Contemporary History*, 1 (2004): 51–71 (authors' translation).

40. On the fields of work, cf. ibid., 56–69; Jost Dülffer, "Der Niedergang Europas im Zeitalter der Gewalt: Das 20. Jahrhundert," in Heinz Duchhardt and Andreas Kunz, eds., 'Europäische Geschichte' als historiographisches Problem (Mainz, 1997), 105–28.
41. For France, cf. Pierre Nora. ed., Les lieux de mémoire, 7 vols. (Paris, 1984–92); for Germany: Étienne François and Hagen Schulze, eds., Deutsche Erinnerungsorte, 3 vols. (Munich, 2001); for Austria: Moritz Csáky, ed., Orte des Gedächtnisses (Vienna, 2000); for Italy: Mario Isnenghi, ed., I luoghi della memoria, 3 vols. (Rome, Bari, 1987/1997); Pim Den Boer and Willem Frijhoff, eds., Lieux de mémoire et identités nationales (Amsterdam, 1993).
42. Cf. for example Jacques Le Rider, Moritz Csáky, and Monika Sommer, eds., Transnationale Gedächtnisorte in Zentraleuropa (Innsbruck, 2002). Also, see the special issue Europäische lieux de mémoire? of the Jahrbuch für europäische Geschichte, 3 (2002), especially the contributions therein by Günther Lottes, "Europäische Erinnerung und europäische Erinnerungsorte?" 81–92 and Gustavo Corni, "Umstrittene lieux de mémoire in Europa im 20. Jahrhundert," 93–100.
43. Haupt, "Auf der Suche," (see note 16), 556, 546 (authors' translation). Cf. Stephen Berger, ed., Writing National Histories. Western Europe since 1800 (London, 1999); cf. the international conference of the Academy of Sciences and Literature and the Institute for European History: Nationale Geschichtskulturen – Bilanz, Ausstrahlung, Europabezogenheit (Mainz, 9 September – 2 October 2004).
44. Cf. Dülffer's skeptical conclusions in "Europäische Zeitgeschichte" (see note 39), 67. At the latest since 2003, the difficulties associated with the Center against Expulsions in Berlin clearly exemplify this. The national ascription of victims and perpetrators apparently obstructs the foundation of such a center in the country of the perpetrators in the spirit of joint, reconciliatory remembrance.
45. This is also pointed out by Frevert in "Europeanizing German History" (see note 8), 14f. Further studies are pending. For Germany, cf. James M. Diehl, The Thanks of the Fatherland. German Veterans after the Second World War (Chapel Hill, 1993); Jörg Echternkamp, "Mit dem Krieg seinen Frieden schließen – Wehrmacht und Weltkrieg in der Veteranenkultur (1945–1960)," in Thomas Kühne, ed., Von der Kriegskultur zur Friedenskultur? Zum Wandel der politischen Mentalität in Deutschland nach 1945 (Münster, 2000), 78–93 (= Jahrbuch für Historische Friedensforschung, 9); Thomas Kühne, "Zwischen Vernichtungskrieg und Freizeitgesellschaft. Die Veteranenkultur der Bundesrepublik (1945–1995)," in Klaus Naumann, ed., Nachkrieg in Deutschland (Hamburg, 2001), 90–113; Thomas Kühne, Kameradschaft. Die Soldaten des nationalsozialistischen Krieges und das 20. Jahrhundert (Göttingen, 2006), 209–70.
46. An overview of this transformation of the different cultures of remembrance is given by the contributions in Flacke, Mythen der Nationen, 1945 (see note 22).
47. Dan Diner, Das Jahrhundert verstehen. Eine universalhistorische Deutung (Munich, 1999). Cf. the Stockholm Declaration at http://taskforce.ushmm.org.
48. Daniel Levy and Nathan Sznaider, Erinnerung im globalen Zeitalter: Der Holocaust (Frankfurt/M., 2001), also: idem, ed. Ulrich Beck (Frankfurt/M., 2007); Volkhard Knigge and Norbert Frei, eds., Verbrechen erinnern. Die Auseinandersetzung mit Holocaust und Völkermord (Munich, 2002); Claudia Lenz, ed., Erinnerungskulturen im Dialog. Europäische Perspektiven auf die NS-Vergangenheit (Hamburg, 2002).
49. Cf. Assmann, "Europe: A Community of Memory?" (see note 24), 14.
50. Ibid., 19–22.
51. On this term, cf. Konrad H. Jarausch and Martin Sabrow, eds., Die historische Meistererzählung. Deutungslinien der deutschen Nationalgeschichte nach 1945 (Göttingen, 2002); Alexander Nützenadel and Wolfgang Schieder, eds., Zeitgeschichte als Problem. Nationale Traditionen und Perspektiven der Forschung in Europa (Göttingen, 2004) (= Sonderheft Geschichte und Gesellschaft).

52. Cf. Heinz-Gerhard Haupt and Jürgen Kocka, "Historischer Vergleich: Methoden, Aufgaben, Probleme. Eine Einleitung," in Heinz-Gerhard Haupt and Jürgen Kocka, eds., *Geschichte und Vergleich. Ansätze und Ergebnisse international vergleichender Geschichtsschreibung* (Frankfurt/M., 1996) 9–47, 33f.; Rainer Hudemann (ed.), *Europa im Blick der Historiker. Europäische Integration im 20. Jahrhundert. Bewußtsein und Institutionen* (Munich, 1995); Heinz Duchhardt and Andreas Kunz, eds., "Europäische Geschichte" als historiographisches Problem (Mainz, 1997); Johannes Paulmann, "Internationaler Vergleich und interkultureller Transfer. Zwei Forschungsansätze zur europäischen Geschichte des 18. bis 20. Jahrhunderts," in *Historische Zeitschrift*, 267 (1998): 649–85; Wolfgang Schmale, "Europäische Geschichte als historische Disziplin. Überlegungen zu einer 'Europäistik'," in *Zeitschrift für Geschichtswissenschaft*, 46 (1998): 389–405.
53. Cf. the definition of the Tübinger Sonderforschungsbereich 437: "Kriegserfahrungen. Krieg und Gesellschaft in der Neuzeit," accessible at http://www.uni-tuebingen.de/SFB437/T.htm (accessed 13 February 2006).
54. Haupt ("Auf der Suche," [see note 16], 546) refers to Hagen Schulze, *Phoenix Europa: die Moderne. Von 1740 bis heute* (Berlin, 1998). Cf. Woolf (see note 15), 329.
55. Cf. Norbert Frei, *Transnationale Vergangenheitspolitik. Der Umgang mit deutschen Kriegsverbrechern in Europa nach dem Zweiten Weltkrieg* (Göttingen, 2006).
56. Cf. in contrast Christoph Cornelißen, Lutz Klinkhammer and Wolfgang Schwentker, eds., *Erinnerungskulturen. Deutschland, Italien und Japan seit 1945* (Frankfurt/M., 2003); Flacke, *Mythen der Nationen, 1945* (see note 22); Pieter Lagrou, *The Legacy of Nazi Occupation. Patriotic Memory and National Recovery in Western Europe, 1945–1965* (Cambridge, 2000) (= Studies in the Social and Cultural History of Modern Warfare, 8), and Pieter Lagrou, *Mémoires patriotiques et Occupation nazie. Résistants, requis et déportés en Europe occidentale, 1945–1965* (Paris, 2003); Jörg Echternkamp, "Die Inszenierung des Krieges in Europa. Kriegsbilder zwischen Protest und Propaganda," in Wulf Köpke and Bernd Schmelzer, eds., *Das gemeinsame Haus Europa. Handbuch zur europäischen Kulturgeschichte* (Hamburg, 1999) 410–24; cf. the fifteen country case studies on the cycles of judicial prosecution of German war crimes and National Socialist atrocities in Frei (see note 55). Cf. also the comparisons between dictatorships: Richard Bessel, ed., *Fascist Italy and Nazi Germany: Comparisons and Contrasts* (Cambridge, 1996); Ian Kershaw and Moshe Lewin, *Stalinism and Nazism. Dictatorships in Comparison* (Cambridge, 1997); Henry Rousso, ed., *Stalinisme et nazisme. Histoire et mémoire comparée* (Brussels, 1999).
57. Cf. the conference reports: Annika Kropf and Holger Kozminski, "Être en guerre. Erfahrung und Erinnerung. Der Zweite Weltkrieg in Europa. Internationales Kolloquium des Deutschen Historischen Instituts Paris und des Militärgeschichtlichen Forschungsamtes, Potsdam in Zusammenarbeit mit den Deutschen Historischen Instituten London, Moskau, Rom und Warschau und dem Institut d'histoire du temps présent Paris," in *MGZ*, 65, no. 2 (2006): 545–53, and Matthieu Osmont, "Être en guerre. Expérience et mémoire de la Seconde Guerre mondiale en Europe. Colloque international de l'Institut historique allemand de Paris et des Instituts historique allemands de Londres, Moscou, Rome et Varsovie et l'Institut d'histoire du temps présent Paris, les 3 et 4 avril 2006," in *Francia*, 33, no. 3 (2007): 121–28.
58. Jaques Revel, ed., *Les jeux d'échelles. La micro-analyse à l'expérience* (Paris, 1996).
59. Cf. Pierre Le Goïc's contribution to this volume as well as Luc Capdevila, *Les Bretons au lendemain de l'Occupation. Imaginaire et comportement d'une sortie de guerre, 1944–1945* (Rennes, 1999).
60. Cf. Dorothee Wierling's, but also Chantal Kesteloot's and Piotr Madajczyk's contributions to this volume.
61. Iwona Irwin-Zarecka, *Frames of Remembrance* (New Brunswick, 1994), especially 115–31.
62. Gerhardt P. Groß, ed., *Die vergessene Front – der Osten 1914/15. Ereignis, Wirkung, Nachwirkung* (Paderborn, 2006).

63. Cf. for an overview: Dieter Langewiesche, *Nation, Nationalismus, Nationalstaat in Deutschland und Europa* (Munich, 2000); Hans-Ulrich Wehler, *Nationalismus. Geschichte, Formen, Folgen* (Munich, 2001); Siegfried Weichlein, *Nationalbewegungen und Nationalismus in Europa* (Darmstadt, 2006).
64. For example Zygmunt Baumann, *Moderne und Ambivalenz. Das Ende der Eindeutigkeit* (Frankfurt/M., 1995); James Scott, *Seeing Like a State. How Certain Schemes to Improve the Human Condition Have Failed* (New Haven/CT, 1998); Paul Weindling, *Epidemics and Genocide in Eastern Europe, 1890–1945* (Oxford, 2000).
65. Assmann, "Europe: A Community of Memory?" (see note 24), 22. "If national memory is not taught within a common framework of shared historical consciousness, the project of a United States of Europe will remain an empty dream." (23).
66. Cf. also Henry Rousso, "Das Dilemma eines europäischen Gedächtnisses," in *Zeithistorische Forschungen/Studies in Contemporary History*, 1 (2004), 363–78, http://www.zeithistorische-forschungen.de/16126041-Rousso-3-2004, as well as Henry Rousso, "Vers une mondialisation de la mémoire," in *Vingtième Siècle. Revue d'histoire*, 94 (2007): 3–11.
67. Assmann, "Europe: A Community of Memory?" (see note 24), 37.
68. The editors would like to express their gratitude to Eva Schissler and Sandra Lustig for translating the contributions that make up this volume into English.

LIST OF CONTRIBUTORS

Richard Bessel is Professor of Twentieth Century History at the University of York.

Philippe Buton is Professor of Contemporary History at the University of Reims.

Mark Connelly is Professor of Modern British Military History at the University of Kent.

Jörg Echternkamp is Fellow at the *Militärgeschichtliches Forschungsamt*, Potsdam, and has been visiting lecturer at the University of Paris 1 (Sorbonne-Panthéon) and Martin Luther University of Halle-Wittenberg.

Filippo Focardi is Lecturer of Contemporary History at the University of Padua.

Gabriella Gribaudi is Professor of Contemporary History at the Faculty of Sociology at the University of Naples Federico II, and a member of the board of the historical review *Quaderni storici*.

Chantal Kesteloot is Senior Research Fellow of the Centre d'Études Guerre et Sociétés Contemporaines, CEGES in Bruxelles

Sergei Kudryashov is Research Fellow at the German Historical Institute in Moscow

Pierre Le Goïc is Research Fellow of the Centre de Recherche Bretonne et Celtique at Brest University (UMR 6038 du CNRS).

Piotr Madajczyk is Professor at the Polish Academy of Science in Warsaw.

Benoît Majerus was Lecturer at the University of Luxembourg and is now Postdoctoral researcher FNRS at the Free University of Brussels.

Stefan Martens is Deputy Director of the *German Historical Institute*, Paris and was visiting lecturer at the University of Paris 1 (Sorbonne-Panthéon) and the Institut d'Études Politiques, Paris.

John A. Ramsden (†) was Emeritus Professor of History at Queen Mary, University of London, having retired in 2008.

Henry Rousso is Director of Research at the French National Scientific Research Center (CNRS). From 1994 to 2005 he was the director of the Institute of Contemporary History (IHTP) and has been a professor at the University of Paris X (Nanterre) since 2001.

Axel Schildt is director of the Research Center for Contemporary History in Hamburg (FZH). Since 2001 he has been a professor of Modern History at the University of Hamburg.

Dietmar Süß has been a research fellow at the Historical Institute of the University of Jena since 2007.

Dorothee Wierling is deputy director of the Research Center for Contemporary History in Hamburg (FZH).

BIBLIOGRAPHY

Ackermann, Volker, "Das Schweigen der Flüchtlingskinder. Psychische Folgen von Krieg, Flucht und Vertreibung bei den Deutschen," in *Geschichte und Gesellschaft*, 30 (2004), 434–64.
Addison, Paul, *The Road to 1945* (London, 1975).
—— and Calder, Angus, eds, *Time to Kill: the Soldier's Perception of War in the West, 1939–1945* (London, 1997).
Aldgate, Anthony, Jeffrey Richards, *Britain Can Take It* (Oxford, 1986).
d'Almeida, Fabrice, *La vie mondaine sous le nazisme* (Paris, 2006).
Altrichter, Helmut and Walther L. Bernecker, *Geschichte Europas im 20. Jahrhundert* (Stuttgart, 2004).
Ansorg, Leonore, *Kinder im Klassenkampf: die Geschichte der Pionierorganisation von 1948 – Ende der Fünfziger Jahre* (Berlin, 1997).
Arnold, Jörg, "'Krieg kann nur der Wahnsinn der Menschheit sein!' Zur Deutungsgeschichte des Luftangriffs vom 22. Oktober 1943 in Kassel," in Dietmar Süß, ed., *Deutschland im Luftkrieg. Geschichte und Erinnerung* (Munich, 2006), 135–49.
Assmann, Aleida, *Der lange Schatten der Vergangenheit. Erinnerungskultur und Geschichtspolitik* (Munich, 2006).
——, "A Community of Memory? Twentieth Annual Lecture of the GHI Washington," in *GHI Washington Bulletin*, 40 (2007), 11–25; "Kommentar von Peter Novick und Replik von A. Assmann", ibid., 27–38.
Asmuss, Burkhard et al., eds, *Der Krieg und seine Folgen. 1945. Kriegsende und Erinnerungspolitik in Deutschland* (Berlin, 2005).
Audoin-Rouzeau, Stéphane, Annette Becker, Christian Ingrao and Henry Rousso, eds, *La Violence de guerre, 1914–1945. Approches comparées des deux conflits mondiaux* (Brussels, Paris, 2002).
Azéma, Jean-Pierre, *De Munich à la Libération (1938–1944)* (Paris, 2002).
—— and Bédarida, François, eds, *1938–1948. Les années de tourmente: De Munich à Prague. Dictionaire critique* (Paris, 1995).
Bachmann, Klaus and Kranz, Jerzy, *Verlorene Heimat. Die Vertreibungsdebatte in Polen* (Bonn, 1998).
Baumann, Zygmunt, *Moderne und Ambivalenz. Das Ende der Eindeutigkeit* (Frankfurt/M., 1995).
Beardmore, George, *Civilians at War: Journals, 1938–1946* (Oxford, 1986).
Beaupré, Nicolas, Anne Duménil, and Christian Ingrao, eds, *1914–1945. L'ère de la guerre*, 2 vols. (Paris, 2004).
Becker, Jean-Jacques, Jay M. Winter, Gerd Krumeich, Annette Becker and Stéphane Audoin-Rouzeau, eds, *Guerres et cultures 1914–1918* (Paris, 1994).
Bedeschi, Giulio, ed., *Fronte greco-albanese: c'ero anch'io* (Milan, 1977).
——, ed., *Fronte jugoslavo-balcanico: c'ero anch'io* (Milan, 1985).

Behrenbeck, Sabine, *Der Kult um die toten Helden. Nationalsozialistische Mythen, Riten und Symbole* (Vierow, bei Greifswald, 1996).
———, "Between Pain and Silence. Remembering the Victims of Violence in Germany after 1949," in Richard Bessel and Dirk Schumann, eds, *Life after Death. Approaches to a Cultural and Social History of Europe During the 1940s and 1950s* (Cambridge, New York, 2003), 37–64.
———, "The Transformation of Sacrifice: German Identity between Heroic Narrative and Economic Success," in Paul Betts and Greg Eghigian, eds, *Pain and Prosperity. Reconsidering Twentieth-Century German History* (Stanford, 2003), 134–35.
Behrends, Jan C., "Soll und Haben. Freundschaftsdiskurs und Vertrauensressourcen in der staatssozialistischen Diktatur," in Ute Frevert, ed., *Vertrauen. Historische Annäherungen* (Göttingen, 2003) 338–66.
Behrens, Sonja von, *Die Zeit der "Polendörfer"* (Petershagen, 2005).
Bendel, Rainer, Aufbruch aus dem Glauben? Katholische Heimatvertriebene in den gesellschaftlichen Transformationen der Nachkriegszeit 1945–1965 (Cologne et al., 2003).
Bendotti, Angelo, Mario Pel liccioli andEugenia Valtulina, eds, *Prigionieri in Germania. La memoria degli internati militari* (Bergamo, 1990).
Benz, Wolfgang (ed.), *Die Vertreibung der Deutschen aus dem Osten. Ursachen, Ereignisse, Folgen* (Frankfurt/M., 1985).
Bergander, Götz *Dresden im Luftkrieg* (Würzburg, 1998) (first edition 1977).
———, "Vom Gerücht zur Legende. Der Luftkrieg über Deutschland im Spiegel von Tatsachen, Erlebeter Geschichte, Erinnerung, Erinnerungsverzerrung", in Thomas Stamm-Kuhlmann, Jürgen Elvert, Birgit Aschmann and Jens Hohensee, eds., *Geschichtsbilder. Festschrift für Michael Saleswki zum 65 Geburtstag* (Stuttgart, 2003), 591–616.
Berger, Stephen, ed., *Writing National Histories. Western Europe since 1800* (London, 1999).
Berlin, Isaiah, *Mr Churchill in 1940* (London, 1964).
Bernecker, Walther L., *Europa zwischen den Weltkriegen 1914–1945* (Stuttgart, 2002).
Bessel, Richard *Political Violence and the Rise of Nazism* (Yale, 1984).
———, *Germany after the First World War* (Oxford, 1993).
———, ed., *Fascist Italy and Nazi Germany: Comparisons and Contrasts* (Cambridge, 1996).
———, ed., *Life after Death. Approaches to a Cultural and Social History of Europe during the 1940s and 1950s* (Cambridge, 2003).
———, *Nazism and War* (London, 2004).
——— and Dirk Schumann, eds, *Life After Death. Approaches to a Cultural and Social History of Europe During the 1940s and 1950s* (Cambridge, 2003).
Besselièvre, Jean-Yves, "Les bombardements de Brest, 1940–1944," in *Revue historique des armées*, 211 (1998), 97–108.
Betz, Albrecht and Stefan Martens, eds, *Les intellectuels et l'occupation. Collaborer, partir, résister* (Paris, 2004).
Beutler, Ulrich, "Über den Dokumentarfilm 'Fascist Legacy' von Ken Kirby. Ein Beitrag zur längst fälligen Diskussion über die italienischen Kriegsverbrechen," in *Geschichte und Region – Storia e Regione*, XIII, 2 (2004), p. 175–88.
Beyen, Marnix *Een bewoonbare geschiedenis. De omgang met het nationale verleden in België en Nederland, 1938–1947*, Doctorat (Leuven, 1999).
———, *Oorlog & Verleden. Nationale geschiedenis in België en Nederland, 1938–1947* (Amsterdam, 2002).
Biddle, Tami David, "Wartime Reaction", in Paul Addison and Jeremy A. Crang, eds., *Firestorm. The Bombing of Dresden*, 1945 (London, 2006), 96–122.
Biess, Frank, "Men of Reconstruction – The Reconstruction of Men. Returning POWs in East and West Germany, 1945–1955," in Karen Hagemann and Stefanie Schüler

Springorum, eds, *Home/Front. The Military, War and Gender in Twentieth-Century Germany* (Oxford, New York, 2002).
Bock, Fabienne, *Les sociétés, la guerre la paix, 1911–1946* (Paris, 2003).
Boelke, Willi A., *Der Schwarzmarkt 1945–1948. Vom Überleben nach dem Kriege* (Braunschweig, 1986).
Boer, Pim den and Willem Frijhoff, eds, *Lieux de mémoire et identités nationales* (Amsterdam, 1993).
Böhler, Jochen, *Auftakt zum Vernichtungskrieg. Die Wehrmacht in Polen 1939* (Frankfurt/M., 2006).
Boldorf, Marcel, *Sozialfürsorge in der SBZ/DDR 1945–1953: Ursachen, Ausmaß und Bewältigung der Nachkriegsarmut* (Stuttgart, 1998).
Bonwetsch, Bernd, "Die Sowjetunion im Zweiten Weltkrieg 1941–1945," in *Jahrbuch für historische Kommunismusforschung*, 9 (2005), 14–43.
Borg, Alan, *War Memorials: From Antiquity to the Present Day* (London, 1991).
Borries, Bodo von, *Jugend und Geschichte. Ein europäischer Kulturvergleich aus deutscher Sicht* (Opladen, 1999).
———, "Narrating European History," in Sharon Macdonald and Katja Fausser, eds, *Approaches to European Historical Consciousness: Reflections and Provocations* (Hamburg, 2000), 152–62.
Bourke, Joanna, *An Intimate History of Killing. Face-to-Face Killing in Twentieth-Century Warfare* (London, 1999).
Bowle, John, *The Unity of European History. A Political and Cultural Survey* (London, 1948, revised and enlarged ed. London, 1970) [german ed.: *Geschichte Europas. Von der Vorgeschichte bis ins 20. Jahrhundert* (Munich, 4. ed.. 1993)].
Braese, Stephan, "Bombenkrieg und literarische Gegenwart: zu W.G. Sebald und Dieter Forte," in *Mittelweg* 36, 11 (2002/03), 4–24.
Brague, Réme, *Europa. Eine exzentrische Identität* (Frankfurt/M., 1993).
Brelie-Lewien, Dagmar von der, "Abendland und Sozialismus," in Lehnert, Detlef and Klaus Megerle, eds, *Politische Teilkulturen zwischen Integration und Polarisierung* (Opladen, 1990), 188–219.
Brivati, Brian and Harriet Jones, eds, *What Difference Did the War Make?* (Leicester, 1993).
Brown, Anthony Montague, *Long Sunset: Memoirs of Winston Churchill's Last Private Secretary* (London, 1995).
Brown, Malcolm, *Britain and 1940* (London, 2000).
Brunswig, Hans, *Feuersturm über Hamburg. Die Luftangriffe auf Hamburg im 2. Weltkrieg und ihre Folgen* (Stuttgart, 2003).
Brzoza, Czesław, *Polska w czasach niepodległości i drugiej wojny światowej (1918–1945)* (Kraków, 2001).
Burgwyn, H. James, *Mussolini's Conquest of Yugoslavia 1941–1943* (New York, 2005).
Buschmann, Nikolaus and Dieter Langewiesche, eds, *Der Krieg in den Gründungsmythen europäischer Nationen und der USA* (Frankfurt/M., 2003).
Buton, Philippe, *Les lendemains qui déchantent. Le Parti communiste français à la Libération* (Paris, 1993).
———, *La joie douloureuse. La Libération de la France* (Brussels, 2004).
———, "La memoria collettiva francese della seconda guerra mondiale, crisi d'identità e consolidamento democratico," in *Ventunesimo Secolo*, 7 (2005), 61–81.
———, "La Francia della Liberazione e la guerra civile," in *Memoria e ricerca*, 21 (2006), 101–11.
Cabanes, Bruno and Édouard Husson, eds, *Les sociétés en guerre 1911–1946* (Paris, 2003).
Calder, Angus, *The People's War: Britain 1939–1945* (London, 1969).
———, *The Myth of the Blitz* (London, 1991).

—— and Dorothy Sheridan, eds, *Speak for Yourself: a Mass Observation anthology* (London, 1984).
Capdevilla, Luc, *Les Bretons au lendemain de l'Occupation. Imaginaire et comportement d'une sortie de guerre, 1944–1945* (Rennes, 1999).
Capogreco, Carlo Spartaco, "Una storia rimossa dell'Italia fascista. L'internamento dei civili jugoslavi (1941–1943)," in *Studi Storici*, 42 (2001), 204–30.
——, *I campi del duce. L'internamento civile nell'Italia fascista (1940–1943)* (Torino, 2004).
Cardini, Franco, *La culture de la guerre X^e–XVIIIe siècle* (Paris, 1992) [1st ed. Firenze, 1982].
Carlier, Claude and Stefan Martens, eds, *La France et l'Allemagne en guerre. Septembre 1939–novembre 1942, actes du colloque de Wiesbaden, 17–19 mars 1988* (Paris, 1990).
Chapman, James, *The British at War: Cinema and Propaganda, 1939–1945*, (London, 1998).
Chassaigne, Philippe et al., eds, *Les sociétés, la guerre la paix, 1911–1946* (Paris, 2003).
Chickering, Roger and Stig Förster, eds, *The Shadows of Total War. Europe, East Asia, and the United States, 1919–1939* (Cambridge, 2003).
——, —— and Bernd Greiner, eds, *A World at Total War. Global Conflict and the Politics of Destruction, 1937–1945* (Cambridge, 2005).
Clarke, Peter, *A Question of Leadership. Gladstone to Thatcher* (London, 1991).
Clout, Hugh D., *After the Ruins: Restoring the Countryside in Northern France after the Great War* (Exeter, 1996).
Cohen, Deborah, *The War Come Home. Disabled Veterans in Britain and Germany, 1914–1939* (Berkeley, Los Angeles, London, 2001).
Collotti, Enzo, "Sul razzismo antislavo," in Alberto Burgio, ed., *Nel nome della razza. Il razzismo nella storia d'Italia 1870–1945* (Bologna, 1999), 33–61.
——, *Fascismo e antifascismo. Rimozioni, revisioni, negazioni* (Roma, Bari, 2000).
——, *L'Europa nazista. Il progetto di un Nuovo ordine europeo 1939–1945* (Firenze, 2002).
—— and Teodoro Sala, *Le potenze dell'Asse e la Jugoslavia. Saggi e documenti 1941–1943* (Milan, 1974).
——, —— and Giorgio Vaccarino, *L'italia nell'Europa danubiana durante la seconda guerra mondiale* (Milan, 1967).
Connelly, Mark, *Reaching for the Stars: A New Interpretation of Bomber Command in the Second World War* (London, 2001).
——, *The Great War: Ritual and Memory* (London, 2001).
——, *British Film Guides: The Charge of the Light Brigade* (London, 2003).
——, *We Can Take It! Britain and the Memory of the Second World War* (London, 2004).
"Consequences and Sequels of the Second World War, Montréal, 2. September 1995, 18e Congrès international des sciences historiques," in *Bulletin du Comité international d'histoire de la Deuxième guerre mondiale*, 27/28, 1995.
Conze, Vanessa, *Das Europa der Deutschen. Ideen von Europa in Deutschland zwischen Reichstradition und Westorientierung (1920–1970)* (Munich, 2005).
Conze, Werner, "Staats- und Nationalpolitik. Kontinuitätsbruch und Neubeginn," in Wenrer Conze and M. Rainer Lepsius, eds, *Sozialgeschichte der Bundesrepublik Deutschland. Beiträge zum Kontinuitätsproblem* (Stuttgart, 1983), 441–67.
Cornelißen, Christoph, "Was heißt Erinnerungskultur? Begriff – Methoden – Perspektiven," in *Geschichte in Wissenschaft und Unterricht*, 54 (2003), 548–63.
——, ed., *Diktatur - Krieg – Vertreibung. Erinnerungskulturen in Tschechien, der Slowakei und Deutschland seit 1945* (Essen, 2005).
——, Lutz Klinkhammer, and Wolfgang Schwentker, eds, *Erinnerungskulturen. Deutschland, Italien und Japan seit 1945* (Frankfurt/M., 2003).
Corrigan, Gordon, *Blood, Sweat and Arrogance: the myths of Churchill's War* (London, 2006).
Coward, Noel, *The Lyrics of Noel Coward* (London, 1978).
Crane, C.C., *Bombs, Cities and Civilians, American Airpower Stategy in World War II* (Lawrence, 1993).

Croft, David and Jimmy Perry, *Dad's Army: The Complete Scripts* (London, 2003).
Csáky, Moritz, ed., *Orte des Gedächtnisses* (Vienna, 2000).
Cuzzi, Marco, *L'occupazione italiana della Slovenia 1941–1943* (Rome, 1998).
Czubiński, Antoni, *Druga wojna światowa 1939–1945* (Poznań, 1999).
———, *Historia Drugiej Wojny Światowej 1939–1945, Dom Wydawniczy Rebis – Wydawnictwo Poznańskie* (Poznań, 2004).
Daly, Peter, Hans Walter Frishkopf, Trudis E. Goldsmith-Reber and Horst Richter, eds, *Images of Germany* (New York, 2000).
Davies, Norman, *Europe. A History* (Oxford, 1996).
De Haan, Ido, *Na de ondergang. De herinnering aan de Jodenvervolging in Nederland 1945–1995* (Den Haag, 1997).
De Jong, Lou, *Het Koninkrijk der Nederlanden in de Tweede Wereldoorlog, Epiloog* (Amsterdam, 1988).
Del Boca, Angelo, *Italiani brava gente? Un mito duro a morire* (Vicenza, 2005).
Dewael, Patrick, *Respect mutuel. Les dangers du Vlaams Blok* (Brussels, 2002).
Diehl, James M., *The Thanks of the Fatherland. German Veterans after the Second World War* (Chapel Hill, 1993).
Dietz, Burkhard, Helmut Gabel and Ulrich Tiedau, eds, *Griff nach dem Westen. Die 'Westforschung' der völkisch-nationalen Wissenschaften zum nordwesteuropäischen Raum (1919–1960)* (Münster et al., 2003).
Dietzsch, Ina, *Grenzen überschreiben? Deutsch-deutsche Briefwechsel 1948–1989* (Cologne et al., 2004).
Diner, Dan, *Das Jahrhundert verstehen. Eine universalhistorische Deutung* (Munich, 1999).
Di Sante, Costantino, ed., *Italiani senza onore. I crimini in Jugoslavia e i processi negati (1941–1951)* (Verona, 2005).
Domansky, Elisabeth and Harald Welzer, eds, *Eine offene Geschichte. Zur kommunikativen Tradierung der nationalsozialistischen Vergangenheit* (Tübingen, 1999).
Donnelly, Mark, *Britain in the Second World War* (London, 1999).
Donnelly, Peter, ed., *Mrs. Milburn's Diaries: An Englishwoman's day-to-day reflections, 1939–1945* (London, 1989).
Dröge, Franz, *Der zerredete Widerstand. Zur Soziologie und Publizistik des Gerüchts im 2. Weltkrieg* (Düsseldorf, 1970).
Duchhardt, Heinz and Andreas Kunz, eds, *"Europäische Geschichte" als historiographisches Problem* (Mainz, 1997).
Dülffer, Jost, "Der Niedergang Europas im Zeitalter der Gewalt: Das 20. Jahrhundert", in Heinz Duchhardt and Andreas Kunz, eds, *"Europäische Geschichte" als historiographisches Problem* (Mainz, 1997), 105–28.
———, *Im Zeichen der Gewalt. Frieden und Krieg im 19. und 20. Jahrhundert*, ed. by Martin Kröger, Ulrich S. Soénius and Stefan Wunsch (Cologne, Vienna, 2003).
———, "Europäische Zeitgeschichte – Narrative und historiographische Perspektiven", in *Zeithistorische Forschungen / Studies in Contemporary History*, 1 (2004), 51–71.
Duménil, Anne, Nicolas Beaupré and Christian Ingrao, eds, *L'ère de la guerre. Vol. 1: Violence, mobilisation, deuil. Vol. 2: Nazisme, occupation, pratiques génocides* (Paris, 2004).
Dybkowska, Alicja, Jan Żaryn and Małgorzata Żaryn, *Polskie dzieje od czasów najdawniejszych do współczesności* (Warsaw, 1996).
Dziurok, Adam, ed., *Armia Krajowa i konspiracja poakowska na ziemi rybnickiej 1942–1947* (Katowice, 2004).
Echternkamp, Jörg, "Die Inszenierung des Krieges in Europa. Kriegsbilder zwischen Protest und Propaganda," in Wulf Köpke and Bernd Schmelzer, eds, *Das gemeinsame Haus Europa. Handbuch zur europäischen Kulturgeschichte* (Hamburg, 1999), 410–24.
———, "Mit dem Krieg seinen Frieden schließen - Wehrmacht und Weltkrieg in der Veteranenkultur (1945–1960) ," in Thomas Kühne, ed., *Von der Kriegskultur zur*

Friedenskultur? Zum Wandel der politischen Mentalität in Deutschland nach 1945 (Münster, 2000), 78–93 (Jahrbuch für Historische Friedensforschung, 9).

———, *Nach dem Krieg. Alltagsnot, Neuorientierung und die Last der Vergangenheit 1945–1949* (Zurich, 2003).

———, "Im Kampf an der inneren und äußeren Front. Grundzüge der deutschen Gesellschaft im Zweiten Weltkrieg," in Id., ed., *Das Deutsche Reich und der Zweite Weltkrieg, Vol. 9/1: Die deutsche Kriegsgesellschaft 1939–1945* (Munich, 2004), 1–92.

———, ed., *Die Deutsche Kriegsgesellschaft 1939–1945* (Munich, 2004/05), (Das Deutsche Reich und der Zweite Weltkrieg, 9).

———, *Kriegsschauplatz Deutschland 1945. Leben in Angst, Hoffnung auf Frieden: Feldpost aus der Heimat und von der Front* (Paderborn, 2006).

———, Weil Lenders, Ralph Trost and Veit Veltzke, eds, *Krieg in der Grenzregion. Bombenkrieg und Kriegsende in Westdeutschland und den Niederlanden 1944/45* (Münster, 2007), (Studien zur Geschichte und Kultur Nordwesteuropas).

——— and Sven Oliver Müller, eds, *Die Politik der Nation. Deutscher Nationalismus in Krieg und Krisen 1760–1960* (Munich, 2002).

Eder, Angelika, "Displaced Persons – 'Heimatlose Ausländer' als Arbeitskräfte in Westdeutschland," in *Archiv für Sozialgeschichte*, 42 (2002), 1–17.

Eismann, Gaël, "La politique répressive du Militärbefehlshaber in Frankreich, un cas singulier en Europe occupée (1940–1944)?," in *Revue Européenne d'Histoire Sociale – Histoire & Sociétés*, 17 (2006), 44–55.

——— and Stefan Martens, eds, *Occupation et répression militaire allemandes 1939–1945. La politique de "maintien de l'ordre" en Europe occupée* (Paris, 2007).

Endres, Rudolf, ed., *Bayerns vierter Stamm. Die Integration der Flüchtlinge und Heimatvertriebenen nach 1945* (Cologne, Weimar, Vienna, 1998).

Erker, Paul, *Ernährungskrise und Nachkriegsgesellschaft. Bauern und Arbeiterschaft in Bayern 1945–1953* (Stuttgart, 1990).

Erll, Astrid, *Kollektives Gedächtnis und Erinnerungskulturen* (Stuttgart, 2005).

"... et wor alles net esou einfach". *Questions sur le Luxembourg et la Deuxième Guerre mondiale: contributions historiques accompagnant l'exposition. Ein Lesebuch zur Austellung* (Luxembourg, 2002).

Evans, Martin and Ken Lunn, eds, *War and Memory in the Twentieth Century* (Oxford, 1997).

Faulenbach, Bernd, ed., *"Transformationen" der Erinnerungskulturen in Europa nach 1989* (Essen, 2006).

Ferenc, Tone, *La provincia "italiana" di Lubiana. Documenti 1941–1942* (Udine, 1994).

———, *"Si ammazza troppo poco". Condannati a morte-Ostaggi-Passati per le armi nella Provincia di Lubiana 1941–1943* (Ljubljana, 1999).

———, *Rab-arbe-Arbissima. Confinamenti-Rastrellamenti-Internamenti nella Provincia di Lubiana 1941–1943* (Ljubljana, 2000).

Ferro, Marc, *Questions sur la Seconde Guerre mondiale* (Paris, 2007).

Fielding, Steven, Nick Tiratsoo and Peter Thompson, *England Arise* (Manchester, 1995).

Fitzgibbon, Constantine, *The Blitz* (London, 1957).

Flacke, Monika, ed., *Mythen der Nationen: ein europäisches Panorama. Eine Ausstellung des Deutschen Historischen Museums; Begleitband zur Ausstellung vom 20. März 1998 bis 9. Juni 1998* (Berlin, 1998).

Focardi, Filippo, "'Bravo italiano' e 'cattivo tedesco': riflessioni sulla genesi di due immagini incrociate," in *Storia e Memoria*, V (1996), 55–83.

———, "La questione della punizione dei criminali di guerra in Italia dopo la fine del secondo conflitto mondiale," in *Quellen und Forschungen aus italienischen Archiven und Bibliotheken*, 80 (2000), 543–624.

———, "La memoria della guerra e il mito del 'bravo italiano': origine e affermazione di un autoritratto collettivo," in *Italia Contemporanea*, 220–221 (2000), 93–99.

———, "L'Italia fascista come potenza occupante nel giudizio dell'opinione pubblica italiana: la questione dei criminali di guerra (1943–1948)," in *Qualestoria*, 1 (2002), 157–83.
———, "Gedenktage und politische Öffenlichkeit in Italien 1945–1995," in Christoph Cornelissen, Lutz Klinkhammer and Wolfgang Schwentker, eds, *Erinnerungskulturen. Deutschland, Italien und Japan seit 1945* (Frankfurt/M., 2003), 210–21.
——— and Lutz Klinkhammer, "The question of Fascist Italy's war crimes: the costruction of a self-acquitting myth (1943–1948)," in *Journal of Modern Italian Studies*, 9 (2004), 330–48.
———, "I crimini impuniti dei 'bravi italiani'," in *Contemporanea*, 7 (2005), 329–35.
———, *La guerra della memoria. La Resistenza nel dibattito politico italiano dal 1945 a oggi* (Laterza, 2005).
———, "Criminali impuniti. Cause e responsabilità della mancata Norimberga italiana," in *Il mito del buon italiano tra repressione del ribellismo e guerra ai civili* (Milan, 2007).
——— and Lutz Klinkhammer, "La questione dei 'criminali di guerra' italiani e una Commissione di inchiesta dimenticata," in *Contemporanea*, 4 (2001), 497–528.
Foot, M.R.D., "Winston Churchill", in Herbert van Thal, ed., *The Prime Ministers* (London, 1975).
François, Étienne, "Meisererzählungen und Dammbrüche. Die Erinnerung an den Zweiten Weltkrieg zwischen Nationalisierung und Universalisierung," in Monika Flacke, ed., *Mythen der Nationen. 1945 – Arena der Erinnerungen*, Vol. 1 (Mainz, 2004), 13–28.
——— and Hagen Schulze, eds, *Deutsche Erinnerungsorte*, 3 Vols. (Munich, 2001).
——— and ———, eds, *Deutsche Erinnerungsorte. Eine Auswahl* (Munich, 2005).
Frantzioch, Marion, *Die Vertriebenen. Hemmnisse, Antriebskräfte und Wege ihrer Integration in der Bundesrepublik Deutschland* (Berlin, 1987).
Freckmann, Klaus, "Luxemburg – ein Teil des deutschen Reiches? Zur Kontinuität der landes- und volkskundlichen Kulturraumforschung und ihr Verhältnis zur kulturellen Identität Luxemburgs im 20. Jahrhundert," in Burkhard Dietz, Helmut Gabel and Ulrich Tiedau, eds, *Griff nach dem Westen. Die "Westforschung" der völkisch-nationalen Wissenschaften zum nordwesteuropäischen Raum (1919–1960)* (Münster et al., 2003), 473–92.
Frei, Norbert, *Vergangenheitspolitik. Die Anfänge der Bundesrepublik und die NS-Vergangenheit* (Munich, 1996).
———, *Karrieren im Zwielicht. Hitlers Eliten nach 1945* (Frankfurt/M., 2001).
———, ed., *Transnationale Vergangenheitspolitik. Der Umgang mit deutschen Kriegsverbrechern in Europa nach dem Zweiten Weltkrieg* (Göttingen, 2006).
Frémeaux, Jacques and Michèle Battesti, eds, *Sorties de Guerre* (Vincennes, 2005), (Cahiers du Centre d'Études d'Histoire de la Défense, 24).
Frevert, Ute, *Eurovisionen. Ansichten guter Europäer im 19. und 20. Jahrhundert* (Frankfurt/M., 2003).
———, "Europeanizing German History. Eighteenth Annual Lecture of the GHI Washington, November 18, 2004," in *GHI Washington Bulletin*, 36 (2005), 9–31.
Friedrich, Jörg, *Die kalte Amnestie. NS-Täter in der Bundesrepublik* (Frankfurt/M., 1984).
———, *Der Brand. Deutschland im Bombenkrieg 1940–1945* (Munich, 2002).
Friedrich, Klaus-Peter, "Frühe Bestrebungen zu einer 'Katholisierung' des ehemaligen NS-Lagers Auschwitz," in *Zeitschrift für Ostmitteleuropa-Forschung*, 54 (2005), 216–41.
Gardner, Brian, ed., *The Terrible Rain: the War Poets, 1939–1945* (London, 1966).
Gentile, Carlo, Lutz Klinkhammer and Steffen Prauser, *I nazisti. I rapporti italo-tedeschi nelle foto dell'Istituto Luce* (Rome, 2003).
Geyer, Michael, "Cold War Angst: The Case of West-German Opposition to Rearmament and Nuclear Weapons," in Hanna Schissler, ed., *The Miracle Years. A Cultural History of West Germany, 1949–1968* (Princeton, Oxford, 2001).
Gilbert, Martin, *Never Despair, 1945–1965, Winston S. Churchill*, Vol. 8 (London, 1988).

Girault, René, ed., *Identité et conscience européene au XXe siècle* (Paris, 1994).
Goeken-Haidl, Ulrike, *Der Weg zurück. Die Repatriierung sowjetischer Zwangsarbeiter und Kriegsgefangener während und nach dem Zweiten Weltkrieg* (Essen, 2006).
Goltermann, Svenja, "Im Wahn der Gewalt. Massentod, Opferdiskurs und Psychiatrie 1945–1956," in Klaus Naumann (ed.), *Nachkrieg in Deutschland* (Hamburg, 2001), 343–63.
Gotovitch, José and Chantal Kesteloot, *Collaboration, répression. Un passé qui résiste* (Brussels, 2002).
Greiner, Bernd, *Die Morgenthau-Legende. Zur Geschichte eines umstrittenen Plans* (Hamburg, 1995).
———, "Zwischen 'Totalem Krieg' und 'Kleinen Kriegen'. Überlegungen zum historischen Ort des Kalten Krieges," in *Mittelweg 36*, 12, 2 (2003), 3–20.
Gribaudi, Gabriella, *Mediatori. Antropologia del potere democristiano nel Mezzogiorno* (Torino 1980, 2nd ed. 1991).
———, *A Eboli. Il mondo meridionale in cent'anni di trasformazione* (Venice, 1990).
———, *Donne, uomini, famiglie. Napoli nel novecento* (Naples, 1999).
———, ed., *Terra bruciata. Le stragi naziste sul fronte meridionale* (Naples, 2003).
———, *Guerra totale: Tra bombe alleate e violenze naziste. Napoli e il fronte meridionale 1940–1944* (Torino et al., 2005), (Nuova cultura, 109).
Gries, Rainer, *Die Rationen-Gesellschaft. Versorgungskampf und Vergleichsmentalität: Leipzig, München und Köln nach dem Kriege* (Münster, 1991).
Groehler, Olaf, *Bombenkrieg gegen Deutschland* (Berlin, 1990).
Große Kracht, Klaus, *Die zankende Zunft. Historische Kontroversen in Deutschland nach 1945* (Göttingen, 2005).
Grosser, Pierre, *Pourquoi la 2^e Guerre mondiale* (Brussels, 1999).
Grotzki, Nina, Gerd Niewerth and Rolf Potthoff, eds, *Als die Steine Feuer fingen. Der Bombenkrieg im Ruhrgebiet* (Essen, 2003).
Hage, Volker, *Zeugen der Zerstörung. Die Literaten und der Luftkrieg* (Frankfurt/M., 2003).
Halle, Uta, "Archäologie und 'Westforschung'", in Burkhard Dietz, Helmut Gabel and Ulrich Tiedau, eds, *Griff nach dem Westen. Die 'Westforschung' der völkisch-nationalen Wissenschaften zum nordwesteuropäischen Raum (1919–1960)* (Münster et al., 2003), 383–406.
Harper, Sue and Vincent Porter, *British Cinema of the 1950s: Decline of Deference* (Oxford, 2003).
Harrison, Tom, *Living through the Blitz* (Harmondworth, 1990).
Haupt, Heinz Gerhard, "Auf der Suche nach der europäischen Geschichte," in *Archiv für Sozialgeschichte*, 42 (2002), 544–56.
——— and Jürgen Kocka, "Historischer Vergleich: Methoden, Aufgaben, Probleme. Eine Einleitung," in Id., eds, *Geschichte und Vergleich. Ansätze und Ergebnisse international vergleichender Geschichtsschreibung* (Frankfurt/M., 1996), 9–47.
Hearnden, Arthur, ed., *The British in Germany* (London, 1978).
Heider, Magdalena, *Politik – Kultur – Kulturbund. Zur Gründungs- und Frühgeschichte des Kulturbundes zur demokratischen Erneuerung Deutschlands 1945–1954 in der SBZ/DDR* (Cologne, 1993).
Heinemann, Elizabeth D., *What Difference Does a Husband Make? Women and Marital Status in Nazi and Postwar Germany* (Berkeley, Los Angeles, London, 1999).
Hennessy, Peter, *Never Again: Britain 1945–1951* (London, 1994).
Herbert, Ulrich, "Die guten und die schlechten Zeiten," in Lutz Niethammer, ed., *"Die Jahre weiß man nicht, wo man die heute hinsetzen soll." Faschismuserfahrung im Ruhrgebiet* (Berlin, Bonn, 1983), 67–96.
———, "Zur Entwicklung der Ruhrarbeiterschaft 1930 bis 1960 aus erfahrungsgeschichtlicher Perspektive," in Lutz Niethammer and Alexander von

Plato, eds, *"Wir kriegen jetzt andere Zeiten." Auf der Suche nach der Erfahrung des Volkes in nachfaschistischen Ländern* (Berlin, Bonn, 1985), 19–51.
———, "Deutsche Eliten nach Hitler," in *Mittelweg 36*, 8 (1999), 66–82.
——— and Axel Schildt, eds, *Kriegsende in Europa. Vom Beginn des deutschen Machtzerfalls bis zur Stabilisierung der Nachkriegsordnung 1944–1948* (Essen, 1998).
Herrebout, Els, *De Duitse Archivschutz in België tijdens de Tweede Wereldoorlog* (Brussels, 1997).
Higonnet, Margaret Randolph, Jane Jenson, Sinya Michel and Margaret Collins Weitz, eds, *Behind the Lines. Gender and the Two Wold Wars* (New Haven, London, 1987).
Hillmann, Jörg and John Zimmermann, eds, *Kriegsende 1945 in Deutschland* (Munich, 2002).
Hirschfeld, Michael, *Katholisches Milieu und Vertriebene. Eine Fallstudie am Beispiel des Oldenburger Landes* (Cologne et al., 2002).
Hoffmann, Dieter et al., eds, *Vertriebene in Deutschland. Interdisziplinäre Ergebnisse und Forschungsperspektiven* (Munich, 2000).
Hoffmann, Egbert A., *Als der Feuertod vom Himmel stürzte. Hamburg Sommer 1943* (Gudensberg-Gleichen, 2003).
Hoffmann, Stefan-Ludwig, "Sakraler Monumentalismus um 1900. Das Leipziger Völkerschlachtdenkmal," in Reinhart Koselleck and Michael Jeismann, eds, *Der politische Totenkult. Kriegerdenkmäler in der Moderne* (Munich, 1994) 276–77.
Horne, John, "War and conflict in contemporary European history, 1914–2004," in *Zeithistorische Forschungen/Studies in Contemporary History*, Online-edition, 1 (2004), H. 3, URL: <http://www.zeithistorische-forschungen.de/16126041-Horne-3-2004>.
——— and Alan Kramer, *German Atrocities, 1914: A History of Denial* (New Haven, 2001).
Hudemann, Rainer, ed., *Europa im Blick der Historiker. Europäische Integration im 20. Jahrhundert. Bewußtsein und Institutionen* (Munich, 1995).
Hürten, Heinz, "Der Topos vom christlichen Abendland in Literatur und Publizistik nach den beiden Weltkriegen," in Albert Langner, ed., *Katholizismus, nationaler Gedanke und Europa seit 1800* (Paderborn, 1985), 131–54.
Ingrao, Christian, *Les chasseurs noirs. Essai sur la Sondereinheit Dirlewanger* (Paris, 2005).
Irwin-Zarecka, Iwona, *Frames of Remembrance* (New Brunswick, 1994).
Isnenghi, Mario, ed., *I luoghi della memoria*, 3 Vols. (Rome, Bari, 1987/1997).
Jacobmeyer, Wolfgang, *Vom Zwangsarbeiter zum heimatlosen Ausländer. Die Displaced Persons in Westdeutschland 1945–1951* (Göttingen, 1985).
Jagodzinski, Zdzisław, *The Katyn Bibliography* (London, 1982).
James, Harold, *Geschichte Europas im 20. Jahrhundert* (Munich, 2004).
Jarausch, Konrad H., "1945 and the Continuities of German History: Reflections on Memory, Historiography, and Politics," in Geoffrey J. Giles, ed., *Stunde Null: The End and the Beginning Fifty Years Ago* (Washington, 1997).
——— and Martin Sabrow, eds, *Die historische Meistererzählung. Deutungslinien der deutschen Nationalgeschichte nach 1945* (Göttingen, 2002).
——— and Hannes Siegrist, eds, *Amerikanisierung und Sowjetisierung in Deutschland 1945–1970* (Frankfurt/M., New York, 1997).
Jeismann, Karl-Ernst, *Geschichte als Horizont der Gegenwart. Über den Zusammenhang von Vergangenheitsdeutung, Gegenwartsverständnis und Zukunftsperspektive* (Paderborn, 1985).
Jeziorański, Jan Nowak, *Courier from Warsaw* (Detroit, 1982).
Judt, Tony, *Postwar: A History of Europe since 1945* (New York, 2005).
Kaarsted, Tage, "Churchill and the Small States of Europe: the Danish Case," in R.A.C. Parker, ed., *Winston Churchill, Studies in Statesmanship* (London, 1995), 106–8.
Kaelble, Hartmut, *Auf dem Weg zu einer europäischen Gesellschaft. Eine Sozialgeschichte Westeuropas, 1880–1980* (Munich, 1987).
———, *Europäer über Europa. Die Entstehung des europäischen Selbstverständnisses im 19. und 20. Jahrhundert* (Frankfurt/M., 2001).

Kaminsky, Annette, *Wohlstand, Schönheit, Glück. Kleine Konsumgeschichte der DDR* (Munich, 2001).
Kämpfer, Frank, "Vom Massengrab zum Heroen-Hügel. Akkulturationsfunktionen sowjetischer Kriegsdenkmäler," in Reinhart Koselleck and Michael Jeismann, eds, *Der politische Totenkult. Kriegerdenkmäler in der Moderne* (Munich, 1994), 327–49.
Karlsch, Rainer, *Allein bezahlt? Die Reparationsleistungen der SBZ/DDR 1945–1953* (Berlin, 1993).
—— and Harm Schröter, eds, *Studien zur Geschichte des Uranbergbaus der Wismut* (St. Katharinen, 1996).
Kaspi, André, *La Deuxième Guerre mondiale. Chronologie commentée* (Brussels, 1995).
Keagan, John, *The Second World War* (London, 1989).
Kellerhoff, Sven Felix and Wieland Giebel, eds, *Als die Tage zu Nächten wurden. Berliner Schicksale im Luftkrieg* (Berlin, 2003).
Kershaw, Ian and Moshe Lewin, *Stalinism and Nazism. Dictatorships in Comparison* (Cambridge, 1997).
Kersten, Krystyna, *Narodziny systemu władzy. Polska 1943–1948* (Warsaw, 1984 and Paris, 1986). [Englisch: *The Establishment of Communist Rule in Poland, 1943–1948* (Berkeley, 1991)].
Kesteloot, Chantal, *Au nom de la Wallonie et de Bruxelles français. Les origines du FDF* (Brussels, 2004).
Kirsch, Jan-Holger, *"Wir haben aus der Geschichte gelernt." Der 8. Mai als politischer Gedenktag in Deutschland* (Cologne, 1999).
Kittel, Manfred, *Die Legende von der "zweiten Schuld." Vergangenheitsbewältigung in der Ära Adenauer* (Berlin, 1993).
Klee, Katja, *Im "Luftschutzkeller des Reiches", Evakuierte in Bayern 1939–1953: Politik, soziale Lage, Erfahrungen* (Munich, 1999).
Kmec, Sonja, Benoît Majerus, Michel Margue and Pit Péporté, eds, *Lieux de mémoire au Luxembourg: Usages du passé et construction nationale/Erinnerungsorte in Luxemburg: Umgang mit der Vergangenheit und Konstruktion der Nation* (Luxembourg, 2007).
Knigge, Volkhard and Norbert Frei, eds, *Verbrechen erinnern. Die Auseinandersetzung mit Holocaust und Völkermord* (Munich, 2002).
Kock, Gerhard, *"Der Führer sorgt für unsere Kinder", Die Kinderlandverschickung im Zweiten Weltkrieg* (Paderborn et al., 1997).
Koselleck, Reinhart, *Vergangene Zukunft. Zur Semantik geschichtlicher Zeiten* (Frankfurt/M., 1989).
—— and Michael Jeismann, eds, *Der politische Totenkult. Kriegerdenkmäler in der Moderne* (Munich, 1994)
Koshar, Rudy, *Germany's Transient Pasts. Preservation and National Memory in the Twentieth Century* (Chapel Hill, 1998).
Krause, Michael, *Flucht vor dem Bombenkrieg. "Umquartierungen" im Zweiten Weltkrieg und die Wiedereingliederung der Evakuierten in Deutschland 1943–1963* (Düsseldorf, 1997).
Kriegel, Annie, "Le Parti communiste français sous la IIIe République (1920–1939): mouvement des effectifs et structures d'organisation", in Id., *Le Pain et les roses: jalons pour une histoire des socialismes (1968)*, new ed. (Paris, 1973), 277–390.
——, *Les communistes français: dans leur premier demi-siècle 1920–1970*, revised ed. (Paris, 1985).
Krumeich, Gerd, "Der 'Ruhrkampf' als Krieg: Überlegungen zu einem verdrängten deutsch-französischen Konflikt", in Gerd Krumeich and Joachim Schröder, eds, *Der Schatten des Weltkriegs. Die Ruhrbesetzung 1923* (Essen, 2004), 9–24.
Kruse, Kai and Wolfgang Kruse, "Kriegerdenkmäler in Bielefeld. Ein lokalhistorischer Beitrag zur Entwicklungsanalyse des deutschen Gefallenenkultes im 19. und 20.

Jahrhundert," in Reinhart Koselleck and Michael Jeismann, eds, *Der politische Totenkult. Kriegerdenkmäler in der Moderne* (Munich, 1994), 91–105.

Kuby, Erich, *Nur noch rauchende Trümmer. Das Ende der Festung Brest. Tagebuch des Soldaten Erich Kuby mit Text des Hörbildes, Plädoyer des Staatsanwalts, Begründung des Urteils* (Hamburg, 1959).

Kudrjaschow, Sergej, "Vojna vokrug vojny. Politicheskaja kon-junktura, ideologicheskie stereotipy i istorija Velikoj Otechestvennoj," in *Voenno-istoricheskij archive*, 12 (2004), 17–25.

———, "Russia and V-Day," in *Everyone's War*, 11 (2005), 33–37.

———, "Ordinary Collaborators. The Case of the Travniki Guards," in *Russia. War, Peace and Diplomacy* (London, 2005), 226–40.

Kühne, Thomas, "Die Viktimisierungsfalle. Wehrmachtsverbrechen, Geschichtswissenschaft und symbolische Ordnung des Militärs," in Michael Th. Greven and Oliver von Wrochem, eds, *Der Krieg in der Nachkriegszeit. Der Zweite Weltkrieg in Politik und Gesellschaft der Bundesrepublik* (Opladen, 2000), 183–96.

Kühne, Thomas, "Zwischen Vernichtungskrieg und Freizeitgesellschaft. Die Veteranenkultur der Bundesrepublik (1945–1995)," in Klaus Naumann, ed., *Nachkrieg in Deutschland* (Hamburg, 2001), 90–113.

Kühne, Thomas, *Kameradschaft. Die Soldaten des nationalsozialistischen Krieges und das 20. Jahrhundert* (Göttingen, 2006).

Kwiet, Konrad, *Reichskommissariat Niederlande. Versuch und Scheitern nationalsozialistischer Neuordnung* (Stuttgart, 1968).

Lagrou, Pieter, "Historiographie de guerre et historiographie du temps présent: cadres institutionnels en Europe occidentale (1945–2000). The Second World War in the XXth Century History," in *Bulletin du Comité international de la Deuxième Guerre mondiale*, 30/31 (1999/2000), 191–215.

———, *The Legacy of Nazi Occupation. Patriotic Memory and National Recovery in Western Europe, 1945–1965* (Cambridge, 2000), (Studies in the Social and Cultural History of Modern Warfare, 8).

———, *Beyond Memory and Commemoration. Coming to Terms With War and Occupation in France After 1945* (London, 2003).

———, "The Nationalisation of Victimhood. Selective Violence and National Grief in Western Europe, 1940–1960," in Richard Bessel and Dirk Schuman, eds, *Life After Death. Approaches to a Cultural and Social History During the 1940s and 1950s* (Cambridge, 2003), 243–57.

———, "L'histoire du temps présent en Europe depuis 1945, ou comment se constitue et se développe un nouveau champ disciplinaire," in *La Revue pour l'histoire du CNRS*, 9 (2003), 4–15.

Lammers, Karl C., Axel Schildt and Detlef Siegfried, eds, *Dynamische Zeiten. Die 60er Jahre in den beiden deutschen Gesellschaften* (Hamburg, 2000, 2003).

Landau, Ludwik, *Kronika lat wojny i okupacji, Państwowe Wydwnictwo Naukowe* (Warsaw, 1962).

Langewiesche, Dieter, *Nation, Nationalismus, Nationalstaat in Deutschland und Europa* (Munich, 2000).

———, "Eskalierte die Kriegsgewalt im Laufe der Geschichte?," in Jörg Baberowski, ed., *Moderne Zeiten? Krieg, Revolution und Gewalt im 20. Jahrhundert* (Göttingen, 2006), 12–29.

Lanzmann, Claude, *Shoah. An Oral History of the Holocaust* (New York, Toronto, 1985).

Latzel, Klaus, *Deutsche Soldaten – nationalsozialistischer Krieg? Kriegserlebnis – Kriegserfahrung 1939–1945* (Paderborn, 1998).

Laux, Stephan, "Flandern im Spiegel der 'wirklichen Volksgeschichte.' Robert Paul Oszwald (1883–1945) als politischer Funktionär, Publizist und Historiker," in Burkhard Dietz, Helmut Gabel and Ulrich Tiedau, eds, *Griff nach dem Westen. Die 'Westforschung' der völkisch-nationalen Wissenschaften zum nordwesteuropäischen Raum (1919–1960)* (Münster et al., 2003), 247–90.

Lehmann, Albrecht, *Gefangenschaft und Heimkehr. Deutsche Kriegsgefangenschaft in der Sowjetunion* (Munich, 1986).

Lemberg, Eugen and Friedrich Edding, eds, *Die Vertriebenen in Westdeutschland. Ihre Eingliederung und ihr Einfluss auf Gesellschaft, Wirtschaft, Politik und Geistesleben*, 3 Vols. (Kiel, 1959).

Lenz, Claudia, ed., *Erinnerungskulturen im Dialog. Europäische Perspektiven auf die NS-Vergangenheit* (Hamburg, 2002).

Lepsius, Rainer M., "Die Europäische Union. Ökonomisch-politische Integration und kulturelle Pluralität," in Reinhold Viehoff and Rien T. Segers, eds, *Kultur, Identität, Europa* (Frankfurt/M., 1999), 201–23.

Le Rider, Jacques, Moritz Csáky and Monika Sommer, eds, *Transnationale Gedächtnisorte in Zentraleuropa* (Innsbruck, 2002).

Levisse-Touzé, Christine and Stefan Martens, eds, *Les femmes dans la Résistance en France* (Paris, 2003).

Levy, Daniel and Nathan Sznaider, *Erinnerung im globalen Zeitalter: Der Holocaust* (Frankfurt/M., 2001).

Lipp, Wolfgang, "Europa als Kulturprozeß," in Id., *Drama Kultur* (Berlin, 1994), 609–26.

Lipski, Jan Józef, "Zwei Vaterländer – zwei Patriotismen. Bemerkungen zum nationalen Größenwahn und zur Xenophobie der Polen," in Georg Ziegler, ed., *Wir müssen uns alles sagen ... Essays zur deutsch-polnischen Nachbarschaft von Jan Józef Lipski* (Gliwice, 1996), 185–228.

Loth, Wilfried and Bernd A. Rusinek, eds, *"Verwandlungszone"? Nationalsozialistische Eliten in der Nachkriegszeit* (Frankfurt/M., New York, 1998).

Lüdtke, Alf and Bernd Weisbrod, *No Man's Land of Violence. Extreme Wars in the 20th Century* (Göttingen, 2006).

Lützeler, Paul-Michael, *Plädoyers für Europa. Stellungnahmen deutschsprachiger Schriftsteller 1915–1949* (Frankfurt/M., 1987).

Machcewicz, Paweł and Krzysztof Persak, *Wokół Jedwabnego*, 2 Vols. (Warsaw, 2002).

MacKenzie, S.P., *The Home Guard* (Oxford, 1995).

Madajczyk, Czesław, *Polityka III Rzeszy w okupowanej Polsce*, 2 Vols. (Warsaw, 1970).

———, *Zamojszczyzna-Sonderlaboratorium SS. Zbiór dokumentów polskich i niemieckich z okresu okupacji hitlerowskiej*, 2 Vols. (Warsaw, 1979).

———, *Faszyzm i okupacje 1938–1945. Wykonywanie okupacji przez państwa Osi w Europie*, 2 Vols. (Poznań, 1983).

———, *Die Okkupationspolitik Nazideutschlands in Polen, 1939–1945* (Berlin, 1987).

———, "Między neutralną współpracą ludności terytoriów okupowanych a kolaboracją z Niemcami," in *Studia nad Faszyzmem i Zbrodniami Hitlerowskimi*, Vol. XXI, 181–96.

Madajczyk, Piotr, *Przyłączenie Śląska Opolskiego do Polski w latach 1945–1948* (Warsaw, 1996).

———, *Niemcy polscy 1944–1989* (Warsaw, 2001).

Mählert, Ulrich, *Die Freie Deutsche Jugend 1945–1949: von den "Antifaschistischen Jugendausschüssen" zur SED-Massenorganisation. Die Erfassung der Jugend in der Sowjetischen Besatzungszone* (Paderborn, 1995).

Mai, Gunther, *Europa 1918–1939. Mentalitäten, Lebensweisen, Politik zwischen den Weltkriegen* (Stuttgart, Berlin, Cologne, 2001).

Maier, Charles S., "Targeting the City: Debates and Silences about the Aerial Bombing of World War II," in *International Review of the Red Cross*, 87 (2005), 429–44.

Majerus, Benoît, "Polizei im besetzten Belgien, 1914–1918 und 1940–1944. Eine vergleichende Studie der Brüsseler Polizei während der beiden Weltkriege," in *Francia – Forschungen zur westeuropäischen Geschichte*, 32/3 (2005), 1–22.

Majerus, Benoît, "Von von Falkenhausen (Ludwig) zu von Falkenhausen (Alexander). Die deutsche Verwaltung Belgiens in den zwei Weltkriegen – Brüche, Kontinuitäten und Lernprozesse," in Günther Kronenbitter, Markus Pöhlmann and Dierk Walter, eds, *Besatzung. Funktion und Gestalt militärischer Fremdherrschaft von der Antike bis zum 20. Jahrhundert* (Paderborn, 2006), 131–33.

Manig, Bernd-Oliver, *Die Politik der Ehre. Die Rehabilitierung der Berufssoldaten in der frühen Bundesrepublik* (Göttingen, 2004).

Mantelli, Brunello, "Die Italiener auf dem Balkan 1941–1943," in Christof Dipper, Lutz Klinkhammer and Alexander Nützenadel, eds, *Europäische Sozialgeschichte. Festschrift für Wolfgang Schieder zum 65. Geburtstag* (Berlin, 2000), 57–74.

——, ed., "L'Italia fascista potenza occupante: lo scacchiere balcanico," in *Qualestoria*, 30 (2002).

Margairaz, Michel, Jacques Portes and Danielle Tartakowski, *Les sociétés, la guerre la paix, 1911 à 1946* (Paris, 2003).

Margalit, Gilad, "Der Luftangriff auf Dresden. Seine Bedeutung für die Erinnerungspolitik der DDR und für die Herauskristallisierung einer historischen Kriegserinnerung im Westen," in Susanne Düwell and Matthias Schmidt, eds, *Narrative der Shoah. Repräsentationen der Vergangenheit in Historiographie, Kunst und Politik* (Paderborn, Munich, Vienna, Zurich, 2002), 189–207.

Martens, Stefan, "Frankreich zwischen 'Histoire contemporaine' und 'Histoire du temps présent'", in *Vierteljahrshefte für Zeitgeschichte*, 55 (2009), 583–616.

—— and Maurice Vaïsse, eds, *Frankreich und Deutschland im Krieg (November 1942–Herbst 1944). Okkupation, Kollaboration, Résistance* (Bonn, 2000).

Marwick, Arthur, *British Society since 1945* (London, 1982).

Matusek, Piotr, Edward Pawłowski and Tadeusz Rawski, *II wojna światowa* (Warsaw, 2005).

Mazower, Mark, *Inside Hitler's Greece* (New Haven, 1993).

——, *Dark Continent. Europe's Twentieth Century* (London, 1998).

Mazur, Zbigniew, "Niemcy czy faszyści? Dwa konkursy w latach 1948–1949 na upamiętnienie niemieckich egzekucji na polskiej ludności cywilnej," in *Przegląd Zachodni* 2005, No. 2, 41–70.

Meinecke, Friedrich, *Die deutsche Katastrophe. Betrachtungen und Erinnerungen* (Wiesbaden, 1946).

Merkel, Ina, *Utopie und Bedürfnis. Die Geschichte der Konsumkultur in der DDR* (Cologne, Weimar, Vienna, 1999).

Merridale, Catherine, *Ivan's War. The Red Army 1939–45* (London, 2005).

Mikkeli, Heikki, *Europe as an idea and an identity* (Basingstoke, 1998).

Milewski, Jan Jerzy and Anna Pyżewska, eds, *Stosunki polsko-białoruskie w województwie białostockim w latach 1939–1956* (Warsawa, 2005).

Millgate, Helen D., ed., *Mr. Brown's War, a diary of the Second World War* (Stroud, Gloucester, 2003).

Milward, Alan S., *The European rescue of the nation state* (London, 1992).

Moeller, Robert G., *War Stories. The Search for a Usable Past in the Federal Republic of Germany* (Berkeley et al., 2001).

Mögenburg, Harm, *Kalter Krieg und Wirtschaftswunder. Die Fünfziger Jahre im geteilten Deutschland* (Frankfurt/M., 1993).

Möhler, Rainer, *Entnazifizierung in Rheinland-Pfalz und im Saarland unter französischer Besatzung von 1945–1952* (Mainz, 1992).

Morgan, Piers, *The Insider, the private diaries of a scandalous decade* (London, 2005).

Mosse, George L., *Fallen Soldiers. Reshaping the Memory of World Wars* (New York, Oxford, 1990).

——, *De la Grand Guerre aux totalitarismes: la brutalisation des sociétés européennes*. Préface de Stéphane Audoin-Rouzeau (Paris, 1999).

Motyka, Grzegorz, Ukraińska partyzantka 1942–1960 (Warsaw, 2006).
Mühlen, Bengt von zur, ed., *Der Todeskampf der Reichshauptstadt* (Berlin-Kleinmachnow, 1994).
Mühlhäuser, Regina, "Vergewaltigungen in Deutschland 1945. Nationaler Opferdiskurs und individuelles Erinnern betroffener Frauen," in Klaus Naumann, ed., *Nachkrieg in Deutschland* (Hamburg, 2001), 384–408.
Müller, Rolf-Dieter, *Der Zweite Weltkrieg* (Stuttgart, 2004), (Gebhardt. Handbuch der deutschen Geschichte, 21).
———, *Der letzte deutsche Krieg 1939–1945* (Stuttgart, 2005).
Muracciole, Jean-François, *La France et les Français pendant la Seconde Guerre mondiale* (Paris, 2004).
Naimark, Norman, *Die Russen in Deutschland, Die sowjetische Besatzungszone 1945–1949* (Berlin, 1997).
Nałęcz, Tomasz, in Henryk Samsonowicz, Janusz Tazbir, Tadeusz Łepkowski and Tomasz Nałęcz, eds, *Polska. Losy państwa i narodu do 1939 roku* (Warsaw, 2003), 447–65.
Namysło, Aleksandra and Tomasz Kurpierz, eds, *Podziemie niepodległościowe na Podbeskidziu w latach 1939–1947* (Bielsko-Biała, 2002).
Neumann, Vera, *Nicht der Rede wert. Die Privatisierung der Kriegsfolgen in der frühen Bundesrepublik. Lebensgeschichtliche Erinnerungen* (Munich, 1999).
Nicholas, Siân, *The Echo of War: Home Front Propaganda and the Wartime BBC, 1939–1945* (Manchester, 1996).
Niedhart, Gottfried and Dieter Riesenberger, eds, *Lernen aus dem Krieg? Deutsche Nachkriegszeiten 1918 und 1945* (Munich, 1992).
Niethammer, Lutz, *Die Mitläuferfabrik. Die Entnazifizierung am Beispiel Bayerns* (Berlin, 1982).
———, "Zum Wandel der Kontinuitätsdiskussion," in Ludolf Herbst, ed., *Westdeutschland 1945–1955. Unterwerfung, Kontrolle, Integration* (Munich, 1986), 65–83.
——— and Alexander von Plato, eds, *Lebensgeschichte und Sozialkultur im Ruhrgebiet*, 3 Vols. (Bonn, 1983–1985).
———, ——— and Dorothee Wierling, *Die volkseigene Erfahrung. Archäologie des Lebens in der Industrieprovinz der DDR*, Berlin 1991.
Niwiński, Piotr, ed., *Opór wobec systemów totalitarnych na Wileńszczyźnie w okresie II wojny światowej* (Gdańsk, 2003).
Noakes, Lucy, "Making Histories: Experiencing the Blitz in London's Museums in the 1990s," in *War and memory in the Twentieth Century*, ed. by Martin Evans and Ken Lunn (Oxford, 1997), 89–104.
———, *War and the British* (London, 1998).
Nolte, Paul, *Die Ordnung der deutschen Gesellschaft. Selbstentwurf und Selbstbeschreibung im 20. Jahrhundert* (Munich, 2000).
Nora, Pierre (ed.), *Les lieux de mémoire*, 7 Vols. (Paris, 1984–1992).
Nützenadel, Alexander and Wolfgang Schieder, eds, *Zeitgeschichte als Problem. Nationale Traditionen und Perspektiven der Forschung in Europa* (Göttingen, 2004).
Ogley, Bob, *Kent at War* (Westerham, 2002).
Oliva, Gianni, "Si ammazza troppo poco." *I crimini di guerra italiani 1940–43* (Milan, 2006).
Orzechowski, Jan, *Aby pamięć nie zginęła. Służba Zwycięstwu Polski, Związek Walki Zbrojnej, Armia Krajowa na terenie powiatu grajewskiego w latach okupacji 1939–1944* (Towarzystwo Miłośników Rajgrodu, Rajgród, 1997).
Ostrowski, Kazimierz, *Hitlerowska polityka podatkowa w Generalnym Gubernatorstwie* (Kraków, 1977).
Overmans, Rüdiger, *Soldaten hinter Stacheldraht. Deutsche Kriegsgefangene des Zweiten Weltkriegs* (Berlin, Munich, 2000).
———, *Deutsche militärische Verluste im Zweiten Weltkrieg* (Munich, 1999).

Passerini, Luisa, ed. Matthias, *L'identità culturale europea. Idee, sentimenti, relazione* (Scandicci, 1998).
Paulmann, Johannes, "Internationaler Vergleich und interkultureller Transfer. Zwei Forschungsansätze zur europäischen Geschichte des 18. bis 20. Jahrhunderts," in *Historische Zeitschrift*, 267 (1998), 649–85.
Pawełczyńska, Anna, *Żywa historia – Pamięć i ocena lat okupacji* (Warsaw, 1977).
Pedaliu, Effie G. H., "Britain and the 'Handover' of Italian War Criminals to Yugoslavia, 1945–48." in *Journal of Contemporary History*, 39 (2004), 503–29.
Petersen, Jens, "Der Ort der Resistenza in Geschichte und Gegenwart Italiens," in *Quellen und Forschungen aus italienischen Archiven und Bibliotheken*, 72 (1992), 550–71.
Pingel, Falk, "Europa im Geschichtsbuch," in Stiftung Haus der Geschichte der Bundesrepublik (ed.), *The Culture of European History in the 21st Century* (Bonn, 1999), 215–37.
———, ed., *Macht Europa Schule? Die Darstellung Europas in Schulbüchern der europäischen Gemeinschaft* (Frankfurt/M., 1995).
Plato, Alexander von and Wolfgang Meinecke, *Alte Heimat – Neue Zeit: Flüchtlinge, Umgesiedelte, Vertriebene in der Sowjetischen Besatzungszone und in der DDR* (Berlin, 1991).
Podlaski, Kazimierz (Bohdan Skaradziński), *Białorusini, Litwini, Ukraińcy* (Białystok, 1990).
Poggio, Pier Paolo and Bruna Micheletti, eds, *L'Italia in guerra 1940–1945* (Brescia, 1992).
Poleszak, Stanisław and Adam Puławski, eds, *Podziemie zbrojne na Lubelszczyźnie wobec dwóch totalitaryzmów* (Warsaw, 2005).
Ponteville, Isabelle and Chantal Kesteloot, "Dossier: Enfants de résistant ou de collaborateur: grandir sans père ou mère," in *'30–'50. Bulletin du CEGES*, 37 (2002), I–XL.
Ponting, Clive, *1940: Myth and Reality* (London, 1990).
Popitz, Heinrich, *Phänomene der Macht. Autorität, Herrschaft, Gewalt und Technik* (Tübingen, 1986).
Prauser, Steffen, "Les crimes de guerre allemands en Italie," in Gaël Eismann and Stefan Martens, eds, *Occupation et répression militaire allemandes 1939–1945. La politique de "maitien de l'ordre" en Europe occpée* (Paris, 2007), 89–103.
Prost, Antoine, *Guerres, paix et sociétés, 1911–1946* (Paris, 2003).
Pupo, Raoul, *Il lungo esodo. Istria: le persecuzioni, le foibe, l'esilio* (Milan, 2005).
——— and Roberto Spazzali, *Foibe* (Milan, 2003).
Ramsden, John, *"That will depend on who writes the History;" Winston Churchill as his own historian*, Inaugural Lectures (Queen Mary and Westfield College, 1996).
———, "Mr. Churchill goes to Fulton," in James W. Muller, ed., *Churchill's "Iron Curtain" Speech Fifty Years Later* (Columbia, Missouri, 1999).
———, *The Dambusters* (London, 2002).
———, *Man of the Century: Winston Churchill and his legend since 1945* (London, 2003).
———, *Don't Mention the War: The British and the Germans since 1890* (London, 2006).
Rauh-Kühne, Cornelia, "Die Entnazifizierung und die deutsche Gesellschaft," in *Archiv für Sozialgeschichte*, 35 (1995), 35–70.
Reichel, Peter, *Politik mit der Erinnerung. Gedächtnisorte im Streit um die nationalsozialistische Vergangenheit* (Munich, 1995).
———, *Vergangenheitsbewältigung in Deutschland. Die Auseinandersetzung mit der NS-Diktatur von 1945 bis heute* (Munich, 2001).
Reif-Spirek, Peter and Bodo Ritscher, eds, *Speziallager in der SBZ. Gedenkstätten mit "doppelter Vergangenheit"* (Berlin, 1999).
Reinhard, Oliver, Matthias Neutzner and Wolfang Hesse, eds, *Das rote Leuchten. Dresden und der Bombenkrieg* (Dresden, 2005).
Reiss, Matthias, *"Die Schwarzen waren unsere Freunde": Deutsche Kriegsgefangene in der amerikanischen Gesellschaft, 1942–1946* (Paderborn, 2002).
Revel, Jacques, *Les jeux d'échelles. La micro-analyse à l'expérience* (Paris, 1996).

Reynaud, Paul, "Churchill and France," in Charles Eade, ed., *Churchill by his Contemporaries* (London, 1953).
Reynebeau, Marc, *Het nut van het verleden* (Tielt, Lannoo, 2007).
Reynolds, David, *In Command of History, Churchill Fighting and Writing the Second World War* (London, 2004).
Rioux, Jean-Pierre, "L'épuration en France, 1944–1945," in *L'Histoire*, 5 (1978), 24–32.
———, *La France de la Quatrième République. I. L'ardeur et la nécessité, 1944–1952* (Paris, 1980).
Rochat, Giorgio, *Le guerre italiane 1935–1943. Dall'impero d'Etiopia alla disfatta* (Torino, 2005).
Rodogno, Davide, *Il nuovo ordine mediterraneo. Le politiche di occupazione dell'Italia fascista in Europa (1940–1943)* (Torino, 2003).
Röhr, Werner, ed., *Okkupation und Kollaboration (1938–1945). Beiträge zu Konzeption und Praxis der Kollaboration in der deutschen Okkupationspolitik* (Berlin, Heidelberg, 1994).
Romeyk, Horst, *Verwaltungs- und Behördengeschichte der Rheinprovinz 1914–1945* (Düsseldorf, 1985).
Rose, Sonya, *Which People's War?* (Oxford, 2003).
Rosenfeld, Gabriel D., *Munich and Memory: Architecture, Monuments and the Legacy of the Third Reich* (Berkeley, 2000).
———, *The World Hitler Never Made* (Cambridge, 2005).
Rossi, Elena Aga, *L'inganno reciproco. L'armistizio tra l'Italia e gli angloamericani del settembre 1943* (Rome, 1993).
———, *Una nazione allo sbando. L'armistizio italiano del settembre 1943 e le sue conseguenze* (Bologna, 2003) (1st ed. 1993).
Roszkowski, Wojciech, *Historia Polski 1914–2001* (Warsaw, 2002).
Rothenberger, Karl-Heinz, *Die Hungerjahre nach dem Zweiten Weltkrieg. Ernährungs- und Landwirtschaft in Rheinland-Pfalz 1945–1950* (Boppard, 1980).
Rousso, Henry, *Syndrome de Vichy de 1944 à nos jours* (Paris, 1990).
———, "L'épuration en France, une histoire inachevée," in *Vingtième Siècle*, 33 (1992), 78–105.
———, *La Hantise du passé. Entretien avec Philippe Petit* (Paris, 1998).
——— (ed.), *Stalinisme et nazisme. Histoire et mémoire comparée* (Brussels, 1999).
———, *Vichy. L'événement, la mémoire, l'histoire* (Paris, 2001).
———, "Das Dilemma eines europäischen Gedächtnisses," in *Zeithistorische Forschungen*, 1 (2004), http://www.zeithistorische-forschungen.de/16126041-Rousso-3-2004.
——— and Éric Conan, *Vichy. Un passé qui ne passé pas* (Paris, 1994).
Rudolph, Hartmut, *Evangelische Kirche und Vertriebene 1945 bis 1972*, 2 Vols. (Göttingen, 1984/85).
Rüsen, Jörn, *Historische Orientierung. Über die Arbeit des Geschichtsbewußtseins, sich in der Zeit zurechtzufinden* (Cologne, 1994).
Rusinek, Bernd-A., ed., *Kriegsende 1945. Verbrechen, Katastrophen, Befreiungen in nationaler und internationaler Perspektive* (Göttingen, 2004).
Sabrow, Martin, Ralph Jessen und Klaus Große Kracht, eds, *Zeitgeschichte als Streitgeschichte. Große Kontroversen seit 1945* (Munich, 2003).
Saerens, Lieven, *Étrangers dans la Métropole. Histoire des Juifs d'Anvers* (Brussels, 2005).
Salewski, Michael, *Geschichte Europas. Staaten und Nationen von der Antike bis zur Gegenwart* (Munich, 2000).
———, *Deutschland und der Zweite Weltkrieg.* (Paderborn, 2005).
Salzborn, Samuel, *Grenzenlose Heimat. Geschichte, Gegenwart und Zukunft der Vertriebenenverbände* (Berlin, 2000).
Samerski, Stefan, ed., *Die Renaissance der Nationalpatrone. Erinnerungskulturen in Ostmitteleuropa im 20./21. Jahrhundert* (Cologne, 2007).

Santarelli, Lidia, "Il sistema dell'occupazione italiana in Grecia. Aspetti e problemi di ricerca," in *Annali dell'Istituto milanese per la storia dell'età contemporanea, della resistenza e del movimento operaio*, 5 (2000), 365–79.

———, "Fra coabitazione e conflitto: invasione italiana e popolazione civile nella Grecia occupata (primavera-estate 1941)", in *Qualestoria* 30 (2002), 143–155.

———, "La violenza taciuta. I crimini degli italiani nella Grecia occupata," in Baldissara, Luca and Paolo Pezzino, eds, *Crimini e memorie di guerra* (Napels, 2004), 271–291.

Schildt, Axel, "Die Atombombe und der Wiederaufbau. Luftschutz, Stadtplanungskonzepte und Wohnungsbau 1950–1956," in *1999. Zeitschrift für Sozialgeschichte des 20. und 21. Jahrhunderts*, 2, 4 (1987), 52–67.

———, *Die Grindelhochhäuser. Eine Sozialgeschichte der ersten deutschen Wohnhochhausanlage. Hamburg-Grindelberg, 1945–1956* (Hamburg, 1988).

———, "Nachkriegszeit. Möglichkeiten und Probleme einer Periodisierung der westdeutschen Geschichte nach dem Zweiten Weltkrieg und ihrer Einordnung in die Geschichte des 20. Jahrhunderts," in *Geschichte in Wissenschaft und Unterricht*, 44 (1993), 567–584.

———, *Moderne Zeiten. Freizeit, Massenmedien und 'Zeitgeist' in der Bundesrepublik der 50er Jahre* (Hamburg, 1995)

———, "NS-Eliten in der Bundesrepublik Deutschland," in *Geschichte, Politik und ihre Didaktik*, 24 (1996), 20–32.

———, *Zwischen Abendland und Amerika* (Munich, 1999).

———, "'German Angst'. Überlegungen zur Mentalitätsgeschichte der Bundesrepublik," in Daniela Münkel and Jutta Schwarzkopf, eds, *Geschichte als Experiment. Studien zu Politik, Kultur und Alltag im 19. und 20. Jahrhundert. Festschrift für Adelheid von Saldern* (Frankfurt/M., New York, 2004), 87–97.

———, ed., *Hamburg im Dritten Reich* (Göttingen, 2005).

———, ed., *Deutsche Geschichte im 20. Jahrhundert. Ein Lexikon* (Munich, 2005).

———, *Die Sozialgeschichte der Bundesrepublik Deutschland bis 1989/90* (Munich, 2007).

——— and Arnold Sywottek, eds, *Modernisierung im Wiederaufbau. Die westdeutsche Gesellschaft der 50er Jahre* (Bonn, 1993, 2nd ed.1998).

Schilmar, Boris, *Europadiskurs im deutschen Exil 1933–1945* (Munich, 2004) (Pariser Historische Studien, 67).

Schmale, Wolfgang, "Europäische Geschichte als historische Disziplin. Überlegungen zu einer 'Europäistik'," in *Zeitschrift für Geschichtswissenschaft*, 46 (1998), 389–405.

———, *Geschichte Europas* (Vienna, 2000).

Schüle, Annegret, Thomas Ahbe and Rainer Gries, eds, *Die DDR aus generationengeschichtlicher Perspektive. Eine Inventur* (Leipzig, 2006).

Schulze, Hagen, *Phoenix Europa: die Moderne. Von 1740 bis heute* (Berlin, 1998).

Schulze, Rainer et al., eds, *Flüchtlinge und Vertriebene in der westdeutschen Nachkriegsgeschichte. Bilanzierung der Forschung und Perspektiven für die künftige Forschungsarbeit* (Hildesheim, 1987).

Schuster, Armin, *Die Entnazifizierung in Hessen 1945–1954. Vergangenheitspolitik in der Nachkriegszeit* (Wiesbaden, 1999).

Schwarz, Guri, *Ritrovare se stessi. Gli ebrei nell'Italia postfascista* (Rome, Bari, 2004).

Scott, James, *Seeing Like a State. How Certain Schemes to Improve the Human Condition Have Failed* (New Haven, 1998).

Sebald, Winfried G., *Luftkrieg und Literatur. Mit einem Essay zu Alfred Andersch* (Munich, Vienna, 1999).

"The Second World War in XXth Century History, Oslo, 12. August 2000, 19e Congrès international des sciences historiques," in *Bulletin des Comité international d'histoire de la Deuxième Guerre mondiale*, 30/31, 2000.

Shelah, Menachem, *Un debito di gratitudine. Storia dei rapporti tra l'Esercito italiano e gli ebrei in Dalmazia (1941–1943)* (Rome, 1991).
Shephard, Ben, *Aftwer Daybreak: the Liberation of Belsen* (London, 2006).
Siegfried, André, *Tableau politique de la France de l'Ouest (1913)* (Paris, 1995).
Sinfield, Alan, *Literature, Politics and Culture in Post–War Britain* (Oxford, 1989).
Skubiszewski, Krzysztof, *Pieniądz na terytorium okupowanym* (Poznań, 1960).
Smith, Malcolm, *Britain and 1940: History, Myth and Popular Memory* (London, 2000).
Speth, Rudolf, "Europäische Geschichtsbilder heute," in Petra Bock and Edgar Wolfrum, eds, *Umkämpfte Vergangenheit* (Göttingen, 1999), 159–75.
Stan i perspektywy badań historycznych lat wojny i okupacji, Główna Komisja Badania Zbrodni Hitlerowskich w Polsce (Warsaw, 1988).
Steinberg, Jonathan, *All or Nothing. The Axis and the Holocaust 1941–1943* (London, New York, 1990).
Stickler, Matthias, *"Ostdeutsch heißt Gesamtdeutsch." Organisation, Selbstverständnis und heimatpolitische Zielsetzungen der deutschen Vertriebenenverbände 1949–1972* (Düsseldorf, 2004).
Stöver, Bernd, *Die Befreiung vom Kommunismus. Amerikanische Liberation Policy im Kalten Krieg 1947–1991* (Cologne, 2002).
Stüber, Gabriele, *Der Kampf gegen den Hunger 1945–1950. Die Ernährungslage in der britischen Zone Deutschlands, insbesondere in Schleswig-Holstein und Hamburg* (Neumünster, 1984).
Summerfield, Penny, *Women Workers in the Second World War* (London, 1984).
———, *Reconstructing Women's Wartime Lives: Discourse and Subjectivity in Oral Histories of the Second World War* (Manchester, 1998).
Süß, Dietmar, "Wiedergutmachung von unten? Katholische Vergangenheitsbewältigung und die Entstehung des Maximilian-Kolbe-Werkes," in Hans Günter Hockerts and Christiane Kuller, eds, *Nach der Verfolgung: Wiedergutmachung nationalsozialistischen Unrechts in Deutschland?* (Munich, 2003), 157–75.
———, *Kumpel und Genossen. Arbeiterschaft, Betrieb und Sozialdemokratie in der bayerischen Montanindustrie 1945–1976* (Munich, 2003).
———, "'Massaker und Mongolensturm'. Anmerkungen zu Jörg Friedrichs umstrittenem Buch: 'Der Brand. Deutschland im Bombenkrieg 1940–1945'," in *Historisches Jahrbuch*, 124 (2004), 521–43.
———, "Erinnerungen an den Luftkrieg in Deutschland und England," in *Aus Politik und Zeitgeschichte*, 18/19 (2005),19–26.
———, ed., *Deutschland im Luftkrieg. Geschichte und Erinnerung* (Munich, 2006).
———, "Der 'Kommissar der Heimatfront': Joseph Goebbels als Reichsinspekteur für den zivilen Luftschutz," in *Beiträge zur Geschichte des Nationalsozialismus* 22 (2006).
Sywottek, Arnold, "Tabuisierung und Anpassung in Ost und West. Bemerkungen zur deutschen Geschichte nach 1945," in Thomas Koebner et al., eds, *Deutschland nach Hitler. Zukunftspläne im Exil und aus der Besatzungszeit 1939–1949* (Opladen, 1987), 229–60.
Szarota, Tomasz, *Okupowanej Warszawy dzień powszedni (Studium Historyczne)* (Warsaw, 1973).
Taylor, Frederic, *Dresden. Dienstag, 13. Februar 1945: militärische Logik oder blanker Terror?* (Munich, 2004).
Taylor, Philip M., ed.. *Britain and the Cinema in the Second World War* (Manchester, 1988).
Terkel, Studs, *The Good War. An Oral History of World War Two* (New York, 1984).
Thamer, Hans-Ulrich, *Verführung und Gewalt. Deutschland 1933–1945* (Berlin, 1986, 3rd ed. 1996).
———, ed., *Zwischen Loyalität und Resistenz. Soziale Konflikte und politische Repression während der NS-Herrschaft in Westfalen* (Münster, 1996).
———, *Nationalsozialismus* (Stuttgart, 2002).

———, ed., *Die Errichtung der Diktatur. Transformationsprozesse in der Sowjetischen Besatzungszone und in der frühen DDR* (Münster, 2003).
Thewes, Guy, "La recherche historique sur la Deuxième Guerre mondiale au Luxembourg. Orientations et perspectives," in *"... et wor alles net esou einfach"*. *Questions sur le Luxembourg et la Deuxième Guerre mondiale: contributions historiques accompagnant l'exposition: ein Lesebuch zur Austellung* (Luxembourg, 2002), 16–20.
Thießen, Malte, "Gedenken an 'Operation Gomorrha.' Zur Erinnerungskultur des Bombenkrieges von 1945 bis heute," in *Zeitschrift für Geschichtswissenschaft*, 53 (2005), 46–61.
Thoss, Bruno and Hans-Erich Volkmann, eds, *Erster Weltkrieg – Zweiter Weltkrieg: ein Vergleich. Krieg, Kriegserlebnis, Kriegeserfahrung in Deutschland* (Paderborn, 2002).
Thrills, Adrian, *You're Not Singing Anymore* (London, 1998).
Timmermann, Heiner, ed., *Die Idee Europa in Geschichte, Politik und Wirtschaft* (Berlin, 1998).
Torzecki, Ryszard, *Kwestia ukraińska w polityce III Rzeszy* (Warsaw, 1972).
Trausch, Gilbert, "La stratégie du faible: le Luxembourg pendant la Première Guerre mondiale (1914–1919)," in Id., ed., *Le rôle et la place des petits pays en Europe au XXᵉ siècle* (Baden-Baden, 2005), 45–176.
Trittel, Günter J., *Hunger und Politik. Die Ernährungskrise in der Bizone (1945–1949)* (Frankfurt/M., New York, 1990).
Ullrich, Klaus, Peter Seifert, Brigitte Müller and Horst Sauer, eds, *Deutsche Demokratische Republik* (Leipzig, 1989).
Vaccarino, Giorgio, "L'occupazione italiana in Grecia," in Pier Paolo Poggio and Bruna Micheletti, eds, *L'Italia in guerra 1940–45* (Brescia, 1992), 237–57.
Valdevit, Giampaolo, ed., *Foibe. Il peso del passato. Venezia Giulia 1943–1945* (Venedig, 1997).
Van den Berghe, Gie, "'Geen holocaustmuseum'," in *Cahiers d'Histoire du Temps Présent (30/60) – Bijdragen tot de Eigentijdse Geschiedenis* (30/60), SOMA/CEGES, 13/14 (2004), 287–310.
van Den Doel, Wim (red.), *Plaatsen van herinnering. Nederland in de twintigste eeuw* (Amsterdam, 2005).
Van den Wijngaert, Mark, Bruno De Wever, Fabrice Maerten, Dirk Luyten and Patrick Nefors, *Luc Vandeweyer en Marnix Beyen, België tijdens de Tweede Wereldoorlog* (Antwerpen, 2004).
Van Doorslaer, Rudi, "Gebruikt verleden. De politieke nalatenschap van de Tweede Wereldoorlog in België, 1945–2000," in Gita Deneckere and Bruno De Wever, eds, *Geschiedenis maken. Liber amicorum Herman Balthazar*, Gent, Tijdsbeeld i.s.m. Universiteit Gent – Vakgroep Nieuwste Geschiedenis/Amsab – Instituut voor Sociale Geschiedenis (Gent, 2003).
Vergnon, Gilles and Michèle Battesti, eds, *Les associations d'anciens résistants et la fabrique de la mémoire de la Seconde Guerre mondiale* (Vincennes, 2006), (Cahiers du Centre d'Études d'Histoire de la Défense, 28).
Vollnhals, Clemens (in Cooperation with Thomas Schlemmer), *Entnazifizierung, politische Säuberung und Rehabilitierung in den vier Besatzungszonen 1945–1949* (Munich, 1991).
"Vom Neuschreiben der Geschichte. Erinnerungspolitik nach 1945 und 1989," in *Transit – Europäische Revue*, 15 (1998).
Vos, Chris, *Televisie en bezetting. Een onderzoek naar de documentaire verbeelding van de Tweede Wereldoorlog in Nederland* (Hilversum, 1995).
Wagner, Patrick, *Displaced Persons in Hamburg. Stationen einer halbherzigen Integration 1945–1958* (Hamburg, 1997).
Wallerang, Mathias, *Luxemburg unter nationalsozialistischer Besatzung. Luxemburger berichten* (Mainz, 1997).
Weber, Eugen, *The Hollow Years. France in the 1930s* (London, 1995).

Wegner, Bernd, "Hitler, der Zweite Weltkrieg und die Choreographie des Untergangs," in *Geschichte und Gesellschaft*, 26 (2000), 492–518.
Wehler, Hans-Ulrich, *Nationalismus. Geschichte, Formen, Folgen* (Munich, 2001).
Weichlein, Siegfried, *Nationalbewegungen und Nationalismus in Europa* (Darmstadt, 2006).
Weidenfeld, Werner, ed., *Die Identität Europas* (Munich, 1985).
Weight, Richard, *Patriots: National Identity in Britain, 1940–2000* (London, 2002).
Weinberg, Gerald L., *A World at Arms. A Global History of World War II* (New York, 1994).
Weindling, Paul, *Epidemics and Genocide in Eastern Europe, 1890–1945* (Oxford, 2000).
Weldon Whalen, Robert, *Bitter Wounds. German Victims of the Great War, 1914–1939* (Ithica, London, 1984).
Welzer, Harald, Sabine Moller and Karoline Tschugnall, *"Opa war kein Nazi!" Nationalsozialismus und Holocaust im Familiengedächtnis* (Frankfurt/M., 2002).
Wette, Wolfram, Ricarda Bremer and Detlef Vogel, eds, *Das letzte halbe Jahr. Stimmungsberichte der Wehrmachtpropaganda 1944/45* (Essen, 2001).
Wiegand, Lutz, "Kriegsfolgengesetzgebung in der Bundesrepublik Deutschland," in *Archiv für Sozialgeschichte*, 35 (1995), 71–90.
Wierling, Dorothee, *Mädchen für Alles. Lebensgeschichte und Arbeitsalltag städtischer Dienstmädchen um die Jahrhundertwende* (Berlin, Bonn, 1987).
———, "The Hitler Youth Generation in the GDR: Insecurities, Ambitions and Dilemmas," in Konrad Jarausch, ed., *Dictatorship as Experience* (New York, Oxford, 1999), 307–24.
———, *Geboren im Jahr Eins. Der Jahrgang 1949 in der DDR. Versuch einer Kollektivbiographie* (Berlin, 2002).
———, "Oral History", in Michael Maurer, ed., *Aufriß der Historischen Wissenschaften*, Vol. 7 (Stuttgart, 2003), 81–152.
Wildt, Michael, *Der Traum vom Sattwerden. Hunger und Protest, Schwarzmarkt und Selbsthilfe* (Hamburg, 1986).
Wille, Manfred, ed., *Sie hatten alles verloren: Flüchtlinge und Vertriebene in der sowjetischen Besatzungszone Deutschlands* (Wiesbaden, 1993).
Wilson, Kevin and Willem Johannis van der Dussen, eds, *The History of the Idea of Europe* (London, 1993).
Winter, Jay, *Sites of Memory, Sites of Mourning. The Great War in European Cultural History* (Cambridge, New York, 1995).
——— and Antoine Prost, *The Great War in History. Debates and Controversies, 1914 to the Present* (Cambridge, 2005).
——— and Emmanuel Sivan, eds, *War and Remembrance in the Twentieth Century* (Cambridge, 1999).
Withuis, Jolande, *Erkenning. Van oorlogstrauma naar klaagkultuur* (Amsterdam, 2002).
Wolfrum, Edgar, *Geglückte Demokratie. Die Geschichte der Bundesrepublik Deutschland von ihren Anfängen bis zur Gegenwart* (Stuttgart, 2006).
Wood, E. Thomas and Stanislaw M. Jankowski, *Jan Karski, Einer gegen den Holocaust. Als Kurier in geheimer Mission* (Gerlingen, 1997).
Woolf, Stuart, "Europe and its Historians," in *Contemporary European History*, 12 (2003), 323–37.
World War II and the aftermath in the Netherlands. The victims, the benefits, the remembrance and the lessons to the future, ed. by the Ministry of Health, Welfare and Sport (The Hague, 2000).
Wóycicka, Zofia, "Zur Internationalität der Gedenkkultur. Die Gedenkstätte Auschwitz-Birkenau im Spannungsfeld zwischen Ost und West 1954–1978," in *Archiv für Sozialgeschichte*, 45 (2005), 269–92.
Zuccotti, Susan, *The Italians and the Holocaust: persecution, rescue and survival* (New York, 1987).

INDEX OF NAMES

A
Adenauer, Konrad, 198, 205, 207
Albert II., King of Belgium, 42
Angelini, Giuseppe, 139, 144n30
Ansip, Andrus, 252
Asquith, Anthony, 61
Attlee, Clement, 41, 60

B
Badoglio, Pietro, 120, 139, 145n36
Beardmore, George, 47
Bernières, Louis de, 146n51
Best, Werner, 14
Bevin, Ernest, 61–62
Blair, Tony, 49
Bodens, Wilhelm-Josef, 16
Böll, Heinrich, 199
Bonaparte, Napoléon, 47, 48, 237
Bone, Muirhead, 57
Boorman, John, 64
Boorman, Pratt, 58
Borg, Alan, 53
Boussard, Germanin, 157
Boussard, Robert, 157
Boussard, Yvonne, 157
Brandt, Willy, 228n34
Brezhnev, Leonid, 93, 100, 104, 241
Brown, Richard, 47
Brownlow, Kevin, 42
Brusilov, Aleksey, 90
Bukharin, Nikolay, 91
Bush, George W., 49

C
Cage, Nicolas, 146n51
Calder, Angus, 65, 66, 67
Chamberlain, Neville, 60
Churchill, Winston S., 40–45, 47–49, 53, 55, 57, 60

Chuykov, Vasily, 98
Coward, Noel, 45, 46
Craushaar, Harry von, 14
Cruise, Tom, 27
Cruz, Penelope, 146n51

D
Dahrendorf, Ralf, 198
Dartevelle, André, 27
Darwin, James, 41
De Gaulle, Charles, 128, 150, 176, 178, 241
Deighten, Len, 42
De Micco, Vincenzina, 133n19
Dethleffsen, Erich, 229–230
Dimitrov, Georgy, 223, 228n27
Dobrobabin, Ivan, 101, 113n50
Dönitz, Karl, 201
Doriot, Jacques, 177
Down, Lesley-Ann, 64
Ducci, Roberto, 138, 144n22

E
Eden, Anthony, 45
Eichhorn, Lisa, 64
Elizabeth, Queen, 55
Enzensberger, Hans Magnus, 199

F
Falkenhausen, Alexander von, 12
Falkenhausen, Ludwig von, 12
Faraday, Michael, 41
Fawlty, Basil, 44
Ford, Harrison, 64
Fortuyn, Pim, 31
Frank, Anne 33
Frank, Hans, 16
Friedrich, Jörg, 180, 188, 190, 191

G
Gance, Abel, 236
George VI., King of the United Kingdom, 55
Gere, Richard, 64
Giganti, Vico, 126
Gilliat, Sidney, 62
Goebbels, Joseph, 184, 185, 186, 190
Gorbachev, Mikhail, 93, 104, 218
Gorges, Konrad, 17
Göring, Hermann, 182
Grass, Günter, 199, 208
Graziani, Rodolfo, 145n36

H
Habermas, Jürgen, 198
Harbou, Bodo von, 12
Heath, Edward, 49
Herriot, Édouard, 41
Heynowski, Walter, 228n25
Himmler, Heinrich, 16
Hitler, Adolf, 3, 12, 14, 17, 40, 47, 59, 71, 73, 87, 95–98, 108, 118–119, 136, 177, 186, 190, 198, 201, 221, 224, 233–234, 250, 251

I
Ilves, Toomas Hendrik, 252

J
Jennings, Humphrey, 55
Juin, Alphonse, 128

K
Kaprov, Ilya, 99
Keitel, Wilhelm, 230
Kennedy, John F., 241
Khrushchev, Nikita, 93, 103, 104, 113n43
Kohl, Helmut, 198, 233, 261
Köhler, Ludwig, 15
Kollwitz, Käthe, 233

294 | Index of Names

Krivitsky, Aleksandr, 99, 100–101
Kuby, Erich, 148–149, 151–158, 158n3, 159n15, 159n18, 160n28, 160n30
Kuby, Lene, 154

L
Lahr, Claude, 27
Langlois, Suzanne, 148–158, 158n5, 158n7, 160n25-26
Launder, Frank, 62
Lenin, Vladimir I., 90, 92, 101, 178
Ley, Robert, 186, 187
Lo Fabio, Pasqualina, 133n17
Longo, Luigi, 141
Louis XIV, King, 47–48
Luciolli, Mario, 138
Lutyens, Edward, 232
Lynn, Dame Vera, 44, 65

M
Macmillan, Harold, 241
Madden, John, 146n
Malyshev, Vyacheslav, 99, 112n26
Mameli, Goffredo, 116
Mandato, Maria, 124
Manning, Bernard, 44
Manson, H.A., 55
Margaret, Princess of Windsor, 42
Marochetti, Carlo, 56
Mason, Herbert A., 55
Medvedev, Dimitry, 107
Meinecke, Friedrich, 199
Mekhlis, Lev, 111n
Mercier, Cardinal, 16
Milburn, Clara, 46, 47
Milton, John, 41
Mitterrand, François, 261
Molotov, Vyacheslav M., 113n45
Montgomery, Bernard, 50
Morgenthau, Henry jr., 201
Mussolini, Benito, 118–121, 132n6, 135–137

N
Navarra, Pio Leonardo, Bishop of Terracina, 123
Nazarbayev, Nursultan, 103
Nicolaus II., Tsar, 90, 94–95
Niemöller, Martin, 43

O
Olivier, Laurence, 61
Ortenberg, David, 99
Oszwald, Robert Paul, 14, 16

P
Panfilov, Ivan, 99–101, 103
Pavelić, Ante, 135
Pavlov, Ivan, 59
Pesch, Ludwig, 14
Pétain, Philippe, 3
Petri, Franz, 14, 16
Philip II., King of Spain, 47–48
Pitt, William, 47
Postyshev, P., 111n20
Priestly, J.B., 45, 65
Pushkin, Aleksandr, 111n20
Putin, Vladimir, 89, 102, 106, 107, 252

R
Ramcke, Hermann, 152–153
Reeder, Eggert, 12–15
Reese, Werner, 14
Reynaud, Paul, 41
Reynolds, Quentin, 56–57
Richard, The Lionheart, 56
Roatta, Mario, 138–140, 144n27, 144n30
Roc, Patricia, 62
Romano, Annamaria, 133n18
Rundstedt, Gerd von, 247

S
Saerens, Lieven, 36
Sandt, Maximilian von, 14
Sayers, Dorothy L., 48
Scanell, Vernon, 54
Scheumann, Gerhard, 228n25
Schmidt, Helmut, 241
Schmithüsen, Josef, 17
Schubarth, Winfried, 229–230
Schwerin von Krosigk, Lutz Graf, 201
Sebald, Winfried Georg, 191
Sellinger, Margaret, 64
Seyss-Inquart, Arthur, 16
Shakespeare, William, 41
Siegfried, André, 161
Simon, Gustav, 17
Simonov, Konstantin, 105
Spaak, Paul-Henri, 42
Spahn, Martin, 14
Sparing, Rudolf, 187

Spradberry, Walter, 57
Stalin, Joseph, 7, 87, 91–100, 102–106, 108–109, 110n9, 111n16, 111n20, 111n23, 112n26, 112n31, 113n39, 113n41, 113n45, 140, 219–220, 223, 238, 250, 261
Stokar, Walter von, 16
Suvorov, Viktor, 96
Suykerbuyck, Hermann, 25
Svechin, Aleksandr, 96, 112n35

T
Thatcher, Margaret, 43–44, 48–49, 60
Thedieck, Franz, 13–14
Titmuss, Richard, 59, 65
Tito, Broz Josip, 140
Trotsky, Leon, 91, 93, 111n24

U
Ulbricht, Walter, 217

V
Vandertaelen, Luckas, 28
Vansittart, Lord Robert, 201
Voscherau, Henning von, 191

W
Wehler, Hans-Ulrich, 199
Weizsäcker, Richard von, 191, 199, 209n10
Wilhelm II, Emperor of Germany, 47
Wilkening, Rolf, 14
Wilkinson, Sir George, 57
Williams, Vaughan, 56
Wilson, Harold, 48
Wren, Sir Christopher, 57

Y
Yeltsin, Boris, 101–102, 106
Yeremenko, Andrey, 98
York, Susanna, 65

Z
Zanussi, Giacomo, 139, 144n28, 144n30
Zhdanov, Andrey, 92
Zhukov, Gregory, 102–103, 108, 230
Zinovyev, Grigory, 92, 95

Index of Places

A
Aachen, 12, 14, 182
Africa, 54, 118–120, 142, 240, 261
   see North Africa
Albania, 135, 137, 139
Algeria, 231
Allendorf, 229
Allensbach, 199
Alps, 166, 171
Alsace, 173
Amsterdam, 33
Antwerp, 32, 36
Anzio, 122–123
Apennine, 129
Aquitaine, 164
Ardennes, 17, 25, 27, 171, 239, 246
Argentina, 44
Arlington, 237
Asia, 207, 259, 261
Atlantic, 148, 175
Attica, 135
Aube, 171, 175
Augsburg, 183–184
Aurunci, 128
Auschwitz, 21, 24, 31–32, 34, 83n18, 240, 257
Australia, 49
Austria, 16, 70, 130, 251

B
Baghdad, 147
Balkans, 4, 119, 135–142, 142n1, 143n5, 256
Bardine di San Terenzio, 130
Bavaria, 181, 204
   Upper Bavaria, 181
Belarusia, 77
Belgium, 6, 10–18, 19n, 21–37, 41, 48, 54, 246, 259, 261
Bellona, 124, 126
Berlin, 11, 16, 47, 81, 138, 183–185, 215, 218, 229–231, 233, 238, 240–241, 249, 261
   East Berlin, 215
   West Berlin, 215
Bonn, 12, 16–17, 138, 197
Breendonk, 33
Bremen, 19n
Brest, 148–158, 158n3–5, 159n11–13, 159n15, 159n22, 160n24, 237–238
Brest-Litovsk, 237
Brindisi, 118
Brittany, 148, 166, 171, 175–176
Brussels, 12, 25, 247, 254, 263n2
Buchenwald, 218, 223, 228n26

C
Campania, 131
Campodimele, 128
Cancello Arnone, 133n19
Canterbury, 59
Caphalonia, 146n51
Capua, 124
Carditello, 124
Cassino, 123, 127, 133n16
Champagne, 238
Channel Islands, 42
China, 240
Ciociaria, 128
Civitella, 130
Cologne, 12–14, 184
Copenhagen, 41
Corsica, 166, 171
Coventry, 238
Crimea, 80
Croatia, 135, 137–138, 140
Czechoslovakia, 44, 204

D
Dalmatia, 135, 138, 146n56
Denmark, 41–42
Dortmund, 183
Dossin, 33
Douaumont, 232
Dresden, 185–188, 190, 195n27, 215, 221–222, 227n23, 233, 238
Dubosekovo, 99
Dunkirk, 53, 55
Dutch East Indies, 231

E
Elbe, 185, 187, 233
Epirus, 135
Estonia, 88, 252
Ethiopia, 145n
Eupen, 13–14

F
Falkland Islands, 65
Finland, 252
Fiume, 138
Flanders, 16, 25, 29, 32–33, 35, 36, 38n10, 39n25
Flensburg, 201
Florence, 133n6
Foggia, 131
Formia, 123, 131
France, 2–3, 6, 10–12, 15, 19n20, 31, 41, 44, 47, 54, 117–118, 127–128, 138, 142n1, 145n36, 147–158, 161–178, 179n9, 231–234, 236, 238, 240–241, 246, 251, 256, 259, 261, 263n1, 264n12, 267n41
Franche-Comté, 175
Freiburg, 115n
French Indo-China, 231
Frosinone, 128

G
Gaeta, 123, 127
Genoa, 118, 120, 133n6
Gentioux, 236

296 | Index of Places

Germany, 3–5, 7, 10–13, 15–17, 18n3, 19n16, 21, 35, 38n17, 44, 48–50, 61, 70–72, 75–81, 88–91, 95–96, 99, 101, 108–110, 115n60, 116–121, 123–131, 136–139, 141, 148–150, 152, 155–156, 177, 180–193, 232, 234–236, 239, 241, 243n20, 244n32, 250–251, 257, 259, 261, 263n1, 264n12, 267n41, 267n45
  FRG, 7, 190–191, 197–208, 213n50, 217–218, 222–225, 226n4, 228n24, 230–235, 239, 242n3, 259
  GDR, 7, 190, 197, 204, 214–225, 226n3, 227n18, 228n25–26, 228n30, 228n32, 231, 233, 241, 242n3, 259
Gouvy, 246
Great Britain, 3, 6, 40–50, 53–68, 117–119, 121–122, 140–141, 144n30, 145n36, 148–150, 155, 158n, 177, 182, 221, 232–233, 236, 244n32, 259, 261
Greece, 135–137, 139, 141, 142n3, 143n5, 146n47

H
Halbe, 239
Hamburg, 120, 184, 186, 189, 191, 196n58, 228n28, 238, 240
Hesse, 204
Hiroshima, 125
Houffalize, 246–247
Hungary, 70, 130, 252

I
India, 240
Indo-China *see* French Indo-China
Indonesia, 240
Ipswich, 47
Iraq, 222
Istria, 146n56
Italy, 4, 54, 116–132, 132n2–4, 132n6, 135–142, 143n8, 144n23, 145n36–38, 146n50, 146n54, 146n56, 259
Iwo Jima, 237

J
Japan, 38n17, 133n21
Jedwabne, 79, 81, 84n27, 85n31
Jersey, 42
Jerusalem, 43
Jura, 171

K
Karlshorst, 230
Kassel, 189
Katýn, 75–76, 109
Kazakhstan, 101, 103
Kent, 58–59
Kenya, 231
Kiev, 238
Koblenz, 17
Korea, 109, 206, 222, 231
Kosovo, 135
Kuybyshev, 111n20

L
Languedoc, 166
La Spezia, 118
Latvia, 88
Lazio, 123, 131
Leningrad (St. Petersburg), 61, 89, 92, 95–96
Lenola, 128, 131
Liège, 12, 14
Lithuania, 77–88
London, 44–45, 49–50, 55, 56, 57, 58, 145n37, 230
Lorraine, 164, 166, 173, 241
Lower Saxony, 204
Lübeck, 184
Lublin, 84n
Luneberg, (Lüneburg), 50
Luxembourg, 10–18, 21–37, 38n11, 38n16, 246, 259
  City, 17

M
Maastricht, 253
Macedonia, 135
Malaya, 231
Malines, 33
Malmédy, 13–14
Manchester, 44
Marburg, 229
Massif Central, 164, 171, 175
Mechelen, 33

Mediterranean, 142n1, 164
Milan, 118, 120
Minsk, 238
Minturno, 123, 133n16
Monte Cassino, 127, 239
  s. Cassino
Montenegro, 135
Morocco, 128–129
Moscow, 76, 89, 92, 99, 101, 108, 115n60, 205, 252
Mosel, 17
Munich, 183, 190–191, 196n45, 233, 250
Münster, 12, 16, 183

N
Naples, 118, 120–122, 124, 126, 133n18
Near East, 261
Neiße, 235, 244n21
Netherlands, 10–18, 21–37, 41, 259
Nola 124
Nord (Department), 164, 166, 176
Normandy, 54, 149, 171
North Africa, 54, 118–120, 128, 142
  see Africa
North Sea, 238
Norway, 41
Nuremberg, 184, 201

O
Oder, 215–216, 235, 244n21
Oder-Neiße, 235, 244n21
Ourthe, 247

P
Pakistan, 240
Paris, 8, 15, 74, 164, 166, 176, 263n1
Pas-de-Calais, 164, 166, 171
Peloponnesus, 135
Péronne, 230
Petrograd s. St. Petersburg
Picardy, 164, 166
Plymouth, 58
Poland, 2, 7, 10, 13, 44, 49, 70–81, 252, 259, 265n24
Potsdam, 109, 263n1
Prussia, 13, 54, 200–201
Pyrenees, 171

R
Rab, 136
Rhine, 10, 13, 17

Index of Places | 297

Rhineland, 3, 10–12, 15, 17–18, 19n20, 183
Rhône, 164
Rome, 118, 121, 127, 133n6, 140
Rostock, 184
Rotterdam, 238
Ruhr, 3, 10–13, 18, 182
Russia, 7, 17, 44, 60–61, 67, 70, 86–109, 110n8, 206, 219–220, 222, 229, 238, 252, 259, 265n24

S
Saarbrücken, 184
Saarland, 12
Sachsenhausen, 218
Salerno, 116, 122, 127
Sant'Anna di Stazzema, 130
Sarajevo, 147
Schleswig-Holstein, 204
Scotland, 44, 56
Seelow Heights, 216
Seine, 171
Seine Maritime, 164, 166
Serbia, 90, 137
Sevastopol, 238
Siberia, 205
Sicily, 122
Sisciano, 133n17
Slovenia, 135–136, 138, 140, 143n5
Smolensk, 76
Somme, 232, 234
Sonnino, 123
Soviet Union, 7, 60–61, 71–72, 75–80, 86–109, 110n8, 111n18–19, 111n22, 145n36, 214–225, 227n18, 234–238, 241, 252, 261
South America, 44
Spain, 25, 47, 49, 144n30
Srebrenica, 31
Staffordshire, 47
Stalingrad (Volgograd), 61, 89, 205, 231, 237, 239
St. Avold, 241
St. Petersburg, *see* Leningrad
Stockholm, 257
Sudeten, 204, 235
Sussex, 49
Switzerland, 251

T
Tallinn, 252
Taranto, 118
Teano, 126
Terracina, 123
The Hague, 31
Thessaly, 135
Thiepval, 232
Torre del Greco, 122
Trentino, 127
Treptow, 238
Trier, 17
Turin, 118, 120
Turkey, 240

U
Ukraine, 77, 79, 81, 84n26, 88, 113n50
United States of America, 40–41, 43–44, 49, 56, 64, 65, 118, 121–126, 128, 140–141, 145n36, 148–149, 152, 156, 177, 221–222, 237, 241, 246, 249, 257, 259
Ural, 96

V
Val di Chiana, 130
Valmontone, 123
Vatican, 121, 123
Venetia, 127
Venezia Giulia, 140
Venice, 133n
Verdun, 3, 261
Versailles, 3, 10, 12–13, 90
Vichy, 251
Vietnam, 222, 228n25
Virginia, 237
Vitebsk, 237
Volgograd, *see* Stalingrad
Volokolamsk, 103
Vosges, 171

W
Wales, 44
Wallonia, 19n16, 25, 29, 33, 39n25
Warsaw, 72, 81, 230, 238
Washington, 49, 115n60
Weimar, 12–13, 199, 250
Westphalia, 181, 183
Wilhelmshaven, 183

Y
Yale, 263n1
Yalta, 75, 80
Yonne, 171, 175
Yugoslavia, 31, 135–137, 139–140, 142, 144n30

CPSIA information can be obtained
at www.ICGtesting.com
Printed in the USA
BVHW041656221221
624700BV00008B/51